Volume I **Crime and Insanity in England**

B

Crime and Insanity in England

Volume one : *The Historical Perspective*

NIGEL WALKER

Reader in Criminology
University of
Oxford

at the University Press
EDINBURGH

© Nigel Walker 1968
EDINBURGH UNIVERSITY PRESS
22 George Square, Edinburgh 8
North America
Aldine Publishing Company
320 West Adams Street, Chicago
Australia and New Zealand
Hodder & Stoughton Ltd.
Africa, Oxford University Press
India, P. C. Manaktala & Sons
Far East, M. Graham Brash & Son
Printed in Great Britain
at The Kynoch Press, Birmingham
85224 017 1

Library of Congress
Catalog Card Number 68-19882

To my daughter Valerie

Preface

This volume, which is being published before its sequel is complete, began as a mere historical introduction to a contemporary survey of the use of hospital orders under the Mental Health Act of 1959. At that time I imagined that the history of the law's ways of dealing with mentally disordered offenders was so simple and well documented that a couple of chapters would dispose of it. But as I tried to write those chapters I found that the simplicity was the result of oversimplification, and that the well-known documents made incomplete sense at best. All sorts of questions seemed to be unanswered. Was no notice taken of insanity before Bracton? Were the centuries which separated him from, say, Blackstone as uneventful as the books suggested? Against what sort of accusations could insanity be offered as a defence during that period? What happened to those who succeeded in doing so? How did Scotland, whose common law on this subject was not so very different from England's, develop the notion of diminished responsibility? What was the reason for Henry VIII's often-quoted legislation of 1542? Was Queen Victoria really as stupid about *mens rea* in 1883 as Lytton Strachey made out? Was Sergeant Boshears' acquittal in 1961 as unprecedented as Lord Bathurst said?

Although these are some of the questions which I think I have managed to answer, there are others which I certainly have not. When and how did the practice of pardoning the insane felon develop into an acquittal or special verdict? Was a death sentence which had been respited because of insanity ever carried out after the felon's recovery? Has the defence of insanity ever been accepted in a summary court? I mention these examples because in my efforts to make sense of the information which I have been able to collect I may have papered over some cracks.

Nevertheless, when recognised authorities did answer my questions I assumed at first that their answers were reliable. I soon found that even this assumption was dangerous. A social historian stated that before 1800 insane persons who committed crimes were held fully responsible, and that until Hadfield's case the possibility of lucid intervals was not recognised by the law: neither is even approximately true. A history of the insanity defence in the nineteenth century implied that the special verdict was changed to 'guilty but insane' before M'Naghten's trial, which in fact occurred forty years earlier. A continental jurist hinted that the M'Naghten Rules had been anticipated by an article in the French penal code of 1810, although their only common feature is that they deal with insane offenders. A well-known textbook of criminal law said that the defence of insanity was not often set up except in capital cases, at a time when the statistics showed the opposite. It would be unfair to name the authors of these myths in the preface to a book that must contain at least as many errors. If the need for unremitting scepticism has been demonstrated, that is enough.

The relationship between the two volumes of this work also requires some explanation. In spite of their close connection, each is reasonably self-contained. This first volume deals with what might be called the traditional legal issues, although not always from a lawyer's point of view. The second volume will be concerned with the problems of the psychiatrist and the penal administrator in their efforts to sidestep the traditional questions.

N.D.W, *March* 1967
Nuffield College, Oxford

Contents

Tables and Figures

Acknowledgments

I should like to record my gratitude to the considerable number of
people who have so generously helped me with advice, information,
criticism, and corrections:

Professor Rupert Cross, All Souls College, Oxford

Professor Bernard Diamond, School of Criminology, University
of California

Dr Gerald Gordon, Department of Criminal Law and Criminology,
University of Edinburgh

Professor S.L. Greenslade, Christ Church, Oxford

The Director of Public Prosecutions and his staff

The Home Office and its Prison Department

Dr Richard Hunter, National Hospital for Nervous Diseases,
London

Mr John Kaye, The Queen's College, Oxford

Mr V.D. Lipman, formerly of Nuffield College, Oxford

Dr Ida Macalpine, London

Mrs Sarah McCabe, Penal Research Unit, Oxford

Mr Anthony Platt, then of the School of Criminology,
University of California

Professor D.D. Reid, London School of Hygiene
and Tropical Medicine

I also want to record my thanks to the Warden and Fellows of
Nuffield College for grants for research assistance, to the research
assistants themselves (Miss Norma Wright, Mr Rhoddri Howell,
Mr Steven Hartz, and Mrs Lavender Millen), to Miss Joan Watson
for her help with the indexes, and to Miss Bond, Miss Chapman,
and Miss Murphy, who produced the typescript.

Introduction

The subject of these two volumes is the attempt of the English penal system, at each stage of its development, to deal with that awkward phenomenon, the irrational infringement of the criminal law. There is, of course, a point of view which regards all crime as attributable to some degree of mental abnormality, and so–on the assumption that normal minds are always rational–to irrationality. As I hope to show in volume II, however, this belief–which is traceable to the armchair psychology of the age of reason–is now not only untenable but also less fashionable, though not quite unheard of among penal reformers. Most criminal offences arise either from normal motives, such as acquisitiveness, or from inadvertence in the performance of normal activities, such as the driving of a car. It is the exceptional offence which springs from an abnormal motive, such as exhibitionism, or from a delusion, for example of persecution, or from very poor self-control, as some assaults do. *How* exceptional such offences are is certainly a matter for argument or, better still, for research. Their frequency is probably underestimated by lawyers, overestimated by psychiatrists.

Whether this is the case or not, it is important to distinguish between mental abnormality and mental disorder, whether one is concerned with offenders or with any other category of people. The mentally abnormal include gifted mathematicians, homosexuals, Close Brethren, pot-holers and clairvoyants, but by no means all members of these groups would be diagnosed as mentally *disordered* by the typical psychiatrist. No doubt some would; and perhaps the percentage which would is higher in some of these groups than it would be in a comparable sample of the population at large. The remainder, however, would neither be recognised by the psychiatrist as exhibiting the symptoms or combinations of symptoms which are described in his textbooks, nor respond to the remedial techniques which he has learned to apply to his patients; that is, their abnormalities would not disappear or become less marked under his treatment.

It is not easy to define the special subdivision of mental abnormality which we call 'mental disorder' in a way that will enable us to say what is or is not mental disorder in cultures that are very different from our own. In societies of the European type a workable definition would be 'those mental abnormalities with which psychiatrists attempt to deal'. It is true that according to this definition a few abnormalities–of which homosexuality

c

is an example – would sometimes be disorders and sometimes not, according to the prevailing attitudes of psychiatrists in the society or decade in question. But awkwardnesses of that sort are inseparable from sociological definitions.

What would, of course, be ridiculous would be a definition which implied that when there were no psychiatrists there were no mental disorders. But when I am discussing the forms or prevalence of mental disorder in medieval England I mean those abnormalities which present-day psychiatrists whom I regard as orthodox would try to treat or care for. There is then no illogicality in pointing out that at earlier stages in our history some mental disorders were likely to be regarded as treason, demoniacal possession or religious heterodoxy, while some merely went unrecognised; or that even if an abnormality were not mistaken for one of these forms of wickedness the medieval equivalent of psychiatric treatment might well be administered by a priest or even a gaoler. Physical medicine had to establish itself as a professional skill before psychiatry could emerge as a special form of it. Even today it is assumed that only a medically qualified person is qualified to diagnose and supervise the treatment of mental disorders, although scientific research work on the problems of diagnosis is largely done by clinical psychologists, and an increasing amount of psychotherapy is being delegated to people whose training is not in medicine.

What criterion is used by psychiatrists in deciding whether this or that abnormality should be dealt with in their hospitals, clinics and textbooks is, of course, another fascinating question. It cannot simply be the success of their techniques in *removing* or *alleviating* the abnormality, for they diagnose as disorders many conditions for which they can do little or nothing. It may be their assumption that the abnormality can be *explained* in their terms, although in the case of many disorders, notably schizophrenia, this assumption has not yet been vindicated. A pessimistic psychiatrist might merely claim that at least he is successful with his *prognoses*, that is, his forecasts of the future course of the abnormalities which he regards as within his province; and although this is not always true it is a safer criterion than the others.

In a history which extends from the tenth to the twentieth century, a minor problem is the choice of terms in which to refer to the various categories and types of mental disorders. I have already explained the difference between 'mental abnormality' and 'mental disorder', although the two are often used as synonyms. 'Mental disorders' (the widest term in the Mental Health Act of 1959) are subdivided into three main groups: 'subnormality' of intelligence and general competence (which is of course a matter of degree); 'mental illness'; and the disorders of personality which – for better or worse – have been statutorily labelled 'psychopathic disorder'. (The last of these is of such historical and sociological interest that a chapter will be devoted to it in volume II.)

These terms have almost completely superseded those of nineteenth-century legislation. 'Insanity', 'lunacy', 'mental deficiency', 'idiocy', 'imbecility' and 'feeble-mindedness' became unpopular with physicians, administrators and legislators not so much because of their antiquity or lack of precision as because they had passed into common parlance and so become intolerably blunt. The euphemisms of one generation become the insults of the next.

'Lunacy', 'insanity' and 'idiocy' are, of course, much older than the nineteenth century, and in earlier works are interspersed with medieval terms such as 'frenzy', 'madness', or lawyers' phrases such as 'non compos mentis' (not in control of his mind), 'de non saine memoire'(of disordered wits), 'fatuitas a nativitate' (folly from birth). Apart from the very ancient distinction between 'folly from birth' and the other forms of disorder, these terms were usually interchangeable, and it would be a mistake to relate any of them to some more precise subdivision of mental illness.

My terminology will be a deliberate mixture of contemporary words (or almost literal translations of these when they were in Latin or legal French) and modern psychiatric language. The former are used when I am trying to see the problem through contemporary eyes, the latter when I am trying to relate it to the facts – or what we now believe to be the facts – of mental disorder, for example when wondering what sorts of disorder qualified for the term 'furor' in Bracton's day.

There are not so many problems of definition when we turn to the concept of 'crime'. A crime is behaviour of the sort that is penalised under the criminal law. This simple semantic rule has been unnecessarily confused by people who either apply the word to behaviour which in their opinion *ought* to be officially penalised (as in the phrase 'crimes against humanity') or confine it to the more serious breaches of the criminal law (as the Scots do). For this reason the term 'criminal offence' or simply 'offence' is sometimes used to connote any breach of the criminal law however serious or trivial, and for the sake of clarity I shall usually resort to these terms. Again, it is true that in some small or primitive societies what we should call 'criminal law' is not clearly distinguishable from 'civil law', and sometimes neither are really distinct from custom. But with the possible exception of Northumbria in the eighth century, the states of English society with which this book is concerned had advanced beyond that stage. They differed from twentieth-century England in treating only a handful of very serious acts as criminal, and in leaving the control of other misbehaviour to civil law, to the Church, or to unofficial retaliation. The shores of the criminal law have expanded enormously since the time of the Norman Conquest; and at the height of the puritan ascendancy its highwater mark included most forms of behaviour of which strict protestants disapproved. That tide has been receding for some time, and we now leave many areas of morality to the civil law or to unofficial sanctions. We are more formal in prosecuting, trying and punishing minor transgressions of the law than the high-handed justices of the peace used to be, and perhaps to this extent the coast-line of the criminal law is more clearly marked than it was. But despite all such differences it is possible to discuss infringements of it without too much ambiguity throughout the period we are considering.

This book is concerned with the problems which arise when a person who is identified as a criminal is also recognised as being mentally disordered. If we consider only the numbers of people to whom this has happened these problems are negligible. Even today, less than one in every hundred persons charged with an indictable or non-indictable offence – to say nothing of motoring offences – is officially dealt with in one of the special ways which we reserve for the mentally disordered; and although this happens on some 2,000 occasions a year many of the offenders involved belong to a 'stage army' who appear in the courts, disappear into the wings of the mental health service, and reappear in the dock not many months later. In earlier centuries, when fewer types of behaviour were criminal, when even those that were occurred less often in a small population, and when the penalties for them were drastic and in many cases final, this stage army was even smaller, and its members must have made fewer appearances.

This is not to belittle the prevalence or incidence[1] of mental disorder in the population. Both are notoriously difficult to estimate. The most conservative estimate of prevalence is based on the number of patients 'on the books' of hospitals for the mentally ill or subnormal at a given date. In 1960, according to the Registrar-General, they amounted to 408 out of every 100,000 males and 445 out of every 100,000 females of all ages.[2] By no means all of these, of course, were confined in the hospitals: some were on 'day parole' for work or recreation; some were even living at home with their families for trial periods. A more comprehensive estimate would of course include also those members of the population who would have been diagnosed as suffering from a mental disorder had a psychiatrist had the opportunity of making a diagnosis. The best estimate of this kind is probably that of Watts, Cawte and Kuenssberg,[3] which was based on a survey in which 261 general practitioners, scattered throughout England, Wales and Scotland, took part in 1961; the population 'at risk' of being counted was just over one million (that is, about one-fiftieth of the total population of the island). To be counted, a person had to be among the patients of one of these doctors and be sufficiently disordered to be recognised as such by his doctor. The doctors who took part were a willing, and therefore biased, selection of those who were invited to do so, and were for this reason probably readier than average to recognise mental disorders: but if anything that was an advantage, since it must have meant that they differed less from psychiatrists in this respect than the average practitioner.

The results of this very interesting survey will be referred to in more detail in volume II. For the present it is sufficient to note the authors' final estimate of the total prevalence of diagnosable mental disorder in England and Wales. On the not too artificial assumption that none of the cases recorded in their survey were also 'on the books of a hospital', they combined their rates with those of the Registrar-General, and arrived at the following table (Table 1).

Very roughly, then, about twelve people in every thousand of our population would be diagnosed by a modern English psychiatrist as mentally disordered. Three of these twelve would be mentally retarded; three would be suffering from depression, with or without intervals of manic

TABLE 1. Estimated prevalence of mental disorder in England and Wales in 1961

	Hospital population at 31st December 1960 as rates per 100,000 of the home population of all ages			Other diagnosable cases at 1st November 1961 as rates per 100,000 of the home population of all ages		
	males	females	both	males	females	both
Mentally ill	262	330	296	486	817	651
Mentally retarded	146	115	130	97	82	89
Both	408	445	426	583	899	740
						426
						1,166

excitement. Two would be suffering from schizophrenia in one of its many varieties. Two would be suffering from anxiety states of greater or lesser intensity. One would be suffering from one of the mental disorders of senility. The twelfth would be an example of one of the many less frequent types of disorder, some due to infection, some to brain damage, some to rare genetic mutations, some to endocrine abnormalities or disturbances, and some simply to an adverse environment in their formative years. Seven of the twelve would be women, for females seem more prone to depressive illnesses and (by reason of greater longevity) to the disorders of senility; it is only among the mentally retarded and the psychopathic that males show a definite preponderance.

In a population of 46 million, these people probably number rather more than half a million, of whom a little more than a third are 'on the books' of a hospital at any one time. It is very hard to estimate what percentage of this considerable number become entangled in the criminal law as a result of their disorders, but it must be very small indeed. Most manifestations of mental illness or subnormality do not constitute offences. It is no breach of the law to be dirty, unkempt, inconsequential, bewildered, tearful, statuesque or stupid, or to grimace, talk to oneself, or lock oneself into one's home.

It is true that some acts of the disordered can be treated as offences: shouting obscenities in public, wearing too little clothing, sleeping in a park, taking or damaging someone else's property, making sexual advances to the unwilling or immature, and attacking other people, are all examples. But many incidents of this kind do not lead to criminal charges even when the perpetrator is mentally normal. He may be undetected; the person affronted may be too forgiving, easygoing, ignorant, embarrassed, or antagonistic to authority to do anything about him. If he is reported, the evidence may be too weak to support a charge, or the police may regard the offence as too trivial for anything but a warning.

All these factors operate to protect the mentally disordered as well as the normal offender. Moreover, if his condition is sufficiently obvious, it may persuade a member of the public or a constable not to invoke the law where they would otherwise have done so. This is especially likely if he is known to be already in the care of a psychiatrist or institution. By looking after so many of our mentally ill or subnormal citizens in hospitals we not only reduce their opportunities and temptations for giving offence, but secure more tolerance for them when they succumb. Many a patient who has committed a theft, indecency or attack while on parole from a mental hospital is simply brought back to it, usually by the local police.

Mentally disordered offenders are very far from being a natural category in the sense that the albino, the haemophiliac or the typhoid carrier is. They are a selection from a group of people who suffer from heterogeneous disorders. The process of selection picks out those whose behaviour is sufficiently offensive to be treated as criminal, sufficiently incautious or frequent to lead to detection, and sufficiently irrational to convince both psychiatrists and lawyers that it is a symptom of disorder. But although they are a tiny and biased selection, the problems which they present are neither negligible nor uninteresting. It is not merely that the harm which may be done by a disordered person is sometimes terrible and irremediable. Nor is it merely that the stage army is a demonstration of a failure in the system devised by administrators, legislators and psychiatrists (an aspect which will be discussed in volume II). The mentally disordered offender raises questions which have troubled theologians, moral philosophers and lawyers throughout the Christian era. A great deal of this first volume is concerned with the attempts of lawyers to reconcile the demands of expediency with their moral principles.

At first sight the most remarkable aspect of this corner of the criminal law is the slowness with which it has developed in the thousand years since the first recorded mention of the insane offender in England. But on reconsideration this becomes less astonishing, for several reasons. One of these is, of course, the fact that an essential feature of any legal code, however sophisticated, is its stability: the Medes and Persians were neither the first nor the last civilisation to recognise this. Innovations must always be suspect, and accepted only when experience has shown that there is a recurring difficulty which can be circumvented in no other way, or only in troublesome ways. Revision may occasionally be dictated by an autocrat (such as Henry VIII) or imposed by the sentiment of the community; but more often than not the pre-existing law eventually reasserts itself, unless the situation recurs with sufficient frequency.

It was this sufficient frequency that was lacking in the case of insane crimes. Until the seventeenth century they were in all probability so rare that no single judge saw more than one or two recognisable examples in his comparatively short career. The explanation of their rarity is not simply that conditions which would now be acknowledged as pathological went undiagnosed, or that many incidents which would lead to prosecution today were not regarded as breaches of the law, or were left to private litigation. What must not be forgotten is that the mere number of insane or feeble-minded persons in this country was far smaller than it is today. Even the artificial assumption that the prevalence of all mental disorders per thousand of the population has remained unaltered would mean that for every forty such cases today there would be only one at the time of the Norman Conquest, when the population of England numbered about one million. Not until the eighteenth century did the sharp increase begin which raised the population from six million to forty-six million in two hundred years.

An even more interesting possibility, however, is that the mental disorders most frequently associated with the incidents which were treated as crimes in earlier centuries were *relatively* as well as absolutely more uncommon: in other words, that a million Englishmen in Norman or Tudor times contained fewer examples of what are now recognised as mental disorders than do a million Englishmen today. Certainly there are mental illnesses which must have been more or less prevalent at different eras. The various forms of cerebral deterioration, for example, which may affect people after middle age but are rare before that, must have been extremely infrequent in the days when the average expectation of life of a one-year-old child was about forty years, as it was throughout the Middle Ages. The mental illnesses which often accompany the last stages of alcoholism must have been very rare until distilled spirits became cheap and available in the early eighteenth century. If syphilis was unheard of, or at least very rare, in England before the sixteenth century, the 'general paralysis of the insane' which filled so many beds in modern asylums until effective cures for syphilis were discovered must have been unknown. (Indeed, it has been suggested that it was not until the Napoleonic Wars that the neurotropic strain of the spirochaete, which is responsible for those cases of syphilis that end in mental deterioration, became common.)[4]

A few types of mental disorder were probably commoner. Those due to deficiencies of nutrition, such as pellagra and Wernicke's disease, must have been more frequent in the Middle Ages than today. Poisoning by ergot (which can occur in flour) or by lead (which was used for cooking utensils) must have been a greater risk than it is now.

As I shall show in volume II, however, the mental disorders which are responsible for most of the crimes of the mentally disordered fall into three groups – the schizophrenias, the manic-depressive psychoses, and the non-specific form of low intelligence. Were these less common than they are nowadays? This is a harder question to answer, and the answers must be much more tentative.

The term schizophrenia – which means not 'split personality' as so many people believe, but 'the cut-off mind' – is applied to a wide variety of patients whose combinations of symptoms are so diverse that it seems necessary to adopt one of two hypotheses. It is possible that there are several distinct forms of mental illness, which have different causes, different prognoses and different responses to different forms of treatment, but which have so many symptoms in common that diagnosticians are not yet able to assign patients to one or the other with much confidence or agreement. Psychiatrists of the Kraepelinian school distinguish, for example, the catatonic type (in which the striking symptom is the patient's immobility and willingness to remain in whatever posture he is induced to assume); the paranoid type (of which delusions of persecution are the main feature); the hebephrenic type (in which deterioration of reasoning and bizarre ideas are characteristic); and 'simple' schizophrenia, in which delusions, hallucinations and catatonic posturing do not appear, but the patient simply loses drive, will-power and sense of responsibility, and his emotions become shallow or inappropriate so that he is labelled 'heartless'. But even the most rigid Kraepelinian would admit that there are very few 'pure' examples of each type.

The other view, which has been held by Meyer and his numerous followers, is that this great variety of symptoms is attributable to the diverse ways in which different types of personality react to stressful situations. An extreme form of this view, which is held by some psychoanalytically oriented doctors such as R. D. Laing, is that these reactions are almost wholly attributable to the severity and timing of the stress, especially certain kinds of stress in childhood and adolescence. A less extreme view is that there is some underlying constitutional factor which prevents the patient from reacting to the stress in a more rational or effective way. On either form of the hypothesis, however, the diversity of schizophrenic symptoms is due not to different forms of the disorder, but to the different ways in which each individual's personality breaks down.

Social psychiatrists, who tend to emphasise the importance of the human environment in the causation of mental illness, often cite as evidence the abnormally low rates of disorders such as schizophrenia in small, cohesive communities such as the Hutterite villages of the American Middle West. If, as is generally supposed, these resemble the rural communities of mediaeval Europe, it seems reasonable to infer that the mediaeval villager was less likely than the twentieth-century city-dweller to have a schizophrenic breakdown.

Most psychiatric textbooks, however, emphasise the importance of heredity in the causation of schizophrenia, and point to evidence from the studies of blood-relatives of schizophrenics. Particularly impressive is the fact that if one member of a pair of twins is recognised to be schizophrenic, there is a higher than average probability that the other will also be, *but especially if the twins are identical* – that is, originated from a single *ovum*.[5] This evidence does not, of course, mean that heredity is the only factor which determines whether one becomes schizophrenic or not; it is worth noting that even the identical twin of a schizophrenic by no means always manifests schizophrenia. But it suggests that the incidence of schizophrenia in a population must owe a great deal to the mechanics of inheritance.

Another group of mental illnesses which accounts for a substantial number of acts of violence is what are called the 'affective psychoses', that is, manic or depressive states, often alternating in the same individual. Although manic states, unlike some forms of schizophrenia, are not usually accompanied by the desire to do physical harm, attempts to restrain or interfere with the sufferer's wild and restless behaviour may provoke him to violence; or if, as sometimes happens, he insists on stripping naked, he may be charged with indecent exposure. More common, however, is the depressive state which leads to suicidal and murderous acts. One of the commonest forms of murder in this country today is committed by the husband or wife whose pathological despair for the future leads them to kill their children and then, in many cases, themselves. Here again, the evidence from studies of twins seems to support the hypothesis that heredity plays an important part in the affective psychoses, although there are undoubtedly some forms of depression which are reactions to environmental stress, infection, and other non-genetic causes.

Another major subdivision of mentally disordered offenders is what used to be called the mentally defective, but is now known as the mentally subnormal. Subnormality too takes various forms, some of them due to brain damage, others to congenital malformation of the brain, to endocrine or metabolic abnormalities, or to infectious or poisonous substances. But such forms of subnormality are rare, severe, and so incapacitating that the sufferer can seldom lead a sufficiently active life to commit breaches of the law. By far the commonest form is mere low intelligence resulting not from specific damage or malformation of the brain but from the considerable variation in inherited intelligence which seems to be inevitable in a freely breeding population.

It is usually assumed that disorders in whose causation heredity plays an important part become more prevalent in a population as its care for its sick and handicapped members becomes more general and effective. Theoretically, this makes it more likely that its more eccentric or stupider members will survive and breed. An even more disquieting observation is that, in more than one civilised country, there is a tendency for the less intelligent to have larger – and less intelligent – families than the more intelligent, although it has been suggested that our intelligentsia has lately developed a taste for larger families. It is true that the establishment of large numbers of asylums for the insane and institutions for the mentally defective, which in England began in the eighteenth century, may have introduced a counteracting factor by preventing the inmates from breeding as freely as they would have. If so – and it is by no means certain whether this has interfered greatly with the fertility of the mentally disordered – the modern tendency to regard the return of the patient to the community as the proper aim of hospital psychiatry is busily reducing whatever eugenic effect the institution used to have.

It is a curious fact, however, that attempts to measure the theoretically likely increases in the prevalence of mental disorders have had largely negative results. There have been two major investigations in Britain in which the intelligence of pre-war schoolchildren was compared with that of post-war children, and in neither case had the average test score declined; indeed, there seemed to have been a slight increase, although this may have been due to greater familiarity with tests on the part of post-war children.[6] It is true that the periods spanned by these investigations were comparatively short – fifteen and thirteen years respectively – and that the techniques used have been criticised. It is conceivable that there had been a slight decline which was more than compensated by the greater sophistication of the post-war children, and that if the tests had been separated by a longer interval, such as fifty years, there would have been a decline sufficient to reveal itself in spite of the masking factors. On the other hand, geneticists have responded to the challenge of these negative results by devising explanatory models which do *not* make it inevitable that the average intelligence of a population should decline.

There have been no similar comparisons in Britain of the incidence of mental illness in different generations. Attempts of this kind, however, have been made in the USA, of which the most thorough is undoubtedly that of Goldhamer and Marshall.[7] It is also remarkable because it succeeded in comparing periods as wide apart as the eighteen-eighties and the nineteen-thirties. The investigation was based on records of admissions of patients to institutions for the insane in Massachusetts, and took considerable precautions against distortions due to differences in social class, immigration, and age composition. The authors' main conclusions were:

1. . . . age-specific first admission rates for ages under 50 are revealed to be just as high during the last half of the nineteenth century as they are today.

2. There has been a very marked increase in the age-specific admission rates in the older age-groups. [They attribute this chiefly to an increased tendency to commit cases of senile mental disorder to hospital, but mention the possibility that the actual incidence of arteriosclerosis has increased.]

Although Goldhamer and Marshall took pains to make sure that they were comparing first admissions of *psychotics*, and not of mental defectives, epileptics, alcoholics and neurotics, they admit that in nineteenth-century Massachusetts one had to be more severely disordered than today in order to be admitted to an institution. But this means that *if there was a difference* between the incidence of the psychoses of early and middle life in the eighteen-eighties and nineteen-thirties, that incidence was almost certainly *higher* in the eighteen-eighties. In other words, as in the case of intelligence, such evidence as there is contradicts the assumption from genetics that the incidence of psychosis is bound to increase under civilised conditions. The possible exception is the incidence of those mental disorders which are more or less confined to people past middle age; but since the question is whether the relatively young population of pre-industrial England was more or less prone to severe mental illness than corresponding age-groups today, that is irrelevant.

Summed up, such evidence as there is suggests that while mental disorders due to syphilis, alcohol and senility must have been extremely rare in England until later periods in its history, the disorders which are responsible for the great majority of serious crimes were probably no less frequent in relation to the population at risk.

For the development of the law, however, it is absolute rather than relative frequency which is important. The tight organisation of the system of criminal trial which was achieved under the Plantagenet kings meant, among other things, that cases in which the accused appeared to be insane were not finally disposed of locally, but were discussed by the king's travelling justices and even by the king with his council. Even when it became the practice to dispose of the insane at the trial itself, it was usually the judges sallying out from the capital who did so, and not the local magistrates. Consequently it was the *actual* rarity of these cases, and not their relative frequency, which was important. Time and again, as we shall see, the judges cast about for a similar case to guide them, and often came to the conclusion that the circumstances with which they were faced were without precedent, although this was not in fact so. Even in the twentieth century it was possible for a Government spokesman in the House of Lords to say that Sergeant Boshears' case was unprecedented, although crimes by 'sleep-walkers' are merely very rare (see chapter 10).

Perhaps the best illustration of the importance of sheer numbers is to be found in the chapters dealing with diminished responsibility. Although this defence[8] was originally devised in Scotland in the middle of the nineteenth century and imported into the English law of murder in 1957, its scope in England has widened much more rapidly in the last ten years than in Scotland. The reason is probably that in Scotland not only are murders much less common than in England, but also the mentally disordered murderer is more often committed to a mental hospital without being tried. Consequently it is very rarely that a Scots judge has to try a case in which this defence is offered, and when he does he casts back to pre-war definitions of the concept. In contrast, there were 284 successful defences of this kind in England from 1957 to 1965, and its scope has widened so as to include states of mind which in Scotland would be rejected unhesitatingly. It is not that Scots judges are more hard-headed or their English colleagues more soft-hearted; simply that to make people devote continuous thought and discussion to an issue examples of it must be sufficiently frequent.

The legal history of England is, of course, infinitely better documented than its psychiatric history, although many of the documents still lie unpublished in the Public Record Office and elsewhere, accessible only from half-past nine till five on weekdays, and intelligible only to a scholarly handful of lawyers. Nevertheless the published documents have their own dangers. In comparison with most of the sources of social history they have the virtue of considerable accuracy; but this very accuracy distracts attention from their chief deficiency. By their nature they are almost always reports of atypical cases. It is of course atypical cases which are supposed to make legal history, but as we shall see when we reach the age of statistics, the most celebrated cases seem to have remarkably little effect on the numerical trends. The chapter on insanity on arraignment mentions at least two cases which never reached the law reports but which had as much effect on procedure as any that did.

There is also a tendency to assume that the earliest recorded case was the first of its kind. No doubt this is often so; but not always. Here again sleep-walkers provide a good example. When modern legal writers began to take notice of crimes committed by sleep-walkers, one of them discovered Fraser's case in the Scottish law reports, and it has been enshrined in the textbooks. As I shall show, however, in chapter 10, at least one similar case occurred in seventeenth-century England and another in the middle of the nineteenth century, although neither seems – for reasons which will be discussed – to have been recorded in the law reports.

There is a sense, of course, in which only the reported cases can make legal history; for it is only the case in the law reports of which judges can be expected to take notice in deciding what the law must be. For example, Hadfield is usually assumed to have been the first person to be acquitted as insane by an English court without being able to satisfy either the 'wild beast test' or the 'right-wrong test'. This is almost certainly not so; in chapter 3 I have been able to describe more than one case in the previous century in which the accused was acquitted although it is hardly conceivable that he or she could have satisfied either of the traditional tests. Yet Hadfield is regarded as a maker of history, while they are forgotten. For his trial was recorded in full in the series of 'State Trials', while theirs were described only in the Old Bailey Sessions Papers or in a rather new publication called *The Times*. There were of course more differences than that. Miss Broadric's victim, for example, was merely a renegade lover, but Hadfield's target was the king. Hadfield's case led to legislation; hers did not. Legal historians, however, would no doubt have argued – if they had compared the cases – that the most important difference was that her acquittal was the irrational result of compassion for a woman wronged, whereas Hadfield's was achieved only by the cold logic with which Erskine exposed the weakness of the traditional tests, and that for this reason Hadfield made new law while she did not.

Even this argument, however, would be an oversimplification. As we shall see, not only was Erskine's logic far from impressive, but his battle-scarred client must have had an emotional effect upon the court, although of a different sort from Miss Broadric's appeal. Moreover the picture we are offered, in which English courts firmly hold to the traditional tests throughout the eighteenth century, rejecting the insanity of Arnold and Ferrers, and suddenly undergoing enlightenment in 1800, is also misleading. I hope to show that for several decades before Hadfield, during the earlier part of George III's reign, there were unmistakable examples of a greater leniency towards the insane, not only on the part of jurors but also on the part of judges, Privy Councillors, and the Home Secretary. If so, Hadfield's judges did not summon up the wind of change but were bowing before it.

A recurring problem then in the interpretation of most of the documents on which this history is based is to decide whether the incident recorded is typical of its time or is being recorded for the very reason that it is unusual. It is a fairly safe assumption that legal reporters record what seems to them new, even if the explanation is merely that it is very rare. On the other hand, the opposite assumption should probably be made in the case of the early plea rolls, on which so much of chapter 1 is based, for they were intended to be complete records and not merely selections. Privy Council minutes certainly seem to be very complete records. But when one is interpreting the documents in eighteenth-century State Papers or the early Home Department files, the situation is more complex. Even if one assumes – as is probable even in the case of eighteenth-century bureaucracy – that the papers are more or less complete for the years in question, their very nature limits the inferences that can be drawn from them. It can be inferred that judges in George III's reign were not *always* content to leave the sanity of the accused to the good sense of the jury; that mental disorder short of the legally required severity was *now and again* urged as a reason for mercy, and that – rather less often – it was actually taken into account in deciding whether to interfere with the course of the law. Safe inferences can also be made about the *procedure* for dealing with such cases. But that is all.

A final word of explanation is perhaps needed about the sequence in which topics are dealt with in the remaining chapters. Instead of chronicling all the relevant events of a century or a decade in a single chapter, I have tried to trace the development of one theme at a time. Thus the first six chapters are concerned with what can broadly be called 'insanity as a defence'.[8] There follows a chapter on the first of the ways in which a less difficult escape route was provided by legislation for a restricted class of offender – the infanticidal mother. This is followed by a similar development, the introduction of the defence of diminished responsibility: chapter 8 describes its Scottish origins and the following chapter its importation into England. Next is an account of that rare defence[8] 'automatism' and the allied topic of drunkenness. The reactions of English monarchs to insane attacks upon them are dealt with in chapter 11. The following chapters deal with the use of the royal mercy to interfere with the course of the law in cases of insanity, at first as a step taken by the king and his advisers, later as a function of the Home Secretary. The subject of the penultimate chapter is insanity as an obstacle to trial.

This volume is thus intended to cover what might be called the traditional approach of the law to the problem of the insane offender. Towards the end of the nineteenth century it is possible to detect the beginnings of the entirely different approach which culminated in the Mental Health Act of 1959. This will be dealt with in the second volume, which will also describe a sample of the offenders who are dealt with under that Act.

Notes

1 By 'prevalence' epidemiologists mean the number of people suffering from a disorder at a given time ('point prevalence') or within a given short period ('period prevalence'). This should be distinguished from 'incidence', which means the number of examples of a disorder which begin during a specified period (such as a year); and from 'expectancy', which means the probability that an individual of a stated age – for example, at birth or at one or more years of age – will suffer from the disorder at least once during his lifetime. See D.D.Reid, *Epidemiological Methods in the Study of Mental Disorders* (World Health Organisation Public Health Papers No. 2, 1960, Geneva).

2 See the Registrar-General's *Statistical Review of England and Wales for the year* 1960: *Supplement on Mental Health*, HMSO.

3 C.A.H.Watts, E.C.Cawte, and E.V.Kuenssberg, 'Survey of Mental Illness in General Practice', in (1964), 2, *British Medical Journal* 1351–.

4 See E.H.Hare's article in (1959), 105, *Journal of Mental Science* 594–.

5 See the impressive summaries of genetic studies in the chapter by J.Shields and E.Slater in H.J.Eysenck's (ed.) *Handbook of Abnormal Psychology* (London, 1960), and in the article by V. Cowie and E.Slater in E.W.T.H.Fleming (ed.) *Recent Progress in Psychiatry*, III (London, 1959).

6 See *The Trend of Scottish Intelligence* by the Scottish Council for Research in Education (London, 1949); and the article by R.B. Cattell on 'The Fate of National Intelligence' in (1950), 42, *The Eugenic Review*, 136. The evidence is reviewed by Cowie and Slater, *loc. cit.* (n 5).

7 H.Goldhamer and A.W.Marshall, *Psychosis and Civilisation* (Illinois, 1949).

8 Throughout this book the term 'defence' will be used so as to include both issues – such as insanity – which not only must be raised by the accused but also lay on him the burden of proof, and issues – such as non-insane automatism – which must be raised by the defence although the burden of disproof is borne by the prosecution.

Chapter I. **Saxons and Normans**

To form some idea of the laws and customs which governed the fate of the insane offender in pre-Norman England is difficult but not quite hopeless. Limited but informative glimpses are provided by two independent texts. One of these was taken by Thorpe from a manuscript in the Burgundian Library at Brussels, which apparently gives both a Latin and an Anglo-Saxon version; it belongs to a period not later than the beginning of the eleventh century, and probably earlier.[1] Thorpe ascribed it to Egbert, the eighth-century Archbishop of York and member of the royal family of Northumbria, who founded what was almost a university in that barbarous country, and was probably the author of the Penitentials which go by his name. Like other Saxon penitentials they dealt, *inter alia*, with homicide and other serious breaches of law or morals.

The secular code treated most forms of homicide, as well as injuries short of death, as matters for compensation under the threat of the feud: a system summed up later in the phrase 'buy off the spear or bear it'. The amount of compensation due was determined not by the extent to which the offender was to blame but by the status of the victim and the seriousness of the harm. The Church, however, was concerned not with liability for restitution but with culpability for sin. Even in Egbert's day the man of violence had to make his peace not only with the victim's kinsmen but also with God – or at least the bishop. The Church tried to impose a higher standard of conduct than mere compliance with secular law and custom. The latter treated the slaying of a man as justified if the rules of the feud had been observed (for example, if compensation had been demanded and withheld); but the Church required a penance for any slaying. Even for an accidental killing a year's fasting was prescribed; and for homicide committed in anger and with premeditation (*per furorem et odii meditatione*) Egbert's Penitentials laid down a penance of five years.[1]

The passage in the Burgundian Library manuscript, however, sounds more like a description of secular law than a passage from a penitential:

If a man fall out of his senses or wits, and it come to pass that he kill someone, let his kinsmen pay for the victim, and preserve the slayer against aught else of that kind. If anyone kill him before it is made known whether his friends are willing to intercede for him, those who kill him must pay for him to his kin.[2]

There is nothing here about penance: simply a straightforward rule for ensuring that compensation was paid for an insane killer's victim, and that the insane man did not become in turn the victim of the spear. It is doubtful whether the passage should in fact be attributed to Egbert; but it is almost certain that it describes what at some period and at some place in pre-Norman England was the proper way to deal with such a situation.

By the eleventh century the control of violence and dishonesty – such as it was – was no longer left entirely to what we might loosely call the civil law of compensation and retaliation. There were by this time certain wrongs – open murder, open theft, arson, housebreaking, and treachery to one's lord – which were 'botless'; that is, which could not be wiped out by compensation but were punishable by death and the forfeiture of property (unless the offender, being 'in the king's mercy', could secure a pardon). In other words, there was a crude but distinguishable criminal law. Like the civil law from which it had emerged, it was based more or less on the principle of strict liability. Just as a man who did harm by accident had to pay compensation, so accident did not completely excuse him if he committed a botless wrong. But here too the Church had eventually succeeded in modifying the secular law. Since the bishops were usually the only people who enjoyed both sufficient standing and sufficient acquaintance with canon law it was usually a bishop who drafted the laws of the kings. Consequently, if his word was not quite law, the law at least used his words. One of the manuscript versions of the tenth-century laws of Æthelred – which are believed to have been drafted by Archbishop Wulfstan – contains a passage which reads more like a sermon than a law, but was no doubt intended as a statement of an important general principle:

> . . . And if it happens that a man commits a misdeed involuntarily, or unintentionally, the case is different from that of one who offends of his own free will, voluntarily and intentionally; and likewise he who is an involuntary agent of his misdeeds should always be entitled to clemency and better terms owing to the fact that he acted as an involuntary agent.
>
> Careful discrimination shall be made in judging every deed, and the judgement shall be ordered with justice, according to the nature of the deed . . . in affairs both religious and secular; and, through the fear of God, mercy and leniency and some measure of forbearance shall be shown towards those who have need of them. For all of us have need that our Lord grant us his mercy frequently and often. Amen.[3]

It is impossible to be sure whether this insertion represents actual practice in Æthelred's kingdom or is mere preaching. However that may be, even Wulfstan did not feel able to go to the length of recommending complete exemption from the penalty simply because the misdeed was involuntary. But the passage clearly embodies the idea that intention, or the absence of it, is relevant.

The laws of Æthelred's successor, Cnut, laid as much, if not more, emphasis on the importance of intention:

> . . . we must make due allowance and carefully distinguish between

age and youth, wealth and poverty, freemen and slaves, the sound and the sick. [This is an echo from Æthelred's laws.]

And discrimination with regard to these circumstances must be shown both in [imposing] ecclesiastical amends and in [passing] secular judgement.

Likewise, in many cases of evildoing, when a man is an involuntary agent, he is more entitled to clemency because he acted as he did from compulsion.

And if anyone does anything unintentionally, the case is entirely different from that of one who acts deliberately.[4]

There is a bureaucratic caution about the wording of these rules which is not entirely due to the translation. Like Wulfstan, the draftsman neither says nor implies that any of the circumstances which he mentions are grounds for complete exemption: all that they justify is *leniency*, which is a very different thing. It is disappointing not to find any mention of madness among these mitigating circumstances. Must we infer that the custom described in the Burgundian Library manuscript did not hold in Cnut's kingdom? After all, it *may* have come from Egbert's Northumbria, as Thorpe believed. Another possibility is that it was easier to deal with the problem of the insane slayer in a system which relied on private compensation than in one which regarded at least the most serious offences as calling for deterrent penalties such as death or mutilation, as Cnut's did. It is all very well to make a madman's family pay for the harm he has done; but to impose physical punishment on them would be rough justice indeed.

Nevertheless it is highly unlikely that Anglo-Saxon custom had ceased to provide for the insane offender. For the so-called Laws of Henry I contain a passage which seems to describe very much the same custom as the undoubtedly Anglo-Saxon text from the Burgundian Library. Whether the Laws were compiled in the reign of Henry I (1100–1135) or Henry II (1154–1189), they are undoubtedly describing the practices of southern Britain before the innovations of Henry II.[5] Moreover, since the Normans, unlike more modern colonisers, did not sweep away the indigenous system of law enforcement or its rules – for their own was hardly more sophisticated – many of the 'Laws of Henry the First' are thought to be statements of customs which survived the Conquest. Among these is probably the following passage:

If a person be deaf and dumb, so that he cannot put or answer questions, let his father pay his forfeitures.

Insane persons and evildoers of a like sort should be guarded and treated leniently by their parents.[6]

Succinct as this precept is, several inferences can be drawn from it. In the first place, the word 'misericorditer' is probably more significant than it seems at first sight. 'Misericordia' was the technical term for the king's mercy, and 'misericorditer' probably means not merely 'with pity', but 'with leniency' or even 'without punishment'. Secondly, it seems clear that even when the insane person had been an 'evildoer' (maleficus) it was for his parents to keep him in such a way that he could not do further

D

harm, and probably – as in the case of the deaf and dumb – to pay his forfeitures.

This is entirely consistent with the earlier fragment, and suggests that although the Laws of Cnut and his predecessors were silent on the subject there was in fact a traditional custom for dealing with such problems. It is after all quite plain that their laws were not complete codes but more often edicts meant to deal with serious problems, such as cattle-stealing, and not with exceedingly rare events such as crimes by madmen.

The silence of Cnut's laws on the subject is paralleled by the omission of any mention of it from that well-known twelfth-century treatise *On the Laws and Customs of the Kingdom of England*, which is usually attributed to Henry 11's chief justiciar, Ranulph de Glanville (?–1190). The fourteenth book of *Glanville*, which deals with procedure in criminal cases, makes no reference to madness or idiocy. Since the plea rolls and treatises of the next century contain several cases or passages concerned with mad felons, are we to infer that there was an important modification in the law after this part of *Glanville* was written? Certainly the main impact of Roman law on this country did not take place until the thirteenth century, and as we shall see the official doctrine of Bracton and Fleta on this subject was derived from the Digest. On the other hand, to assume that twelfth-century law or custom ignored it would require us to dismiss the *Laws of Henry the First*. The answer is probably that the fourteenth book of *Glanville* should not be regarded as a comprehensive statement of the criminal law; after all, it ends by pointing out that its aim is to deal only with the king's court, and not with thefts and other pleas within the jurisdiction of the sheriff, which are heard and determined according to the varying customs of the county courts. Moreover, it is equally silent on the subject of children accused of felony, although in an earlier book we are told how they should be dealt with (by waiting until they are old enough to be appealed of felony – that is, until they reach the age of twelve). Richardson and Sayles are probably right when they suggest that Book XIV is no more than

> a guide to the procedure in criminal cases, especially where it might
> be easy for the inexperienced to go astray. The author assumes that
> we shall know that . . . a man is standing his trial whom the
> hundred jury have declared to be defamed of a certain felony, and
> the men from the four neighbouring townships have concurred
> with the hundredors. There is to be no trial in the modern sense
> of the word. The suspect will go to the ordeal; if he is unfree, to the
> water; if he is a freeman, to the hot iron. If he fails in the ordeal he
> will be hanged or mutilated.[7]

If so, it is at least possible that mental disorder was something which was taken into account – on the rare occasions when it was spectacular enough to be recognised – at an earlier stage, when the hundredors were discussing the case. Certainly it was not the sort of thing which trial by ordeal could be expected to diagnose. Indeed, the ordeal was presided over by priests, who might well have taken the view that it should not be applied to a person whom they regarded as morally guiltless, whatever the ordeal might prove that he had *done*. This supposition is not irreconcilable with what we know of the way in which insane offenders were dealt with in the following century. By that time there had been two important developments. Henry 11 had established a system of prosecution by the Crown and trial by itinerant justices for the serious crimes which came to be known as 'felonies'. Trial by ordeal, which was becoming discredited even in his time, was finally discountenanced early in the thirteenth century by the withdrawal of the clergy from the ceremony; its place was taken by the jury. The suspect was not merely presented for trial by the decision of a jury: it was a jury – perhaps at first the same jury – which tried him. The petty jury, as it came to be called, had to compete for prestige with a traditional form of trial in which the outcome was believed to be decided by the Deity himself; and they must at first have had their qualms about their capacity for this supernatural task. Certainly it was several centuries before they acquired quite the same superstitious authority.

Even in the late thirteenth century, when trial by jury was firmly established, the insane offender was occasionally disposed of without trial. The case of Richard of Cheddestan, so vividly described in the documents reproduced on pp 20–23, shows that as late as 1270 the Sheriff of Norfolk simply confined this homicidal man in prison. The facts were so clear that trial must have seemed unnecessary. This was not quite the way, however, in which the new machinery of justice was supposed to function. Everyone was happier if the facts had been formally stated by the jurors on their oath: and this was one of the steps which the king took, six years later, to tidy up the Norwich affair. Other thirteenth-century cases demonstrate that in such cases the usual procedure was for the jury to certify the facts and for the king to decide what should be done with the offender. The York plea rolls for the year 1212 record a case in which

> The King must be consulted about an idiot who is in the prison
> because in his witlessness he confessed that he is a thief, although
> in fact he is not to blame.[8]

It is possible that the king's justices could then order the lunatic to be indefinitely detained: Bracton's notebook mentions a woman called Matilda who in 1226 had difficulty in claiming an inheritance because another claimant, Ralph, was

> ... out of his wits and senses, for in this state he killed a man and
> came before the justices and confessed that he had killed him ...
> and he is in the prison, and will be for ever so long as he shall live,
> by order of the justices for that death.[9]

More probably, however, the justices simply ordered (or confirmed) the man's detention for the time being, and reported to the king, whose authority was required for his indefinite detention.

Later in the century there is a still more precise description of what happened to the insane murderer. In 1280 a Nottingham jury had to deal with a man who had hanged his daughter in a frenetic state.[10] The jury certified that he 'did as aforesaid, and not feloniously or through malice aforethought'. The justices therefore delayed in passing judgment until

This document and the one on page 22 will be found in file C/154/34 at the Public Record Office, by whose permission they are reproduced here. I am indebted to Mr Kaye for drawing my attention to them and deciphering them. The translations (which appear on the facing page in each case) are mine.

Edward, by the grace of God King of England, Lord of Ireland and Duke of Aquitaine, to his beloved and loyal John de Lovetot, greetings. On behalf of Richard of Cheddestan, taken and held in our prison at Norwich, it has been stated to us that when he, more than six years ago, was suffering from a frenzied seizure and in that frenzy killed his wife and two children, our then Sheriff of Norfolk, who had heard tell of this deed, took Richard and confined him in the aforesaid prison, where he is wretchedly detained. We therefore, wishing to know the truth of the aforesaid matter, depute you to enquire on oath of the knights, and other trustworthy and law-abiding men of the county from whom the truth may best be got, whether the aforesaid Richard, under the influence of the aforesaid frenzy, acted thus or otherwise, and if otherwise how and in what fashion, and whether the aforesaid Richard is restored to his former soundness of mind, or whether it would be dangerous if he were released from the prison on the ground that he was ill. And therefore we instruct you that on a given time and place to be arranged by you for this purpose you hold this inquiry, and having done so plainly and publicly report to us briefly and without delay. Accordingly we also instruct our Sheriff of the aforesaid county that at a time and place which you will make known to him he shall cause to appear before you such knights and other trustworthy and law-abiding men as are needed for getting at the truth of these matters. In witness whereof we have had these letters patent drawn up. In my presence at Westminster on the 25th day of July in the fourth year of our reign.

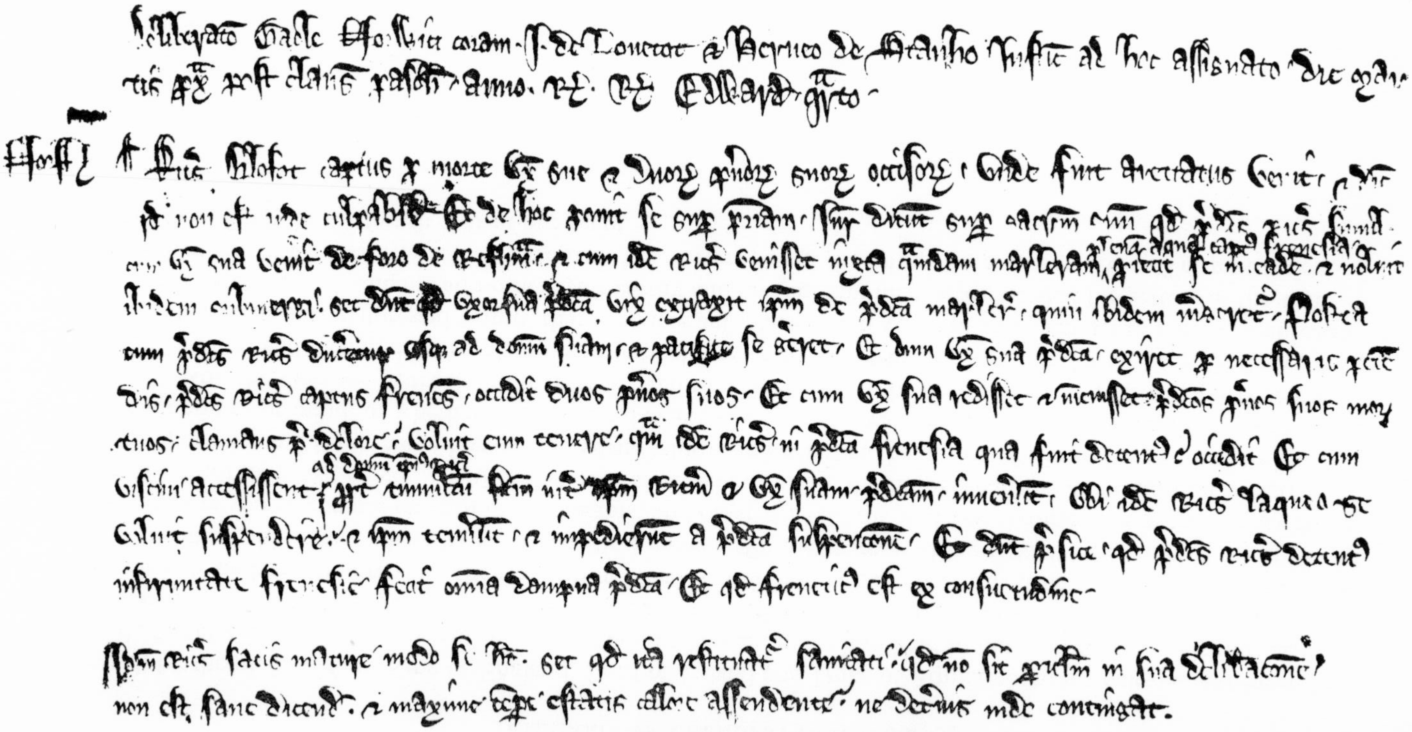

Delivery of Norwich gaol before J. de Lovetot and Henry de Stanho, Justices deputed for this purpose, on the first day of March after Easter in the fourth year of King Edward:

The Sheriff of Norfolk [states that] Richard Blofot, in custody for the death of his wife and two slain children, the reason for his arrest, appeared and says that he is not guilty thereof; and for this places himself upon his country. The jurors say on their oath that the aforesaid Richard, together with his wife, came from Reepham market; and when the same Richard had come near a certain marl-pit full of water he was seized with a frenzy and cast himself into it, wishing to drown there. But, they say, his wife with much difficulty dragged him from the aforesaid marl-pit before he drowned. Later Richard was taken to his home with his wife and children and behaved peacefully. And while his aforesaid wife was away from his home in search of necessaries the aforesaid Richard was seized with frenzy and killed his two children. And when his wife returned and found her aforesaid children dead, she cried out in grief and tried to hold him, but was killed by Richard in the grip of the aforesaid frenzy. And when the neighbours, summoned by the noise made by Richard and his aforesaid wife, reached the house they found the same Richard trying to hang himself from a roof-beam, and they held him and prevented him from doing so. And they say clearly that the aforesaid Richard in the grip of a frenzied sickness did all the aforesaid harm, and that he is continually frenzied.

The same Richard is well enough; but it cannot safely be said that he is so restored to soundness of mind that there would not be danger in setting him free, especially when the heat of summer is increasing, lest worse befall.

they had received instructions from the king. The king's orders were eventually that he should be handed over to the custody of 'manucaptores' to be brought before the king's bench in case anyone wanted to proceed against him. His goods and lands were also to be seized; but he was to be allowed sustenance from them, and the persons charged with their management were not to commit any waste.

The king must be consulted not because the jury or justices were at a loss but because it was not for them to interfere with the normal course of the law by excusing him from the automatic penalty for his felony. This is demonstrated by two cases of the year 1292 in the record of the Eyre of Cumberland.[11] A lunatic who had burned a man's house was convicted by the justices but released on their authority; and in the following year they were fined for taking this step without consulting the king. The temptation to arrive at the same result by a quicker method than consulting the king must have been very strong in a remote county such as Cumberland, for in the same Eyre a coroner was gaoled for overstepping himself by countenancing a false finding, to the effect that a man 'was a lunatic and had set fire to a house in his frenzy, and not with malice aforethought'.[12] So that when Matilda claimed that her Ralph would be in prison so long as he lived 'by order of the justices' she may have been referring to a similar action on the part of the local justices (although it is also possible that they had simply ordered him to be confined until the king confirmed that he was not to die).

This state of affairs represented a compromise between a legal system founded on strict liability and the ecclesiastical insistence on the importance of *mens rea*. On the one hand the harm done must be acknowledged by the legal process; on the other hand the legal process could not be carried to its grim conclusion if the harm was unintentional. So there must be interference with the due process of law by the one person who could properly interfere – the king.

It is quite conceivable that in such cases the petty jury who 'found' that the accused had been mad at the time of his act were simply doing what the hundredors had done. Whether a man was an idiot or a madman was a matter of local knowledge, and they were therefore the obvious people to ask. It is clear that the central government wished to have control over the trial and disposal of persons who committed serious crimes, including the insane. It may well be, therefore, that the lunatic who would in Glanville's day have been put away without being presented for trial by ordeal now had to come before the petty jury and the king's justices, and be reported eventually to the king.

The insanity of the accused was not the only circumstance that obliged the justices to consult the king. A royal pardon was needed if he had killed by accident or self-defence, or if he was an infant. But whereas the chattels of the accused seem to have been forfeit in those cases, this does not seem to have been so if he was insane. Fitzherbert notes that 'if a woman become demented and out of her wits and kill her lord, she does not forfeit any of her heritage or free property, but when she comes to her senses she possesses her property as before',[13] and he is referring to a case of 1228.

Elsewhere he cites a case of 1330 in which a woman who was known to be mad had drowned herself, but since the jury said that she was only mad from time to time her chattels were forfeit: the implication is that if she had been mad continuously they would not have been.[14]

Nevertheless the king was interested in the property of the madman as well as his person; nor was this interest confined to criminal cases. The wardship of the person and land of a recognised lunatic or idiot – which could sometimes be quite a profitable responsibility – had by now passed out of the hands of his parents, first into those of his feudal lord and then into the hands of the crown. The Statute on the King's Prerogative (which was drawn up between 1255 and 1290[15]) makes it clear that

> The King has the custody of the lands of natural fools (*fatuorum naturalium*), taking their profits without waste, finding them their necessaries . . . and after their death must return them to the rightful heirs. . . . He must also see to it that when anyone who formerly had memory and understanding is no longer in his right mind (*compos mentis suae*) – as some may be between lucid intervals – their lands and tenements are safely kept without waste or destruction; that they and their families live and are maintained from the profits; and that what is left from maintaining them is reasonably kept for their use when they have recovered their memories. . . . The king shall take nothing to his own use, and if the person dies in that state shall distribute the remainder for his soul by the advice of theOrdinary.

It is noticeable that by this time idiocy and madness are distinguished. The former is recognised as a permanent condition, sometimes defined as existing 'from birth'; and there is therefore no reason why the king should not take the profits from idiots' estates during their lifetimes, so long as he provides them with their 'necessaries'. Madness, on the other hand, is a temporary condition, and the sufferer who recovers has a right not only to his estates but to the profits which it yielded while he was temporarily out of his mind.

The estates of idiots continued to be a source of royal income until the end of the eighteenth century. The administration of madmen's property was delegated either to a local administrator (such as the mayor of a city)[16] or – probably a later development – to a committee. But the history of this part of the civil law and administration is outside the scope of this book, and will be mentioned only when it is relevant to the problems of the penal system.[17]

The period during which it became the regular practice to acquit the insane accused instead of leaving him to be pardoned by the king cannot be identified with certainty. Holdsworth seems to regard the fact that the chattels were not forfeit in the cases I have cited as evidence that the accused was acquitted[18]: but the finding of the Cumberland jury in 1292 suggests that this can hardly have been so in the case of the woman who 'killed her lord' in 1228 (unless we suppose that the practice had become fairly common but that Edward I tried to stamp it out, perhaps for pecuniary reasons). However that may be, the earliest clear case of acquittal which I have found belongs to 1505:

A man was accused of the murder of an infant. It was found that at the time of the murder the felon was of unsound mind (de non saine memoire). Wherefore it was decided that he should go free (qu'il ira quite). To be noted.[19]

What seems almost certain is that when Bracton compiled his treatise *On the Laws and Customs of England* in the middle of the thirteenth century it was not yet the practice of courts to acquit the insane offender as they later did. Yet Bracton, the first medieval English jurist to deal with the subject, writes as if that was what they should have done. After a brief discussion of accidental homicide he continues:

... for a crime is not committed unless the will to harm be present. Misdeeds are distinguished both by will and by intention [and theft is not committed without the thought of thieving]. And then there is what can be said about the child and the madman, for the one is protected by his innocence of design, the other by the misfortune of his deed. In misdeeds we look to the will and not the outcome. . . .[20]

Fleta, writing a generation or so later, reproduces this passage almost word for word.

The explanation is probably that Bracton was not describing procedure but expounding principles. The principle in this case was that intention is all-important when it is a question of a crime. To this doctrine he was trying to link, in a coherent way, the leniency with which madmen – and children – were in practice treated when they had broken the law. The arguments with which he sought to do this, however, were borrowed from the Roman law in which he was so learned and did not quite fit the actual procedure of the courts, although they justified the final outcome – a royal pardon.

Let me sum up at this point the hypothesis which seems to fit most neatly the scanty facts which we have – the passages from the so-called Laws of Henry I and from the Burgundian Library's manuscript, the silence of the Laws of Cnut and of Glanville's treatise on the subject, the procedure followed by thirteenth-century courts and its inconsistency with Bracton's Romanesque pronouncements. I suggest that the pre-Norman practice in dealing with serious offences by the insane, such as homicide, was to make the offender's family pay and look after him, and that this was done without presenting him formally for trial: local knowledge of his insanity settled the matter without the necessity for that. This practice would be consistent with the silence of Cnut and Glanville, although, as we have seen, it is not the only possible explanation of it. On this view, the transition to a more modern procedure began when juries were substituted for the ordeal as a method of trial, and when Henry II and his successors made efforts to improve the system of law enforcement by appointing their own justiciars to see that justice was done. Since the petty jury consisted of local men, it was perfectly reasonable to ask them to declare to the king's justice or the coroner whether the accused had really been mad when he committed the offence; this was no real breach with the ancient practice. But since they were now doing so at the extremely formal stage of trial, they must be careful not to override the law by acquitting a man who had in fact committed an offence. Only the king could do that, although at a later period his courts were finally allowed to. What Bracton was expounding was a justification for the end result of this procedure, whereby a madman escaped the penalty for his act.

All this is speculative. The most that can be claimed for it is that it makes sense of what is otherwise a series of apparently inconsistent pronouncements and cases. What is missing is of course confirmation of the hypothesis that insane offenders were dealt with informally and without trial in the days of Cnut and the twelfth-century Norman kings. If one rejects my hypothesis, the alternative seems to be the conclusion that during this period persons who were recognised as insane (and there can be no doubt that the pre-Norman English recognised some instances of insanity) were presented for trial, usually by ordeal, and suffered the penalty; and that it was only when jury trial had been established that mercy was shown to them, perhaps under the influence of Roman law. This seems to me to underestimate both the continuity and the sophistication of criminal procedure in the eleventh and twelfth centuries and to fit the known facts less neatly. But that is as far as the argument can be carried.

We must now take a closer look at Bracton, for the passage which has just been quoted has curious features. The remark that children are excused by their 'innocence of intent', madmen by the 'misfortune of the deed' is a more or less *verbatim* quotation from Modestinus[21] but with a difference. Modestinus refers to 'the misfortune of his *fate*' (*infelicitas fati*), but Bracton's manuscripts refer to 'the misfortune of his *deed*' (*infelicitas facti*), a phrase which Fleta simply copied and translators have simply translated without questioning its sense. Modestinus was referring to one of the justifications which Roman law offered for treating the insane offenders with leniency: that his madness was punishment enough (*satis furore ipso punitur*),[22] and was explaining that the reasons for excusing children and madmen were rather different. It is true that elsewhere in the Digest there was authority for the view that the madman has 'no will': but Modestinus argued that he should be excused punishment for a crime because of his misfortune. We shall find this argument cropping up now and again in Coke, Hume, and elsewhere. It has nothing to do with intention or its absence: if it has a modern analogy this might be the argument that a man who has been severely injured in a motoring accident should not be prosecuted for his careless driving.

Nevertheless it is clear that for Bracton madmen as well as children were examples of offenders who lacked the intention necessary for guilt. He may well have simply incorporated Modestinus' remark without reflecting on its irrelevance, especially if his text or memory rendered it as 'the misfortune of the deed'. For elsewhere, when he is discussing the incapacity of the insane in civil actions, he reasons that the person who is mad (*furiosus*) or of unsound mind (*non sanae mentis*) – the two are treated as synonyms – is totally lacking in 'discretion' (*discretionem*):

Such are not very different from animals who lack understanding (*ratio*), and no transaction is valid that is entered into with them while their madness lasts. For some of them sometimes enjoy lucid intervals, other suffer from continuous madness. . . .[23]

What was meant by lack of 'discretion' or 'understanding'? In the psychology of Bracton's day '*ratio*' could signify either understanding of the nature of one's act or knowledge of its wrongness, and it was recognised that madmen might lack either.[24] In the passage quoted, however, Bracton was talking about madmen's contracts, not their crimes, and almost certainly had in mind their understanding of the nature of their acts. Almost certainly, too, this is what 'discretion' meant. For if a child committed a felony the question was whether he had reached the age of discretion, which in the thirteenth century was not seven but twelve; and the usual test was his ability to count up to twelve pence, or perform tasks involved in his father's occupation, such as measuring cloth. It was probably not until the time of Spigurnel, Edward II's judge, that it became the practice to ask whether the child could tell good from evil, and children of seven – the crucial age in Roman law – were in danger of being hanged or burned.[25] In Bracton's day discretion seems to have meant 'knowing what was what', and it was this sort of common sense that was lacking in both children and the insane.

What sorts and degrees of disorder were recognised as justifications for exemption? In the recorded cases the accused is usually described in terms suggesting mental illness ('furiosus', 'frenetico passione detentus', 'insanus', 'demes', 'de non saine memoire') rather than mental defect which would be represented by such terms as 'fatuitas'. It is possible that Ralph's 'amentia' was 'witlessness', but 'amens et extra sensum' may well mean 'out of his normal wits and senses'. As for the degree of mental illness required, Bracton explains in the passage quoted that the terms he uses ('furiosus vel non sanae mentis') mean a total lack of 'discretion' and 'understanding', an animal-like state.

What sort of behaviour was likely to qualify for this description? Nothing can be inferred from Bracton's use of the word 'brutus', for although this was later translated into 'the *wild* beast test' it meant no more than 'dumb animal' would to us – a creature lacking rationality.[25] Nor does 'frenetico passione detentus' help us much, for it means no more than 'seized by a mad disorder'. Nevertheless, the constantly recurring word 'furiosus' suggests violent, excited behaviour, and could fairly be translated 'raving mad'.[26] There are one or two disorders which sometimes give rise to states of spectacular and obviously unreasoning violence. Epilepsy is one, and the term 'furor epilepticus' is still popular with Continental psychiatrists. Again, some such states are ascribed by psychiatrists to schizophrenia of the catatonic type:

Schizophrenia sometimes begins with a sudden burst of wild excitement. . . . The degree of restlessness and excitation may exceed everything known in psychiatry, except perhaps some epileptic furors. The patient cries, hits, bites, breaks and destroys everything he can lay hand on, runs up and down, fights everybody

and keeps moving day and night. . . . Horror or rage may be
expressed in the patient's face, but often the expression is
blank. . . .[27]

It is reasonable to assume that it was states of this kind which were
accepted by Bracton and his contemporaries as justifying the description
'furiosus'.

As in Roman law, it was recognised that a man might be 'furiosus' at one
time but in his right mind at another. We have already seen that both
Bracton and the Statute on the King's Prerogative are careful to explain
this, and there is even a recorded case of this same century from the rolls
of Cumberland in which a man who was on his way to the gallows to be
hanged for homicide was rescued by a band of his friends. When the res-
cuers in turn were brought to trial, one was found to be a lunatic, although
'from time to time he enjoys lucid intervals',[28] and he is ordered to be kept
in custody 'until the will of our lord the king thereon be known'.

To what sorts of crime did the exemption of the insane apply in Bracton's day? The special position of treason is discussed in chapter 11. There
were few felonies – homicide, rape, arson, grand larceny and robbery –
and no such thing as a misdemeanour. The cases which have already been
cited in this chapter include homicide and arson: but what about theft?
Bracton mentions it in the *locus classicus* ('theft is not committed without
the thought of thieving'); but that sentence may well be a later interpola-
tion, and in any case the writer may have had children rather than madmen
in mind. There are, however, two recorded cases of the thirteenth century
in which a mentally disordered person seems to have been involved in
theft. In one the king is to be consulted about 'an idiot who is in prison
because in his witlessness he confessed that he was a thief: but he is not
to blame'.[8] In the other 'Richard of Brent . . . accused of larceny, came
and defended all of it an put himself upon the country [i.e. accepted trial
by jury]. And the twelve jurors . . . say that they do not suspect him, save
of a fowl which he took in his madness at a time when he was lunatic.
Therefore let him be under pledges until more be known'.[29] But whether
the taking of the fowl was grand larceny depends on its value, and is not
certain; nor is it clear whether in the other case the idiot's confession was
believed or dismissed. What we do know is that by Hale's time the doctrine
seems to have been that the defence of insanity applied only to capital
crimes; and in the next chapter I shall argue that it would have made little
sense to apply it to lesser crimes. It is hardly surprising, however, that
there are no indisputable records of robbery, grand larceny, or rape by
persons recognised as madmen or idiots. These crimes are usually attributed to motives which we regard as natural, so that they do not prompt
us to question the sanity of the perpetrator as readily as do crimes of personal violence, and especially violence against a near relative such as a wife
or child. No doubt in those days, as now, robbery, theft, and rape were
occasionally committed by men whom we would regard as mentally ill
or subnormal: but it is unlikely that their disorder would be spectacular
enough to be recognised.

Finally, what can be said about the disposal and treatment of the insane offender in Saxon and Norman times? As we have seen, it was the family's duty to keep him under control. Indeed, who else could have been made responsible in a society whose few solid buildings were for defence against a much greater danger from without, the ever-present possibility of an invasion? Even Plato, when he drafted his utopian *Laws*, could not propose a better arrangement: 'if anyone be insane, let him not be seen openly in the town, but let his kinsfolk watch over him as best they may, under penalty of a fine'.[30] This cannot, however, have been an easy matter in times when the ordinary dwelling was built of wood and wattle. Madmen sometimes had to be tied to one of the roof-props or kept among the cattle. Perhaps because of faith in their healing powers, but more probably because they were more solid, churches were sometimes used as what modern legislators would call 'places of safety': in 1286 a Suffolk jury certified that a man who had killed a woman while 'furiosus' was lying bound in the Church of St Nicholas at Yarmouth.[31] When the first prisons began to be provided – usually in fortresses or bishops' palaces – they were an obvious place for the violent lunatic: Matilda's kinsman Ralph was in prison in 1226, and it seems to have been assumed by her – although it may have suited her case to do so – that he would be there for the rest of his life.

The administrators, however, were more interested in the proper administration of the madman's property than in the supervision of his behaviour. In fourteenth-century Bristol the custom was that

> . . . the mayor must see that his goods and chattels are taken and given to his nearest friends to look after until he recovers his sound mind. And his friends must place a sufficient guard on the persons of such madmen as will ensure that they come to no harm or loss and that they do not harm to others.[16]

The mayor (no doubt as the king's representative) must see that the madman's property was not misappropriated, but was not responsible for his person: that was still a matter for his 'friends', who must be presumed to include his relatives.

As for techniques of care and treatment, other writings once attributed to Egbert, and certainly Anglo-Saxon in origin, testify to the concern of the Church with the problem of insanity among its members. Nobody who had ever been observed to have an insane seizure ('qui palam aliquando arrepti sunt') could be admitted to clerical status, and if they had been they must be removed from it. There also are obscure fragments which seem to talk of religious exercises and daily exorcism for those who are out of their wits or agitated by spirits ('amentibus quaecunque sunt conferenda' and 'omni die exorcistae inerguminis manus imponant').[32] Saxon techniques for treating the insane were a mixture of religion, magic, herbal medicine, and chastisement. Madmen were taken to saints in the hope of miraculous cures. Others were ducked in streams, ponds, or springs (especially holy ones): for faith in the curative properties of water has inspired many a psychiatric device, from the cucking-stools of mediaeval England to the 'surprise-baths' of Georgian times and the flannel-baths of twentieth-century asylums. As for pharmacology, a collection of medicinal recipes by a tenth-century scribe named Cild contains several for 'fiend-sick' men. Many were based on emetics: 'take a spew-drink . . . lupin, bishopwort, henbane, cropleek. Pound them together, add ale for a liquid, let it stand for a night and add fifty libcorns . . . and holy water' – a powerful draught indeed. Another herbal brew had to be drunk out of a church bell, and there were similar remedies for the feeble-minded. A child with epilepsy (or convulsions?) should be given the brain of a mountain goat which had been drawn through a ring. As some of the remedies had to be taken at certain phases of the moon it is evident that some sorts of madness were already associated with its influence. Finally there is the stand-by on which so many madhouses came to rely in later centuries: 'in case a man be mad, take a skin of mere-swine [porpoise], work it into a whip, and swinge the man with it: soon he will be well. Amen'.[33]

Reliance on these crude techniques was not altogether inexcusable. Purges and emetics are extremely weakening, and so is flogging. Alone or in combination they must often have reduced the violent lunatic to a state in which he was at least quiescent, and his quiescence could be taken for a cure. Moreover, since the more spectacular symptoms of mental illnesses tend to fluctuate in severity, and even to disappear and reappear at intervals, treatment sometimes coincides with spontaneous remission, and produces an illusion of effectiveness which has occasionally deceived even modern psychiatrists. Finally, whatever else was achieved by confinement and restraint in the poorest of shelter, coupled with scanty feeding interrupted by purges and emetics, one effect must have been to hasten the patient's death, to the relief of both his relatives and their medical advisers.

It is true that by Bracton's day the influence of Continental schools of medicine, and particularly of Salerno, had introduced ideas which were both less superstitious and less unpleasant. Gilbertus Anglicus[34] advises rest and careful diet instead of pilgrimages and purges. Bartholomaeus[35] favours head-shaving and music, with purges and surgery only as last resorts. Neither mentions flogging. No doubt writers such as these were followed by physicians who had charge of wealthy or important patients. But as we shall see the old ideas died hard, and the treatment of the ordinary madman continued to be unscientific and brutal.

Notes

1 See A. W. Haddan and W. Stubbs, *Councils and Ecclesiastical Documents relating to Great Britain and Northern Ireland*, III (Oxford, 1869), 413; and B. Thorpe, *Ancient Laws and Institutes of England*, II (London, 1840).

2 See Thorpe, op. cit. Additamenta 29, 'si homo quis animo suo vel mente sua exciderit, et ei aliquem occidere evenerit, solvant pro homine propinqui ejus, et eum contra simile quid servent. Si quis inscienter eum occiderit, antequam cognitum erat num amici ejus pro eo intevenire vellent, solvant pro homine propinquis ejus homines qui eum occiderint'.

3 From Miss A.J.Robertson's translation in her *Laws of the Kings of England*, VI Æthelred 52 (Cambridge, 1925).

4 Ibid., p. 209.

5 See T.F.Plucknett, *Edward the First and Criminal Law* (Cambridge, 1960), 45; and H.G.Richardson and G.O.Sayles, *Law and Legislation from Æthelberht to Magna Carta* (Edinburgh, 1966), 43.

6 See F.Liebermann, *Die Gesetze der Angelsachsen*, I (Halle, 1898), 595:

> Si quis a nativitate surdus et mutus sit, ut sua vel alterius nequeat irrogata [sc. interrogata?] confiteri, emendet pater ejus forisfacta sua.
>
> Insanos et ejusmodi maleficos debent parentes sui misericorditer custodire.

7 H.G.Richardson and G.O.Sayles, op. cit. (n5), 107.

8 Selden Society Publications, *Select Pleas of the Crown*, I (London, 1887) 66:

> Loquendum cum rege de quodam stulto qui est in prisona eo quod per demenciam cognovit se esse latronem sed non est culpabilis.

9 See F. W. Maitland (ed.), Bracton's Notebook, III (1887), 660–1 :

> . . . amens et extra sensum, ita quod per amenciam suam occidit quendam hominem et venit coram justiciariis et cognovit quod eum occiderat . . . et est in prisona et erit in perpetuum quamdiu vixerit per praeceptum justiciariorum pro morte illa.

10 'frenetico passione detentus'. I am indebted to Mr J.M.Kaye of the Queen's College for notes on this (and other) cases which he has found in the original plea rolls.

11 I owe this case, too, to Mr Kaye.

12 '. . . lunaticus fuit et in furore suo combussit domum, et non per feloniam excogitatam.' This is another of Mr Kaye's cases.

13 Forfeiture 33, 12 Henry III: 'Nota, si feme devient demes et hors de memorie, et issint esteant occis son baron, el ne forfeta rien de son heritage ou de son franc tenement quod nota, mes quant el vient a sa memor el occupa sa trē come devant.'

14 Corone 324, 3 Edward III: 'Pres. fuit q̄ un feme quant el fuit enfrenzy aver naye l y m p son gree demene dd· fuit de le dozyn si le malady se mist de jour en jour ou p̄ foies, p̄ q̄ les cateux fuer forfets.'

15 According to Holdsworth: see his *History of English Law*, I (London 1903). 473 n.

16 See the Selden Society Publications, II *Borough Customs* (London, 1906), 150: 'Et de hominibus dementibus quod maior capere faciat bona eorum et catalla et ea liberare proximis amicis eorundem custodienda quousque ad bonam memoriam pervenerint. Et quod eorum amici super corpora hujusmodi demencium talem ponant custodiam quod [nec?] malum nec dampnum eis eveniant nec quod ipsi aliis malum faciant.'

17 Some of it will be found in Holdsworth, op. cit. (n15), some in

D. H. Tuke's *Chapters in the History of the Insane in the British Isles* (London, 1882). For the last two hundred years see the two volumes by Kathleen Jones, *Lunacy, Law and Conscience* (London, 1955) and *Mental Health and Social Policy* (London, 1960).

18 See Holdsworth, op. cit. (n15), 111, 372, n9.

19 Yearbooks of Henry VII, 21 Michaelmas Term, plea 16.

20 Bracton, *De Legibus et Consuetudinibus Angliae*, Woodbine ed. (Yale, 1915):

> . . . quia crimen non contrahitur nisi voluntas nocendi intercedat. [Et voluntas et propositum distinguunt maleficia, et furtum non committitur sine affectu furandi.] Et secundum quod dici poterit de infante et furioso, cum alterum innocentia consilii tueatur et alterum facti [*sic*] infelicitas excuset. In maleficiis autem spectatur voluntas et non exitus . . .

The words in square brackets may not have been part of the original text. For 'infelicitas' other manuscripts read 'imbecillitas' and 'infedelitas', an indication, perhaps, that the copyists were conscious that the phrase did not make complete sense.

21 821.11: 'furiosus si hominem occiderit, lege Cornelia non tenetur, cum eum fati infelicitas excuset.'

22 Digest 1.18.14

23 Bracton, op. cit. (n20), IV, 308: 'Tales enim non multum distant a brutis quae ratione carent, nec valere debet quod cum talibus agitur durante furore. Possunt enim quidam aliquando dilucidis gaudere intervallis, et quidem habent furorem perpetuum.' The comparison between the insane and animals was so influential in the course of the next six centuries that it would be interesting to trace it to its ultimate source. It is unlikely that it was Bracton's own inspiration, and not merely because he was not given to inspirations of this kind. He makes the comparison twice, in exactly the same words (once in the passage quoted and again when discussing suicide by the insane: op. cit., 11, p. 424), which suggests that it was a traditional argument. Moreover, it can be found in Continental jurists who, though later than Bracton, are unlikely to have been influenced by him: for example, in Matthaeus (loc. cit. in ch. 8, n3).

24 This is clearly illustrated by Gilbertus Anglicus, more or less a contemporary of Bracton, in his *Compendium Medicinae* (Book II) when he explains the difference between melancholy and mania. He records the case of 'a melancholic who, given charge of glass vessels belonging to his master, saw a friend passing and said to him "Would you like these?" The friend said "Yes", and the melancholic threw them at his feet, smashing them. In this case the imagination was not damaged, because he recognised his friend. It was his understanding (*ratio*) that was damaged, because he did not know that the vessels would break. The other case . . . is that of a maniac who was escaping from his father. The latter was at his heels and he turned and struck him. When his father said "Son, why do you strike your father?" he fell at his father's feet, begging

E

his forgiveness. In this case the imagination was damaged, since he did not recognise his father. His understanding (*ratio*) was not damaged, since he knew it was wrong to strike him.'

25 See A. M. Platt, *The Criminal Responsibility of the Mentally Ill in England* (1965): unpublished thesis in the library of the University of California, Berkeley.

26 In Egbert's Penitentials, however (see n1), 'furor' is used at least once in a context in which it must have its modern meaning of 'fury' rather than its original meaning of 'madness': 'si laicus homicidium fecerit per furorem et odii meditatione, IV vel V vel VI annos peniteat' – one of the longest penances prescribed, much longer than the year prescribed for accidental homicide.

27 See W. Mayer-Gross, E. Slater, and M. Roth, *Clinical Psychiatry*, 1954 ed. (London), 250.

28 'Per tempora autem gaudet lucidis intervallis: from another of Mr Kaye's cases.

29 From pleas heard at Ilchester in 1225: 'Ricardus de Brente . . . rettatus de latrocinio venit et defendit totum et ponit se super patriam. Et xij juratores et villate Brente (etc. . . .) dicunt quod non malecredunt eum nisi de uno pullo quem cepit in furore tempore quo fuit lunaticus. Et ideo sub plegiis (sit) quousque plus sciatur,' (Selden Society Publications, *Select Pleas of the Crown*, I, 119).

30 Plato, *The Laws*, XI, 934.

31 Another of Mr Kaye's cases. The *Narrenschiffen*, in which boatloads of fools and madmen sailed the rivers of mediaeval Europe, do not seem to have been used in Britain, perhaps because its rivers are smaller and less easily navigable.

32 See Thorpe, op. cit. (n1), 11.

33 See T. O. Cockayne, *Leechdoms, wortcunning and starcraft of early England* (London, 1865).

34 Op. cit. (n24).

35 See Bartholomaeus Anglicus' *De Proprietatibus Rerum*, an encyclopaedic work of the late thirteenth century.

Chapter 2. **From Bracton to Hale**

The four centuries which separate Bracton from Hale were a period of
clarification rather than progress. Few and far between as cases of insane
felons were, the experience of trying them led to new distinctions and
minor refinements of procedure, but not to any redefinition of the test of
criminal insanity. As we shall see in chapters 12 and 14, it was during this
period that justifications were devised for refraining from hanging the
felon who became insane after conviction, and the practice of exempting
some idiots and madmen from being tried at all was established. But so far
as the trial of felony was concerned Bracton's word was still regarded as
law. It is true that, as we shall see, some interpretations of Bracton's
principle were more generous to the accused than Bracton himself would
have been; but even these were probably enunciated by people who did not
realise that they were being more generous.

The clearest statement of the law and its procedures at any single time
in this period is to be found in the *History of the Pleas of the Crown*, which
was found among the unpublished writings of Sir Matthew Hale after his
death in 1676 (but was not immediately published). Unlike earlier writers,
such as Coke (1552–1634), who had been content with a few notes on the
subject and were more interested in the testamentary or contractual capacity of idiots and madmen, Hale devoted an entire chapter, the fourth, to
'the defects of ideocy, madness and lunacy in reference to criminal offences
and punishments'. This chapter is not merely the most detailed description of seventeenth-century practice: after its belated publication in 1736
it had more influence on lawyers of the eighteenth and nineteenth century
than any other single work on the subject.

Moreover, Hale was not only a lawyer. He must have been the first, if
not the only, Lord Chief Justice of England to interest himself in the psychological theories of his day. Nor was his interest merely the superficial
attention of the well informed, for among his writings was a thoughtful
book called *The primitive origination of mankind, considered and examined
according to the light of nature*, the second chapter of which is a discussion
of the psychological and physiological differences between man and animals. The acquaintance with Aristotle, Plutarch, and Galen which he
displays is not surprising in a man who spent part of his youth at Oxford
and had intended to enter the Church; but it is clear that he had also read
the contemporary writer Descartes. It is true that the chapter has nothing

to say about disorders of the mind, but after all its author was trying to demonstrate man's superiority to the rest of creation.

Where he does deal with mental disorder, in chapter I V of his *History of the Pleas of the Crown*, he writes clearly and with confidence. Although his terminology is very different, most of the distinctions which he draws can still be found in our present law. It is true that most of them are traceable to earlier authorities; but his very lack of originality makes it all the more likely that he was really describing the law and practice of his day – an assumption which cannot so safely be made where Coke is concerned.

Under the term 'ideocy' he distinguishes the disorder which was statutorily classified as 'idiocy' or 'imbecility' until the euphemistic legislation of 1959 substituted 'severe subnormality'. The distinction between low intelligence and mental illness in English law is at least as old as the thirteenth-century Statute of the King's Prerogative which dealt with the management of their property and which was described in the previous chapter. Synonymous with 'ideocy' so far as Hale was concerned were 'fatuitas a nativitate' (stupidity from birth) and 'dementia naturalis' (inborn witlessness); and Hale's predecessor Coke, writing a generation or two before him, distinguished two degrees of stupidity, 'fatuitas' and 'stultitia', the latter being less severe; but since Coke says that 'stultitia' includes someone who 'knows not good from evil', it was probably severe enough to serve as an excuse.[1]

Certainly some degree of stupidity could be the basis for a successful defence of insanity. By Henry VIII's reign (1509–47) – and very probably earlier than that – a crude but by no means ridiculous form of intelligence test was used to determine whether a person was an idiot, at least when it was a question of the management of his property. '. . . He who shall be said to be a Sot and Idiot from birth', explains Fitzherbert, 'is such a person who cannot account or number twenty-pence, nor can tell who was his Father or Mother, nor how old he is &c, so as it may appear that he hath no understanding of Reason what shall be for his Profit or what for his Loss. But if he hath such understanding that he know and understand his letters, and do read by Teaching or information of another Man, then it seemeth that he is not a Sot, nor a natural idiot.'[2] As we have seen, primitive intelligence tests of this kind were used in Glanville's day to decide whether a child had reached the age of discretion. Apparently, if Fitzherbert is to be read *au pied de la lettre*, a man was not an idiot unless he failed on all these counts. Although the test itself was no mean achievement for so unscientific an age, the technique of administration would horrify modern psychologists, as an example will show. In 1743 the unfortunate Henry Roberts, who was trying to satisfy a Lord Chancellor's Commission that he was fit to manage his own estate, was put into a private room with a jury, who (he said)

> . . . came around me and asked their questions together, without giving me time to answer. They asked me what a lamb and what a calf was called at one, two and three years old. They gave me a sum of money to tell, which I miscounted; and then I heard them say

'He is not capable of managing his affairs, we will return him
incapable. . . .'[3]

Men who had been born deaf or dumb were presumed by law to be idiots,
since they probably did not understand the law or its penalties. They
were to be treated as responsible only if they could be shown to have
'understanding', and Hale adds that 'great caution is to be used'[4] in coming
to this conclusion – an attitude that contrasts strongly with the stringent
test applied to the mentally ill.

Hale implies that tests of this kind were relevant in criminal trials, but
not conclusive. 'These, though they may be evidences, yet they are too
narrow and conclude not always; for "ideocy or not" is a question of fact
triable by jury, and sometimes by inspection.' Throughout his chapter on
ideocy, madness, and lunacy he defends the jury system with a sturdy
chauvinism:

Now touching the trial of this incapacity . . . this is a matter of
great difficulty, partly from the ease of counterfeiting this disability,
when it is to excuse a nocent, and partly from the variety of degrees
of this infirmity. . . .

Yet the law of England hath afforded the best method of trial that
is possible of this and all other matters of fact, namely by a jury of
twelve men all concurring in the same judgement, by the testimony
of witnesses viva voce in the presence of the judge and jury, and by
the inspection and direction of the judge. . . .[4]

A more or less contemporary case shows the jury dealing with a thief of
low intelligence. In 1685

Francis Tims, of the Parish of Stepney, Indicted [at the Old
Bailey] for Stealing a Silver Cup from Thomas Middleton, the third
of March last. The Evidence against the Prisoner that he lodged at
Middleton's House, and Middleton's Wife missing of the said Cup
made inquiry of the Prisoner whether he knew what was become
of the Cup, he confessed that he had taken it and offered it to Sale
for 20s. But the Prisoner appearing to be little less than a Fool, he
was Acquitted[5].

It is unfortunate that the Old Bailey Sessions Papers, from which this
report is taken, were not compiled by lawyers; the shorthand writers were
more interested in unusual or salacious features of the trial than in the
judge's rulings or summing-up. In this case, however, it seems clear that
the reason for the acquittal was subnormality of intelligence.

Severe mental illness is described under the general heading of 'dementia
accidentalis' to distinguish it from the witlessness which exists from birth;
and Hale lists various possible causes from which it may arise:

. . . sometimes from the distemper of the humours of the body, as
deep melancholy or adust [i.e. burnt-up] choler; sometimes from the
violence of a disease, as fever or palsy; sometimes from concussion
or hurt of the brain, or its membranes or organs. . . .[4]

Like Coke, he distinguishes the 'interpolated' dementia of 'lunacy', with
its 'lucid intervals', from the 'permanent', fixed dementia of 'phrenesis
or madness'. As Coke said, a lunatic 'hath sometimes his understanding,

and sometimes not'.[6] The periodic nature of some mental illnesses had been recognised by the law at least as early as the thirteenth century (see the previous chapter), so that a man who was in his senses at his trial was not in logic debarred from pleading insanity in his defence. But his sanity would be a handicap, for the onus was on him to show that his crime had *not* been committed in a lucid interval. We shall see in chapter 8 that Hale's contemporary in Scotland, the Bluidy Mackenzie, would have given the accused the benefit of the doubt; but that was in another country.

Even more important – as we shall see when we come to the trials of the eighteenth and nineteenth centuries – was the distinction between total and partial insanity. The test of insanity which was applied by the courts was still as stringent as it had been in the thirteenth century, Bracton had defined the 'furious' man as 'totally lacking in discernment. and 'not much above the beasts, which lack reason'. Four centuries later Coke[7] and Hale[4] insist that the condition must be 'absolute madness and deprivation of memorie', and Hale justifies the exemption of demented felons from capital punishment by explaining that 'they have not the use of understanding, and act not as reasonable creatures, but their actions are in effect in the condition of brutes'.[4] We shall see, too, that by the eighteenth century at the trials of Arnold and Ferrers, Bracton's phrase 'not much above the beasts' has been crystallised into a rigid and narrow test.

It was not that lawyers failed to recognise less severe abnormalities of mind. Hale explains:

> There is a partial insanity of mind . . . ; some persons that have a
> competent use of reason in respect of some subjects, are yet under a
> particular dementia in respect of some particular discourses,
> subjects or applications; or else it is partial in respect of degrees;
> and this is the condition of very many, especially melancholy
> persons, who for the most part discover their defect in excessive
> fears or griefs, and yet are not wholly destitute of the use of reason;
> and this partial insanity seems not to excuse them in the committing
> of any offence for its matter capital; for doubtless most persons,
> that are felons of themselves, and others are under a degree of partial
> insanity when they commit these offences. . . . The best measure that
> I can think of is this; such a person as labouring under melancholy
> tempers hath yet ordinarily as great an understanding, as ordinarily
> a child of fourteen hath, is such a person as may be guilty of
> treason or felony. . . .[4]

The notion of 'partial insanity' was to exercise the minds of lawyers, psychiatrists, and Royal Commissions for the next three centuries. Although Hale, as always, offers the clearest exposition of it, he was by no means the first lawyer to recognise it. Coke does not mention it, but it can be found in a pamphlet in which the Elizabethan lawyer-priest, Richard Cosin, discusses the trial of William Hacket and his fellow conspirators for treason.[8] Hacket, a religious fanatic who at times believed himself to be Christ, and may have been suffering from alcoholism or an early stage of neurotropic syphilis, was tried in 1592, along with two followers, for treason and blasphemy. His insane prayers and other outbursts in the course of his trial, though they did not prevent him from being hanged and drawn, raised a posthumous argument as to whether he should have been excused as insane. The loyal Cosin argued that whether Hacket's disorder was feigned or not, it did not amount to dementia, in which there is a complete loss of understanding. Cosin describes other kinds of disorder in which this does not occur, and in particular '. . . a kind of Inconstancy voide in deede of perfite soundnes of mind, yet such, as that he which hath it can observe and doe the common offices of this life among men, in some reasonable and tolerable sort'. Since this is not much more than a rather free translation from Cicero's Tusculan Questions (Book III), it is clear that Cosin was influenced by his classical education rather than contemporary medical thinking. Physicians who were interested in disorders of the mind were not unheard of in sixteenth-century Elizabethan England. Bartholomaeus Anglicus' encyclopaedic work, with its chapters on mental illness, had been translated into English a hundred years before Cosin's pamphlet was written. Juan Luis Vives the Spaniard had been a favourite of Catherine of Aragon and Sir Thomas More, although he left England before publishing his *De Anima et Vita* (1538). Elyot, Langton, Boorde, and Barrough all expounded the Galenic view of mental illness in more or less orthodox fashion under the later Tudors. But they were concerned more with causation and cure than with legal or moral culpability, so that where such questions were concerned lawyers could hardly be blamed for looking to Rome for guidance; and Rome meant both the Christian Church (of which Cosin was a priest) and the classical authorities.

Finally, Hale distinguishes a third type of disorder, the *dementia affectata*, or 'induced witlessness'. Since the examples he gives are mental states induced by drink or drugs such as nux vomica or aconite this corresponds roughly to what modern psychiatrists would call 'toxic disorders'. Like Coke, Hale is insistent that mere drunkenness cannot excuse; but he adds two riders. The first is not very important, although it reminds us – if we need a reminder – that even physicians are fallible. If a man's toxic state were due to 'the unskilfulness of his physician or the contrivance of his enemies', his 'phrenzy' was to be judged like any other. More important was the concession that if heavy drinking had caused 'an habitual or fixed phrenzy' he should be treated by the law as if it were involuntarily contracted[4] – a principle that was to save several Victorian alcoholics from the gallows.

So much for the doctrine. Had the underlying justifications changed since Bracton's day? Hale is concerned with more practical questions of procedure and types of disorder, and has nothing explicit to say on this subject. Coke merely reels off a string of maxims:

> In criminal causes, as felony &c., the act of a madman shall not be imputed to him, for that in these causes *actus non facit reum nisi mens sit rea*, and he is *amens* (id est) *sine mente*, without his mind or discretion; and *furiosus solo furore punitur*, a madman is only punished by his madness. And so it is of an infant until he be of the age of 14, which in law is accounted the age of discretion.[9]

Notice how conscientiously he preserves the ancient justification from the Digest that the madman is punished enough by his madness, but makes no attempt to reconcile it with the completely inconsistent argument that the madman is not to be blamed for his act. Notice, too, that the exemption of madmen is again linked to the age of discretion of children, but not to the minimum age of criminal responsibility. By Coke's time it was fairly firmly established that the ability to tell good from evil was the crucial test when a child was on trial for felony, and evidence of concealment was evidence of this ability. Children below seven (the end of infancy in Roman law and the traditional age for first confession in the Church) were presumed incapable of making this distinction. But Coke compares the madman not to the child under seven but to the child under fourteen, who may or may not know the difference between good and evil, but is in any case deemed not to have full discretion, that is, not to appreciate the full significance of acts such as the disposal of property. Hale, too, sees an analogy between the madman and the child under fourteen. In the passage on partial insanity quoted above he says 'such a person as labouring under melancholy tempers hath yet ordinarily as great an understanding as ordinarily a child of fourteen hath, is such a person as may be guilty of treason or felony'.

The point is important because it emphasises the awkwardness of the argument that the madman did not have a guilty mind. The maxim '*actus non facit reum nisi mens sit rea*' is so often repeated when the exemption of the insane is under discussion that its applicability to the insane is never questioned. It is simply assumed that the madman has no guilty intention. But if we consider the sort of crimes with which Coke and Hale were concerned – which were usually homicides – it is at once obvious that this assumption needs refining. In all but the exceptional case the madman obviously does mean to kill or at least seriously injure his victim; in other words, what Bracton called the 'will to harm' was not lacking. Instances in which a mentally ill or subnormal person has manifestly killed under a complete misapprehension of what he is doing are easier to bring under the maxim, but much rarer. Yet throughout the period we are considering juries were, with the approval of judges, acquitting people who committed insane but intentional acts.

Why did they do so? There were at least two possible justifications. They might have felt that the madman knew and intended what he was doing only to a limited extent. Like a child, he might mean to kill without appreciating the horror and permanence of death. Or they may have thought that his moral sense was in some way impaired, so that he did not know that he was doing wrong. The fact, however, that the madman tended to be compared to the child under the age of fourteen rather than the child under seven suggests that – at first at least – it was failure to appreciate the true nature and quality of his act that was supposed to be his defect. The notion of inability to tell right from wrong was familiar to physicians in Bracton's day (see p. 28 and note 24). But not until later did the law concede its relevance, first in the case of children, and eventually in the case of the insane. The earliest passage known to me in which inability to tell right from wrong is clearly imputed to the mentally disordered is by Dalton, a contemporary of Coke:

> . . . if one that is *'non compos mentis'*, or an ideot, kill a man, this is no felony, for they have not knowledge of Good and Evil, nor can have a felonious intent, nor a will or mind to do harm. . . .[10]

Coke himself described the feeble-minded man (*stultus*) as 'imprudent, improvident, unable to tell good from evil' (*ignorans mali et boni*). Since the feeble-minded resemble children more than do the insane, it is possible that the child's inability to tell right from wrong was first ascribed to the former and later extended to the insane.

However that may be, we shall see in the next chapter that by 1724 a judge was actually telling a jury that this was part of the test of criminal insanity. The 'right-wrong test', as it came to be called, must have filled a gap of which earlier lawyers and judges were almost but not quite conscious, by making it logically justifiable to excuse the madman who intended his act. It was the most important of the few and minor modifications which took place between Bracton's day and Hadfield's trial.

So much for the underlying logic of Hale and his predecessors. What does he have to say about procedure? We saw in the previous chapter that by the sixteenth century and probably earlier it was the practice for courts to deal with obviously mad felons instead of leaving them to the mercy of the king. Exactly what did the courts do? Hale's explanation (which is given not in the chapter on mental disorders but in the preceding one, which deals with infancy) is not as straightforward as could be wished:

> . . . in all cases of infancy, insanity, &c., if a person uncapable to commit a felony be indicted by the grand inquest, and thereupon arraigned, the petit jury may either find him generally *not guilty*, or they may find the matter specially, that he committed the fact, but that he was *non compos*, or that he was under the age of fourteen . . . and had not discretion to discern between good and evil, & *non per feloniam*; and thereupon the court gives judgment of acquittal. . . .[11]

The special finding was almost certainly a survival from the days when the jury left the madman to be pardoned by the king. Hale explains elsewhere[12] that such findings were still obligatory in cases of homicide by self-defence, but optional when the killer had been insane. The reason why it was sometimes preferred to an acquittal in cases of homicide was that the latter left a technical loose end: every homicide ought if possible to be ascribed to its author either by a coroner's inquest or by a trial, so that strictly speaking an acquittal necessitated another inquest. If the jury did return a special verdict, it was to the effect that A had killed B, but had done so in self-defence or while insane, as the case might be. Then it was open to the judge to call the crime murder or manslaughter: although Hale says that he had rarely known judgment to be given for murder in such cases, it was not unheard of. The next step was a pardon, which could be regarded as a certainty. Pardons for homicides in self-defence are not hard to find among the State Papers of the sixteenth and seventeenth centuries, but pardons following on special findings of insanity must have been most uncommon, for I have found only one example, and that was the most unusual case of Colonel Culpeper, which is described in chapter 10.

What action followed an acquittal on the ground of insanity? Was the accused person simply set free? Hale describes the case of 'a woman of Aylesbury' who had killed her newborn child in 'a temporary phrenzy' but thereafter had soon recovered her understanding (his account will be found in the chapter dealing with infanticide). It is conceivable that after her acquittal she was allowed to return to her husband. But if the accused seemed to constitute a continuing danger to others something more than this was necessary. What was probably a common arrangement is described in Mr Justice Gould's report on the case of Matthew Clay, the insane burglar, which is quoted in chapter 12. Clay's father was willing to take care of him, and the judge proposed that the father should enter into a recognisance – for the considerable sum of £20 – before a justice of the peace, which would bind him to take 'due care' of his son and prevent him from committing future offences. It is true that in Clay's case the jury had failed to acquit him; but the judge took the view that he should have been acquitted, and was proposing the sort of arrangement which would no doubt have followed an acquittal.

So convenient and inexpensive a solution, however, was possible only when the accused was lucky enough to have a relative who was willing and able to look after him. What happened in other cases? Neither Coke nor Hale answer this question; but Blackstone does. He explains that under the common law 'persons deprived of their reason might be confined until they recovered their senses, without waiting for . . . special authority from the crown'. He adds, however, that by his time a statutory procedure had been 'chalked out for imprisoning, chaining and sending them to their proper homes'.[13] He was referring to the vagrancy legislation of 1744, which allowed two justices to order this to be done. But could the judge who had tried an insane offender make a similar order? At Hadfield's trial the Attorney-General seems to have told the court that they could do so. 'It is laid down in some of the books', he said, 'that by the common law the judges of every court are competent to direct the confinement of a person under such circumstances.' Lord Kenyon, however, did not think it was quite so straightforward. 'That may be, Mr Attorney-General; but at present we can only remand him to the confinement he came from. . . .' He seems to imply that all he could do was send Hadfield back to Newgate gaol; and this appears to be confirmed by what Baron Eyre said in 1784 after the acquittal of William Walker (a lunatic from a workhouse whose trial is referred to in the next chapter):

> This man must not be discharged, unless the parish officers, to save the expences, come and take him away; he must be carried before a magistrate, confined, and taken proper care of.

Eyre too seemed to think that he himself could not make the necessary order and that this must be done by the justices. All that he could do was direct that Walker should not be released until the necessary arrangements for his confinement had been made.

Admittedly, if the magistrates did order confinement, the obvious, indeed often the only, place where a troublesome or dangerous lunatic could be securely detained was the gaol; and even this was sometimes so decrepit that its inmates had to be chained to the walls or floor to prevent escape. The gaoling of the insane was neither as unjust nor as inhumane as it sounds to modern ears. Private madhouses were few until the end of the eighteenth century, and in any case were beyond the means of all but the well-to-do. Bethlem served London as a public madhouse from 1377, but its capacity was limited, and it was not until 1751 that the foundation of St Luke's provided London with another public repository for the insane. In Bristol, the largest city outside London until the industrial revolution, St Peter's Workhouse, with its ward for the insane, was not founded until 1696. The rest of England had nothing comparable until the growth of urban populations in northern towns led to the foundation of the first public asylums – Manchester's Lunatics Hospital in 1763 and York Asylum in 1777.

Families with large houses or estates could keep a lunatic chained up away from sight and hearing, but this was out of the question for the rural labourer or urban artisan. For them the economic and psychological burden of a madman in the household must have been almost or completely intolerable. Many a family simply thrust him out of their home, to become a vagrant and so find his own way to the gaol or the house of correction. The vagrancy legislation of the eighteenth century expressly distinguished lunatics as a special subdivision of this social problem. Nor was there any control over the liberation of the madman. On the contrary, the common law was that he could be confined only until he recovered his senses, and since the mentally disordered were both an expense and a nuisance to their families or the parish, the result must have been the setting free of many a dangerous schizophrenic during one of his 'lucid intervals'. The consequences were vividly described by the Attorney-General in the House of Commons when he introduced the legislation of 1800. 'It has been found that persons who have done the most shocking acts, and who have been acquitted on the grounds of being deranged in their intellects, having been allowed to go at large have afterwards committed similar acts again; there are several instances of His Majesty's subjects having lost their lives for want of a due provision in this respect. . . .' As he said, 'these unhappy persons . . . generally . . . are of low habits and connexions, and seldom have any friends to take care of them'.[14]

There can have been little to choose between the penal and psychiatric establishments of this era. From the sixteenth to the nineteenth century Bethlem was under the management of the same governors as Bridewell, and at one time its keepers had to be paid a fee, like gaolers, before they would release an inmate. Even the eighteenth-century madhouses, like the poor law institutions and asylums which began to multiply at that time, were custodial rather than remedial in their aims. The physician John Aikin (1747–1822) compared pauper hospitals with prisons: John Howard

(1726(?)–90) found both in need of the same improvements. Typhus visited both with such impartiality that it had two names, 'gaol-fever' and 'hospital-fever'. When Bentham (1748–1832) designed his 'Panopticon or inspection-house' he meant it to serve either as prison or as asylum. As for private madhouses, repeated scandals over the way in which sane people with property were committed to them by greedy relatives led eventually to the Act of 1774 for their regulation. (Unfortunately this not only excluded pauper lunatics from its ambit – even when they were inmates of private madhouses – but failed in its own limited objectives.)

Indeed, except by a few enlightened physicians, no very clear distinction was drawn between penal and psychiatric treatment. Dr Battie, who is described in the next chapter, told a Committee of the House of Commons in 1763 how a woman 'perfectly in her senses' was brought by her husband to a private madhouse which was under the doctor's direction. When Dr Battie insisted that he should take his wife home, the husband said with surprise that 'he understood the House to be a sort of Bridewell or place of correction'.[15]

To what sort of charges was insanity a defence? 'In capitals', says Hale; that is, to charges of treason or most felonies (by his time there were a few felonies which were not capital, at least on first conviction). Presumably he included even 'clergyable' felonies, since they were in law capital even if everyone convicted of them could escape hanging by claiming benefit of clergy. Felonies, however, did not in his day include serious injury which did not cause death and did not amount to attempted murder: this was merely a 'trespass', and as such could only be the subject of a civil action. As Brydall explained a few years after Hale:

. . . in Civil Trespasses and Injuries, that are of an inferiour
Nature, the Law doth rather consider the Damage of the Party
wronged than the Malice of him that was the Wrongdoer. And
therefore, if an Infant . . . or a Madman kill another, he shall not
be impeached thereof; but if they put out a Man's Eye, or do him
like corporal Hurt, they shall be punished in trespass.[16]

As for misdemeanours and the few non-capital felonies, there was so little to choose between their penalties and the treatment of the insane that to raise the defence of insanity in such cases would have seemed pointless to Hale and his predecessors. Imprisonment, as we have seen, was a recognised way of restraining madmen as well as a minor punishment. Whipping, another penalty for trivial misbehaviour, had been prescribed for insanity since the time of Cild the Saxon. A reminiscence of Sir Thomas More (1478–1535) illustrates what must have been the prevalent attitude:

Another was one, whyche after that he had fallen into ye frantike
heresyes, fell soone after in to playne open fransye byside. And all
be it that he had therfore ben put uppe in bedelem [Bethlem], and
afterwarde by betynge and correcyon gathered hys remembraunce
to him, and began to come agayne to hym selfe beynge theruppon
set at lyberty and walkynge about abrode, hys olde fansyes beganne
to fall agayne in his hed. And I was fro dyvers good holy places
advertised, that he used in his wanderynge aboute, to come into the

chyrche, & there make many madde toyes and trifles, to the trouble
of good people in the dyvyne servyce and specially wold he be most
besy in the time of most sylence, whyle the preste was at the secretes
of the masse about ye levacyon. And if he spied any woman
knelynge at a forme yf her hed hynge any thynge low in her medyta-
cyons, than wolde he stele behynde her, & yf he were not letted
wolde laboure to lyfte up all her clothes & caste them quyte over
her hed, wheruppon I being advertised of the pageauntes, and
bynge sent unto and requyred by very devout relygyouse folke, to
take some other order wyth him caused him as he came wanderynge
by my dore, to be taken by the constables and bounden to a tre in
the strete before the whole towne, and there they stryped him with
roddys therfore tyl he waxed wery and somwhat lenger. And it
appered well that hys remembraunce was good inough, save yt wente
about in grasynge tyll it was beten home. For he could then very
well reherse his fawtes hym selfe, and speke and trete very well,
and promyse to do afterwarde as well. And veryly god be thanked I
here none harme of hym now.[17]

More's anecdote demonstrates several interesting points. One is that although the lunatic's sacrilegious behaviour and indecent assaults caused
scandal, the possibility of bringing him to summary trial does not seem
even to have been considered. On the other hand, what we should regard
as a judicial punishment was imposed without any formality by order of a
local knight (for presumably Sir Thomas was not acting in his capacity as
Lord Chancellor). It was regarded as a corrective which was as effective
with lunatics as with normal men. The question whether a man known
to be a bedlamite should have been excused from this form of punishment
would therefore have seemed to Sir Thomas to miss the point.

Nor had people's outlook changed by Hale's day. The constable of
Great Staughton in Huntingdonshire recorded in 1690 that he had been
'Paid in charges taking up a distracted woman, watching [i.e. guarding]
her and whipping her next day, eight shillings and sixpence'.[18]

Other techniques of treatment were equally traditional. It is true that
exorcism and magic had now gone out of fashion – at least among educated townsmen – and the public now looked to the physician rather than
the priest for cures. But purges and emetics were still as popular with
physicians as with Saxon wise-men, and the discoveries of the centuries
had merely added more exotic poisons to our native herbs.

The survival or revival of old remedies is especially striking in the history of psychiatry. The Celtic ritual of 'dowsing' the madman in a well or
spring was preserved in the medieval practice of ducking witches and
scolds, and was resurrected by a Dutch physician and mystic, van Helmonth (1577–1644), as a cure for the distracted. His patients were stripped
naked, and with their hands bound behind them were lowered head first
into a great vessel of water

   . . . and there left [wrote van Helmonth's son] until he judged
that their upper Parts were drowned. It may happen indeed that
some through fear, or because they are not strong enough to stand

out this Method, may miscarry and die; and it is therefore fitting that permission should be sought from the Magistrate for the exercising of this practice, as is usual for the cutting of the stone, which is likewise a doubtful operation. . . .[19]

His method was copied by Willis (1621–75), the Oxford physician and natural philosopher, and in the eighteenth and nineteenth centuries was modified into the 'surprise bath', a less dangerous apparatus which let fall an unexpected douche of cold water on the unsuspecting patient. Under the imposing title of 'the cataractick cure' it was specially recommended by the Aberdeen school of physicians for hallucinations and – by a rather crude reasoning – for hydrophobia. In the early twentieth century its place was taken by warm baths, in which the patient was immobilised in long wraps of flannel. In the 1939–45 war the technique of ducking was revived as a device for terrifying prisoners under interrogation. The rationale has of course varied. The Celts looked on their wells and springs as places of purification. The witch-hunters used water as a test of innocence; the duckers of scolds saw it as a mild deterrent. Van Helmonth thought that it drove out fiery essences. To the Aberdeen school the shock was the essential part of the treatment. In contrast, the advocates of flannel baths saw them as relaxing influences, even when the patient had to be forcibly put into them. The interrogators of Germany or Algeria, who were at least realistic, knew that the experience of drowning is demoralising in the extreme; no doubt it reduces even a madman to temporary docility. But whatever the rationale, the ingredient of the treatment was water.

Almost as ancient a remedy as water was wine. Dr Shaw (1694–1763) specially recommended 'the juice of the grape' for 'the Hippo', as hysteria in males was called in his day. (Since Hippocrates had observed this disorder only in women, and had attributed it to displacement of the womb (hysteron), a sound classical education made it impossible for the eighteenth-century physician to diagnose 'hysteria' in a man: a philological superstition which survived in some medical schools into the second half of the nineteenth century.)

Remedies which were fashionable for physical disorders were optimistically applied to mental illnesses as well. Bloodletting and cupping were used almost indiscriminately for every ailment from gout to epilepsy. The swinging chair, which Dr Smyth (1741–1821) had found so effective in cases of pulmonary tuberculosis, was soon adopted for the insane, and Cox's Rotatory Machine was recommended in a psychiatric textbook as late as 1828.[20] Wesley the preacher (1703–91), though offensively critical of the bloodletting in Bethlem, himself had great faith in an electrical machine, with which (he records) he one day 'ordered several persons to be electrified'.[21] Nor was this a passing enthusiasm, for some years later (1756) he claimed that from it 'while hundreds, perhaps thousands, have received unspeakable good I have not known one man, woman or child who has received any hurt thereby'.[21] Since his machine was probably incapable of generating more than ten volts, casualties were certainly unlikely. By 1759, however, Wesley was more psychotherapeutically oriented, and was offering psychological explanations of bodily afflictions.

It was not until the second half of the eighteenth century that there were encouraging developments, such as the notion of 'moral management', in the care of the insane, and not until the early nineteenth century that special provision was made for the criminal lunatic. These and other developments will be described in volume II. Meanwhile this account of the insane delinquent in the sixteenth and seventeenth centuries would be incomplete without a mention of some other ways in which mental illness could incur reprisals from an unenlightened community. The most obvious example is of course the persecution of witches.

Although Saxon law dealt sternly with sorcerers, the wholesale persecution of sorcery and heresy was an achievement of the post-Renaissance church. The early priesthood laid more emphasis on the comparatively humane techniques of exorcism, and it was the Inquisition which, in Europe at least, fanned the primitive fear of magic into the flames of the auto-da-fé. The Inquisition failed to establish a foothold in England, but its manual on the detection and disposal of witches, the 'Malleus Maleficarum', compiled by two German priests in the last quarter of the fifteenth century, exercised great influence on English minds, with the rather paradoxical result that it was not until the Reformation that the series of statutes against sorcery began. 'Invocations or conjurations of spirits, witchcrafts inchantments or sorceries' became felonies without benefit of clergy or sanctuary. The sharp division of opinions on the subject led to frequent repeals and re-enactments of these statutes, and much depended on the enlightenment or superstition of the sovereign of the day: James VI of Scotland, a country which has always been more hag-ridden than England, was personally responsible for reviving witch-hunts after his accession to the English throne. It was not until the early eighteenth century that legislation finally put an end to the persecution.

Two sorts of person were especially likely to fall under suspicion of being in league with devils: scientists[22] and the mentally ill. Of the latter, some were men or women who shared the popular belief in sorcerers and witches, wished and believed themselves to have supernatural powers, and therefore spontaneously took part in the practices and rituals which led to their arraignment. Like the spiritualist mediums of the twentieth century – or at least whose who are sincere – these unfortunates were merely suggestible to the point of hysteria. Others were undoubtedly schizophrenics whose strange behaviour alarmed their neighbours and whose distortions of reality confirmed their reputation for dealings with the supernatural. The schizophrenias seem to be as old as civilisation, but the content of the hallucinations or delusions which are among their symptoms seems to be determined by the ideas of the day. In the twentieth century paranoid delusions often concentrate on radio or television as the occult means by which the sufferer is being persecuted, or tormented with sexual sensations. In the imaginations of the Middle Ages the powers of darkness took the place of radiation, and paranoid women attributed their sexual excitement to the devil instead of the BBC. Hallucinations, too, whether they consisted of apparitions or of voices, took a fashionable form, and so confirmed the superstition.

Hale himself, though he had to try and sentence at least one pair of witches, has little to say on the subject in his writings; he devotes a chapter to heresy but not to witchcraft. But fifty years earlier Coke, though no friend of the Scottish James, wrote with approval of the King's new legislation against 'witchcraft, sorcery, charme and inchantment'. In Scotland itself, Hale's contemporary the Bluidy Mackenzie prosecuted both witches and covenanters with equal, though discriminating, enthusiasm.

Another, much less serious, charge which was often brought against women was that of being a 'scold'. A scold was a woman – practically never a man – who was given to persistent abuse of her neighbours or of anyone who crossed her path. In the Middle Ages 'common scold' was a recognised description: 'eadem Katerina est communis scolde' said the court rolls of Maldon for 1467. Shakespeare's Katharina was another:

> Saw you no more? Mark'd you not how her sister
> Began to scold and raise up such a storm
> That mortal ears might hardly endure the din?[23]

In Blackstone's day such behaviour was still a misdemeanour. 'A common scold, *communis rixatrix* (for our law Latin confines it to the feminine gender), is a public nuisance to her neighbours.'[24]

Tranio may not have been serious when he suggested that Katharina the Shrew was 'stark mad'; but it seems very likely that many scolds were really suffering from forms of mental illness, perhaps hysteria or paranoia. Admittedly scolding is a rare (though not unheard of) symptom today. It may be that compulsive talking or nagging (which, like scolding, are women's failings) are milder forms of it. In any case, there are fashions in symptoms, and hysterics are notoriously imitative in their eccentricities. St Vitus' dance, or the convulsions of the exorcists' and the mesmerists' patients, are examples of imitative symptoms which have now disappeared.

The usual punishment for the scold was ducking in water. By Tudor times this rough and ready treatment had been refined by the introduction of the device variously called the trebuchet, castigatory, or cucking-stool. This was a seat of sorts into which the scold was strapped, and which pivoted on an axle in such a way that she could be tipped head first into a pond or river.[25] This is a much more terrifying procedure than it sounds: the immersion of a helpless person in water is known as a most effective way of reducing their resistance to interrogation, and has been reported from places as far apart as Algeria and Viet-Nam. It is probably more than mere coincidence that it was also a traditional form of treatment for the insane. In medieval England it was used for other minor misdemeanants as well as scolds; yet it was so closely associated with the latter in the popular mind that Coke mistakenly derives 'cucking-stool' from the Saxon *Guck*, which (he says) 'signifieth to scould or brawl'. But the penalty varied from region to region. The Scots, for example, sometimes used 'the branks', a device probably imported from the Low Countries: it consisted of a metal frame which fitted over the scold's head and forced a spur-like rod deep into her mouth, making it impossible for her to move her tongue without lacerating it.

Although male witches were not unheard of, the delusions of men more often took the form known as blasphemy, heresy, or even treason. Hacket's behaviour, which has already been described, was tried by Parliament as treason, presumably because he preached the overthrow of the existing ecclesiastical hierarchy. Some heretics and blasphemers were merely atheists or agnostics who were unfortunate enough to be born ahead of their time and foolish enough to voice their opinions; an example was Robert Fisher, who in 1596 was handed over to his Archbishop for punishment because he had said 'that Christe was no saviour and the gospell a fable'.[26] Others were plainly insane, like John Moore, who in 1561 believed himself to be Christ and convinced at least one follower of his divinity. He was a Bedlamite, but that did not save him from being brought out of Bethlem to be confronted with his deluded follower, who had been brought from the Marshalsea prison: both were whipped until they 'confessed Christ to be in Heaven'.[27] During the religious ferments of the sixteenth and seventeenth centuries, in which many a sect was born, either to grow like the Quakers or die out like the Milleniaries, a man who believed himself Christ could often collect a small following of simple-minded men and women–especially women–to worship, serve, and feed him.

One of these was James Naylor, whose case threatened to split Cromwell's Parliament in 1656. He was a Yorkshireman who had served with Lambert's troop until disabled by sickness in Scotland. At home he was a member of an independent church until he was expelled for blasphemy and lewdness with a married woman (reports of his later conduct also illustrate the strong sexual attraction which religious fanatics seem to have for women). After wandering up and down the country he found his way to the Cornwall Quakers, having by this time collected a small band of followers, most of them women. They were gaoled as vagrants by one of Cromwell's majors but later released by an Order in Council, for Cromwell was embarrassed by the intolerance of some of his commanders. Naylor probably believed himself to be Christ (although in a less chaste incarnation), and as his band passed through Somerset and entered Bristol women threw garments in front of him and sang 'Holy, Holy, Holy'. This and other incidents led to his arrest and appearance before a Parliament which contained a strong element of bigoted presbyterians. After a special committee had interrogated him there was much debate as to whether his behaviour could be retrospectively declared to be the crime of blasphemy or, what seems to have been worse, 'horrid blasphemy'. The extremists wanted him executed, if possible by stoning in true biblical fashion, but the moderates prevailed. His tongue was pierced with a red-hot iron, and he was kept in Bridewell until released three years later, in very poor health, by the new Parliament. Throughout the debates there was no sign that even the most tolerant members had doubts of his sanity; once he is referred to as 'deluded', but this is not used as an argument for exempting him completely from punishment, nor is the possibility of sending him to Bethlem mentioned.[28]

F

In politics as in religion extremist groups have an attraction for the un-balanced, which probably lies in the emotional companionship created by enthusiasm for a common cause. Like anarchists, suffragettes, and campaigners for nuclear disarmament, the armies which gathered round men like Tyler or Monmouth must have had their lunatic fringes. At least one of the Young Pretender's officers was so insane that (apparently with his co-operation) his wife and her maid used to strap him to his bed at night for their protection and his. This was James Bradshaw, a young man in his twenties who joined Bonnie Prince Charlie at Manchester in the Forty-Five and was commissioned as a captain. Captured at Culloden, he was tried for treason, and his defence of insanity, though founded on fact, was rejected.[29]

So much for theory, procedure, and public outlook at the beginning of the eighteenth century. We shall see in the next chapter how trials were actually conducted in that century.

Notes

1 Sir Edward Coke, *Reports* (London, 1600–15), Part IV, Beverley's case: 'levius est esse stultum quam fatuum, sc. imprudens, improvidus, ignorans mali et boni'.

2 A. Fitzherbert, *La Nouvelle Natura Brevium*, 1567 ed. (London, 1524), 233:
   Et q̄ serra dit sot & idiot a sa neiftvē est tiel pson q̄ ne scieȓ accompt en nomber xx. deniers, ne sciē dire q̄ fuit son pere ou mere, ou de q̄l age & c. issint q̄ il poet appere, q il naveȓ ascun entendement de reason q̄ sere a son pfit, ou a son dam̄, mes sil ad tiel intelligens, q̄ il scier apprendȓ & a conuftr lȓes, & de lier p instruction & informacion de auȓ home, doqs semble q̄ il nest sot ne ideot naturalt.

3 From an anonymous pamphlet of 1747, published in London and quoted by R. Hunter and I. Macalpine, *Three Hundred Years of Psychiatry, 1535–1860* (Oxford, 1963), 375.

4 Sir Matthew Hale, *Historia Placitorum Coronae*, I (London, 1736), ch. IV.

5 From the series of *Proceedings on the King's Commissions of the Peace and Oyer and Terminer, and Gaol-Delivery of Newgate, held for the City of London and County of Middlesex, at Justice-Hall, in the Old-Bayly . . .* , for 4 and 5 June 1685. See the note in the bibliography under 'Old Bailey Sessions Papers'.

6 Sir Edward Coke, *First Part of the Institutes of the Laws of England* (known as *Coke upon Littleton*) (1628), Lib. 3, section 405.

7 Coke, *Third Part of the Institutes of the Laws of England* (London, 1644), ch. I.

8 Richard Cosin, *The Conspiracie for Pretended Reformation! viz. presbyteriall discipline* (London, 1592).

9 Coke, op. cit. (n7), ch. XII.

10 M. Dalton, *The Country Justice* (London, 1618).
   I am indebted to Mr A. M. Platt, op. cit. (ch. 1, n24), for drawing
   my attention to this passage.
11 Hale, op. cit. (n4), ch. 111.
12 Ibid, vol. 11, 305.
13. Sir William Blackstone, *Commentaries on the Laws of England*
   (London, 1765–9), Book 1v, ch. 2. He was referring to
   17 Geo. 11, c. 5.
14 Hansard for 30 June 1800, cols. 389–90.
15 See the 'Report from the Committee appointed to inquire into the
   State of the private Madhouses in this Kingdom' in the *House of
   Commons Journal* for 1763, pp. 486–9.
16 John Brydall, *Non Compos Mentis* (London, 1700).
17 Sir Thomas More, *The apologye of syr T. More, knyght* (London,
   1533).
18 Quoted by D. H. Tuke in *Chapters in the History of the Insane in
   the British Isles* (London, 1882).
19 For this and other descriptions of seventeenth- and eighteenth-
   century techniques of treatment, see Hunter and Macalpine, op. cit.
   (n3).
20 See Sir Alexander Morison's *Causes of Mental Disease* (London,
   1828), where it is illustrated. The machine was said to be in use in
   most British public asylums at this time.
21 Wesley, John, *The Journal of the Rev. John Wesley*, ed. N. Curnock
   (London, 1909–16).
22 In the sixteenth century science was often called 'natural magic' and
   scientists were frequently confused with sorcerers. Anatomists were
   in particular danger because their interest in the human corpse was
   misunderstood. Coke relates how 'a man was taken in Southwark
   with a head and face of a dead man, and with a book of sorcerey in
   his Male (i.e. wallet)'. He escaped death by a technicality, and only
   the head and the book were burned; but Coke remarks that if he
   had been convicted he would have suffered the same fate.
23 *The Taming of the Shrew*, 1, 1.
24 Blackstone, op. cit, (n13), 1v, ch. 13.
25 See the monograph by J. W. Spargo, *Juridical Folk-lore in England
   as illustrated by the Cucking-stool* (Duke University Press, 1944).
26 See G. D. Nokes, *History of the Crime of Blasphemy* (London, 1928),
   11.
27 Holinshed's Chronicle, 111, 1194.
28 See Thomas Burton's *Diary*, 1, ed. J. Rutt, (London, 1828), and
   Hargrave's State Trials, 11 (London, 1776 ed.), cols. 265–.
29 See Hargrave's State Trials, 1x (1776 ed.), cols. 575–.

Chapter 3. **Some Eighteenth-century Trials**

In most historical accounts of this subject the eighteenth century is usually dismissed in a sentence or two. 'Insanity was until 1800 ineffective as a defence against a criminal charge' says one social historian; 'In certain cases an individual jury might refuse to convict where the prisoner was obviously insane, but as a general rule the criminally insane went to gaols and bridewells in exactly the same way as other prisoners.' This is doubly misleading. In the first place, gaols and bridewells were the places to which offenders were usually sent if they *were* found insane; it was the gallows or the plantations which awaited most of those who were not. More misleading still, however, is the myth that the year 1800 marked the birth of the defence of insanity.

There are several reasons for this impression. The trial which led to Hadfield's acquittal in 1800 was a spectacular one, fully and vividly reported in the 'State Trials' series.[1] The three eighteenth-century offenders whose attempts at insanity defences were recorded in the same series (Arnold, Bradshaw, and Ferrers) were all unsuccessful, and it was inevitable that this should be contrasted with Hadfield's success. Secondly, Hadfield's trial led to the first statute[2] which expressly provided for a special verdict (although as we have seen special verdicts were occasionally returned under the common law before that). Finally, the eighteenth century is regarded, and not without justification, as a grim period in our penal history. It was the century during which the number of capital crimes was said to have reached two hundred, and in which it was still possible for a boy of nine to be hanged and for countless other children to be transported. The theft of goods worth more than forty shillings was still capital.

What is sometimes overlooked is that the very harshness of such sentences and the rigidity of the law which compelled judges to pronounce them led to several expedients for circumventing the law. The best known of these was juries' practice of saving a thief from the gallows by valuing the stolen goods at less than forty shillings (even when the goods themselves consisted of several guineas!); but it is a mistake to assume that these were always mutinous juries. Judges themselves would sometimes invite the jury to adopt this solution, no doubt because it was preferable to the other popular expedient, an unreasonable acquittal. Other devices included the royal pardon, which will be dealt with in chapter 12.

Nor were judges and juries completely unreceptive to the idea that the accused might have been out of his wits at the time of his crime. The trials of Arnold and Ferrers have often been cited to demonstrate how strictly the criteria of insanity were applied by criminal courts; but it is a demonstration which assumes that these were typical cases. In fact they could hardly have been less typical. Ferrers was an earl, and was therefore tried in the House of Lords. His crime was of the kind that antagonises juries, and he would have been lucky to be acquitted even if he had been tried in the first half of the twentieth century. It was inevitable that the trial of a nobleman by his peers should be considered worthy of inclusion in the 'State Trials' series; but the inclusion of Arnold's case needs a little more explanation. It was included *not* because the defence of insanity was so rare, but because his attempt to murder Lord Onslow was regarded – by Lord Onslow at least – as part of a plot against the king. Among the state papers of George 11 in the Public Record Office can be found a letter[3] from Onslow to a Mr Cracherode about the need for a shorthand writer to report the trial. The letter (which is reproduced overleaf) hints that Arnold's crime was one 'very much concerning His Majesty's safety, for my life was not the only one that was intended to be taken away'. It is for this reason that Arnold's case is the earliest example of a defence of insanity for which we have a report of the entire proceedings.

Nevertheless, although it must not be regarded as typical, the report is of great interest. It illustrates, among other things, the difficulties under which persons on trial for felony laboured at this period – difficulties which must have been at their worst when the defence was insanity. The law did not allow Arnold to be represented by counsel. A Mr Hungerford petitioned on his behalf that he should at least be allowed a solicitor by him for the purpose of calling his witnesses, but even this was opposed by the prosecution as unprecedented (a somewhat curious argument when the right to call witnesses on oath had only recently been granted to persons accused of felony). Mr Justice Tracy upheld the prosecution's view, but as the trial proceeded did in fact allow the solicitor to suggest questions which he, as judge, should put to witnesses. It was regarded as proper at this period for the judge to look after the interests of the accused, although many of them hardly troubled to do so.

Arnold pleaded not guilty to a charge of maliciously and wilfully shooting at and wounding Lord Onslow. The prosecution's case was that seven months previously, when Lord Onslow and some other gentlemen were returning on their horses from a fox-hunt, Arnold came up the lane towards them with a cocked gun. One of the gentlemen, a Mr Flutter, asked him what he meant by this. 'The man makes no answer, goes on a pace or two, turns back, takes aim, and shoots at this noble Lord. The blast being so near it struck him off his horse. . . .' Fortunately the gun was loaded with small shot, and Onslow was not killed. Arnold, who had proceeded on his way, was captured and brought back to the spot. When he saw that he had failed to kill Onslow he made as if to finish him off, but this was prevented.

Witnesses testified that Arnold had made preparations for his crime.

From the State Papers (Domestic) of George II in the Public Record Office. A transcription is printed on p. 72, n3.

That same day he had bought powder and shot, asking for the biggest shot in stock (fortunately there was only 'the second size'). He had enquired at a house nearby if Lord Onslow was out hunting, and had said 'God damn him, if I see him I will shoot my Lord Onslow.'

By this time Arnold himself had interrupted in a most unfortunate way:

Prisoner. I have had my gun go off several times in my hand; but never till now had this accident.

Serjeant Cheshire. He never before shot a lord in the shoulder! He can ask both questions when he holds up his head; but if his guilt makes him hold it down, I can't help it.

Soon after, however, his solicitor desired the judge to ask a prosecution witness whether he did not believe the prisoner to be a madman. The judge complied, and the witness agreed that he 'thought he was not right in his senses, he took to swearing so much . . . he would talk strange things . . . he was very often so, a great many of the neighbours knew it'.

At the conclusion of the prosecution's evidence Arnold was asked by the judge what he had to say. There was a long pause:

Prisoner. With humble submission, I don't know what to say. May God forgive me; if it is my fault I am sorry for it. I don't know what to say more. . . .

Justice Tracy. How came you to attempt this?

Prisoner. I don't know how it happened.

Justice Tracy. And what was the cause? It don't appear that this noble lord ever did you the least injury. Call your witnesses for the prisoner. . . .

Called on the prisoner's behalf, his brother Nathaniel testified that Edward had been strange and troublesome since he was young. He would not settle to any apprenticeships or to live with his family. 'I have caught him under my own hayrick in a morning, when he might have been in his own bed. . . .' As an adult, he lived by himself in a cottage with neither stool nor pan nor bed. Nathaniel regarded him as mad, but under cross-examination admitted that he had not thought him 'so much a madman to be chained', and that he had trusted him with the money to pay his rent.

Other members of his family and the local community gave evidence of his insanity. He was known as 'Mad Ned Arnold', given to irrational antics and minor acts of violence and damage. A servant remarked:

I always found him in great disorder, always complaining of my
Lord Onslow's bewitching him, and he had sent into his chamber
devils and imps and he had no rest, and he could not go a-fishing
for my Lord Onslow was with him. . . .

Mary Martin, who kept the public house, described how he had sat there 'scratching his bosom, and feeling and looking down into his bosom, cursing and swearing; and he said my Lord Onslow was in his bosom, and he had such a power over him that he could neither eat nor drink nor sleep nor be at ease for him'.

Other witnesses testified that in the Marshalsea prison, after his arrest, Arnold had accused Onslow of being 'the occasion of all the troubles in the nation'. The prosecution objected that evidence of behaviour subsequent to the crime should not be heard, as it was likely to be feigned, but the judge allowed it. Thus the way was paved for the introduction in later trials of medical witnesses who had examined the accused after his crime, although it should be noted that no such witnesses were called in defence of Arnold.

Both counsel for the prosecution made closing speeches: neither Arnold nor his solicitor attempted to do so. Mr Justice Tracy addressed the jury. The evidence as to fact (which he summarised very thoroughly) was clear and unchallenged, the only question was:

> . . . whether this man hath the use of his reason and senses. If he was under the visitation of God, and could not distinguish between good and evil, and did not know what he did, though he committed the greatest offence yet he could not be guilty of any offence against any law whatsoever: for guilt arises from the mind, and the wicked will and intention of the man. If a man be deprived of his reason, and consequently of his intention, he cannot be guilty: and if that be the case, though he had actually killed Lord Onslow, he is exempted from punishment: punishment is intended for example, and to deter other persons from wicked designs; but the punishment of a madman, a person that hath no design, can have no example. This is on one side. On the other side we must be very cautious; it is not every frantic and idle humour of a man that will exempt him from justice, and the punishment of the law. When a man is guilty of a great offence it must be very plain and clear before a man is allowed such an exemption; therefore it is not every kind of frantic humour, or something unaccountable in a man's actions, that points him out to be such a madman as is to be exempted from punishment: it must be a man that is totally deprived of his understanding and memory, and doth not know what he is doing, no more than an infant, than a brute or a wild beast, such a one is never the object of punishment; therefore I must leave it to your consideration, whether the condition this man was in, as it is represented to you on one side or the other, doth shew a man, who knew what he was doing, and was able to distinguish whether he was doing good or evil, and understood what he did: and it is observed they admit he was a lunatic and not an idiot. A man that is an idiot, that is born so, never recovers, but a lunatic may, and hath his intervals; and they admit he was a lunatic. You are to consider what he was at this day, when he committed this fact. Then you have a great many circumstances about the buying of the powder and the shot; his going backward and forward: and if you believe he was sensible, and had the use of his reason, and understood what he did, then he is not within the exemptions of the law, but is as subject to punishment as any other person.'

Tracy's summing-up is particularly interesting because it shows that while Bracton's criterion of insanity – total deprivation of reason – was still the theoretical foundation of the test, a superstructure had been added. In the first place, 'brutus', which merely meant 'animal' as distinct from 'human', had become 'brute or wild beast' – a phrase which must have conjured up a rather different picture from the subdued figure in the dock. Secondly, the tendency to talk of infants and madmen in the same breath is now very evident, and the question is not merely whether he 'knew what he was doing' but also whether he was 'able to distinguish whether he was doing good or evil', a question which, as we have seen, was originally applied to children. Tracy does not make it clear whether inability *either* to know what he was doing *or* to know that it was wrong would have excused Arnold; he speaks as if the two went together. It was not until the nineteenth century that they became clearly separate alternative tests.

To return to Arnold: the summing-up was plainly unfavourable to his defence, and the jury did not take long to find him guilty. He was sentenced to death, but Lord Onslow, with some magnanimity, interceded to secure a reprieve for him, and he spent the remaining thirty years of his life in the gaol at Southwark.

As I have shown in the previous chapter, however, successful defences of insanity were not completely unheard of even in the seventeenth century, nor is there any reason to suppose that by Arnold's time the attitude of the courts had become stricter. Tracy might well have been less hostile to Arnold if it had not been for the political suspicions which Onslow had aroused. A few years later, in 1731, an Old Bailey jury were persuaded to return a special verdict on evidence of insanity which was – to modern eyes at least – no more impressive than in Arnold's case. This was at the trial of Edward Stafford, which is recorded in the Old Bailey Sessions Papers.[4] Largely because this series was compiled not by legally qualified reporters but by shorthand writers who seldom picked up points of law and did not often trouble to record the judge's summing-up, it is not often referred to by legal historians. But as a source of information about the eighteenth-century system of prosecution and sentencing, to say nothing of the light they throw on the actual behaviour of criminals, victims and witnesses, they deserve a great deal more attention.

Edward Stafford, brother of Lord Stafford, was tried for the murder of Thomas Manwaring outside a coffee-house in Holborn. Manwaring seems to have been one of those frequenters of coffee-houses who were willing to earn money by running errands, and Stafford sent him for some snuff. Perhaps because he failed to fetch any, Stafford seems to have pricked him with his sword, for he cried out to passers-by that he had been stabbed. When taken to an apothecary's and stripped Manwaring showed no traces of blood, but was hustled back to the coffee-house by a porter who wanted him to charge Stafford before a constable. Stafford was said to have asked 'Are you the scrub rascal that will have a constable charged with me?' The terrified Manwaring denied this, but Stafford exclaimed 'I have not killed you but God damn you I will kill you!' and gave him a mortal sword thrust. Stafford walked back into the coffee-house 'with a Bravado, shaking his hands and stepping boldly along'. He was nearly mobbed, but gave up his sword and was taken before a Justice of the Peace, by which time he was in a very chastened frame of mind.

Most of the eye-witnesses who gave evidence said they had seen no sign that he was 'fuddled' or suffering from any 'disorder'. They were clearly prejudiced against him, however, and one of them admitted that 'the prisoner afterwards strutted and gave himself such airs that although he did not seem to be in a passion, yet he appeared . . . to be distracted'. More than a dozen other witnesses testified to his eccentricities and delusions. He was haunted by the noise of a spinning-wheel, and thought that he was bewitched, and persecuted by devils. Lord Stafford and his niece, Lady Plowden, told the court that his increasingly wild and aggressive behaviour had so alarmed them that a doctor had been sent for to arrange for his confinement, but before the doctor could be found the 'accident' happened. Although no doctor gave evidence, the jury were convinced and their verdict was reported as 'lunacy' – presumably an example of the special finding mentioned by Hale.

It is unfortunate that as usual the Sessions Papers do not record the judge's summing-up, for it would have been interesting to compare what he said about Stafford's defence with what Tracy said to Arnold's jury. Although Stafford's witnesses were more numerous and impressive, his delusions were hardly more marked than Arnold's. Moreover, whereas Arnold's delusions centred on Lord Onslow and provided him with a motive, if not a legal justification, for attacking him, the eye-witnesses' accounts of Stafford's attack on Manwaring do not sound as if it was connected with his delusions. It is true that this is an anachronistic point, for it was not until the nineteenth century that courts took an interest in the content of the madman's delusion and the extent to which it motivated and justified his deed. From what Stafford was alleged to have said and done, however, it would have been hard to argue that he did not know what he was doing, or that he was unable to tell right from wrong. In other words, even by the standards of his day, Stafford was luckier than Arnold. His jury – who must have been respectable men of property – were no doubt impressed not only with his long procession of witnesses but also with his rank. If so, the trial of Earl Ferrers illustrates the disadvantage of trial by one's peers, although admittedly Ferrers' disorder was less obvious than either Arnold's or Stafford's. His trial is of interest chiefly because it provides the earliest recorded example of psychiatric testimony in a criminal trial.

Earl Ferrers was tried before the House of Lords in April 1760 for the murder of his factor Johnson. His trial, which took place with much ceremony before a large gathering of his peers, took three days, which was much longer than most criminal trials of that day; but the result was the same as it had been in Arnold's case. Like Arnold, Ferrers was not allowed to be represented by counsel except, as we shall see, when a point of law arose. Otherwise he had to conduct his own defence, examining and cross-examining witnesses called by himself and the prosecution, and submitting his own written statement in conclusion.

The story, as presented for the Crown by the Attorney-General, was this. Johnson had been in the service of Ferrers' family since his youth, and two years earlier, when a quarrel between Ferrers and his wife led to a legal separation by private bill, Johnson had been appointed receiver of the estates. Although this appointment was made with Ferrers' approval, he soon fell out with Johnson, who would not always administer the trust in accordance with his directions. Ferrers began to suspect him of conspiring with his enemies and of frustrating a contract which Ferrers had hoped to obtain for the sale of coal on his land. He gave Johnson notice to quit a farm which had been leased to him by the trustees, but failed to break the lease. Three months before the trial Ferrers invited Johnson to his house, took him to his parlour, and locked the door. After a long argument Ferrers was heard to shout 'Down upon your knees; your time is come; you must die' and immediately shot the kneeling man in the stomach below the heart. The shot was not immediately fatal; though in great pain Johnson was able to rise and be assisted upstairs to bed. Ferrers, who seems to have alternated between hate and remorse, sent for a surgeon and for Johnson's daughter: when the latter arrived he told her that he had deliberately shot her father. Johnson did not die until next morning, and meanwhile Ferrers pestered the surgeon with enquiries as to whether he would recover. Later that evening the Earl took to the bottle, went up to Johnson's room and forced the wounded man to confess to being a villain. The surgeon, who was clearly terrified of Ferrers, pacified him by saying that Johnson was in no danger, but in the small hours, with the help of six or seven armed men, smuggled the dying man back to his own home, where he expired a few hours later. The posse then surrounded Ferrers' house, and after an abortive attempt at an armed escape he surrendered.

The Crown's witnesses took little time: their evidence was plain, and Ferrers' cross-examination of them was neither lengthy nor skilful, although it was by no means irrational. Their lordships also had the right of questioning witnesses, and the sudden interjections of occasional questions from their benches must have increased the awe and confusion of the commoners who were testifying. When called on for his defence, Ferrers explained that his case was:

. . . what my family have considered for me, and they have engaged all the evidence that are to be examined upon this unhappy occasion, who I really have not seen; I do not well know what they have to say: I should therefore hope your lordships will give me all the assistance that is possible in their examination. My lords . . . the ground of this defence has been a family complaint; and I have heard that my own family have of late endeavoured to prove me such [sc. a lunatic]. The defence I mean is occasional insanity of mind; and I am convinced from recollecting within myself, that, at the time of this action, I could not know what I was about. . . .

The witnesses whom he called testified that not only he but also his uncle and aunt were regarded as lunatics. His uncle had in fact died in a madhouse, probably in Bethlem. For it was the Physician Superintendent of Bethlem, Dr John Monro, whom Ferrers called on his behalf and examined in person. (Monro was the second in a formidable dynasty of four Monros who, father and son, superintended Bethlem for over a century.) His evidence might have been more effective if Ferrers himself and not merely his uncle had been his patient. He was thus testifying not to Ferrers' insanity but on the subject of insanity in general, and it was obvious that he found some of the unfortunate earl's questions clumsy and embarrassing:

Q. Did you know the late earl Ferrers?
A. I did.
Q. Did you know him in any, and what, distemper?
A. I attended him as a physician when he was under the unhappy influence of lunacy.
Q. Have you heard all the evidence that has been given in this cause, on the charge against earl Ferrers[5] on both sides?
A. I have.
Q. You are desired to mention what are the usual symptoms of lunacy.
A. Uncommon fury, not caused by liquor, but very frequently raised by it; many others there are which tend to violence against other persons or against themselves: I do not know a stronger, or more constant or a more unerring sympton of lunacy than jealousy, or suspicion without cause or grounds: there are many others too long to enumerate.
Q. Has the carrying of arms been generally a circumstance of lunacy?

This was a most ill-advised question; for if Monro said 'Yes' he would have been ridiculed by their lordships, who must often have gone armed about the countryside. If he replied 'No', he would appear to be undermining Ferrers' case. But Monro, who was no fool, extricated himself with a cautious reply:

A. I have known it to be so, but not generally.
Q. Please to inform their lordships whether any, and which of the circumstances which have been proved by the witnesses are symptoms of lunacy.
Attorney-General. My lords, if the noble lord means to insist upon that question, I object to it.
Lord High Steward. Lord Ferrers, do you desire your counsel to be heard upon that?
A. I do.

Since this was a point of law, the accused man was allowed the assistance of counsel, and had the good sense to accept it:

Earl of Hardwicke. My lords, this question is too general, tending to ask the doctor's opinion upon the result of the evidence, and is very rightly objected to by the counsel for the crown: if the noble lord at the bar will divide the question, and ask whether this or that particular fact is a symptom of lunacy, I dare say they will not object to it.
Attorney-General. My lords, I shall not.
Earl Ferrers. My lords, I submit to have it go on in the way recommended by Lord Hardwicke. Please to inform their lordships whether quarrelling with friends without cause is a symptom of lunacy.
Monro. Very frequently one.

Earl Ferrers. Whether being naturally suspicious is a sympton of lunacy?
Monro. Yes, it is, without cause, a constant one.
Earl Ferrers. Whether going armed where there is no danger is a symptom of lunacy?

Ferrers had not learned to avoid this unwise topic, and was trying, by a more carefully phrased question, to get a more favourable answer from the psychiatrist. If anything, the answer was less forthcoming than before:

Monro. That must be according to the circumstances.

Ferrers tries once more:

Q. Whether going *generally* armed where there is no *apparent* danger is a symptom of lunacy?

Monro capitulates:

A. I should think it was.

Ferrers' rather fumbling examination continues:

Q. Whether spitting in the looking-glass, clenching the fist, and making mouths is a symptom of lunacy?
A. I have frequently seen such in lunatic persons.
Q. Whether walking in the room, talking to himself, and making odd gestures, are symptoms of lunacy?
A. Very common ones.
Q. Is quarrelling without cause a symptom of lunacy?
A. It is a very frequent attendant upon such unhappy complaints, and they are generally malicious.
Q. Whether drinking coffee hot out of the spout of the pot is a symptom of lunacy?
A. I should think it one in the present case; it is not a general one.

Monro is doing his best to help the accused without damaging his own reputation: but Ferrers' next question is disastrous:

Q. Whether lunatics, when they are angered with or without cause, know what they are doing?

Had Monro felt able to say 'No' he might have saved Ferrers' life. Either he had lost patience or, like many a psychiatrist in later generations, he did not realise the crucial importance of his reply in the eyes of the law:

A. Sometimes, as well as I do now.

Ferrers changes the subject.

Q. Is it common to have such a disorder in families in the blood?
A. Unfortunately too common.
Q. Whether lunatics, in their intervals, are conscious of their being lunatics?
A. They are conscious of it; many both in and out of their intervals; very few that are not.

A good point had been made. For most of his hearers must have thought it paradoxical that a man whose defence was insanity should be able to conduct a rational, if not very skilful, defence.

Q. Whether lunatics are apt to be seized with fits of rage on a sudden?
A. Very often.
Q. Without any apparent cause?
A. Without any apparent cause.
Q. Is there any other way of discovering whether a man is lunatic or not, but by the irregularity of his behaviour or his pulse?
A. By the irregularity of his behaviour; I know of no other method; the pulse discovers nothing in general.
A lord. Please to inform their lordships whether a person under an immediate visitation from God of madness, has not commonly a fever?
Monro. Seldom or never, unless it may be at the first attack of the distemper, or in some very violent fit.

Finally Ferrers submitted a written summary of his case. One passage in it frankly exposes its failure to meet the strict requirements of the day:
... If they [the witnesses] have not directly proved me so insane as not to know the difference between a moral and an immoral action, they have at least proved that I was able to be driven and hurried into that unhappy condition upon very slight occasions. . . . If I could have controlled my rage, I am answerable for the consequences of it. But if I could not, and if it was the mere effect of a distempered brain, I am not answerable for the consequences. . . .
In effect, he was attempting a defence based on what later came to be known as 'irresistible impulse'. Two hundred years later it would have been listened to seriously, if not actually accepted in his case. But the Solicitor General's closing speech made short work of it:
If there be a total permanent want of reason, it will acquit the prisoner. If there be a total temporary want of it, when the offence was committed, it will acquit the prisoner: but if there be only a partial degree of insanity, mixed with a partial degree of reason; not a full and complete use of reason but (as Lord Hale carefully and emphatically expresses himself) a competent use of it, sufficient to have restrained those passions, which produced the crime . . .
not a very happy phrase, since Ferrers' argument was that his reason was *not* sufficient to restrain his passions –
if there be thought and design; a faculty to distinguish the nature of actions; to discern the differences between moral good and evil, then upon the fact of the offence proved, the judgment of the law must take place.
The Solicitor General went on to deal with the psychiatric evidence. He pointed out that the three principal types of behaviour which had been put to Monro as 'marks of lunacy' had been common fury, jealousy, and suspicion with causeless quarrelling, and the carrying of arms. All these might merely prove a bad heart and a vicious mind; and Monro could not have said, and did not say, that every man who exhibited them was a

lunatic. The Solicitor General concluded his speech with the observation:
My lords, in some sense, every crime proceeds from insanity [an
echo from Hale]. All cruelty, all brutality, all revenge, all injustice,
is insanity. There were philosophers, in ancient times, who held
this opinion. . . .

My lords, the opinion is right in philosophy but dangerous in
judicature. It may have a useful and a noble influence, to regulate
the conduct of men; to control their important passions; to teach
them that virtue is the perfection of reason, as reason itself is the
perfection of human nature; but not to extenuate crimes, nor to
excuse those punishments, which the law adjudges to be their due.

Unlike an ordinary jury, their lordships were not given the benefit of a
judicial summing-up. They had no difficulty, however, in coming to a
unanimous verdict. Ferrers was pronounced guilty by each of the hundred
and seventeen peers present, including the earl who had acted as his legal
adviser. At his hanging the newly devised mechanics of the drop failed to
work properly, and the executioner had to resort to the old practice of
jumping on the back of the slowly strangling man.

This was not the only criminal trial in which Dr Monro was a witness.
In 1780, for example, he attended the Old Bailey in order to testify that
one Richard Hyde, indicted for rioting, had been observed by him to be
insane eight years before. (Even in those days witnesses seem to have
found attendance at court a great waste of time, for after Monro had waited
at the Old Bailey for 'several days with great inconvenience' counsel for
the Crown eventually allowed his statement to be read in his absence.)[6] It
was very rarely, however, that the accused was able to call a medical witness. Not until 1798 have I found another such case. In that year Dr Leo,
who was one of the physicians employed by the Society for Visiting the
Sick and Charitable Deeds (a body set up by the London community of
Sephardic Jews), appeared two or three times at the Old Bailey on behalf
of Jews accused of shoplifting, which usually, for some reason, involved
the theft of ribbons.[7] In 1800, when a Post Office employee called Piers
was tried for embezzling letters,[8] the chief witness to his insanity was a Dr
Willis (probably not the famous Francis Willis who put George III under
'moral management' in 1788 and who would by 1800 have been in his
eighties, but one of his two sons who themselves attended the king on later
occasions). In each of these cases the physician was able to testify that he
had been treating the accused's insanity *before* the offence. Unless the
prisoner was well-to-do, or a member of a community which looked after
its own as the London Jews seem to have done, he was unlikely to have
been able to pay for the services of a physician, and consequently most
unlikely to be able to produce one who would testify to his state of mind
before the crime.

By the seventeen-eighties there can be no doubt that not only juries but
some judges as well were perfectly ready to give their blessing to a defence
of insanity. In 1783, when William Harris was tried for a capital larceny,
a witness testified that he had seemed insane all the while that he had been
in gaol: whereupon Baron Hotham said to the jury 'Then you will acquit

him to be sure, gentlemen".[9] In the following year, when William Walker, a pauper in a workhouse, was accused of the murder of his wife there, Baron Eyre devoted a considerable time to making sure that the jury returned a special verdict. His summing-up made no mention of 'wild beasts' or the ability to tell right from wrong; indeed, at times he sounded like a twentieth-century judge describing a case of 'irresistible impulse':

Where men suffer their passions to get the better of their reasons
. . . they must answer for the consequences; but rage which is the effect of distemper is brought upon them by the act of God, and not by themselves, and they are not answerable for what they do in those moments. The man's afterwards coming to his senses will not alter the . . . case, if it was committed under the impression of insanity, and the mind disturbed and deprived of its powers of governing the man. . . .[10]

The contrast between the judge's attitude in such cases and the summing-up of Tracy at Arnold's trial is striking. Was it merely the difference between two generations' interpretation of the law? This can hardly be so, for in the next chapter we shall find Mansfield treating Bellingham as severely as Tracy handled Arnold. Was it the difference between the personalities of individual judges? This is possible: there are not enough reported cases to confirm or refute the hypothesis. What is more probable, however, is that these contrasting cases were simply illustrations of a tendency which is also detectable in nineteenth- and twentieth-century cases: the tendency to apply the law strictly when trying the unpopular offender, but to forget it when trying the merely unfortunate.

A notable example of leniency was the trial of Miss Broadric in 1795, which was mentioned in the course of Hadfield's trial. The only contemporary account which I have been able to find is in *The Times* for 18th July 1795; but it is sufficiently detailed to be interesting; and since it is not as accessible as the State Trials, I have reproduced it in Appendix F. Miss Broadric seems to have been a lady of easy virtue who was taken up by a Mr Errington after his divorce from his first wife. After a while, however, Mr Errington deserted Miss Broadric to contract another marriage, with the result that Miss Broadric pursued him to his country home and shot him with a pistol and a leaden bullet. She was tried at Chelmsford, and made an excellent impression on *The Times*' correspondent by appearing in deep mourning, 'greatly agitated and almost fainting'; but during most of the trial 'showed great presence of mind and behaved with great propriety'. The prosecution's evidence showed that the crime was premeditated: Miss Broadric had journeyed to Mr Errington's house, had been shown by the new Mrs Errington into her husband's room, and had then shot him, after which she threw the pistol down saying 'Hang me or do with me as you please!' When searched she was found to have a second loaded pistol which she said she had meant for herself. It must thus have been clear that she knew what she was doing and that she was committing a crime. Her counsel, however, elicited from his witnesses that her mother and sister had both been afflicted with 'a constitutional insanity'; that she frequently talked oddly, and spoke of doing away with herself; that she had thrown scalding water over her chairwoman for not cleaning the stairs to her liking; that she used to walk about Kennington like a soldier doing his exercise; in short that she was 'whimsical' and 'maddish like'.

Lord Chief Baron Kenyon, who was to preside over Hadfield's trial five years later, summed up in what *The Times* called 'a very human and affecting manner', and although he reviewed the evidence on both sides most impartially Miss Broadric had evidently won the sympathy of the court, for the jury acquitted her without leaving their box and to the open satisfaction of the spectators. She was ordered to be detained. No doubt the consideration which really turned the scale so decidedly in her favour was that she was a woman who had been treated badly – although to do Mr Errington justice she must have been an alarming mistress and had apparently forfeited the affection of at least one previous lover. However that may be, her defence of insanity presented the jury with an excuse to save her from the death sentence. Had Mr Errington shot her instead, it is doubtful whether similar evidence of mental disorder – which does not seem to have amounted to more than what would now be called psychopathy – would have saved him.

One or two other features of the Old Bailey trials of this period are worth noting. The accused can now expect more help from counsel than Arnlod could. The famous Garrow, who later became a judge, often appears on behalf of prisoners who can hardly have afforded the fee to which he was accustomed (perhaps there was a system of dock briefs for capital cases by this period?). Moreover, the prisoner's counsel is allowed to call and examine his witnesses and to cross-examine the prosecution's witnesses, although he cannot yet make a speech. Even when he is not assisted by counsel, the accused himself – to say nothing of his friends who appear on his behalf – is often quite clearly aware of the possibilities of insanity as a last line of defence. 'I was out of my senses', said one Denis Rearden. 'There is nobody in their right senses would take such a tool to kill a person.' A helpful, but unwise, friend added that 'Sometimes, when he was drunk, he used to behave like a madman.'

Courts were also sophisticated enough to be aware of the danger of false confessions by lunatics. In the seventeen-sixties a woman called Mary Davis or Cavenhau, who was suicidally minded, gave considerable trouble to the agencies of law enforcement. On one occasion she confessed to the murder of a bastard child, but failed to satisfy Sir John Fielding, the magistrate, that the child had ever existed. Thereupon she went to Gloucester, where she managed to get herself put on trial for the murder of the probably mythical baby, but was acquitted for the same reason. A few years later she confessed to robbing and murdering a turnpike man, and after trying to hang herself in Clerkenwell bridewell was brought to trial at the Old Bailey, where she was again acquitted because her confession was disbelieved. In the following year she was once more on trial at the Old Bailey, this time for a petty larceny; and although this time it was a defective indictment that led to her acquittal the court 'recommended her to the Governors of Bedlam, as a proper object of that charity'.[11]

G

Another point worth noting is that by this time the defence is not confined to what Hale called 'capitals', but is sometimes accepted in the case of non-capital thefts. If Hale was correct in his assumption – and there is no evidence that he was not – exactly when and why did this development take place? It is impossible to do more than speculate; and I can only suggest that it may have been connected with the growing importance of transportation as substitute for hanging. Since this was a non-capital penalty which was more to be feared than the fate of the lunatic, it created a situation in which there was some point in deciding whether the offender was insane, even if everyone knew that his life was not at stake. But it must be admitted that there is no direct evidence to support this hypothesis.

From the middle of the century onward the Sessions Papers seem sufficiently complete, and examples of the insanity defence sufficiently frequent, to justify one or two statistical generalisations. Since the continuous judicial statistics for England and Wales do not begin until 1834, the Sessions Papers provide a means of anticipating the age of statistics by roughly a century. To indicate what reliance can be placed on my figures I must explain briefly how they were compiled. The Sessions Papers themselves number each case consecutively throughout the twelve months of each mayor's term of office, and although there are occasional mistakes in the numbering they thus provide a ready-made count of the number of trials. To identify insanity defences, however, it was necessary to scrutinise the more or less verbatim statements attributed to each prisoner and his witnesses, if any. Since the average annual number of trials at mid-century was slightly over 400 and rose to more than 2,000 by the eighteen-thirties, the task of scrutinising each defence for the whole period would have been enormous, and after the seventeen-sixties I had to be content with selected quinquennia, although at one or two points – for example, just before and after Hadfield's trial – it seemed advisable to cover longer periods. Even so, the search involved glancing briefly, and often not so briefly, at the accounts of more than 50,000 trials.[12]

Three types of error were possible. Sometimes the report of the case was so short and formal, containing no more than the name of the accused, the offence, the verdict, and the sentence, that it was possible that the reporter had not been present. Such entries are rather frequent during the seventeen-thirties but less common thereafter; and I have therefore not tabulated figures for the period before 1740. The second possibility of error was simply that of overlooking an instance, as I am sure we must have done now and again. The third was the difficulty of deciding whether to classify a statement by the prisoner or a witness as an instance. For example, intoxication was often put forward as a defence or mitigating circumstance throughout this period, and as we shall see in chapter 10 it occasionally led to an acquittal. Quite often the prisoner was said to be like a madman when drunk; but such cases were not counted. Nor were cases in which witnesses to the prisoner's character added that he or she was 'rather silly and stupid' or 'weak in her intellect'. On the other hand, 'brain-fever', stories of head injuries followed by odd behaviour (if not

TABLE 2. Old Bailey trials during selected periods between 1740 and 1913 in which the sanity of the accused was questioned

| Period | Trials at which the prisoner's | | | | 'Success-rate', i.e. cols. B+D as % of A+C[f] | Frequency of A+C[e] per 1,000 accused persons |
| | fitness for trial was questioned | – successfully | mental state was considered as an excuse | – and accepted | | |
	A[d]	B	C	D[e]	E	F
1740–4	—	—	9	3	28·5%	4·6
1745–9	—	—	15	5		
1750–4	—	—	11	2		
1755–9	1	1	16	7	50·0%	7·2
1760–4	1	—	17	9		
1765–9	—	—	15	8		
1780–4	—	—	12	7	41·3%	4·4
1790–4	3	3	11	4		
1795–9	1	—	19	5		
1800[a]	1	—	2	1		
1801–5	—	—	23	12	50·0%	4·7
1806–10	2	2	22	7		
1811–5	1	1	14	9		
1834–6[b]	2	2	23	12	56·0%	2·9
1851–3	6	4	23	7	37·9%	6·4
1881–4	2	2	38	15	42·5%	7·9
1909–13[c]	5	5	51	34	69·6%	13·0

The laboriousness of the task ruled out the examination of the entire series. A few quinquennia were therefore selected around dates which were of interest, and the gaps between them were filled in when it became clear that the period was of special interest. In the nineteenth century the annual numbers of trials increased greatly, and periods of three or four years, which yielded as many cases as eighteenth-century quinquennia, were examined: since other statistical information was available, greater intervals were allowed. The total number of trials scanned was about 55,000.

[a] The year of Hadfield's trial has been deliberately excluded in calculating the rates in columns E and F.

[b] The period was chosen because the published national judicial statistics begin in 1834.

[c] The series ended in April 1913, not with a whimper but a bang – the trial of Mrs Pankhurst for trying to blow up a building.

[d] The figures exclude cases of deaf-mutism.

[e] These figures are included in the previous column.

[f] Columns A and B must be included because of the likelihood that if the prisoner's fitness for trial had not been questioned his mental state would have been considered as an excuse, and because in some early cases it is not clear whether the case should be classified as an instance of A or C.

combined with drunkenness), and 'the falling sickness' were counted. To the extent that we made errors in this classification, they were like the other types of error – in the direction of an underestimate.

Table 2 is the result. For each selected period it shows the numbers of defendants whose mental state was considered as a possible reason for postponing trial or for excusing them from punishment, and the cases in which this course was taken. The last two columns show two sets of calculated statistics. One is what I have called 'the success-rate'; that is, the defendants who were excused either trial or punishment shown as a percentage of those whose mental state was considered. The other is the frequency with which the mental state of the defendant was considered, expressed as a rate per 1,000 defendants. For this purpose the early quinquennia have been grouped together in order that the rates might be based on larger numbers and so be more reliable.

The table shows, for example, that while an insane defendant's chances of success were slightly lower just before than just after Hadfield's trial in 1800, the change was by no means as marked as the usual historical account assumes. Indeed, his chances seem to have been as high just after the middle of the eighteenth century as they were in the early nineteenth century. Another interesting feature of the table is the frequency for this period, which – with an important exception – remains at about 4½ per 1,000 defendants from the seventeen-forties until the end of the Napoleonic Wars. The exception is the period from 1755 to 1769, when the frequency seems to have been markedly higher – about 7 per 1,000. This leads to the even more interesting observation that it was apparently during this period that the 'success rate' first reached the level of about 50 per cent, which it was to maintain, with small fluctuations, for another eighty years. During the preceding period, from 1740 to 1754, it seems to have been markedly lower.

What explanation can be offered for these phenomena – the increases in frequency and success rate just after the middle of the century? In the first place, we must always consider the possibility that the differences are the result of mere chance. The probability of this, however, can be calculated and is rather low (for example, the odds against the explanation of the differing success rates in terms of chance are about twelve to one, and in the case of the frequencies they are even higher). In other words, we would not be justified in dismissing the differences as fortuitous.[13]

Another possibility is that the explanation lies in some change of legal procedure which was favourable to the defendant. If so, it must have been a change which did not favour defendants in general, for the acquittal rate for all defendants at the Old Bailey during both periods seems to have been roughly 30 per cent. Nevertheless at least one procedural development was taking place at this time which might well have helped the defendant who was mentally handicapped. In the early seventeen-fifties the defendant's counsel was occasionally allowed not merely to suggest questions which the judge might put to witnesses (as he was allowed to do in Arnold's case) but to put such questions himself. I therefore analysed the trials of the defendants whose mental state was considered to see

FIGURE 1. Frequencies and success-rates of Old Bailey trials in which the sanity
of the accused was questioned (based on table 2)

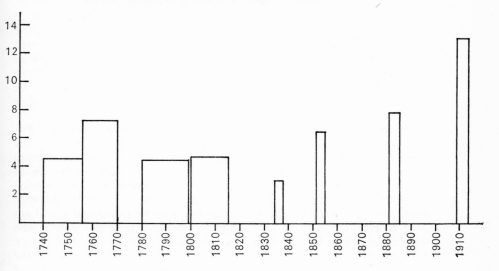

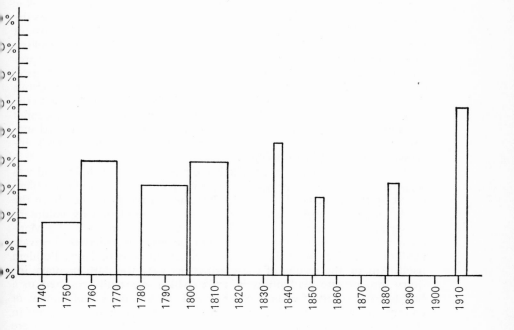

whether those whose counsel was clearly recorded as intervening in this way were more often successful than the others. Unfortunately for this hypothesis the result was negative: there was no significant difference.

Since we cannot dismiss the figures as the result of chance or improvements in procedure, we must look for signs of genuine changes either in the pattern of crime or in attitudes to mental disorder. For example, the insane defendants of the later period (1755–69) were more often accused of thefts than those of the earlier period (60 per cent compared with 40 per cent) and more of them were women (38 per cent compared with 26 per cent). Neither stealing nor being a woman, however, seemed to be associated with a more than average chance of being excused from trial or punishment by reason of insanity.

On the whole, therefore, we must seriously consider two fairly straightforward explanations. One is that the figures really do reflect what they seem to – an increase in the relative frequency with which lunatics and idiots appeared in the dock at the Old Bailey. To account for this we do not have to suppose a sharp increase in the national incidence of mental disorder, as a result, for instance, of gin-drinking or syphilis (although both were spreading at this time). All that need be postulated is a slight over-representation of the mentally disordered among the people who were moving into London from the provincial countryside. Although we have no direct evidence of this, it was a not unlikely consequence of the vagrancy legislation of the seventeen-forties, which made it the duty of local justices to order the detention of wandering lunatics by the parish overseers. In theory this should have reduced the numbers of insane vagrants: in practice it is very likely that it merely drove them towards the metropolis. Parishes were unwilling to be burdened with the cost of vagrants' upkeep, and the incentive to move them on instead of locking them up was strong. The wandering lunatic himself may well have preferred a precarious freedom to the barbarities of the local bridewell, gaol, or workhouse. (Even the humane regimes of modern provincial hospitals do not dissuade many a chronic schizophrenic from finding his way to the anonymity of Paddington or Waterloo.) If this explanation – which cannot be more than speculative – is at least part of the truth, the increased success rate of the period 1755–69 was one result of the Old Bailey's increasing familiarity with insane offenders.

However this may be, an unmistakable phenomenon of this period was a growing public awareness of the special nature of the social problem posed by the mentally disordered. This showed itself not merely in the crude legislation against vagrancy, but in the foundation by voluntary subscription of hospitals for the insane – St Luke's in 1751, the Manchester Lunatic Hospital in 1763 – and in the growing criticisms of private madhouses and even of that ancient stronghold of psychiatry, Bethlem itself. Among the results of these criticisms were the parliamentary inquiry into private madhouses in 1763 (which eventually resulted in a half-hearted statute for their control) and the gradual establishment of county asylums. During this same period there had been improvements in the training of doctors, and among the new generation of physicians were some who took a not unprofitable interest in the care and treatment of the insane.

One of these was William Battie. Already a physician of some repute – he had been Harveian Orator in 1746 – Battie had purchased himself membership of the Bethlem governors in 1742, at the cost of a £50 subscription, and was evidently dissatisfied with its regime. It was largely due to his initiative that St Luke's Hospital for Lunaticks was founded in 1751, and he became its chief physician. Not long afterwards he acquired his own private madhouse. He was probably the first English physician of status to make psychiatry his business, and – more important still – to teach it systematically to new entrants to his profession.

Some idea of what he taught can be got from his *Treatise on Madness*, which he published in 1758. It is an interesting mixture of dogma and enlightenment. For example, although he recognised that idiocy seldom responded to treatment, he suggests that it may sometimes be useful 'if nothing contraindicates [a phrase with a very modern sound] to shake the whole frame by vomits, cathartics, errhines [i.e. medicinal snuffs] and all sorts of tolerable irritation'. At the same time he is quick to point out that no specific for madness proper has yet been discovered, only techniques for treating its symptoms. Many patients, he argued, recovered if simply confined in peaceful surroundings, protected from the upsetting visits of friends and the teasing of sightseers (a remark which was obviously aimed at Bethlem, where the patients were on show as if in a zoo). Some of his generalisations were penetrating; others were disastrous. He observes with acuteness that 'madness hath . . . shared the fate common to so many other distempers of not being precisely defined. . . . Not only several symptoms, which frequently and accidentally accompany it, have been taken into account as constant, necessary and essential, but also the supposed cause, which perhaps never existed, or certainly never acted with such effect, hath been implied in the very names given to this distemper'. Certainly the confusion of diagnosis with causal theories is still one of the unsatisfactory features of psychiatry. Unfortunately he was confident that he himself had detected the essential characteristic of madness, which was 'deluded imagination' – a theory which he owed to the philosopher Locke. This oversimplification was so neat and intelligible that it came to have considerable influence, especially on nineteenth-century judges. Indeed, the book was admirably suited both to the busy practitioner and to the intelligent layman. It was short, elegant, clear, and combined neat aphorisms with practical advice.[14] Its popularity was ensured by a sarcastic rejoinder from Monro of Bethlem, whom Battie had by implication criticised for admitting sightseers but not medical students to his wards.

Battie's influence, however, must have been reinforced by the sheer frequency with which the mental state of the accused was now being brought to the attention of judges. In the Old Bailey alone this happened about three times a year during the seventeen-fifties. How frequently did it happen in the country as a whole? With some hesitation I have tried to estimate this by using the Old Bailey figures as a basis.

There are obvious difficulties and dangers in this calculation. It cannot be done by relating the two populations at risk, since both would themselves be estimates (the first census was not carried out until 1801); and in any case the population at risk of appearing in the Old Bailey could not be estimated from the population of London and Middlesex, since there were other criminal courts in which the Londoner could appear – for instance the Clerkenwell Sessions. Moreover, the London crime rate was almost certainly higher than that of the country as a whole, but by what margin we do not know. The least objectionable estimate would be one based on a comparison between the numbers of successful insanity defences for the Old Bailey and for England and Wales during the earliest years of the published judicial statistics, which begin with the year 1834. In the three years 1834–6 the number of successful insanity defences reported in the Sessions Papers was 12; and the number published for England and Wales as a whole was 53, in other words, about four and a half times the Old Bailey number. On this basis, a conservative and tentative estimate of the frequency of insanity defences in the country as a whole for the period covered by table 2 might be reached by multiplying the Old Bailey figures for each period by four. This would take no account of changes in the ratio between the crime rates of the country as a whole and of the Old Bailey's jurisdiction during the period. All that can be said on this point is that, during the eighteenth century, London probably accounted for a *smaller* share of the country's crime than it did in the eighteen-thirties, in which case a factor of four yields too cautious an estimate.

This would mean that in the seventeen-fifties there were about four successful defences of insanity each year throughout England and Wales and another eight unsuccessful ones. If, as I argued in the Introduction, one of the necessary conditions of change in the legal approach to a problem is that it should present itself to the courts with sufficient frequency, this condition was probably fulfilled by the second half of the eighteenth century, and the change itself took place forty years before Hadfield's case.

Notes

1 T.B.Howell, *A Complete Collection of State Trials and Proceedings for High Treason and other Crimes and Misdemeanours* (London).
2 40 Geo. III, c. 94.
3 Among the State Papers (Domestic) of George II in the Public Record Office, by whose permission it is reproduced. It has been transcribed below:
I have orders from my Lord Townshend & Lord Carteret that the Attorney & Solicitor generall shall by his Majesty's directions attend at Kingston Assizes the tryal of Edward Arnold for his attempt to murther me, the evidence of this fact very much concerning his Majesty's safety, for my life was not the only one that was intended to be taken away; I presume you either have orders already or will speedily have to take heed of this matter; I have ordered Mr Hall (?) my solicitor that takes care of the prosecution for me to wait

upon you to concert proper measures with you on behalf of the
Crown & he will give you a further account of the Case. It is
designed that this tryal be printed, you having acquaintance with
a proper shorthand writer in the late State tryals I must rely upon
you to provide one; My Lord Duke of Newcastle & Mr. Walpole
are both acquainted with what is intended and approve thereof
I am

I should be glad	Sir
to see you at the	Yr assured Freind [sic]
house of Lords on	& humble servt
Monday or Wednesday	
next	ONSLOW

4 See the proceedings for July 14–17, 1731. For a description of the
  Old Bailey Sessions Papers see the bibliography. In the same year
  (in the sessions for April 28 to May 3rd) Richard Cooper unsuccessfully offered a defence of insanity when indicted for murdering the
  woman with whom he lived.

5 Although Ferrers himself was perforce conducting the examination
  he is reported as referring to himself in the third person.

6 Hyde's case (1780), O.B.S.P., case 415.

7 See, for example, Samuel Jacob's case (1798), O.B.S.P., case 470.

8 Piers' case (1800), O.B.S.P., case 315.

9 Harris' case (1783), O.B.S.P., case 7.

10 Walker's case (1784), O.B.S.P., case 388.

11 See (1763), O.B.S.P., cases 428–30, and (1764), O.B.S.P., case 128.

12 In this task I had the able assistance of Mr Steven Hartz of Hert-
  ford College, who undertook much the larger share of the search.

13 The odds given in the text relate only to a comparison of the period
  1740–54 with the period 1755–69. If the numbers are increased by
  adding later periods to the period 1755–69, the odds against an
  explanation in terms of chance become greater still. Odds of twelve
  to one are not high enough to satisfy modern social scientists, who
  deal in large numbers of comparisons, but should be good enough
  for historians, who are seldom able to calculate the probability of
  their inferences, and must often accept lower odds than this
  without realising it.

14 Not all practitioners, however, found it easy going. James Boswell,
  whose brother John spent many years in madhouses, went to see
  Dr Hall of St Luke's in 1775, who told him that he could not
  understand the book.

Chapter 4. **Hadfield and Others**

The previous chapter must have demonstrated that Hadfield's trial in 1800[1] was hardly the historical landmark that it has been made to seem. It was not without its significance, as I shall explain after describing his trial. But it cannot be said to have increased the numbers of offenders who attempted the same defence or who succeeded in it. Successful defences of insanity had been a regular feature of Old Bailey trials for at least sixty years. As table 2 in the previous chapter shows, there was a slight increase about the time of Hadfield's trial in the relative frequency of the defence, but whether this should be attributed to chance or to some other factor it is undoubtedly a fluctuation which began a few years *before* 1800. Nor was Hadfield the first offender to call a physician to testify as to his state of mind. He was not even the first insane assailant of a monarch to escape the gallows. Margaret Nicholson's attack on George III in 1786, and the Privy Council's humane treatment of her, are described in chapter 11. John Frith's attack on him in 1790, and the subsequent trial at the Old Bailey, are discussed in chapter 14.

Admittedly, Hadfield's attack was a much more serious affair. Margaret Nicholson merely made an incompetent thrust with a pen-knife, while John Frith threw a stone. Hadfield used a firearm, and came within a few inches of wounding, if not killing, George III. The 15th May 1800 had been an eventful day for the king, for at a parade of troops which he attended early in the day a member of his entourage had been wounded by a musket which should have been loaded only with powder. That same evening, as the King entered the royal box at Drury Lane theatre, a man in the standing audience fired a pistol at him. The ball passed about a foot above the king's head, through a hollow pilaster, and was later found in the orchestra. A bystander struck the pistol from the man's hand and he was seized by several people. There seems to have been no attempt to do him physical harm: he was simply lifted over the orchestra rail and taken to the musicians' anteroom, where he was interrogated by the king's brother, the Duke of York. The Duke was probably acting in his capacity as a member of the Privy Council, which could and did commit people for trial if their crime concerned the king. The man's face seemed familiar to the Duke, and he reminded the latter that he had been one of his orderlies at the battle of Freymar.

Hadfield, who seemed quite rational to the Duke, was in much greater danger of the gallows than Margaret Nicholson or John Frith. He owed the success of his defence to several lucky circumstances. First, the fact that his target was a royal one meant that his crime was treason and that he had several privileges which were denied to persons accused of mere felonies, even when these were capital. He was given more time in which to prepare his defence and collect witnesses. He was told the exact terms of the charge against him, the nature of the evidence, and the names of the jurors who would try him. Most important of all, he was provided with counsel not merely to advise on points of law and examine witnesses, but also to address the court. What is more, his counsel was no ordinary counsel but the famous Erskine, at the peak of his career at the bar, who had already shown courage and skill in defending such unpopular prisoners as Lord Gordon and Tom Paine. The care with which Erskine prepared Hadfield's case, and the use he made of these privileges, is demonstrated by the fact that several jurors were challenged, that the defence had an apparently inexhaustible list of witnesses to Hadfield's abnormality, and that Erskine had mastered the literature of his subject.

The trial took place six weeks later. Several witnesses for the prosecution described the incident itself with considerable agreement and were not cross-examined by Erskine. The Attorney-General then called the Duke of York. After describing their recognition of each other, the Duke was asked to recollect what Hadfield had said about his act:

A. . . . he said once or twice, at different times, he knew perfectly well that his life was forfeited.

Q. Will your Royal Highness have the goodness to recollect whether there was anything more said by him?

A. He said he was tired of life, and that he regretted nothing but the fate of a woman who was his wife, who would be but a few days longer he supposed his wife; in talking upon the enormity of the crime he had been committing, he said, I think, exactly in these words: 'The worst has not happened yet' or 'has not come yet'.

Q. In the whole of the conversation which your Royal Highness had with this man . . . did he betray in his answers any irregularity from which you could collect a then existing derangement of his understanding?

A. Not the least: on the contrary, he appeared to speak as connectedly as could possibly be. The first conversation at which I was present continued nearly three-quarters of an hour; he was as much collected as possible.

Although this was damaging to his client, Erskine's cross-examination was suitably deferential, and elicited only one important addition to the evidence in chief. He asked the Duke whether Hadfield had explained his phrase 'tired of life':

A. He said he was tired of life, that he thought he should certainly be killed if he were to make an attempt upon his majesty's life.

The Attorney-General swiftly re-examined the witness:

Q. Did he give the answer collectedly, or as a man under any disturbance of mind?

A. No; he was perfectly collected, in my opinion, at the time he
answered.

Other witnesses for the prosecution described how Hadfield had shown
them a pair of pistols which he had just bought on the day of the incident,
and had spoken of going to the theatre. Asked how normal Hadfield's
bearing had been, one said: 'He seemed lower in spirits than I thought I
had usually seen him before.' To the others he had seemed 'as well as ever
I saw him', or 'nothing but as usual'. Since Hadfield's usual behaviour
was little short of bizarre, these phrases were almost Greek in their double-
edged irony; but it was an irony which at this stage only Erskine could
appreciate.

When his turn came, Erskine had no difficulty in producing spectacular
evidence of Hadfield's abnormality. His client had obvious and disfiguring
wounds in the head, acquired in action against the French six years before.
One of these had penetrated the skull, so that Erskine was able to invite
the jury to inspect the membrane of the brain itself. An officer of his
former regiment testified that before Hadfield had been wounded he had
been an excellent soldier, but afterwards had been incoherent, with 'manifest symptoms of derangement'. The regimental surgeon recalled how he
had been compelled to have Hadfield tied to a bed for a fortnight.

Evidence was also given by a Dr 'Creighton' from Bethlem. This was
probably the thirty-eight-year-old Alexander (later Sir Alexander) Crichton, whose recently published *Inquiry into the Nature and Origin of Mental
Derangement* included discussions of insane motives for murder.[2] (He later
became physician to Tsar Alexander I and head of the civil medical department in Russia.) Unlike Drs Leo and Willis, he had not seen the
accused until after the crime (although of course there was plenty of other
testimony as to Hadfield's earlier insanity), so that his role was that of the
modern psychiatric witness.

Crichton's examination of Hadfield had taken place in Newgate as
recently as the previous night, and it had lasted about half an hour. He
had been accompanied by a surgeon and also by a gaoler (until quite late
in the nineteenth century it seems to have been the rule that the governor
or a member of his staff should be present throughout the proceedings[3]).
Crichton's evidence was to the effect that the prisoner's madness was
probably the result of his wounds, and although in law it did not matter
what the cause was this must have made a favourable impression on a
war-time jury. As regards the nature of his madness, he said in answer to
Erskine that

> . . . When any question concerning a common matter is made to
> him, he answers very correctly; but when any question is put to
> him which relates to the subject of his lunacy, he answers irration-
> ally. . . . It requires that the thoughts which have relation to his
> madness should be awakened in his mind, in order to make him
> act unreasonably. . . .

Cross-examination failed to shake him, and when Kenyon himself asked whether Crichton had told Hadfield that he was to be a witness at his trial Crichton was able to deny this. There were lay witnesses, too, of course. Among them were Hadfield's brother and sisters-in-law, who described his periodic fits of terrifying madness, in one of which he had threatened to kill his own child because God had told him to. Erskine thus had little difficulty in establishing his client's insanity. What he could not argue was that Hadfield had been unaware of the nature of his act; not only had he planned it in a more or less rational way, but his very objective – to be executed for treason – showed that he appreciated its probable conse-quences. By the same token Erskine could not contend that Hadfield satisfied the 'right-wrong test', since to appreciate the consequences of the act he must have known that it was unlawful. Erskine might con-ceivably have pointed out that Hadfield imagined himself to be acting under the command of the Almighty, and so presumably to be doing no wrong, though committing a crime; but we must remember that the dis-tinction between morality and legality was by no means familiar to lawyers of his day. Even if the point had occurred to him, he might well have hesitated to rely upon it.

He therefore resorted to a most skilful tactic. First he undermined the established test by arguing that it could not mean what it said. He made great play with Coke's requirement that 'there must be a total deprivation of memory and understanding'. Was anyone but a helpless idiot literally in that condition? Very occasionally the mind was 'laid prostrate by the stroke of frenzy' so that the man was unconscious even of external objects; but such cases were regarded by physicians as examples of delirium rather than mania, were rare, and gave judges no difficulty.

In the cases which gave rise to real difficulty 'reason is not driven from her seat, but distraction sits down upon it along with her, holds her, trembling upon it, and frightens her from her propriety'. The madman reasoned from premises which were false; 'not false from any defect of knowledge of judgment, but because a delusive image, the inseparable companion of real insanity, is thrust upon the subjugated understanding, incapable of resistance because unconscious of attack'. In Hadfield's case the delusion was 'that he must be destroyed, but must not destroy himself'. Erskine's rhetoric was masterly, if a trifle mannered, and the flaw in his logic was concealed by his sleight of hand.

For he had discredited the accepted test by citing it in its least defensible form. Had he, for example, been minded to do it justice, he could have cited Hale's test for *dementia accidentalis*:

> . . . the best measure that I can think of is this: such a person as,
> labouring under melancholy distempers, hath yet ordinarily as
> great understanding as ordinarily a child of fourteen years hath, is
> such a person as may be guilty of treason or felony.

This form of test would, however, have made it hard for him to avoid the question whether Hadfield could tell right from wrong; and as we have seen, this would have been dangerous ground.

But there was no doubt about the effect of his rhetoric – and his procession of witnesses – upon the judges. After a while Lord Kenyon asked if the evidence was nearly finished. 'No, my lord', said Erskine; 'I have twenty more witnesses to examine.' But the judges did not want to sit through repetitions of Hadfield's eccentricities, and the Attorney-General confirmed that he did not wish to challenge any of the evidence. The court then publicly debated what was to be done with Hadfield. 'I do not know that one can run the case very nicely', said Kenyon, 'if you do run it very nicely, to be sure it is an acquittal.' But, he very sensibly argued:

> . . . the prisoner, for his own sake, and for the sake of society at large, must not be discharged; for this is a case which concerns every man of every station, from the king upon the throne to the beggar at the gate; people of both sexes and of all ages may, in an unfortunate frantic hour, fall a sacrifice to this man, who is not under the guidance of sound reason; and therefore it is absolutely necessary for the safety of society that he should be properly disposed of, all mercy and humanity being shown to this most unfortunate creature. . . .

Kenyon seems to have been hinting that Bethlem rather than Newgate was the proper place for Hadfield; but as we saw in chapter 2[4] he took the view that his own powers allowed him to do no more than send the prisoner back to Newgate. Although the formality of the occasion seems to have inhibited the judges and law officers from discussing the situation openly, all those concerned – except possibly Hadfield – knew that a hastily drafted Bill was about to be passed by Parliament in order to provide a clear-cut and foolproof procedure for such cases, and that it would enable Hadfield to be dealt with retrospectively. Meanwhile, however, a verdict of some sort had to be returned. It was suggested to the jury that they should acquit the accused but give their reason for doing so, and this they duly did. A copy of the official record of the verdict was supplied to the Home Office at its request, and is reproduced opposite.

Whether the Act of 1800 'for the safe custody of insane persons charged with offences'[5] would have been drafted and passed with such urgency if Hadfield's target had not been a royal one, or if he had been so obviously insane as to be within the existing definition of insanity, is doubtful. However that may be, its chief provisions were these. Henceforth the only permissible verdict in cases in which the jury was satisfied that the accused was insane at the time of his crime was to be the special verdict which made it clear that the acquittal was on the ground of insanity: the alternative of a plain acquittal was no longer open to them. Secondly, the effect of a special verdict was to be that the court must order the accused 'to be kept in strict custody, in such place and in such manner as to the court shall seem fit, until His Majesty's pleasure be known'; whereupon it would be for His Majesty to give orders for his custody. By a retrospective phrase this part of the Act was applied to offenders who had already been so dealt with by the courts – in other words, to Hadfield. No doubt His Majesty was made responsible simply because there was as yet no precedent for designating the recently created Secretary of State for Home Affairs in any Act.

Thursday next after fifteen Days of the holy —
Trinity in the fortieth year of King George the 3.

Middlesex
The King
ag.st
James Hadfield

The Jury at the Barr here say that the
Prisoner is Not Guilty of the Treason —
whereof he is Indicted being under the
Influence of Insanity at the time when
the several Overt acts mentioned in the
Indictment were Committed and that he did
not fly for it And it appearing to the Court
here that he is Subject to frequent fits of
Insanity And that it is therefore not Consistent
with the safety of his Majesty and his subject
that he should go at large he is now remanded
to the Custody of the Keeper of his Majestys Goal
of Newgate in order to be dealt with according
to Law —

By the Court

The document is numbered 155 in file HO 48/9 at the Public
Record Office, by whose permission it is reproduced here. The
accompanying letter makes it clear that it was a copy for which the
Home Office had made a special request. An explanation of the
phrase 'and that he did not fly for it' will be found in Hale's
History of Pleas of the Crown, II: if the accused had tried to
escape, his goods would have been forfeit even if he had been
acquitted.

A similar arrangement was to govern the disposal of persons found by a jury to be so insane as to be unfit to be tried on indictment. The Act also closed a loophole by applying the same procedure to persons about to be discharged for want of prosecution who appeared to be insane; this was probably designed to thwart the offender who might escape custody through a private prosecution brought by a friend with the express intention of deserting it. Finally, the Act at last made it possible for the justices to confine certain insane persons without the possibility of private bail, so that only two justices, or a higher judicial authority, could release them; this provision was limited to 'any person discovered and apprehended under circumstances that denote a derangement of mind and a purpose of committing an indictable offence'. This power, which seems a fairly sweeping one, could apparently be exercised without any requirement that the justices should have medical evidence on the subject of the derangement of mind.

The significance of these provisions will be discussed in later chapters. For the moment, a curious feature of the drafting of the Act must be mentioned. The section concerned with insanity on arraignment was expressly applied to indictments 'for any offence', whereas the main section which dealt with the special verdict specified only treason, murder, or felony, and thus excluded misdemeanours. The difference is so obvious that it is implausible to attribute it to a drafting error. At a guess, the explanation may lie in Hale's doctrine that the defence of insanity was confined to 'capitals'. No doubt this dated from a time when the penalty for all felonies was capital; but with the introduction of the non-capital penalty of transportation the doctrine may have been modified so that the defence was reserved to felonies (and of course treason).

However that may be, the omission of misdemeanours from the main section eventually, though not immediately, embarrassed the courts. In 1820, for example, when a man called Little was tried for the misdemeanour of assaulting a woman with a stick with intent to murder her, an awkward situation arose. The jury decided that he was insane at the time of his trial and had been at the time of his crime, and acquitted him. The judge – Baron Wood – could not order Little's detention under the main section of the 1800 Act because the offence charged was only a misdemeanour. He got round the difficulty by acting as if Little had been found insane on arraignment (as in one sense he had, although the jury had proceeded to acquit him); and was upheld by his fellow judges when he reserved the case for their consideration.[6] A similar problem seemed likely to arise when John Goode was tried in 1837 for the misdemeanour of uttering seditious words in Queen Victoria's presence (see chapter 11); if he had not been found insane on arraignment the Act of 1800 could not have been applied.[7] It was probably this – and other incidents involving the Queen and lunatics in the first two years of her reign – that led to the inclusion of a section in the Act of 1840 extending the special verdict and its consequences to misdemeanours.[8]

Hadfield himself was eventually committed to Bethlem. According to the anonymous author of *Sketches in Bedlam* (1823) his confinement was by no means uneventful. He escaped once and was recaptured at Dover, an incident which led to his being confined to Newgate Gaol until the opening of the new and more secure wing for criminal lunatics at Bethlem. Even while in Bethlem he killed another patient by knocking him over a bench.

The significance of his case was threefold. From the jurisprudential point of view the statutory special verdict was an attempt at a compromise between two traditional alternatives. It purported to be an acquittal, for it used the words 'not guilty'. On the other hand, it resembled the old special verdict in two ways, by adding the finding that the accused had been insane at the time of his act, and thus enabling the judges to return him to custody. It was an acquittal in name only, for it tacitly admitted that the doctrine of *mens rea* could not safely be applied to the insane. A criminal lunatic might be as morally innocent as a man who had done harm by accident or in self-defence, but the danger of *treating* him as innocent was too great. The solution was to pay lip-service to his innocence but use the law to make sure he remained in custody. Hitherto it had been the civil law that had been used for this purpose; henceforth it was to be the criminal law. As we shall see, however, lawyers have been so strongly influenced by the doctrine of *mens rea* that they have persisted in regarding the special verdict as an acquittal, even to the extent of arguing that the accused could not appeal against it; and even Queen Victoria's intervention did not break the spell.

(It should not be assumed, however, that the result of a successful defence of insanity was invariably a special verdict after the Act of 1800. During the nineteenth and even the twentieth century a jury would occasionally respond to the evidence of insanity with a simple acquittal. Since the judge's charge to the jury is not recorded in any of these cases it is impossible to be sure when the jury were simply being stupid and when they were following his lead. As we shall see in chapter 10, there are circumstances in which abnormal mental states have been held to justify a complete acquittal.)

From the administrative point of view the incident startled the Government into legislation which gave them some control over the subsequent careers of offenders who were found to be insane by the courts. From the judicial point of view, Hadfield – or rather Erskine – established the doctrine that in order to be excused on the grounds of insanity the accused need not be shown to have lacked all understanding, or the ability to distinguish between right and wrong, but could be proved to have suffered from a delusion which prompted his act. Although Erskine thus in effect persuaded Kenyon and his fellow judges to recognise a new criterion of criminal lunacy, this was another development whose importance has been exaggerated. As we shall see, it is very difficult to find any later cases in which Erskine's test clearly saved defendants who would have failed on the other tests. For the M'Naghten Rules of 1843, by insisting that the content of the delusion must be such that if true it would have justified the act in law, restricted its application to vanishing point. At most Erskine persuaded the lawyers to take an interest in the nature of the madman's fantasies.

H

It cannot even be argued that the result of his eloquence was to make courts more sympathetic to the defence of insanity. As has been pointed out, table 2 in the previous chapter shows that the temporary increase in the frequency of such defences had begun before Hadfield's trial. Moreover, it was not long before there were signs of antagonistic reactions in the courts. In the year following, Dr Leo made his third appearance at the Old Bailey, this time in defence of a Jew who had been caught stealing spoons.[9] Mr Justice Grose was clearly suspicious of his *bona fides*:

Court. And perhaps you have known (the accused) sometimes pretend to be mad when they are not?

Leo. I did not know him before these four or five months. . . .

Court. Why did you not insist on his friends confining him?

Leo. I told his wife she should send him to a public place or a private place.

Court. Had he no lucid intervals?

Leo [who evidently knew his law]. Very little or none at all.

Court. Are you particularly versed in this disorder of the human mind?

Leo. I am.

Court. Then you are what is called a mad doctor? [No doubt there was laughter in court at this sally.]

Leo. It is not my particular profession to attend persons under that complaint; I have attended to them; we call it the mania. . . .

Defence counsel's examination was not very effective, and the prosecution took their line from the judge:

Mr Knapp. Upon your oath, were you not present at Bow Street when the prisoner was under examination?

Leo. Upon my oath I was not there. . . .

Mr Knapp. Have you ever given evidence here before?

Leo [almost losing his temper]. I believe that I have. Is that any matter of consequence?

Mr Knapp. Upon your oath, have you or not been examined as a witness here before?

Leo. I never took any notice.

Mr Knapp. Have you not been here twice?

Leo. Yes.

Mr Knapp. Have you not been here more than three times?

Leo. I cannot say.

Mr Knapp. Have you not been here before as a witness and a Jew physician, to give an account of a prisoner as a madman, to get him off upon the ground of insanity?

Leo. I attended here once, but for what defence I have forgot; I do not think I was here more than once.

It was an early example of the mistrust that was to bedevil the relations between the two professions for at least a century and a half.

The accused was convicted and transported for seven years. Within a few years of Hadfield's acquittal, as table 2 demonstrates, the defence of insanity was no commoner at the Old Bailey than it had been twenty years before. Lord Kenyon, who dealt sympathetically with other madmen as well as Hadfield, had died in 1802, and judges such as Lord Mansfield were less enlightened. In 1812, when the paranoid Bellingham shot the Prime Minister, Spencer Perceval, in the lobby of the House of Commons, he was rushed to trial within a matter of days and condemned to death after an extremely adverse charge to the jury from Mansfield. Sensibility was manly in those days, and Mansfield was in tears when he began to speak. Bellingham was perhaps particularly unfortunate, for his victim, unlike Hadfield's, had died, and was more popular than the king. When he spoke in his own defence he made matters worse by implying that his act had been justified by the Government's refusal to pay attention to his complex grievance. Even so, Mansfield's summing-up on the subject of insanity could hardly have been stricter. He told the jury that the only proof of insanity which would excuse Bellingham was 'the most distinct and unquestionable evidence that he was incapable of judging between right and wrong', which must be proved 'beyond all doubt'.[10] Nor was Bellingham the only madman to suffer as a result of this reaction. A farmer called Bowler, who was an epileptic and had been found insane by a civil commission of lunacy, was executed for shooting a neighbour with intent to kill him.[11] 'Very barbarous' was a later judge's comment on his trial.

Notes

1 R. v. Hadfield (1800), 27 State Trials (New Series) at 1281.
2 See R. Hunter and I. Macalpine, *Three Hundred Years of Psychiatry* (London, 1963).
3 In 1863, for example, Forbes Winslow was accompanied by the prison governor when he interviewed Townley (see chapter 13).
4 See page 42.
5. 40 George III, c. 94.
6 R. v. Little (1821) Russ. & Ry. 430.
7 R. v. Goode (1837) 7 Adolphus & Ellis 536.
8 3 & 4 Victoria, c. 54.
9 R. v. Lawrence (1801), O.B.S.P., case 446.
10 Although the source usually cited for Mansfield's charge is a short extract from it which is given in the 1826 edition of Russell's *Treatise on Crimes and Misdemeanours* (London), the full text can be found in the verbatim account of Bellingham's trial in (1812), O.B.S.P., case 433. The two versions are compared in Appendix D
11 R. v. Bowler (1812), O.B.S.P., case 527.

Chapter 5. M'Naghten's Case and the Rules

Between Bellingham's trial in 1812 and M'Naghten's[1] in 1843 important changes took place in the system of law enforcement, trial, and punishment. Fielding's Bow Street Runners, who had fought a guerilla war against London's criminals, were gradually superseded by Peel's Metropolitan Police, an innovation which was copied, spontaneously or under compulsion, by the provinces. As we shall see in later chapters, it was often the policeman who had to cope with the disturbances created by the mentally disordered. In court he became an increasingly frequent and important witness, as can be seen from the Old Bailey proceedings of the eighteen-thirties. Another sort of witness who began to make his appearance at this period was the gaol surgeon. The reforms in Newgate and the provincial gaols which took place under Peel's administration included the appointment of surgeons or physicians, and in the eighteen-thirties Mr Murdo appeared several times to give evidence on the state of mind of prisoners from Newgate. It is true that similar evidence was also given on the same or other occasions by the Governor or one of his turnkeys, as in earlier decades; but the prison doctor was clearly in process of assuming the authority which was later to become a decisive factor in so many trials of the insane. As for the conduct of the defence, the right to be not merely assisted but also represented by counsel, which had hitherto been limited to trials for treason, was extended to felonies and misdemeanours in 1836. But for this, M'Naghten might well have shared the fate of Bellingham, whose crime so closely resembled his.

The consequences of the court's verdict were also changing. In the eighteenth century a convicted person went to the gallows, the colonies, the hulks or – if his crime was one which the court felt able to treat leniently – to the House of Correction, the pillory or the branding iron. If he was acquitted as insane, he might be consigned to a gaol or to the care of relatives. The result was that lawyers and administrators were more familiar with the madman who had been excused punishment than with his counterpart who had not, for the latter had usually been removed beyond their ken. During the first half of the nineteenth century this situation was radically altered. Capital punishment was restricted until in practice it was retained only for murder. The transports and the hulks were replaced by the State Penitentiaries in and around London. Offenders whom the courts had excused from punishment because of their insanity were gradually transferred from the gaols to the asylums, and eventually most of them were concentrated in Broadmoor. Sightseers ceased to be admitted to Bethlem, and the newer asylums were deliberately sited away from the towns in the peace of the countryside. The lunatic was no longer a familiar sight, and this was especially true of the criminal lunatic. In the penitentiaries and local gaols it was the uncertifiable but nevertheless disordered prisoner who now presented a problem. Some of the consequences of this new state of affairs will be discussed in the next volume. One result, however, was that, when every custodial institution was familiar with the phenomenon of the insane convict, the court's choice between punishment and the special verdict no longer seemed so irrevocable or infallible.

It was during this period, too, that the age of reason gave place to the age of statistics. Soon after the first census in 1801 there were attempts to collect national figures on the subject of trials and sentences and the populations of gaols. It was not until 1834, however, that a continuous series of judicial statistics was inaugurated.[2] From that year onward the parliamentary papers include annual judicial statistics showing, for the country as a whole as well as for each county, the fates of persons committed for trial at assizes or quarter sessions, and distinguishing those who were acquitted or found unfit for trial because of their mental condition. Instead of measuring trends by the records of a single court – however important – we can henceforward use national statistics.

It is unfortunate that these do not show the numbers of trials in which the issue of the prisoner's sanity was unsuccessfully raised, since a comparison of these with the numbers of successful instances would be the best possible measure of changes in the strictness with which the courts interpreted criminal responsibility or fitness to plead. To some extent this can be remedied by counting successful and unsuccessful insanity defences in the Old Bailey Sessions Papers, which continued to be published until the spring of 1913. This is an extremely laborious task, however, and could not be carried out for more than a few selected years. At the beginning of the period, as we saw from table 2, the defence succeeded in roughly half the cases in which it was raised: at the end of the period its success rate was about two-thirds. I shall discuss this slight upward trend at the end of the following chapter.

So far as the judicial statistics are concerned, the best that can be done is to show persons found unfit for trial and persons who successfully offered insanity defences as percentages of persons arraigned for trial. Since the distinction between the person who was deemed unfit for trial and the person who was found to have been insane at the time of the act depended partly on the judgment of individual doctors, partly on the extent to which his state of mind had improved or deteriorated between the crime and the trial, and partly on the strictness of the court, the two outcomes are to some extent complementary, so that a clearer picture of the trend is given by showing both as a combined percentage of persons arraigned for trial, and this is done in the final column of table 3. This chapter, however, is concerned with insanity as a defence, and the

TABLE 3. Murderers[a] found unfit to plead or acquitted as insane from 1834 to 1965

Period	A Persons for trial (as annual averages)	B Unfit to plead	C Acquitted as insane	D Found of diminished responsibility
		(as percentages of A)		
1834–43	65·3	2·0%	7·5%	—
1844–53	72·6	4·7%	7·5%	—
1854–63	68·0	5·7%	10·1%	—
1864–73	63·7	5·8%	9·6%	—
1874–83	63·6	8·8%	10·4%	—
1884–93	68·4	11·4%	11·0%	—
1894–1907	62·6	8·2%	22·6%	—
1908–13	70·7	7·8%	26·4%	—
1914–18	52·2	15·1%	26·0%	—
1919–22	74·0	10·5%	20·6%	—
1923–30	54·8	14·2%	28·1%	—
1931–38	56·5	16·2%	31·2%	—
1939–45	No figures published for the period of the War			
1946–56	72·4	21·2%	22·5%	—
1957–64	103·9	11·1%	6·3%	28·5%

[a] Strictly speaking, persons brought to trial on indictment for murder.

B+C+D   *'Landmarks' used as dividing points*

(*as percentages of A*)

9·5%	
	M'Naghten's case
12·2%	
15·8%	
	Capital Punishment Commission
15·4%	
19·2%	
	New form of special verdict
22·4%	
30·8%	
	Court of Criminal Appeal created
34·2%	
41·1%	First World War
31·1%	
	Infanticide Act: True's Case: Atkin Committee appointed
42·3%	
	Commons Committee on Capital Punishment
47·4%	
	Second World War
43·7%	
	Homicide Act
45·9%	
	Capital punishment suspended for murder in 1965

development of the concept of unfitness for trial will be dealt with in chapter 14.

Table 3 needs a few more words of explanation. It divides the period covered – 1834–1964 – not into regular decades or quinquennia, but into periods of varying length, chosen because they begin and end with relevant 'landmarks' such as M'Naghten's trial or the Homicide Act of 1957. (The year in which the landmark occurred is usually treated as the last year of the preceding period, but if, like the Homicide Act of 1957, the landmark occurred early in the year, the year is treated as the first of the new era.) The uneven lengths of the periods do not prevent the statistics from being comparable: 'persons for trial' are shown as annual averages, and all other figures are shown as percentages of these. Offences other than murder are excluded because the probable penalties attached to them varied during the hundred and thirty years covered by the table, with the result that a man accused of, say, 'grievous bodily harm' had a much greater incentive to plead insanity in the early part of the period than in the last decade or so. But murderers had the strongest possible incentive throughout, with one or two minor exceptions (the infanticidal mother or the very young murderer, who have been able to count on a reprieve for the last three-quarters of a century, and the new category of non-capital murderer which was created in 1957). For this reason the table ends with 1964, the year before the death penalty for *all* murders was suspended.

Let us return, however, to the eighteen-thirties, not long before M'Naghten's trial. Insanity defences were by then about three times as frequent as they had been in the seventeen-forties and occurred nearly eight times a year at the Old Bailey. This increased frequency was probably due to nothing more than the greater volume of trials, which had multiplied even faster, so that – as table 2 in the previous chapter demonstrates – there were if anything rather fewer insanity defences for every thousand persons tried. Nor had their chances of success risen since the seventeen-sixties: they were still more or less even. It is possible, of course, that this apparent stability conceals a real change of pattern, and that the decreasing severity of penalties for most offences meant that the accused had less incentive to take advantage of this defence than he had in the eighteenth century. But there is no positive evidence that, apart from sheer numbers, the eighteen-thirties differed in any important way from preceding decades.

From now on, however, we must rely largely on the national statistics for murder, the one crime which carried a real risk of the death penalty throughout the next hundred and thirty years and which is more often than any other crime – except perhaps arson – the crime of the mentally disordered. As table 3 shows, 653 persons were brought to trial for murder during the decade immediately before M'Naghten's crime, and almost one in ten were formally exempted from sentence of death either because they were acquitted as insane (7·5 per cent) or because they were found unfit for trial (2·0 per cent). What emerges most clearly from the table is that for the decade *after* his trial the percentage of special verdicts was the same, and that for several decades thereafter it rose only at a very slow rate. The reason why M'Naghten's case had so little effect upon it may shortly become clear.

By the time of his trial the relationship between insanity and legal responsibility – both in its civil and in its criminal aspects – was beginning to be the subject of books by physicians. Until John Haslam published his *Medical Jurisprudence as it relates to Insanity according to the Law of England* in 1817 virtually all books on this subject had been the work of lawyers. Haslam's little book contained some acute and relevant sociological observations. He pointed out, for example, that even visits to Bedlam (which had been allowed in his time) did not convince the layman that people could be insane without spectacular or bizarre behaviour, since the silent, melancholic, and orderly patient either attracted no interest or was assumed to be convalescent – or even to be unjustly confined!

Haslam, however, was more concerned to explain insanity to lawyers than to attack the existing criminal law, which – in so far as he grasped it – he seems to have regarded as reasonable, if not perfect. In any case his reputation had suffered severely from the inquiry of 1815 into the management of Bethlem, which resulted in his dismissal. Although Haslam is now recognised as an important contributor to the progress of English psychiatry,[3] his arrogant and sweeping statements did not endear him to lawyers. On one occasion he was under cross-examination in an action concerning the annulment of a marriage and was asked whether the wife was of sound mind. He replied 'I never saw any human being who was of sound mind.' When counsel objected that this was no answer to his question, Haslam retorted 'I presume the Deity is of sound mind, and he alone.' Counsel asked him how he had assured himself of the Deity's sanity, to which Haslam made the rather lame reply 'From my own reflections during the last fourteen years, and from repeated conversations with the best divines in the country.'[4] As we shall see from the references to him in the House of Lords, such behaviour did a great deal to discredit his profession.

Five years before M'Naghten's trial, however, an American doctor, Isaac Ray, had published what was to become one of the most influential books of the nineteenth century on the subject: *A Treatise on the Medical Jurisprudence of Insanity* (1838), and in the year before the trial the learned, though not very original, Prichard (who was to become a Commissioner for Lunacy in 1845) had published a similar work.[5] Ray, at that time a general practitioner, was more outspoken than any of his predecessors. Since the practice in most American jurisdictions was still to follow the English common law, he could make all his points by attacking English judges and counsel without the tact that was needed where his own courts were concerned. The burden of his argument was that, taken singly or together, such tests as knowledge of the nature of the act, ability to tell right from wrong, or delusion, were much too narrow a test of criminal responsibility, and that in civil law the criterion was far more generous.

Ray was strongly influenced both by French psychiatrists and by French law. The Code Napoléon of 1810 had included a wide exemption for insane offenders:

Il n'y a ni crime ni délit, lorsque le prévenu etait en état de démence au temps de l'action. . . . (Article 10)

A similar principle had been adopted, said Ray, by New York State, which had enacted that

No act done by a person in a state of insanity can be punished as an offence. . . .

In theory this was generous in the extreme. It called for no investigation into the relationship between the 'state of insanity' and the act: all that had to be shown was that at the time of the act the offender was insane. In practice so simple and sweeping a rule could not have been acceptable to lawyers had not the definition of insanity been so strict. Since only severe degrees of disorder were accepted as 'demence' or 'insanity', it would have been pedantic to argue that the act could have had no connection with the disorder.

Ray did not go quite so far as to recommend this formula. What he suggested was that 'if the mental unsoundness, necessary to exempt from punishment, were required by law *to have embraced the criminal act within its sphere of influence,* as much perhaps would then be accomplished as is practicable within a specific enactment'. It was his personal influence on Judge Doe which led the latter to introduce this principle into the criminal law of New Hampshire – an example which was followed nearly a century later by the District of Columbia.

Although Ray's book was republished in this country within a year of its appearance in America and attracted a good deal of attention, M'Naghten's trial was almost certainly the first occasion on which so foreign a point of view was forced upon the attention of an English court.

Like Arnold, Margaret Nicholson, Frith, Hadfield, Bellingham, and most of the assailants of Queen Victoria whose fates are described in chapter 11, M'Naghten suffered from a form of insanity which concentrated his animosity on a person of eminence. He was the illegitimate son of a Glasgow wood-turner, and became his father's apprentice with expectations of becoming his partner. But when the time for this approached his father, who now had younger legitimate children to provide for, decided to employ him as a mere journeyman. The disappointment may have been partly responsible for the gloomy and unsociable disposition for which Daniel M'Naghten was known from his youth onward. After three years as his father's journeyman he broke away to set up on his own as a wood-turner, and thereafter cut his father dead if they passed in the street. He shared a room and bed with a printer, who later told the court how M'Naghten would get up in the middle of the night to pace round the room and utter incoherent sentences. At the same time he was 'a mild, inoffensive and humane man' who enjoyed watching children at play or feeding birds. He was also hard-working, intelligent, and given, like many another young schizophrenic, to 'the study of difficult and abstruse matters'. His eccentricities soon led to his being asked to leave his lodgings, and he took to living in his own workshop. By this stage – five or six years before his trial – he had begun to believe that he was being persecuted and was complaining of pains in the head. Sometimes his persecutors were the police, a comparatively new institution which must have figured in many a delusion of that time. Sometimes they were members of an older organisation, the Church of Rome, which is still a popular scapegoat for paranoid Glaswegians. Whoever they were, they dogged his footsteps when he was alone, laughing at him and throwing straws in his face, but craftily disappeared when he was in company. He applied for protection to his father, to the Sheriff-Substitute, to the Lord Provost; but nothing was done. In despair he gave up his thriving little business and fled to France. But like so many sufferers from paranoia he carried his Furies with him and found them waiting for him at Boulogne. He returned to Glasgow, but now his delusions took a political turn, and he was being victimised by the Tories for voting against them at an election, a belief which was not quite so ridiculous then as in these modern days of secret balloting. He complained again to the Sheriff-Substitute, who warned M'Naghten's father that his son was insane: unfortunately nothing was done to restrain him.

For more than a year before his crime he had been escaping occasionally to London, the refuge of many a sufferer from imaginary persecution, and in the summer of 1842 he entered into a rational and businesslike correspondence with a Londoner who had advertised a partnership (it is tempting to see in much of his behaviour the reflection of his grievance against his father). About this time he bought a pair of pistols. He spent the rest of the year in London, and his animosity had by now begun to centre on the Prime Minister, Sir Robert Peel, who was not only a Tory but also the creator of the metropolitan police force. Early in January 1843 he was observed by police to be hanging about Whitehall near Peel's office, and when asked what he wanted used to walk away.

Since the Prime Minister's private secretary, Drummond, was frequently to be seen leaving and entering the Prime Minister's offices, M'Naghten appears to have mistaken him for Peel himself. On 20th January he followed Drummond up Whitehall to his bank and as he was returning shot him in the back. M'Naghten was pulling another loaded pistol from inside his coat when a constable threw his arms round him; the pistol went off in the struggle but did no further damage. Drummond was able to walk back to the bank and a doctor was summoned, but he died five days later in great pain.

When examined at Bow Street, M'Naghten made a statement which the clerk recorded in these words:

The Tories in my native city have compelled me to do this. They follow and persecute me wherever I go, and have entirely destroyed my peace of mind. They followed me to France, into Scotland and all over England; in fact they follow me wherever I go. . . . They have accused me of crimes of which I am not guilty; in fact they wish to murder me. It can be proved by evidence. That's all I have to say.

Within a fortnight M'Naghten was placed on trial, but his counsel, Cockburn, successfully applied for a postponement to allow evidence of the
accused's state of mind to be procured from Scotland and possibly France,
with the result that the trial did not take place until 3rd March.[6] It was
presided over by Chief Justice Tindal and two other judges, Williams and
Coleridge. It was clear from the start that it was to the bench rather than
the jury that counsel were addressing themselves. Lengthy passages from
earlier cases, from Hale and Hume and Alison, and from psychiatric
treatises, were read aloud by both sides – a precedent which at least one
contemporary judge found intolerable. It was noticeable that the prosecution did not offer any evidence by medical witnesses who had examined
the prisoner, although in fact M'Naghten had undergone a joint examination by two doctors from each side. Since it was clear, however, that
M'Naghten would rely on the defence of insanity, the Solicitor-General
(Sir William Webb-Follett) did his best to undermine it in his opening
speech. Like his predecessor at Ferrers' trial, he conceded that there were
few crimes, above all crimes of this atrocious nature, that were not committed by persons labouring under some 'morbid affection of the mind'
whose motives were difficult to understand. This was especially true of
political assassinations. But such a state of mind did not *excuse* the assassin.
Nor was he excused by a morbid delusion of mind upon some subjects
which could not exist in a wholly sane person – in other words, partial
insanity – if he was able to distinguish right from wrong, and if he acted
in conscious knowledge of the effects of his crime. He cited Hale's *dicta*
on partial insanity with approval, and dismissed Erskine's reasoning in
Hadfield's case as an incomplete and misleading statement of the law
(which it was). If, he stated, the delusion did not lead to an inability to
distinguish right from wrong and to be aware of the consequences of one's
act, it was no defence.

His account of M'Naghten's career stressed the normality and rationality of his behaviour – his successful management of his business and
finances, his studies of natural philosophy and anatomy. Among the
prosecution witnesses were M'Naghten's London landlady, a Glasgow
hairdresser who had been his friend, and the surgeon whose anatomy
classes he had attended. None of them had regarded him as at all unsettled
in his mind, although under cross-examination by defence counsel the
landlady admitted that M'Naghten had seemed sullen and reserved, and
had repeatedly got out of bed moaning in the night.

Like Hadfield, the accused was fortunate enough to have one of the
most able counsels of the time, Alexander Cockburn, QC, who later became Attorney-General in Russell's government and thereafter Lord
Chief Justice. His oratory was more rhetorical than a modern judge or
jury might relish:

I stand in a British court, where Justice, with Mercy for her
handmaid, sits enthroned on the noblest of her altars, dispelling
by the brightness of her presence the clouds which occasionally
gather over human intelligence, and awing into silence by the
holiness of her eternal majesty the angry passions which at times

intrude beyond the threshold of her sanctuary, and force their
way even to the very steps of her throne. . . .

But after some little time on this level he began to get down to business.
The next half-hour was devoted to an historical account of the state of
psychiatric knowledge. He countered the Solicitor-General's appeal to
Hale with criticisms of Hale taken from contemporary psychiatrists,
especially Isaac Ray.

One of Ray's most penetrating observations, of which Cockburn made
skilful use, was that in Hale's day

> . . . insanity was a much less frequent disease than it is now, and
> the popular notions concerning it were derived from the observa-
> tion of those wretched inmates of the madhouses whom chains
> and stripes, cold and filth, had reduced to the stupidity of the
> idiot, or exasperated to the fury of a demon. Those nice shades of
> the disease in which the mind, without being wholly driven from
> its propriety, pertinaciously clings to some absurd delusion, were
> either regarded as something very different from real madness, or
> were too far removed from the common gaze, and too soon con-
> verted by bad management into the more active forms of the
> disease, to enter much into the general idea entertained of mad-
> ness. Could Lord Hale have contemplated the scenes presented by
> the lunatic asylums of our own times, we should undoubtedly have
> received from him a very different doctrine for the regulation of
> the decisions of after generations.

Ray was not the first to make this point: Haslam, for instance, had done
so in 1817. But he was more successful than Haslam in undermining the
still popular notion of insanity as a condition that was either severe and
obvious or completely absent, and in suggesting that this was the result of
observing only cases which were either spectacularly disordered or had
been rendered so by mismanagement.

Cockburn also relied heavily upon Erskine's arguments in defence of
Hadfield, and played upon the disquiet which judges still felt at the
execution of Bowler and Bellingham. But precisely what was the underlying logic of his almost interminable speech? He had to establish not
merely that partial insanity was within the law's interpretation of insanity,
and that M'Naghten was partially insane; but also that his partial insanity
in some way excused him. The latter proposition would have been less
difficult to establish if it had been possible to argue that the accused had
been so affected as to be unaware of what he was doing, or its consequences; but this was ruled out by the evidence. Another line of argument
would have been that he had been so affected as to be unable to distinguish
between right and wrong in general; but this too Cockburn never attempted to assert, probably because he felt that the rationality of most of his
client's conduct made it implausible.

If, on the other hand, he had argued that the nature of M'Naghten's
delusion, while not rendering him generally incapable of telling right
from wrong, had made him feel justified in this particular act, he risked
two rejoinders. One was that this was not sufficient to satisfy at least some

judges, who demanded a *general* incapacity to tell right from wrong. Another was that even if his delusion had been the truth, M'Naghten would not have been acting in self-defence, under physical provocation or under duress of the kind which the law of God or man recognised as excusing homicide. The latter argument would of course have been fallacious, since if we assume that his delusion was true, and that it was M'Naghten's moral sense that was at issue, what mattered was not whether his act was justifiable in the eyes of God or man, but whether it was justifiable in M'Naghten's belief; if so, his partial insanity could have been held to prevent him from knowing whether this particular act was right or wrong. But these points would clearly have been risky ones to argue even before so sophisticated a bench, and Cockburn wisely did not do so.

What Cockburn did argue was that the prisoner's insanity 'takes away from him all power of self-control'. Like Erskine, therefore, he had to persuade the judges to accept a test of insanity that was not really recognised by the criminal law without allowing them to realise what they were doing. And, like Erskine, he managed it. At the end of his speech, when everyone's attention must have been flagging more than a little, he came as near as he dared to a summary of his argument:

> I trust that I have satisfied you by these authorities that the
> disease of partial insanity can exist – that it can lead to a partial or
> total aberration of the moral senses and affections, which may
> render the wretched patient incapable of resisting the delusion,
> and lead him to commit crimes for which morally he cannot be
> held responsible. . . .

The reference to 'aberration of the moral senses and affections' was an attempt to smuggle the new notion past their lordships under the disguise of inability to tell right from wrong.

The witnesses whom Cockburn called gave a very different picture of the accused from that painted by the Solicitor-General. M'Naghten's father, his friends, a sheriff depute and even the Lord Provost of Glasgow testified to his eccentric conduct and his delusions of persecution. Finally four doctors gave evidence. Two of them – E. T. Monro of Bethlem and Sir Alexander Morison – had taken part with the Crown's doctors (who were not called) in a combined interview with the prisoner, and both emphasised that he must have been 'deprived of all self-control' or 'restraint over his actions'.

It was the evidence of the last two medical witnesses, however, which was later to be the subject of criticism, for neither of them had interviewed the accused at any time. They had merely sat in court throughout the trial, listened to the evidence, and no doubt observed M'Naghten's demeanour. Neither of them was particularly distinguished for his expertise in the subject, but one of them was Forbes Winslow.

Winslow was a doctor who had paid for his own medical training by journalism and the writing of students' manuals. He had published a book a few years before[7] in which he argued that most suicides were insane. But his most timely publication was *The Plea of Insanity in Criminal Cases*,[8] which appeared between M'Naghten's crime and the trial, and was opportunely dedicated to the Attorney-General. It was little more than a collection of cases from legal reports and the writings of earlier psychiatrists such as Ray (whose case-histories were already secondhand). Through works such as these Winslow soon acquired a reputation as an authority on insanity, and a few years after M'Naghten's trial he founded a journal and two private asylums. In later life he was frequently called as a medical witness for the defence, and, as we shall see in the next chapter, allied himself with Ray's attack on the test of insanity in the criminal law.

Although he had never met M'Naghten and knew nothing more about him than had been brought out in evidence, he was allowed to testify that he had 'not the slightest hesitation in saying that [M'Naghten] is insane, and that he committed the offence in question whilst afflicted with a delusion, under which he appears to have been labouring for a considerable length of time'. His colleague Dr Philips, a surgeon and lecturer at the Westminster Hospital, supported him. It was undoubtedly this part of the trial which Lord Brougham had in mind when he later referred in the House of Lords to evidence which should not have been heard. No doubt the judges were leaning over backwards to be indulgent to the defence, and there are modern parallels, of which the most notable has been the defence's calling of Dr Stafford-Clark – also a psychiatrist well known to the public – in the Podola case (see chapter 14). But whereas Stafford-Clark was called on to rebut some generalisations about amnesia which the prosecution had elicited from another medical witness (Dr Denis Leigh), Winslow added nothing to the evidence of those experienced alienists who had interviewed M'Naghten before the trial.

Lord Chief Justice Tindal summed up very briefly. The question for the jury was whether at the time of the act the accused had been 'sensible that it was a violation of the law of God or of man'. If they thought that he had been 'capable of distinguishing between right and wrong, then he was a responsible agent and liable to all the penalties the law imposes. . . .' He offered to recapitulate the medical evidence, but pointed out that it had all been on one side. The jury indicated that they required no more and without hesitation brought in a special verdict. M'Naghten was removed to Bethlem Hospital and later became one of the first male patients at Broadmoor, where he died of tuberculosis.

The verdict came as a shock to the public. *The Times*, though full of admiration for British justice and the British jury, was sarcastically sceptical:

. . . still we would, not captiously nor querulously, but in a spirit
of humble and honest earnestness, of hesitating and admiring
uncertainty, and of almost painful dubitation, ask those learned
and philosophic gentlemen to define, for the edification of common-
place people like ourselves, where sanity ends and madness begins,
and what are the outward and palpable signs of the one or the
other. . . .[9]

The Government was pressed in both Houses of Parliament to rectify the law. One Member of Parliament, a Mr Blake, even sought leave to bring in a bill to abolish the plea of insanity in cases of murder or attempted murder, except where it could be proved that the accused was publicly known as a maniac and not afflicted by partial insanity, but he found no supporter.

Not least concerned was the House of Lords, always alarmed at any sign of weakness in the enforcement of the criminal law. At the instance of several peers the Lord Chancellor, Lord Lyndhurst, initiated a debate on 13th March.[10] His speech was a reassuring one:

> . . . there is no doubt with respect to the law – that it is clear,
> distinct, defined; and I think the result upon your Lordships'
> minds will be that . . . it will be quite impossible beneficially to
> alter the law, or to render it better adjusted than it is. . . .

He argued that there had been no departure from the principle established at Hadfield's trial,

> namely that if the party at the time that he committed the act was
> in such a state of mind – in such a state of sanity as to know that
> he was doing a wrong thing – in that case, but not otherwise, he
> was amenable to the law.

He claimed that the law of other countries corresponded precisely with England's, and – a superbly confident aside – 'must of necessity correspond'.

(In support of this astonishing statement he cautiously cited only the Scots jurists Hume and Alison. But the desire to find similarity at all costs has led others into even more specific inaccuracies. Marc Ancel, the French judge, remarks that

> . . . les M'Naghten Rules anglaises . . . malgré leur technicité origi-
> nale . . . peuvent être pratiquement rapprochées de la règle
> énoncée par l'article 64 du Code Pénal Français de 1810. . . .[11]

This has been paraphrased by an historian of English criminal law into the statement that the two are 'virtually identical' and used as an example of the parallelism between English and continental codes. The only similarity is that, like all well-developed criminal codes, both recognise some degree of mental disorder as a complete excuse. They are no more similar than the provisions in both codes for excusing children.)

The Lord Chancellor went on to ask whether their Lordships wanted to legislate so as to punish men who, under the effect of delusion, did not know that they were doing wrong. He suggested that if they were in doubt as to the law they could summon the judges before them to give their opinion (a step for which there were a few precedents). At the same time he promised to lay before the House a bill which, without altering the law on this subject, would make it possible to strengthen precautions against such incidents, although it would never be possible to prevent occasional repetitions. (This was presumably an opportunistic reference to the legislation of 1845 for the regulation of the whole system of asylums and the committal of lunatics, which must then have been at the drafting stage.)[12]

Lord Brougham was as eloquent and provocative as usual: his circumstantial and slightly inaccurate description of M'Naghten's crime drew more than one cry of 'No' from their Lordships. With mock charitableness he supposed that the reports of the trial must be incorrect, since if they were not 'certain evidence was given which ought not to be given, [and] questions were put which the law did not allow to be put. . . .' (the allusion was to the evidence of Drs Winslow and Philips). Nevertheless he agreed with the Lord Chancellor that the law required no change, nor were the judges at fault; and, having taken half an hour to say so, he resumed his seat.

Lords Cottenham and Campbell, who had both been law officers of the Crown, welcomed the suggestion that the judges should be invited to explain themselves, and made it plain that what had caused them anxiety was the 'latitude of definition which medical men were apt to attribute to the notion of insanity'. Lord Cottenham recalled a doctor who had said under cross-examination that very few people had a mind which was altogether sound. Lord Campbell quoted the renowned Haslam to the effect that 'we were all insane', whereupon Brougham interjected 'I have heard him say it.' In contrast to earlier speakers, Campbell thought there was enough discrepancy between the authorities on the accountability of the partially insane and deluded criminal to justify a demand for the clarification of the law.

Three months later, after at least one reminder from their Lordships, the judges appeared in the upper chamber with their answers.[13] The questions which had been put to them were these:

1st. What is the law respecting alleged crimes committed by persons afflicted with insane delusion, in respect of one or more particular subjects or persons: as, for instance, where at the time of the commission of the alleged crime, the accused knew he was acting contrary to law, but did the act complained of with a view, under the influence of insane delusion, of redressing or revenging some supposed grievance or injury, or of producing some supposed public benefit?

2nd. What are the proper questions to be submitted to the jury, when a person alleged to be afflicted with insane delusion respecting one or more particular subjects or persons, is charged with the commission of a crime (murder, for example), and insanity is set up as a defence?

3rd. In what terms ought the question to be left to the jury, as to the prisoner's state of mind at the time when the act was committed?

4th. If a person under an insane delusion as to existing facts, commits an offence in consequence thereof, is he thereby excused?

5th. Can a medical man conversant with the disease of insanity, who never saw the prisoner previously to the trial, but who was present during the whole trial and the examination of all the witnesses, be asked his opinion as to the state of the prisoner's mind at the time of the commission of the alleged crime, or his opinion whether the prisoner was conscious at the time of doing the act, that he was acting contrary to law, or whether he was labouring under any and what delusion at the time?

I

Mr Justice Maule, whose attitude to these questions differed from that of his fellow judges, was allowed to speak first, and then, by common consent, ignored. He deserved more attention than he got, for at least two of his points were worth making. In the first place, he objected to being asked general questions which did not, on the face of it, refer to a particular case. Here he put his finger on what, from a lawyer's point of view, was the unreality of the entire occasion. What was worrying the House was the acquittal of a particular individual; but if discussion were allowed to concentrate on his case it would inevitably cast doubt upon the verdict. Moreover, since the verdict had clearly been in accordance with the Lord Chief Justice's own summing-up, any such doubt would reflect on the competence of the judiciary. The Government had no wish to be put in the position of defending either the verdict in question or the judges' interpretation of the law. The result was a series of questions which, though general in form, were clearly drafted with M'Naghten's case in mind, and it was this aspect of them which Maule found understandably awkward. At a later point in his speech he countered neatly by referring to M'Naghten's case as if it had simply occurred to him as a convenient illustration of what he had in mind.

He would have liked, too, to hear argument about the questions before answering them – a typically judicial point of view. Thirdly, he feared that the judges' answers 'may embarrass the administration of justice when they are cited in criminal trials'. Whatever one may think of his first two objections, there can be no doubt that his third showed foresight.

With these and other reservations, his answer to the first question was that the accused would be responsible for his act. To the second, that the questions for the jury were questions of fact and of law, and as to the latter the judge should define the necessary degree of insanity on the lines of Maule's answer to the first question (a curious reply, since even Maule cannot have regarded his answer to the first question as dealing comprehensively with the responsibility of the insane). As for the third question, there were no terms which the judge was required by law to use (he was right, but there soon would be). The fourth question was answered by his reply to the first. As to the fifth, his reply, though long-winded and pedantic, amounted to 'Yes'. Lord Chief Justice Tindal then gave the views of the rest of the judges:

My Lords, Her Majesty's Judges (with the exception of Mr Justice Maule, who has stated his opinion to your Lordships), in answering the questions proposed to them by your Lordships' House, think it right, in the first place, to state that they have forborne entering into any particular discussion upon these questions, from the extreme and almost insuperable difficulty of applying those answers to cases in which the facts are not brought judicially before them. The facts of each particular case must of necessity present themselves with endless variety, and with every shade of difference in each case; and as it is their duty to declare the law upon each particular case, on facts proved before them, and after hearing argument of counsel thereon, they deem it at once impracticable, and at the same time dangerous to the administration of justice, if it were practicable, to attempt to make minute applications of the principles involved in the answers given by them to your Lordships' questions.

They have therefore confined their answers to the statement of that which they hold to be the law upon the abstract questions by your Lordships; and as they deem it unnecessary, in this peculiar case, to deliver their opinions *seriatim*, and as all concur in the same opinion, they desire me to express such their unanimous opinion to your Lordships.

He then proceeded to deal with the first question:

In answer to which question, assuming that your Lordships' inquiries are confined to those persons who labour under such partial delusions only, and are not in other respects insane, we are of opinion that, notwithstanding the party accused did the act complained of with a view, under the influence of insane delusion, of redressing or revenging some supposed grievance or injury, or of producing some public benefit, he is nevertheless punishable according to the nature of the crime committed, if he knew at the time of committing such crime that he was acting contrary to law; by which expression we understand your Lordships to mean the law of the land.

Since the fourth question also dealt with delusions, the answer to it should be read with this answer:

. . . the answer must of course depend on the nature of the delusion: but, making the same assumption as we did before, namely, that he labours under such partial delusion only, and is not in other respects insane, we think he must be considered in the same situation as to responsibility as if the facts with respect to which the delusion exists were real. For example, if under the influence of his delusion he supposes another man to be in the act of attempting to take away his life, and he kills that man, as he supposes, in self-defence, he would be exempt from punishment. If his delusion was that the deceased had inflicted a serious injury to his character and fortune, and he killed him in revenge for such supposed injury, he would be liable to punishment.

From the legal point of view the answers are unexceptionable. If the insanity of the accused is limited to a delusion, then only a delusion which, if true, would have justified his act in law will excuse him from the penalty. It is true that the answer is not quite consistent with Tindal's exposition of the right-wrong test, for it does not excuse the man whose delusion leads him to consider his act morally though not legally justified. But the objection of later generations of psychiatrists to this part of the Rules has not been this but the underlying assumption that a man could be deluded in this highly restricted way without suffering from any other distortion or impairment of his awareness of reality or his ability to control himself. The Rules established in the minds of several generations of judges the notion that a deluded man could be assumed to be in all other respects normal unless there were evidence to the contrary. It is not of course inconceivable that he should be otherwise normal: but it is unlikely, and especially unlikely if he has committed some act of savage violence. The second and third questions were answered together:

> We have to submit our opinion to be, that the jurors ought to be told in all cases that every man is to be presumed to be sane, and to possess a sufficient degree of reason to be responsible for his crimes, until the contrary be proved to their satisfaction; and that to establish a defence on the ground of insanity, it must be clearly proved that, at the time of the committing of the act, the party accused was labouring under such a defect of reason, from disease of the mind, as not to know the nature and quality of the act he was doing; or, if he did know it, that he did not know he was doing what was wrong. The mode of putting the latter part of the question to the jury on these occasions has generally been, whether the accused at the time of doing the act knew the difference between right and wrong: which mode, though rarely, if ever, leading to any mistake with the jury, is not, as we conceive, so accurate when put generally and in the abstract, as when put with reference to the party's knowledge of right and wrong in respect to the very act with which he is charged. If the question were to be put as to the knowledge of the accused solely and exclusively with reference to the law of the land, it might tend to confound the jury, by inducing them to believe that an actual knowledge of the law of the land was essential in order to lead to a conviction; whereas the law is administered upon the principle that everyone must be taken conclusively to know it, without proof that he does know it. If the accused was conscious that the act was one which he ought not to do, and if that act was at the same time contrary to the law of the land, he is punishable; and the usual course therefore has been to leave the question to the jury, whether the party accused had a sufficient degree of reason to know that he was doing an act that was wrong: and this course we think is correct, accompanied with such observations and explanations as the circumstances of each particular case may require.

It was this answer which came to be regarded as the heart of the Rules, cited by judges and textbooks long after the answers dealing with delusion and medical evidence had ceased to be considered authoritative. It provided judges with clear guidance as to what juries should be told, not merely as regards the burden of proof but also as regards the kind and degree of insanity that was sufficient to excuse the accused. The 'test' of 'criminal insanity', as it came to be called, was a combination of Bracton's so-called 'wild beast test' and Spigurnel's 'right-wrong test'. To satisfy it, the accused must either have been deprived of awareness of what he was doing or have been deprived of awareness that what he was doing was wrong; and it must have been a defect of reason, arising from disease of the mind, and not mere ignorance, mistake, or perversity of opinion, which deprived him of this awareness.

The phrase 'nature and quality of the act' must have seemed to Tindal and his colleagues too clear to need explanation; and indeed it was only after a considerable number of years, when desperate attempts were being made to stretch the meaning of the Rules, that any question was raised as to its meaning (see, for example, the account of Codère's case in the next chapter). But the right-wrong test seemed to call for elucidation. We have seen how Tracy asked the jury whether Arnold 'could distinguish between good and evil', and not whether he knew that it was evil to kill Lord Onslow, although quite conceivably this might have been the only point at which his moral attitude differed from normal. Evidently some judges were still putting the question to the jury in this form, which was far less favourable to the accused than the question 'Did he know that this act was wrong?' – the form in which it had been put to M'Naghten's jury. Tindal's answer was tactfully drafted so as to discourage without totally discrediting the more general version.

Equally important, though less successful, was the effort to deal with the ambiguity of the word 'wrong'. In the early decades of the nineteenth century judges do not seem to have distinguished between moral wrongness and illegality. It is true that Hadfield himself undoubtedly made this distinction, for he relied on the illegality of his act to ensure that he was put to death in accordance with God's wishes: but his counsel made little of this. In Bellingham's case[14] Mansfield refers to 'the laws of God and nature' and 'the law of God and the law of the country', but does so in such a way that it is obvious that for him they meant the same thing. After all, he was talking of murder, and would have found it difficult to conceive of a code of conduct which did not condemn this. His resounding phrase 'the laws of God and nature' was copied by his successors – for example in Offord's case in 1831[14]; and even after M'Naghten's case judges sometimes spoke in the same breath of 'the laws of God and man', as if man were as certain to be in agreement with God as Nature had been. Tindal's explanation seems unequivocal, however, notwithstanding the curious conclusions which later Lord Chief Justices were to draw from it. He was making two points:

a. that only if the act was 'contrary to the law of the land' did any question of punishment arise;

b. but the question was whether 'the accused was conscious that the act was one which he *ought not to do*'.

Since Tindal was careful to distinguish between what was illegal and what one ought not to do, it seems beyond doubt that his 'ought' had a moral and not a legal meaning. His explanation makes complete sense. If the act was not criminal, it did not matter what the accused thought: he was not punishable. If the act was criminal, and the accused knew it to be morally wrong, he was punishable. If the act was criminal but he believed it morally justifiable, he was not punishable. Whether he knew the law was not the question: as Tindal said, 'everyone must be taken conclusively to know it', and he made no exception for madmen. We shall see in the next chapter what his successors made of his efforts.

The last question, which in effect asked whether Winslow's evidence should have been allowed, was an awkward one:

In answer thereto, we state to your Lordships, that we think the medical man, under the circumstances supposed, cannot in strictness be asked his opinion in the terms above stated, because each of those questions involves the determination of the truth of the facts deposed to, which it is for the jury to decide, and the questions are not mere questions upon a matter of science, in which case such evidence is admissible. But where the facts are admitted or not disputed, and the question becomes substantially one of science only, it may be convenient to allow the question to be put in that general form, though the same cannot be insisted on as a matter of right.

In other words, a judge who wanted to give the defence every possible chance – as Tindal had done – could allow this. But at least one of his colleagues, Baron Alderson, felt strongly that there should be more control over medical evidence, and in a later case[15] refused to hear a medical witness in Winslow's position. In another case[16] he even refused to allow defence counsel to read – as Erskine and Cockburn had done – from a medical work, and when counsel protested that this had been allowed in M'Naghten's case he got the sharp reply:

And that shews still more strongly the necessity for a stringent adherence to the rules laid down for our observance. But for the non-interposition of the judge in that case you would not have thought it necessary to make this struggle now.

Having extracted the answers to these questions from the judges, their Lordships did not proceed to discuss their merits, but contented themselves with reasserting their right to put such questions to the judiciary. Nobody was tactless enough to point out that if the judges' answers represented the law M'Naghten should have been convicted. The debate ended on that note of self-congratulation for a good day's work which is so often heard in the upper chamber.

Notes

1 M'Naghten's name has been spelt in almost as many ways as Shakespeare's: Macnaughton, Macnaughten, Macnaghten, M'Naughton, M'Naughten, M'Naghten (see the article by B. L. Diamond in (1964), 25, *Ohio State Law Journal*, 1). The only signature of his that has been found could be McNa(u)ghten, McNa(u)ghtan, or McNa(u)ghton with or without the 'u'. Some authors spell it differently in different passages (see, for example, the report of the Select Committee on Capital Punishment of 1930). I have adopted the spelling used by the Gowers Commission, which is now fashionable and has the distinction of being the only one that cannot be reconciled with the man's own signature.

2 See *Judicial Statistics* in the bibliography.

3 See the chapter devoted to him in D. Leigh's *Historical Development of British Psychiatry*, I (Oxford, 1961).

4 This is one of the many anecdotes in Forbes Winslow's *Lettsomian Lectures on Insanity* (London, 1854).

5 *On the Different Forms of Insanity in relation to Jurisprudence* (London, 1842).

6 For the fullest account of the trial see 'State Trials, New Series', ed. J. Macdonell, 1820, etc. (Eyre and Spottiswode, London). This does not appear, however, to be a complete transcript, and one or two pieces of evidence not reported there can be found in the account in the Annual Register for that year.

7 L. F. Winslow, *The Anatomy of Suicide* (London, 1840).

8 L. F. Winslow, *The Plea of Insanity in Criminal Cases* (London, 1843).

9 A leader in the issue of 6 March 1843.

10 Hansard, Third Series, LXVII, 714.

11 M. Ancel, in his introduction to *Codes Pénaux Européens* (Centre Français de Droit Comparé, Paris).

12 8 & 9 Vict., c. 100.

13 For the complete text see 10 Cl. & Fin. 200. I have omitted those parts of the answers which merely rehearse the original questions, but virtually nothing else is left out.

14 R. v. Bellingham (1812), O.B.S.P., case 433, at p. 272, and R. v. Offord (1831), 5 Car. & P. 168, where Mansfield was cited. Professor Glanville Williams interprets these cases as indicating that early in the nineteenth century judges had 'gone on moral wrong'; but it seems more likely that they simply failed to make the distinction. See the full text of what Mansfield had to say on this subject, in Appendix D.

15 R. v. Frances (1849), 4 Cox 57.

16 R. v. Crouch (1844), 1 Cox 94.

Chapter 6. **The Rules in Action**

It was some little time before the importance of the judges' answers, and their defects, began to be appreciated. English doctors were neither swift nor strong in following the lead of Isaac Ray. In the year before M'Naghten's case a short book entitled *The Different Forms of Insanity in relation to Jurisprudence* had been published by Prichard, the Bristol asylum superintendent who achieved fame not only as the populariser of 'moral insanity' (see volume II) but also as an Egyptologist and anthropologist. But Prichard, like Haslam, was more concerned to instruct than challenge the judges: he was after all what Ray was not, a member of the establishment. His book was much less original and provocative than Ray's, and he did little more than confuse the issue with his talk of moral insanity.

In any case, Prichard died a few years after M'Naghten's case and not long after his appointment as one of the first Commissioners in Lunacy under the legislation of 1845, so that it was left to the more superficial Winslow to carry the torch lit by Ray. By 1854 Winslow was a fully accepted authority on the subject, and he devoted one of his Lettsomian Lectures[1] to the difficulties posed for medical witnesses both by the legal tests of insanity and by counsel's sophistical methods of cross-examination. Although he illustrated and criticised tests such as the right-wrong test, he did not, for some unaccountable reason, mention either M'Naghten's case or the judges' answers to the Lords' questions. He objected strongly to the way in which medical witnesses were questioned by counsel when insanity was an issue and had some good tactical advice for alienists who found themselves in the witness box. But it is not easy to make out from his verbose and anecdotal lectures exactly what he supposed the law to be or how he would have liked to reform it.

Almost inevitably therefore both Winslow's and Ray's points of view came to be confused with the contemporary tendency to widen the definition of insanity by recognising and including new subdivisions of it, such as 'moral insanity' and 'instinctive insanity', examples which were given some prominence in Prichard's books. Ray's main point was that, *whatever was included in insanity*, the exemption of the insane from punishment should not turn on intellectual tests of the kind applied by English judges, but simply on the question whether 'the mental unsoundness . . . embraced the act within the sphere of its influence'; in other words, whether he did it because of his insanity or whether his act was unconnected with his insanity. For the understanding of his point it was unfortunate that he and his contemporaries were also trying to popularise a wider conception of insanity.

The concept of moral insanity and its connection with 'psychopathy' will be dealt with in volume II. Equally important, however, was the notion of 'instinctive' or 'impulsive insanity', which, like moral insanity, had been described by Pinel and imported by Prichard. The latter described it thus:

> In this disorder the will is occasionally under the influence of an impulse, which suddenly drives the person affected to the perpetration of acts of the most revolting kind, to the commission of which he has no motive. The impulse is accompanied by consciousness; but it is in some instances irresistible; some individuals who have felt the approach of this disorder have been known to take precautions against themselves; they have warned, for example, their neighbours and relatives to escape from their reach till the paroxysm should have subsided.

He goes on to explain that while it can take serious forms such as homicidal mania and pyromania, it can also be responsible for behaviour such as kleptomania.

Prichard himself did not think that someone who had struggled with an insane impulse and lost should be excused punishment, and it was hardly surprising that lawyers should have been even more firmly of this view. The young Fitzjames Stephen (1829–94) – at that time a briefless barrister living more by journalism than by legal practice – was highly critical of the notion of 'irresistible impulse' in a paper to the Juridical Society in 1855:

> There may have been many instances of irresistible impulse of this kind, although I fear there is a disposition to confound them with unresisted impulses. . . .[2]

He was prepared to recognise that there might be cases in which the impulse had been irresistible, but pointed out that it should not be assumed either that all insane impulses were of this kind or that irresistible impulses were confined to the insane. 'If a prisoner is to be acquitted it must be because the impulse is irresistible, because the act is not wilful – if he is to be called insane it must be because the impulse is unaccountable. . . . The guilt turns upon the wilfulness of the act and not upon the insanity of the prisoner.'

While it is difficult to find a clear statement of the medical objections to the M'Naghten Rules at this date, the main criticism was probably that they made no allowance for this phenomenon of irresistible impulse. A resolution which Dr Harrington Tuke persuaded the recently established Association of Medical Officers of Asylums for the Insane to adopt at the time of the appointment of the Capital Punishment Commission in 1864[3] condemned the right-wrong test on the grounds that 'the power of distinguishing between right and wrong exists frequently among those who are undoubtedly insane, and is often associated with dangerous and *uncontrollable* delusions' (my italics). What they seem to have meant was that some insane persons should be excused because their delusions led to uncontrollable impulses.

In his own evidence to the Capital Punishment Commission Dr Tuke argued that no insane man should be held responsible to the extent of being punished capitally, although he saw no harm – and indeed considerable corrective value – in applying less irrevocable punishments, such as penal servitude, to them. He also favoured the idea of separating the trial of the prisoner's responsibility from the trial of the facts – an expedient with which California and one or two other American States were later to experiment. In the end the Commission refused to make any recommendation on the law regarding insanity, on the ground that this was not confined to capital cases : the same argument was again found convenient in the nineteen-fifties.

It is interesting to watch Fitzjames Stephen, who in his younger days had so stoutly defended the M'Naghten Rules, later undergoing a change of heart, and especially on the subject of irresistible impulse. His *General View of the Criminal Law*, written in 1861 and 1862, was respectful towards the Rules. Nevertheless, without any apparent sense of disloyalty to them, he was prepared to grant, as a somewhat academic point, that if an impulse were irresistible the accused was entitled to be acquitted because 'the act was not voluntary and was not properly his act'. But 'If the impulse was resistible, the fact that it proceeded from disease is no excuse at all'. Infanticide was the sort of case in which he was readiest to admit the probability that the impulse really was irresistible (see chapter 7). His reading on the subject included Ray, Prichard and Winslow.

By the time he embarked on the codification of the English criminal law in the early eighteen-seventies he was firmly convinced that it should exempt an offender who had been 'prevented by disease affecting the mind . . . from controlling his own conduct'.[4] His proposals were criticised by such influential judges as Bramwell and Cockburn, who was by then Lord Chief Justice, and in any case the Select Committee was opposed to codification. But Stephen did not let the argument rest there. In his *History of the Criminal Law of England*,[5] written with the authority of someone who was now a Queen's Bench Judge, he argued that the Rules were not a complete statement of the law on the subject, at least at the time when they were formulated, although he was prepared to grant that because they had come to be regarded as a complete statement his point had become rather academic. With this reservation he held that the judges had dealt only with examples of the way in which insanity can lead to ignorance or mistake, and had not dealt (for they had not been asked to deal) with cases in which the emotions and the will are affected. He summed up his view as follows :

If it is not, it ought to be the Law of England that no act is a crime if the person who does it is at the time . . . prevented either by defective mental power or by any disease affecting his mind from controlling his own conduct, unless the absence of the power of control has been produced by his own default.

As we shall see in chapter 9, he proposed a solution rather like the verdict of diminished responsibility which his Scottish contemporary, Lord Deas, had introduced.

But since this solution was not yet open to English juries, Stephen was prepared to make sure that they interpreted the law in his way. In 1881 he presided at the trial in Newcastle-on-Tyne of William Davis, a thirty-eight-year-old labourer who had attempted to murder his sister-in-law because, as he told the police, 'the man in the moon told me to do it. I will have to commit murder, as I must be hanged' – a line of reasoning reminiscent of Hadfield's. Medical witnesses testified that he suffered from *delirium tremens* (although sober at the time), and that he would know what he was doing but would be unable to control his actions and unable to distinguish right from wrong. Stephen's summing-up had all the appearance of orthodoxy, for he told the jury that they must follow 'the great test laid down in McNaughten's case', and must ask themselves whether Davis knew at the time that the act he was committing was wrong. But he then did his best to disguise the distinction between self-control and knowledge of right and wrong:

> As I understand the law, any disease which so disturbs the mind
> that you cannot think calmly and rationally of all the different
> reasons to which we refer in considering the rightness and wrong-
> ness of an action . . . may fairly be said to prevent a man from
> knowing that what he did was wrong. . . . Both the doctors agree
> that the prisoner was unable to control his conduct, and that nothing
> short of actual physical restraint would have deterred him. . . . If
> you think there was distinct disease caused by drinking, but differ-
> ing from drunkenness, and that by reason thereof he did not know
> that the act was wrong, you will find a verdict of not guilty on the
> ground of insanity. . . .[6]

The jury did think so.

Since Stephen's formula was more favourable to the accused than the orthodox interpretation of the law, even the creation of the Court of Criminal Appeal in 1907 did not discourage the occasional judge from following his lead. Thus, for example, at the trial of Fryer, a soldier who had strangled his fiancée, Mr Justice Bray explained the M'Naghten Rules to the Gloucester jury, but continued

> That is the recognised law on the subject; but I am bound to say
> it does not seem to me to completely state the law as it now is, and
> for the purpose of today I am going to direct you in the way indi-
> cated by a very learned judge, Fitzjames Stephen, . . . If it is shown
> that he is in such a state of mental disease or infirmity as to deprive
> him of the capacity to control his actions, I think you ought to
> find him what the law calls him – 'insane'.[7]

They did.

In 1922, however, True's case[8] at last gave the Court of Criminal Appeal its opportunity to state an authoritative view. Ronald True had murdered and robbed a prostitute after boasting beforehand that he was going to commit murder. He used a spectacular and unnecessary amount of violence, and this undoubtedly helped to prejudice both public and jury against him. The defence brought witnesses who testified to his bizarre and violent behaviour at other times and to his addiction to morphia. Evidence as to his insanity was given by two psychiatrists and two prison medical officers, including Norwood East, who later became the established authority on forensic psychiatry, and a member of the Prison Commission. They all agreed that he was insane and abnormally deficient in moral sense. The two psychiatrists agreed that he had acted under an uncontrollable impulse; but Norwood East's view was not so clear. He was subjected to a most confusing examination, in which counsel's questions were constantly interrupted by Mr Justice McCardie, who seemed anxious to air his own knowledge both of psychiatry in general and of particulars of the case which had not been brought out in evidence. In his summing-up McCardie made it quite plain to the jury that in his view True had known the nature and wrongness of his act, but told them that they could bring in a special verdict if they thought that he had been 'deprived of the power of controlling his actions'. As to whether this had been so, however, he seemed sceptical, and after an absence of an hour and a half the jury rejected the defence.

The Court of Criminal Appeal, who upheld the verdict, said more or less openly that the judge had been too generous to True when he told the jury that irresistible impulse would have constituted criminal insanity. The M'Naghten Rule, which mentioned only knowledge of the nature and quality of the act or of its wrongness, was 'sufficient and salutary'.

So far as the courts were concerned, that was that. But True himself was reprieved by the Home Secretary on the grounds of his mental condition, and the result was an outcry of protest, culminating in a short debate in the Commons which is described in chapter 13. (It is a measure of the change in popular feeling about capital punishment in England that this was the last case in which a decision *not* to hang a man was so strongly criticised: later protests were all against hanging.) But the Home Secretary's explanation did not completely satisfy his critics, and the Government resorted to the manœuvre of appointing a committee 'to consider what changes, if any, are desirable in the existing law practice and procedure relating to criminal trials in which the plea of insanity as a defence is raised, and whether any, and if so what, changes should be made in the existing law and practice in respect of cases falling within the provisions of section 2(4) of the Criminal Lunatics Act, 1884' (the section dealing with psychiatric inquiries instituted after sentence by the Home Secretary).[9] In composition the Committee was not only overwhelmingly legal (the only non-legal members were the permanent head of the Home Office and one of his senior subordinates); it was also official to an extent that would nowadays be considered quite improper. It contained the two civil servants mentioned, the Attorney-General, the Solicitor General, Senior Treasury Counsel (who had prosecuted True), and the Director of Public Prosecutions. The nearest thing to an unofficial member was Sir Herbert Stephen, son of Fitzjames Stephen, and he was a Clerk of Assize. The chairman was a lord justice of appeal, Lord Atkin (1867–1944).

Clearly Lord Birkenhead, who as Lord Chancellor was responsible for the appointment of the members, was doing his best to ensure that their report would contain no embarrassing surprises. But it did. Although it contained no medical members, the Committee received memoranda from both the British Medical Association and the Association of Medical Officers of Hospitals for the Insane (which had by then changed its title to the Medico-Psychological Association). The latter made a radical proposal which would have abrogated the M'Naghten Rules and in effect substituted Isaac Ray's formula ('Was the accused insane at the time? If so, has it nevertheless been proved . . . that his crime was unrelated to his mental disorder?') Less radical was the British Medical Association's recommendation, which in effect simply added irresistible impulse to the other tests in the M'Naghten Rules. The Atkin Committee preferred this solution, and recommended that 'it should be recognised that a person charged criminally with an offence is irresponsible for his act when the act is committed under an impulse which the prisoner was by mental disease in substance deprived of any power to resist'. The drafting was clumsy but the meaning was plain.

But legislation on these – or any other – lines in this field did not appeal to the Government, who took no steps to implement the report. Eventually Lord Darling introduced a private member's bill which would have enlarged the Rules by excusing those offenders who, through some mental disease, were 'wholly incapable of resisting the impulse to do the act'. But the Lord Chancellor, now Lord Haldane, opposed the bill. Although in theory the idea was right, he argued, in practice it would mean that juries would be asked to decide an impossible question. Moreover, it would allow the defence of insanity to be offered by large numbers of shoplifters, many of whom were kleptomaniacs. This was an odd argument: did he really think that a shoplifter would offer a defence which might lead to indefinite detention in Broadmoor? But if a shoplifter *were* to choose this defence, and really *were* a kleptomaniac, why should he or she have less right to be excused conviction than a murderer? He contended that it was better to rely on the Home Office to ensure, as they did, that no case of 'uncontrollable impulse' was ever executed, but he did not answer the awkward question whether any cases of uncontrollable impulse were ever allowed to go to prison for non-capital crimes such as attempted murder. In the face of official discouragement, Lord Darling found little support, and his bill was rejected by the Lords.

The Select Committee which was set up by the Commons to discuss capital punishment in 1930 recommended a re-examination of the law on insanity, but made no proposals of its own.[10] It was left to the post-war Royal Commission on Capital Punishment to re-open the subject.[11] Although concerned with many other aspects of the death penalty, it discussed the criminal responsibility of the mentally disordered with more comprehensiveness, precision, and understanding than any other officially appointed body has so far done in this country, and its views will be referred to in several of the subsequent chapters.

It was, however, insanity as a defence, with which they, and the witnesses who gave evidence to them, were chiefly concerned. By this time many people – judges as well as psychiatrists – were prepared to say openly that the Rules were being widely stretched by some (though by no means all) judges, and on occasion were not even mentioned at all. There seemed to be a tendency on the part of judges – and there certainly was on the part of juries – simply to ask themselves whether the accused had been shown to have been insane, and if so to decide in his favour without really giving thought to the tests in the Rules. Nevertheless the Commission felt it necessary that the letter of the law should be brought up to date. Like the Atkin Committee they were faced with two schools of witnesses. The Medico-Psychological Association (which had by now added the title 'Royal' to its new name) was no longer in favour of abrogating the Rules, but was content to rely on the 'increasing elasticity' with which they were interpreted. But the abrogation of the Rules was favoured by other witnesses, including the former Home Secretary, Lord Templewood, and all but four members of the Commission (Mr Fox-Andrews, Miss Florence Hancock, Mr Macdonald and Mr Radzinowicz) adopted this solution. They recognised that so long as mere insanity was not acceptable as coextensive with irresponsibility, juries must decide whether this or that insane person should be held responsible in law. What they doubted was whether any up-to-date formula could be devised to help the jury. True the Rules were being honoured only by lip-service; but it was impossible to define an irresponsible state of mind with any precision, and any attempt to do so would inevitably exclude cases which ought to be included. The jury should be left to decide whether the insanity was such that the accused should not be held responsible, a question no more difficult than many others which they had shown themselves capable of deciding, for example in civil actions involving technical or professional negligence. The last of these sentiments echoes Hale's stout confidence in the English jury:

> Yet the law of England hath afforded the best method of trial that
> is possible of this and all other matters of fact, namely by a jury of
> twelve men all concurring in the same judgement. . . .

The Commission's solution was surgery of the heroic kind; but would it have saved that frail patient, criminal responsibility? Lord Cooper, Lord Justice General for Scotland, had already told them roundly that whatever judges said to juries, the latter simply retired and asked themselves 'Is this man mad or is he not?' If there were any juries which did more, the new formula would soon have put a stop to that. The Commission's argument began with the assumption that insanity and irresponsibility were not to be treated as coextensive; but whatever their solution meant in theory that is the result which it would have had in practice. As we shall see in chapter 7, the Infanticide Acts allowed juries to think in this way in the special cases in which mothers murdered their last-born infants; but that is not what the Commission intended. Moreover, their argument glossed over an awkward gap when it said that any attempt at a formula would exclude cases which ought to be included. By what criterion could one tell whether this or that case 'ought' to have been included? Could the criterion be

expressed in words, or was it ineffable? If in words, were they quite un-
suitable for use in a judge's summing-up? No doubt the Commission
could have answered these questions; what is surprising is that they did
not.

Conscious, however, that their solution did not command universal
assent, they offered as a second choice the proposal which the British
Medical Association had persuaded the Atkin Committee to adopt, and
were still urging: the addition of a new question to the tests of the Rules,
namely 'Was the accused incapable of preventing himself from committing
his act?'[12] This time there was only one dissenter, Mr Fox-Andrews, the
only English counsel on the Commission, who preferred that the Rules
should remain unaltered, but if not, be abrogated. His argument in support
of this somewhat difficult position was that the Rules could not be improved, so that those who were dissatisfied with them should be in favour
of their abolition!

There can hardly have been another Commission whose report was
composed so well but to so little purpose. Every one of their major recommendations was rejected by the Conservative Government of 1953, which
– in so far as it could be said to have had a united view on so controversial
a subject as capital punishment – seems to have been trying to preserve
the *status quo ante*. One of the reasons which was given for rejecting the
Commission's proposals on the law of insanity was that they extended
beyond the law on murder. This time-worn argument, which had been
used by the Commissioners of 1864 to justify their refusal to deal with the
same subject, could hardly have been more superficial. The Gowers
Commission had been asked in 1949 to consider 'whether liability under
the criminal law in Great Britain to suffer capital punishment for murder
should be modified, and if so to what extent and by what means. . . .' The
most frequent defence to a charge of murder was insanity; it was seldom
offered to a non-capital charge; and it had never been suggested to them
that they should exclude it from their report. The Government's arguments were clearly opportunistic rather than genuine.

We shall see in later chapters that M'Naghten's ghost faded away not
as the result of any official decision to exorcise it, but simply from neglect,
as the result of the new defence of diminished responsibility. Before I turn
to this part of the story, however, there are other developments to be
described. So far I have concentrated on the main theme: the controversy
over the exhaustiveness or otherwise of the Rules, and their silence on the
subject of irresistible impulses. But there were other issues. The most important was probably the meaning of 'wrong'.

We have seen the form which Spigurnel's right-wrong test took in the
trials of Arnold and Ferrers. Although the M'Naghten Rules were supposed to be a statement of the law as it then was, this is one point on which
Tindal and his colleagues seemed to be embroidering their statement with
a recommendation. In previous trials the question put to the jury had been,
in effect, 'Was the accused able to distinguish righ- from wrong in
general?' – that is, 'could he have given sensible answers to questions
about the rightness and wrongness of different sorts of action?' No doubt

some of Tindal's colleagues had in fact put the question in this way. But collectively they agreed that it should now be phrased in a more practical and more readily answerable form: 'Did he know that what he *was* doing was wrong?' But they hastened to say that the old form of the question 'rarely if ever' led to any mistake with the jury: it was merely not quite so 'accurate' as the form in which they put it.

Did 'knowing that the act was wrong' mean 'recognising that it was generally accepted as morally wrong', or 'believing oneself in its moral wrongness' or 'being aware that it was an infringement of the criminal law'? For a man might recognise that his act would be morally condemned by his fellow men, and yet believe it to be morally right; or he might recognise it to be criminal, and yet either believe that it would not be morally condemned by his fellow men, or believe that they would be mistaken in condemning it.

Before M'Naghten's case, as we have seen, neither judge nor jury distinguished clearly between sinfulness and illegality. But the judges' replies to the Lords' questions show that they certainly did:

> If the accused was conscious that the act was one which he ought
> not to do, and if that act was at the same time contrary to the law
> of the land, he is punishable.

In other words, it was his *knowledge* of its objective moral wrongness, together with the *fact* of its illegality, which made him punishable. Stephen, too, when he defended the Rules in his paper for the Juridical Society in 1855 (loc. cit., p. 75) clearly interpreted them in this way. It was probably Townley's case (described in chapter 13) which made the lawyers think a little more deeply. Townley seems to have realised that to kill his fiancée was against the criminal law, and that it was morally condemned by man (if not God); but he was sure of his right to kill her because he regarded her as his property. His judge, Baron Martin, still assumed like his predecessors that the laws of God and man were fairly similar, but said that 'the mere setting himself up against the law of God and man was not a delusion' – and therefore, since Battie's definition of madness was still influential, it was not an acceptable form of insanity.

It is very difficult to reconcile this with the M'Naghten Rules: indeed, it is not certain that Baron Martin would have been greatly concerned to do so. But Townley's case emphasised the problem posed by the Rules. Was a man to be acquitted if he admitted to knowing that his act was both illegal and morally condemned by his fellow men, yet said that to him it had seemed right? How was one to judge his sincerity? The test would cease to be whether he had 'knowledge' of any objective fact, and would become something quite different. Even 'knowledge' of the moral views of one's fellow men was dangerously close to subjectivity. If objectivity was the aim, the most objective fact was the illegality of the act; and some judges took the view that knowledge of its illegality should be the test.

By the time, therefore, that he came to write his *Digest of the Criminal Law* in 1877 Stephen had to recognise two points of view; and he simply said that 'wrong' meant either morally wrong or illegal. (He did not discuss the rather academic possibility that a man might know his act to be morally wrong yet deludedly believe it to be legal, so that it is not clear whether he would have stuck to his formula through thick and thin.)

The pendulum had begun to swing, and in 1916 it swung further still, when Codère's case came before the Court of Criminal Appeal during the First World War.[13] Georges Codère was a Canadian infantry lieutenant who was known in his regiment as 'Fou Codère', and had been regarded as so abnormal as to be unfit for active command in France. While stationed in England he conceived the idea of murdering a Canadian sergeant, possibly for the latter's money. After trying unsuccessfully to enlist the help of friends (who humoured him but do not seem to have warned the sergeant), he lured his victim to the officers' quarters and battered him to death with great violence, afterwards cutting his throat nearly to the spine. He then asked two of the officers' servants to help him clear up the mess and put the body in a stable. At least one of them, who was both dull-witted and terrified of Codère, obeyed him, and later waited on him at table as he calmly dined with his colonel and major. Codère tried to put the blame for the killing on this servant, but was soon under arrest himself. His defence was insanity, but was rejected by the jury, Mr Justice Darling having told them that 'wrong' meant 'contrary to law'.

His counsel argued before the appellate court that it was not enough that he knew the act to be contrary to law: the jury should have been told that they must acquit him unless they also thought that he knew it to be morally wrong. For some not very clear reason – perhaps as a safety precaution – counsel complicated the issue by resting this argument not merely on the M'Naghten Rules' clear interpretation of 'wrong' which has just been quoted, but also on the phrase 'nature and quality of the act'. He maintained that 'nature' referred to the physical characteristics of the act, but 'quality' referred to its morality. The Court of Criminal Appeal were understandably sceptical about this part of his argument, but less pardonably rejected his interpretation of 'wrong' in the M'Naghten Rules. The Rules said quite plainly that 'if the accused was conscious that the act was one which he ought not to do (i.e. conscious of its moral wrongness) and if that act was at the same time contrary to the law of the land (i.e. as a matter of fact, not of his knowledge) he is punishable'. The clear implication is that if the act was illegal, but he was *not* conscious of its moral wrongness, he was not punishable. Yet although they quoted this very passage the court interpreted it in a perverse sense.

They said that the wrongness of the act could not be judged by the standard of the accused, but only by 'the ordinary standard adopted by reasonable men', and went on to argue that 'once it is clear that the appellant knew that the act was wrong in law, then he was doing an act which he was conscious he ought not to do'. In effect they were maintaining that while the M'Naghten Rules clearly said that the test was knowledge of moral wrongness and not of illegality, in practice knowledge of the former could safely be inferred from proved knowledge of the latter! Yet, as Stephen had emphasised, Hadfield's case had demonstrated that a man

K

could know his act to be illegal yet think it right (as Hadfield must have done, for he was trying to be hanged without breaking God's commandments). They rejected the appeal, but hinted that the Home Secretary ought to reprieve Codère, which he did.

With Windle's case in 1952 the pendulum finally reached its furthest point, and stuck there.[14] Francis Wilfred Windle was 'a man of little resolution and weak character', married to a woman who was eighteen years older and suffering from a mental illness. She talked persistently of suicide, and Windle himself became preoccupied with her state until his workmates were tired of hearing about it. Eventually one of them said 'Give her a dozen aspirins'. Windle gave her a much larger dose than this and killed her, telling the police later that he supposed he would be hanged for what he had done. One doctor at his trial said that he had been suffering from the form of communicated insanity called *folie à deux*, which his wife had no doubt succeeded in imposing on his weak personality. But the judge (Mr Justice, now Lord Devlin) ruled that there was no issue of insanity to be left to the jury. On appeal, counsel put forward more or less the argument that had been attempted in Codère's case (although without the confusing point about the meaning of 'quality'): he argued that the M'Naghten Rules did not apply to a case in which there were no delusions, but that in any case by 'wrong' they meant morally wrong, and that cases such as Hadfield's were precedents for acquitting men who knew they were breaking the law but thought they were acting rightly.

The Lord Chief Justice, Lord Goddard, rejected this view with an argument which was, if anything, even less closely reasoned than his predecessor's in Codère's case:

> Courts of law . . . can only distinguish between that which is in accordance with law and that which is contrary to law. There are many acts which we all know, to use an expression to be found in some of the old cases, are contrary to the law of God and man. In the Decalogue are the commandments 'Thou shalt not kill' and 'Thou shalt not steal'. Such acts are contrary to the law of man and they are contrary to the law of God. In regard to the Seventh Commandment, 'Thou shalt not commit adultery', it will be found that, so far as the criminal law is concerned, though that act is contrary to the law of God, it is not contrary to the law of man. That does not mean that the law encourages adultery: I only say it is not a criminal offence.
>
> The test must be whether an act is contrary to law . . . In the opinion of the court, there is no doubt that the word 'wrong' in the M'Naghten Rules means contrary to law, and does not have some vague meaning which may vary according to the opinion of different persons whether a particular act might not be justified. . . .

Goddard had gone a step further than Lord Reading in Codère's case, and was flatly maintaining that 'wrong' in the M'Naghten Rules meant 'illegal', although it is difficult to see how the crucial passage could be construed thus. Even more curious was the logic with which he tried to show that in any case this is the sensible view. 'Courts of law can only distinguish between that which is in accordance with law and that which is contrary to law.' Granted: but were they being asked to do more? Nobody had suggested that they should decide what was or was not morally wrong. At most they were being asked to accept two propositions. First, that the reasonable man regarded wife-killing as morally wrong. Second, that because of his insanity Windle did not (the fact that they may have doubted both that he was insane and that he believed his action right is irrelevant here). As for the differences between the law of God and the law of man, all that this point did was to dispose of Lord Reading's argument that a person who knew the law of man could be assumed to know what was wrong in the eyes of God.

It is only towards the end of his argument that Goddard hints at what really worried the court. This was the vagueness of the test if 'wrong' meant 'morally wrong'. Certainly there would be occasions – although this was hardly one of them – in which it would not be easy for the court to say whether the reasonable man would have regarded the accused's action as morally wrong or not – for example in the case of a genuine mercy-killing. And although Goddard did not raise it, a curious question *might* be raised in such a case. If 'morally wrong' meant 'regarded by the reasonable man as morally wrong', and if it were likely that the reasonable man would not regard mercy-killing as morally wrong, would this weaken or support the defence of the mercy-killer whose insanity had strengthened his conviction that he was doing right?

However that may be, Windle's case, which is regarded as the last word on the subject, was the final step in the courts' retreat from the test which Spigurnel applied to the young felon in the fourteenth century: whether he knew good from evil. Like most retreats, it was dictated by expediency and carried out in confusion.

Finding cases where a decision has been determined by the precise interpretation of 'the nature and quality of the act' is not easy. In Codère's case, as we have just seen, counsel argued unsuccessfully that 'quality' meant 'morality'; but he did so probably as a safety precaution in case he failed with the argument that 'wrong' meant subjectively wrong. It is significant that discussions of the meaning of 'nature and quality' refer either to cases from other jurisdictions – chiefly Australia and the USA – or to imaginary situations. Stephen instances a man who wounded someone when he thought he was breaking a jar, and another man who strangled someone when he thought he was squeezing an orange; but he does not name the men or give references for their cases.[15] Almost certainly he was using his imagination; and later writers have simply used his illustrations.

According to the M'Naghten Rules the accused's ignorance of the nature, quality, or wrongness of his act should be due to 'a defect of reason, through disease of the mind'. The use of the word 'reason' and the omission of words such as 'will' or 'self-control' is of course consistent with the cognitive nature of the tests themselves, but does not seem to have given rise to any special difficulty.

For the same reason there have been very few actual cases in which the verdict has turned on the precise meaning of 'disease of the mind.' It has been pointed out by J.A.Hobson that although 'insanity' in M'Naghten's day was commonly used, even by doctors, in such a way as to include 'imbecility', the two have since then come to be distinguished, so that a psychiatrist might have to say that an accused was *not* insane *but* an imbecile.[16] Yet even Hobson cites only one case – Straffen's – to support his contention that this has in practice excluded some offenders who would otherwise have satisfied the M'Naghten Rules. Norwood East, who probably gave psychiatric evidence in more criminal trials than any other single doctor in the period between the wars, told the Gowers Commission in 1950 that he had never come across a case in which it had been held that the accused did not come within the Rules because mental deficiency was not a disease of the mind.[17]

The explanation is undoubtedly that if psychiatric witnesses were prepared to testify that the accused's disorder deprived him of the knowledge of what he was doing or of its wrongness, then neither judge nor jury would normally be concerned to draw distinctions between insanity and mental deficiency. Had the tests been less stringent the distinction would have been less academic; but as it was, a person who satisfied one of the tests satisfied the court.

Straffen's case did not occur until two years after Norwood East had given evidence to the Royal Commission. John Straffen was a youth of low intelligence who at the age of 21 had, by his own later admission, strangled at least two very young girls on the outskirts of Bath. When he came to trial he had been found unfit to plead and had been committed to Broadmoor. Six months later he escaped and within a few hours strangled another small girl within a short distance of the hospital. At his second trial[18] his counsel made no attempt to have him found unfit to plead: his defence was that it was not he who killed her but that in any case he was insane within the meaning of the M'Naghten Rules. In support of this second contention counsel pointed out that he had not only been certified as a mental defective at the age of ten but had been found unfit to plead at his first trial the year before. Medical witnesses for the defence also stressed his lack of moral sense and his inadequate appreciation of the wrongness of killing the girls (he claimed to have done it merely to annoy the police). The prosecution's medical witnesses, while agreeing that he was of low intelligence, said that he was neither insane nor completely unaware of the wrongness of killing. Considerable play was made with the fact that he knew 'Thou shalt not kill' to be one of the Commandments and that he knew the penalty for murder.

Mr Justice Cassels' summing-up was clearly unfavourable to Straffen:

. . . ask yourselves whether you are satisfied by the defence that at the time when he did that murder he was insane within the meaning of the criminal law; not that he was feeble-minded; not that he had a lack of moral sense; not that he had no feeling for the victim or her relatives; not that he had no remorse; not that he may be weak in his judgement; not that he fails to appreciate the consequence of his act; but was he insane through a defect of reason caused by disease of the mind, so that either he did not know the nature and quality of his act, or, if he did know it, he did not know it was wrong?

Although he offered the jury a choice between 'not guilty', 'guilty but insane', and 'guilty', it is not surprising that they chose the last of these verdicts. Straffen's appeal, which was not in any case based on this part of his defence, was dismissed, and he would have been hanged if the Home Secretary had not advised a reprieve. He was not sent to a mental hospital but has been kept in various prisons ever since.

It is conceivable that in the few years which remained before the introduction of the defence of diminished responsibility in 1957 there were subsequent cases in which Cassels' policy of distinguishing insanity from mental deficiency was followed. If so, I have not found them. It is even more unlikely that there have been any since 1957.

The distinction between a disease of the mind and a disease of the brain troubled courts for a short period in the middle of the nineteen-fifties. Charlson (whose case is described more fully in chapter 10) had seriously injured his son while in a state of automatism which was attributed by a medical witness to a tumour in his brain. The defence was not insanity but automatism, and he was acquitted. A year later a similar defence was attempted by Kemp, who had caused grievous bodily harm to his wife while in an abnormal state which was the result of hardening of the cerebral arteries. His counsel submitted that his state was not yet a disease of the mind (although at least one of their medical witnesses thought that it might develop into one) and that the proper verdict was therefore a complete acquittal, as in Charlson's case. The prosecution's medical witness thought that the arteriosclerosis had caused 'melancholia', and that this, which was undoubtedly a disease of the mind, had been the cause of Kemp's attack on his wife. Mr Justice Devlin took the view that 'disease of the mind' had not been intended to distinguish between brain and mind, but to make it clear that the 'defect of reason' must not merely be attributable to causes such as a bad upbringing. For safety he added the not altogether consistent argument that arteriosclerosis did seem to affect the mind in a way that could be called a disease. Kemp was therefore less fortunate than Charlson and was found guilty but insane.[19]

Although Devlin had tried to distinguish Kemp's case from Charlson's, the general opinion among judges seems to have been that Charlson had been too fortunate, and that the proper course in his case also would have been to regard his disorder as a disease of the mind and find him guilty but insane. Certainly this is what Lord Denning said when Bratty's case reached the House of Lords (the case is described in chapter 10). Indeed, he went so far as to say that 'any mental disorder which has manifested itself in violence and is prone to recur is a disease of the mind'. This in its turn is open to criticism. The phrase 'mental disorder' makes the dictum sound like a tautology: did he mean to say 'cerebral disorder'? And what about a mental or cerebral disorder which was prone to recur but manifest ted itself not in violence but in theft? Presumably he would have included this had Bratty's crime been theft.

The rule that drunkenness is not insanity, but that prolonged drinking may produce what is a 'disease of the mind', which was firmly established by Hale's time, has remained more or less unaltered since, although one relevant development will be described in the chapter on automatism.

Tindal and his fellow judges had dealt in a particularly logical way with the difficult problem raised by delusion. In order to support a defence of insanity the nature of the delusion must be such that if it had been true the accused would be exempt from punishment. If he thought he was killing him in self-defence he would be excused; if he was revenging himself for an imaginary injury he would not. In practice, however, deluded offenders have been defended on the ground that they did not know the nature and quality of their act, so that this rule is nowadays regarded by authorities such as Professor Glanville Williams as being in desuetude.[20] Glanville Williams has found one case, in 1930, in which a man called Kenneally was charged with wounding a fellow workman with intent to murder him. He had been under the insane delusion that he had received news of his father's death and that the other man had killed him. Even if true this would not have justified his attack, and it was probably for this reason that he was advised by counsel to plead 'guilty'. However that may be, he was sentenced to ten years' penal servitude, and appealed. By that time he had been certified and transferred to an asylum, and the Court of Criminal Appeal reduced his sentence to three years, which probably meant that he would not have to go back to prison when he was discharged. Had he pleaded 'guilty but insane' he would probably have succeeded.[21]

I myself was present at an unusual trial in 1964. A West Indian called Male had been committed for trial at Oxford Assizes for the theft of a piece of cheese and a packet of biscuits from a supermarket. He suffered from the delusion that he was one of the Prophets who had returned to redeem the world, and that he had a right to any food that he needed. His delusion was therefore such that had it been true his taking of the food would not have been larceny, since it would have been done under a *bona fide* claim of right. (In the event, his counsel did not offer a defence of insanity, which could at best have resulted in indefinite detention in a mental hospital. Instead, he took the bolder line that his client was not guilty, since he genuinely believed that he had a right to the food. This defence might well have forced the judge to direct an acquittal; but the latter raised the question of Male's fitness to plead. Another jury was empanelled to try this issue, but decided that Male was fit to plead; at a third trial he pleaded guilty and was made the subject of a hospital order.)

It has always been an essential part of procedure for the accused to bring forward some evidence of insanity if he wished to offer this as a defence. As Tindal and his colleagues put it, 'every man is presumed to be sane until the contrary be proved to [the jury's] satisfaction' and later they used the words 'clearly proved'. Since this in effect seems to saddle the accused with the burden of disproving *mens rea*, it is not easy to reconcile it with the general principle that this is for the prosecution to prove. The difficulty was not recognised in 1843 because the general principle had not been clearly stated; indeed, it was not until 1935 that it was plainly laid down by the House of Lords in Woolmington's case.[22] It was said then, in

passing, that insanity was an exception; but lawyers have had great difficulty in justifying the exception. Glanville Williams does so by arguing
that what rests on the accused is merely an *evidential* burden – that is, the
necessity of producing some evidence pointing to insanity – and that once
this has been done the *persuasive* burden – of arguing that the accused
was not insane within the meaning of the Rules – then lies on the prosecution. But this does not seem to be honoured in practice.

Instead, it was conceded[23] soon after Woolmington's case that while the
burden of proof of insanity rested on the accused, it was not quite so
heavy as the burden which normally rests on the prosecution. Whereas the
latter had to produce evidence which proved *mens rea* (and other matters)
beyond reasonable doubt, the accused's evidence need only point *on a
balance of probabilities* to insanity within the meaning of the Rules.

No evidence need be given by witnesses with psychiatric or indeed
medical qualifications, although nowadays an attempt to set up the defence
without such evidence would have little chance of success. In the eighteenth century, as we have seen, it was exceptional for the accused to be
able to produce a doctor to confirm his insanity: only the well-to-do, or
the London Jew who could call on his society's physician, were in a position to do this. In the eighteen-thirties, although the Newgate surgeon
appeared quite frequently at the Old Bailey to testify to the state of mind of
the accused, his place was sometimes taken by the governor. Even after the
medical profession had been recognised by statute, and asylum doctors
had become acknowledged as specialists, it was not impossible for the
accused to rely on his or her state of mind as a defence without calling a
medical witness. In 1878 Eliza Dart threw her child and then herself into
the Serpentine. Both were rescued and she was indicted for attempted
murder. Although the case is not adequately reported,[24] her defence seems
to have been that her state of mind deprived her of the intention to kill: on
being rescued she had exclaimed 'Save the child, let me die'. The prosecution submitted that if this was her defence she should produce scientific
evidence as to her state of mind, but Mr Justice Brett ruled that it was a
mistake to suppose that this *must* be done: if the facts indicated unsoundness of mind, that was enough. As late as 1910 an Old Bailey jury found
William Backwell (who had shot at a woman friend) guilty but insane on
what appears to have been nothing more than the evidence of himself and
his friends (although it is true that he claimed to be under medical treatment).[25] Although I do not know of any later example, the Privy Council
made it clear in the South Australian case of Brown [26] that this was still
theoretically possible in 1960: 'their Lordships are not of course suggesting that legal insanity cannot be sufficiently proved without medical evidence. The previous and contemporaneous acts of the accused may often
be preferred to medical theory.' Nowadays, however, legal aid and the
National Health Service make it unnecessary as well as unwise for the
defence to dispense with psychiatric testimony.

A much-criticised feature of M'Naghten's trial had been the way in
which the judges had allowed Drs Winslow and Philips, whose only knowledge of M'Naghten had been gained from hearing the evidence of others

and watching his demeanour in court, to testify as to his mental state at the time of his act. Tindal and his colleagues had defended themselves rather half-heartedly on this point in the Rules; they admitted that it was not quite proper, but thought that where the facts were not in dispute the question became 'one of science only', and while it could not be demanded as a right it could be allowed. Six years later, in Frances' case, Baron Alderson and Mr Justice Cresswell (who had been among the judges who composed the Rules) took the line that a physician who had merely been in court throughout the trial could not be asked whether the prisoner was insane: only what were the symptoms of insanity or, assuming particular facts to be true, whether they indicated that the prisoner was insane. To allow more would be to substitute the witness for the jury.[27]

The principle that it is for the jury and not for medical witnesses to decide whether the defence is satisfied has been maintained to the present day, although in Matheson's case[28] (described in chapter 9) the Court of Criminal Appeal conceded that if the medical evidence was 'all one way' a jury's verdict which disregarded it should be set aside. Although Matheson's defence was not insanity but diminished responsibility, no doubt the concession applies to the defence of insanity.

But even if the medical evidence is all one way, it is the duty of the prosecution to probe its soundness, as was made clear in the case of Ahmed Din. He was a Pakistani, aged 46, who lived in Birmingham with his wife and some of his ten children. They had a somewhat younger friend of 29, Ansari, who used to visit them, sharing Din's bed while the wife slept with the children. Din conceived the idea that his wife was unfaithful to him with Ansari and told her to ask Ansari to leave; but she said she could not do so, and denied that the relationship was more than that of 'brother and sister'. Din stabbed Ansari one night in their bed with great ferocity. His defence was diminished responsibility, and two medical witnesses (including a prison medical officer) supported it with a diagnosis of paranoia. They were cross-examined by the prosecution, but only in order to see whether the accused should not be found 'guilty but insane' (see chapter 9). Mr Justice Stable intervened, and elicited from both witnesses the admission that the only evidence of Din's paranoia was his belief that his wife was unfaithful to him with Ansari, and that there had in fact been suspicious occurrences. Neither side had asked the wife to testify. The judge criticised the prosecution for not probing the medical evidence more thoroughly, and told the jury that it was for them to decide whether Din's belief was a delusion or reasonable. The jury then rejected the defence, and on appeal Stable's direction to them was upheld.[29]

A feature of the English system of trial which is the subject of recurrent criticisms is the way in which it treats psychiatric witnesses like any other kind of witness. They must be called either by the defence or by the prosecution; their opinions are elicited by question and answer; they are cross-examined and re-examined; and if they appear to be contradicting each other it is the jury who at the end of the day decides who is telling the truth. Like the witness who identifies an assailant, the psychiatrist is treated as if he is testifying to an ordinary matter of fact. As on so many points, it was Isaac Ray who had the temerity (on the other side of the Atlantic) to question the merits of the system which Hale had extolled so proudly. Ray thought it ridiculous that the jury should be allowed to decide between conflicting medical witnesses, of whom one might be an authority, the other an ignorant nobody. The procedure seemed to him much inferior to its French counterpart, under which the court could appoint *experts* to inquire into the mental state of the accused and report on oath to the court. Bucknill and Forbes Winslow, who greatly resented the way in which he had been cross-examined by counsel, proposed a similar procedure in the eighteen-fifties. Harrington Tuke, another experienced psychiatric witness, suggested it to the Capital Punishment Commission of 1864–6, who ignored him.

The British Medical Association proposed to the Atkin Committee in 1923 that there should be an impartial panel of psychiatric experts to which the accused should be referred if suspected of being mentally disordered, and which would furnish copies of its report both to prosecution and defence. At the trial, they suggested, 'evidence should be tendered in person by the expert or experts who examined the accused, and should be considered by the court in deciding the responsibility or otherwise of the accused'. The Medico-Psychological Association, who submitted a similar proposal, made it clear that the experts should be open to cross-examination by either side, who would also have the right to call their own expert witnesses. Presumably they hoped, not unreasonably, that the authority of the impartial expert would simply make it unprofitable to exercise this right. The Atkin Committee (who included only lawyers and civil servants) gave these ideas short shrift. 'The panel would have to range over the whole of England and Wales, and we think that in some parts of the country there would be a difficulty in finding suitable members. In no case would it be possible to leave medical testimony to members of the panel and thus prevent an accused person calling evidence of his own doctor or doctors not on the panel. The conflict of medical opinion could not by such means be prevented.' One is left with the feeling that they had not really studied the proposals with care.

By the time of the Royal Commission on Capital Punishment of 1949–53 the two medical associations were no longer in favour of the idea; but other medical witnesses were, and the Commission, though they apologised for dealing with it rather briefly, gave it a more thorough consideration than any of their predecessors had done. They admitted that it need not preclude the cross-examination of the impartial experts, nor the calling of other medical witnesses by either side; but the possibility that the jury might give more weight to the impartial experts seems to have struck them as an objection rather than as an advantage. On the whole they seem to have been conscious of difficulty in producing strong arguments against the innovation, and had to fall back on the argument that it 'would mean a fundamental change in the procedure of our courts . . . and would have repercussions so far beyond the limited field of our inquiry that we should not feel justified in recommending it'. This was an appeal to conservatism and their terms of reference rather than to logic.

So much for developments in procedure and interpretation. What was happening in practice? For example, what changes had there been in the success rate of the insanity defence since the eighteen-thirties? So far as trials at the Old Bailey are concerned it is possible to answer this question up to 1912, but not after, since the Sessions Papers ceased to be published in the spring of the following year. Since they had by this time become extremely bulky, containing reports of more than 1,500 cases a year, it was out of the question to examine more than a few short periods. I chose the last four years of the series, and two intermediate periods of three years each. One was in the early eighteen-fifties, nearly a decade after M'Naghten's case, which could by then be presumed to have made some of its impact on the courts. The other was the early eighteen-eighties, and was chosen partly because it was more or less intermediate between the other two, partly in the hope – which was not to be realised – of finding some mention of Queen Victoria's new form of special verdict (see chapter 11).

The result can be seen in table 2. In the eighteen-fifties and eighteen-eighties the frequency of 'insanity cases' seems to have been 6½ and 8 per thousand, higher than in any previous period since the seventeen-sixties; and by the Edwardian years it had risen higher still. Part of the increase may have been due to the tendency to deal with petty offences at summary courts, thus leaving the Old Bailey with a greater concentration of crimes carrying serious penalties; but this was not the case as early as the eighteen-fifties, when many of the charges were trivial ones of uttering counterfeit coins. At least part of the trend must reflect a genuinely greater likelihood that a mentally disordered prisoner would be recognised as such: a trend which must have been at least partly attributable to the increasing efficiency of medical attention. In many of the insanity cases the witnesses included the medical officer of Newgate or other gaols.

On the other hand, the success-rate did not rise with the frequency. If anything it was slightly lower than previously – about four in ten as compared with five in ten. It was not until the end of the century that it began to climb again, until just before the first world war it was about seven in ten. For if we turn to the national statistics in table 3, the picture they present is consistent with this. Although they do not unfortunately give us any information about frequencies or success-rates, they show that from the last decades of the nineteenth century there was a steady rise in the murderer's chances of benefiting from a plea of insanity.

These observations are consistent with, and perhaps lend a greater sharpness to, the impression of the nineteenth century which I have tried to give in the last three chapters. It was not, as is so often supposed, a period during which the eighteenth-century's unwillingness to accept pleas of insanity was gradually relaxed. On the contrary, for most of the century lawyers were becoming increasingly concerned, articulate, and restrictive about such pleas, so that an increase in their frequency, which in the seventeen-fifties had been accompanied by a greater willingness to accept them, now merely meant that more of them were unsuccessful. It was not until the last decades of the nineteenth century that the second major relaxation of attitude commenced. This was not the consequence of any *cause célèbre*, or indeed of any single identifiable event, but a gradual process.

For this was the period during which British psychiatry, which had hitherto been the preserve of a handful of somewhat controversial pundits, began to establish itself as a respectable discipline. The multiplying of asylums recruited more and more doctors. The discoveries, real or apparent, of neurologists opened up the prospects of a scientific basis for alienists' theories. More particularly, the increasing numbers of convicts, many of them serving very long sentences, presented the medical officers of the prisons with psychiatric problems which – as we shall see in volume II – could not be ignored. Moreover, although psychiatry had not yet achieved the popularity with the educated layman which was to have such an impact on the outlook of the twentieth century, its importance was beginning to be appreciated by legislators and lawyers, including – as we have seen – Fitzjames Stephen himself, whose own declining years were to be clouded by mental disorder.

From the first world war onward we must rely on table 3. The percentage of successful pleas of insanity in murder trials continued to rise steadily until 1938. It was exceptionally high during the 1914–18 war, no doubt because the percentage of mentally normal murderers was reduced by the absence of so many able-bodied men from normal life. In contrast, special verdicts were less frequent than usual in the years immediately following the war, when many murders were committed by those mentally normal men when they returned home to find their women unfaithful, jobs hard to get, and civilian life an anticlimax. Although unfortunately no such figures can be obtained for the second world war, there was a similar drop in the percentage of special verdicts in the years of demobilisation.

It is surprising, however, that the percentage continued to rise in the nineteen-twenties. For in 1922 not only did the Court of Criminal Appeal finally rule out irresistible impulse as a defence, but also the Infanticide Act provided mothers who killed their babies with a safer defence than insanity. The inference must be that the effects of these events were more than counterbalanced by a greater readiness on the part of medical witnesses, judges, and juries to consider defences of insanity from male murderers. By the nineteen-thirties nearly one-third of murder trials ended in a special verdict, and nearly one-half ended either in a special verdict or a finding of 'unfit to plead'. But at this point some sort of high-water mark seems to have been reached. Even in the early nineteen-fifties, after the 'demobilisation murders' were over, the combined percentages of murderers found 'unfit to plead' or 'guilty but insane' did not rise above 44 per cent; and, as we shall see in chapter 9, not even the addition of a new defence, diminished responsibility, could raise the percentage much higher.

Notes overleaf

Notes

1 L.F.Winslow, *Lettsomian Lectures on Insanity* (London, 1854): see the third lecture.
2 J.F.Stephen, *On the policy of maintaining the limits at present imposed by law on the criminal responsibility of madmen* in Papers read before the Juridical Society, 1855–8 (London, 1855).
3 Report and Minutes of Evidence before the Royal Commission on Capital Punishment, 1864–6: in British Sessional Papers, 1866, XXI.
4 J.F.Stephen, *Digest of the Criminal Law* (London, 1877).
5 J.F.Stephen, *History of the Criminal Law of England*, (London, 1883).
6 R. v. Davis (1881), 14 Cox 563.
7 R. v. Fryer (1915), 24 Cox 405.
8 R. v. True (1922), 16 Cr. App. R. 164; and see D.Carswell (ed.), *The Trial of Ronald True* (London, 1923) for a full account of the trial and appeal.
9 Report of the Committee on *Insanity and Crime* (1924), Cmd. 2005, HMSO.
10 Report of the Select Committee on *Capital Punishment* (1930), HMSO.
11 Report of the Royal Commission on *Capital Punishment*, 1949–53, Cmnd. 8932. (I shall refer to this as 'The Gowers Commission', partly for the sake of brevity, partly to distinguish it clearly from the Commission of 1864–6.)
12 This recommendation has found more favour in other parts of the Commonwealth than in Britain: see, for example, the Nigerian Criminal Code and the Criminal Justice (Northern Ireland) Act, 1966.
13 R. v. Codère (1916), 12 Cr. App. R. 21.
14 R. v. Windle (1952), 2 Q.B. 883 (C.C.A.).
15. See J.F.Stephen, *A General View of the Criminal Law* (London, 1863).
16 In (1955), 9, *Howard Journal*, 2.
17 loc. cit., p. 119.
18 Fully described by L.Fairfield and E.P.Fullbrook in *The Trial of John Thomas Straffen* (London, 1954).
19 R. v. Kemp (1956), 40 Cr. App. R. 121.
20 Glanville Williams, *Criminal Law: the General Part*, 2nd ed. (London, 1961).
21 R. v. Kenneally (1930), 22 Cr. App. R. 52.
22 R. v. Woolmington (1935), A.C. 475.
23 By the Privy Council in Sodemann's case (1936), 2 A.E.R., 1138.
24 R. v. Dart (1878), 14 Cox 143.
25 R. v. Backwell (1910), CCCSP, p. 492.
26 A.G. for S. Australia v. Brown (1960), 44 Cr. App. R. 100 (P.C.).
27 R. v. Frances (1849), 4 Cox 57.
28 R. v. Matheson (1958), 42 Cr. App. R. 145.
29 R. v. Din (1962), 42 Cr. App. R. 116.

Chapter 7. **Infanticide**

The crime of infanticide is of special interest to both lawyers and psychiatrists. From the legal point of view it is unique in two respects. It provides a special defence which succeeds in glossing over the issue of responsibility, and it confines this defence to women.

From the psychiatric point of view, infanticide is one of the possible manifestations of the mental disorder or disorders to which some women succumb after giving birth. Not long ago these were lumped together under the heading of 'puerperal psychosis'. The symptoms varied from one patient to another, and included delirium, depression, hallucinations, catatonia, and acute anxiety. Various explanations were offered. Puerperal fever resulting from infection was often blamed, on doubtful evidence; but in any case improvements in antiseptic precautions have greatly reduced the incidence of these infections in civilised countries. Psychodynamic explanations were of course offered by Freudian psychiatrists such as Zilboorg. The endocrine system, which certainly undergoes massive readjustments during and after pregnancy, was blamed by the physiologically minded; and if the disorder did not appear until some time after childbirth it was sometimes called 'lactational insanity'. Others suggested that it was an 'exhaustion psychosis'. The most prevalent view at present seems to be that it should not be regarded as a single disorder, but that the physiological and psychological stress of childbirth may trigger off hitherto latent tendencies to one or other of the common psychoses or neuroses, a theory which would account for the great variety of symptoms and prognoses.[1] Whatever the explanation, the juncture at which a woman is most likely to commit homicide is during the period immediately following the birth of her child; and the most likely victim is the child itself, although the mother not infrequently kills, or tries to kill, the rest of her family as well as herself.

Not all infanticides are committed in disordered states of mind. The unmarried woman or girl who finds herself pregnant and, for one reason or another, is prevented from procuring an abortion may succumb to the temptation to dispose of the child either by abandoning it where it will be found in time to save its life or by taking its life before she becomes attached to it. Both Aschaffenburg and Grünhut[2] recognised that in many cases this is the inexperienced girl's substitute for contraception or abortion. In making up their minds whether an illegitimate child had been stillborn or had died by its mother's hands the hard-headed courts of the eighteenth century used to ask whether she had concealed her pregnancy and whether she had summoned help when in childbirth.

Since fornication and adultery were strongly condemned by the Church, the criminal codes of medieval Europe treated this as a particularly heinous form of murder and prescribed hideous deaths for the mother. Even the Code Napoléon retained this as one of its few capital crimes: if the child was murdered before it had been registered, the penalty was the guillotine.[3] The justification was that until registration the child enjoyed less protection than the ordinary citizen from the normal deterrents of the law, since its existence was not known; consequently an exceptional deterrent was required. It was this philosophy of maximum deterrence which prompted Baron Bramwell to argue to the Capital Punishment Commission in 1865[4] that 'the greater the temptation the greater the need for punishment' in such cases.

There were of course practical difficulties in proving murder against the woman who had secretly given birth to a child. The dead baby might have been stillborn, or might have died through her inability to attend to it in the exhaustion of labour. To make sure, however, that the woman should pay the penalty for her sin an Act of 1623[5] provided the death penalty for the mother of an illegitimate child which had been born alive and whose body was disposed of so as to conceal its death. (A later act of 1803[6] allowed a woman to be convicted of this crime only if she had been acquitted of murder, but since the Offences against the Person Act of 1861[7] it has been an offence for the mother or anyone else to attempt, by secretly disposing of the body, to conceal the birth of a child, legitimate or illegitimate, whether it died before, at, or after birth. The 1803 Act reduced the maximum penalty to two years' imprisonment, which was no doubt sufficient to satisfy the juror who thought that the mother deserved some degree of punishment.)

The operation of the law in the seventeenth century is illustrated by Sinah Jones' case, taken from the Old Bailey Sessions Papers for 1688 (13–16 January):

Sinah Jones, of the Parish of St Mary Woolnoth, was Indicted for Murdering her Bastard Male Child, on the eighteenth December last, being Saturday night, by stopping its Breath with a Cloath put in its Mouth; she being a Servant in the House of Mr Cousins. The Evidence against her was plain, the Nurse, the Chair-woman, the Mid-wife, the Master and his Servant, all deposing, that she denying the Key, they broke open her Trunk, where they all saw the Child Dead, wrapped up in a Cloath, with a Rag in the Mouth of it, as big as a Handkerchief, and that the Child being something Warm, they tried all they could to recover Life in it, but to no purpose. The Prisoner said little for herself, but that she knew nothing of the Cloath in the Mouth of the Child, and that she had not her Senses, and was Light-headed. Then the Statute was read to her, wherein, if the Child be found Dead and Concealed, though it were so Born, the Person Concealing it, shall suffer Death as in

case of Murder, except she can prove by one Witness at least, that
the Child so Concealed was born Dead. Upon full evidence, she
was brought in guilty of Murder.

She was sentenced to death; and since this was in a metropolitan jurisdiction the records give no indication whether the court intended to recommend a pardon (see chapter 12).

Of course, if the child was legitimate and the mother had made no attempt to conceal her pregnancy or its birth it was less easy to find a rational motive for her act, and the defence of temporary insanity was more likely to be accepted. Lord Chief Justice Hale was greatly impressed by a case of this sort, perhaps because he himself had presided at the trial:

In the year 1668 at Aylesbury a married woman of good reputation
being delivered of a child and not having slept many nights fell
into a temporary phrenzy, and kild her infant in the absence of any
company; but company coming in, she told them, that she had
killed her infant, and there it lay; she was brought to gaol presently,
and after some sleep she recovered her understanding, but marvelled
how or why she came thither; she was indicted for murder, and upon
her trial the whole matter appearing it was left to the jury with this
direction, that if it did appear, that she had any use of reason when
she did it, they were to find her guilty; but if they found her under
a phrenzy, tho by reason of her late delivery and want of sleep,
they should acquit her; that had there been any occasion to move
her to this fact, as to hide her shame, which is ordinarily the case
of such as are delivered of bastard children and destroy them; or
if there had been jealousy in her husband, that the child had been
none of his, or if she hid the infant, or denied the fact, these had
been evidences, that the phrenzy was counterfeit; but none of these
appearing, and the honesty and virtuous deportment of the woman
in her health being known to the jury, and many circumstance of
insanity appearing, the jury found her not guilty to the satisfaction
of all that heard it.[8]

There were cases in which it was less certain whether the killing of the baby had been an insane or a rational act. Hume describes the trial in 1756 of Agnes Crockat, who had borne a bastard child but had not attempted to conceal the fact. A week after its birth she was given it to suckle and was shortly after found with it dead by her side, saying that the devil had tempted her to kill it. Since there was 'no clear proof of bodily complaint or of a marked transition from a state of disorder to soundness' the jury refused to acquit her on the grounds of insanity, but she was saved by the royal mercy. This was a Scottish case, and I have not been able to find a contemporary example of similar clemency in an English case. What probably saved Englishwomen in such situations – in the cases in which they were saved – was the increasing reluctance of juries to convict for murder in such cases. They would grasp at any suggestion that the baby had been stillborn, or had died in the course of birth, or had been accidentally killed. Even if the signs of deliberate killing were unmistakable, the

mother could benefit from a curious hiatus in the criminal law. To procure a miscarriage was a felony, and wilfully to kill a newborn baby was
murder; but to destroy a child in the course of birth, before it had a separate existence, was no crime. (The gap was not filled until the Infant Life
Preservation Act of 1929[9] made 'child destruction' a crime.)

In the occasional case in which the facts pointed unmistakably to murder and the jury were not prepared to ignore the evidence, they could
recommend the mother to mercy; and by the nineteenth century they
usually did so, with the support of most judges. If the judge was in favour
of mercy, a reprieve was a foregone conclusion (see chapter 12). Executions
of mothers for the murder of their own babies became increasingly rare,
and the last took place in 1849, when Rebecca Smith was allowed to go to
the gallows for poisoning her baby. (What seems to have prevented her
from securing a reprieve was the general dislike of deliberate poisoning,
together with the strong suspicion that she had previously disposed of
several other children in the same way.[10] The jury had recommended her
to mercy, but when asked why gave the unfortunate explanation that it
would give her time to repent!) By the time of the Capital Punishment
Commission of 1864–6 it was 'established practice' in the Home Office to
advise the commutation of the death penalty when a woman was convicted
of murdering her own child while it was under or not much over the age of
twelve months.[11]

All but a few of the judges and other witnesses who gave evidence to the
Capital Punishment Commission thought that there should be some lesser
category of crime into which such cases could be brought. No doubt their
main objective was that the infanticidal mother should be convicted of
something more serious and realistic than concealment of birth. Here
again, however, Fitzjames Stephen was the exception, and expressed what
was the opinion of an increasing number of contemporary alienists:

> . . . women in that condition do get the strongest symptoms of what
> amounts almost to temporary madness, and . . . often hardly know
> what they are about, and will do things which they have no settled
> or deliberate intention whatever of doing. . . .[12]

He was even bold enough to hint that less harm was done by such homicides than in other cases: 'you cannot estimate the loss to the child itself,
you know nothing about it at all. With regard to the public it causes no
alarm, because it is a crime which can be committed only by mothers upon
their newly born children.'

Even the tough-minded Bramwell could on occasion be so swayed by
such feelings as to suspend his judicial insistence on evidence:

> Another case which I remember was one of the most painful cases
> that I ever tried. A young woman had an illegitimate child a year
> old: she was very fond of it and behaved well to it. What particu-
> lar thing so disturbed her I do not know, but I have some reason
> to suppose that she was about to be married and that a person
> had threatened to inform her intended husband that his brother
> was the father of the child. . . . On a Sunday morning the child's
> clothes were hanging before the fire to dry and she was evidently

intending to dress it and take it out and use it well, as she had always done. She cut its throat, and she rushed out into the street and said that she had done so. . . . I cannot in my own mind believe that that woman was as mad as the law would require her to be . . . but it was an act of such a character that the only address to the jury was 'This woman may have had a sudden condition of mind come upon her, in which she really did not know what she was doing'. She was a very decent-looking young woman; everybody in court wept, the counsel on both sides and the jury and everybody; and the result was that she was acquitted.[13]

So much for the M'Naghten Rules! Bramwell was undoubtedly acting with intelligence as well as humanity, but he should have told the jury that the accused must be presumed to have been sane unless the contrary was proved to their satisfaction.

Like everyone else, Bramwell knew very well that the use of the prerogative of mercy had by now turned the whole issue into an academic question: what should the crime be called? He himself wanted the best of both worlds – the deterrent effect of the penalty for murder but the free use of the power to reprieve. Nevertheless, it is a curious fact that for the next half-century there were repeated attempts by English judges to amend this part of the law of murder. It is true that at first these attempts were part of general efforts to tidy up the criminal law, but they continued long after these efforts had been abandoned.

What most judges seem to have found objectionable was the necessity of pronouncing the death sentence on the mothers who were convicted of murder. Their privilege of merely recording it in silence had been abolished in 1861 so far as murder was concerned, and the fact that it was common knowledge that the sentence would never be carried out in such cases made matters worse, if anything, in their eyes. There were several attempts – the last in 1909 – to restore their discretion to record the death sentence instead of pronouncing it. But by this time the idea of giving the judiciary discretion over a matter of life and death seems to have become unpopular, and the proposal was never taken seriously.

Although it was known to be the Home Secretary's practice to reprieve *all* infanticidal mothers, attempts to reform the law itself did not take so sweeping a form. Russell Gurney's Homicide Bill of 1872 included a clause which provided that if a woman murdered her child 'at or soon after birth and whilst deprived of her ordinary powers of self-control by the physical effects of the birth' the judge should have discretion to sentence her not to death but to penal servitude for not less than five years! Two years later a similar Bill introduced by Gurney embodied something more like the present law: the crime was to be manslaughter and not murder if the mother was 'deprived of the power of self-control by any disease or state of mind or body produced by bearing the child whose death is caused'. Both Bills were eventually dropped on the advice of a Select Committee, on the familiar ground that they were partial measures affecting principles of criminal law which extended to other crimes.

A few years later, in 1880, another attempt to amend the law of

L

homicide, including the law on infanticide, was made in a gigantic private members' Bill of 763 clauses, but was equally unsuccessful. In 1908, however, after yet another attempt had been made in the House of Commons to reform the law of homicide in general, the Lord Chancellor himself, Lord Loreburn, tried a new tack in the Lords. He sought to insert in the Children Bill – which sounded a more appropriate place than in fact it was – a clause providing that 'where a woman is convicted of the murder of her infant and that child was under the age of one year, the court may, in lieu of passing a sentence of death, sentence her to penal servitude for life or any less sentence'. He was, of course, a former judge, and his clause would in effect have achieved something like the judicial discretion which existed before 1861 (see chapter 13). His main argument in support of it was that it would avoid the 'solemn mockery' of pronouncing the death sentence. He was successfully opposed by no less a person than the Lord Chief Justice, Lord Alverstone, who preferred to see the discretion vested in the Home Secretary – a point of view which would have shocked several of his successors. The clash between the two lawyers prompted the Bishop of Southwark to suggest that if the Lord Chief Justice did not like the Lord Chancellor's proposal he should take some other action himself.

Lord Alverstone was thus more or less trapped into introducing a Bill of his own, which he did in the following session (1909). His Bill was not entirely consistent with his objection to Lord Loreburn's clause, for it would have restored the judges' discretion to record the death sentence in cases of 'child murder'. In any case, however, the Bill's character was completely altered by Lord James, the eighty-year-old former Attorney-General. He moved an amendment to the effect that if a mother who had not recovered from childbirth killed her infant the judge could direct the jury that they might acquit of murder and convict of manslaughter; and the Lord Chief Justice gave way. In this form the Bill finally reached the Commons in July, when they were already in difficulties with their time-table; and it was probably sheer lack of Parliamentary time which prevented it from proceeding further.

Thirteen years later, Mr Arthur Henderson, the secretary of the Labour Party, successfully introduced a Bill which in principle resembled the amended Bill of 1909, with the difference that it simply left it open to the jury to bring in a verdict of manslaughter instead of murder, and did not permit the judge to direct them to do so. The practical effect of a verdict of manslaughter was that the judge could then award any sentence from penal servitude for life to a fine or even a conditional discharge. Such a verdict was to be permissible (not obligatory) wherever evidence was given that at the time of the killing the woman 'had not recovered from the effect of giving birth to the child', a definition which covered physical as well as mental effects, and which specified no time-limit after the date of the birth. Although it was no wider than the principle on which the Home Secretary was using the prerogative of mercy, the Lord Chancellor (now Lord Birkenhead) condemned it as 'almost terrifying' in its lack of particularity.

He moved an amendment which he had drafted, but which had the approval, he said, of the Director of Public Prosecutions and the Law Officers of the Crown. It restricted the scope of the Bill to those cases

Where a woman unlawfully by any direct means intentionally
causes the death of her *newly born* child, but at the time . . . had
not fully recovered from the effect of giving birth to such child,
and by reason thereof the balance of her mind was disturbed. . . .

In such cases the jury were enabled to find her guilty of the new crime of infanticide, for which the woman could be sentenced as if she were guilty of manslaughter.

Clearly Birkenhead's clause was meant to achieve at least two objects. In the first place, it is clear from his criticism of the Commons' Bill that he meant his clause to restrict the scope of the Bill. This in itself is strange. Did he not know how wide was the class of mothers whom the Home Office was automatically reprieving? And would he have been so quick to claim credit for drafting the clause if he had foreseen quite how restrictive the courts' interpretation would be?

Like some of his predecessors, he seems to have felt the need to draft the clause in such a way that it would be self-justifying – in other words, that the reason for according special treatment to this class of homicide would be evident. Hence his reference to the mother's state of mind. But earlier attempts – for example, in the Homicide Bill of 1872 – referred to women who were 'deprived of their ordinary powers of self-control', and thus in effect would have obliged the court to estimate her ability to help doing what she did. Birkenhead's clause merely stipulated that 'the balance of her mind should be disturbed', without requiring that it be so disturbed as to affect her 'self-control' or 'responsibility'. He explained that he had deliberately chosen a phrase that was not a term of art, but would have to be interpreted *de novo* by the courts; but whether he appreciated that he had unobtrusively simplified the legal relationship between disease of the mind and *actus reus* is less certain.

Another of his objectives was no doubt to give the judges the same wide choice of sentence as they had in cases of manslaughter, without offending legal purists by defining the crime as manslaughter.

In this form the Bill, by now renamed the Infanticide Bill, passed through its remaining stages and received the Royal Assent. It was not of course expected to save a single mother from the gallows, nor did it do so. What it did ensure was that if a mother killed a child that could be regarded as 'newly born' she would certainly not be found guilty of murder.[14] In other words, in such a situation she could invariably hope to have the crime reduced to manslaughter or infanticide, either by the Director of Public Prosecutions or by the court.[15]

But what was meant by 'newly born'? Parliament was not yet quite rid of this King Charles' head. Five years later in 1927 a woman called O'Donoghue, who had killed her thirty-five-day-old infant, was tried by Talbot, J., who ruled that while there was evidence of insanity which could go to the jury, there was none of infanticide, since the child could not be said to be 'newly born'. The accused was sentenced to death (but was of course swiftly reprieved, even before her appeal against this ruling could be rejected by the Court of Criminal Appeal).[16] The judges have been criticised for interpreting the Act so narrowly, but it would be fairer to criticise Lord Birkenhead. Since his clause insisted that the balance of the woman's mind must have been disturbed by the effect of giving birth to the child, the additional requirement that the child should be 'newly born' clearly created the possibility of a situation in which the crime was committed under the after-effects of childbirth, but so long afterwards that the child could not be said to be 'newly born'. The courts must assume that this phrase was meant to add to the meaning of the clause and they had to assign some time-limit which was not straining the language.

A bold attempt to widen the scope of this legislation to correspond more closely both with public feeling and with the Home Secretary's use of the prerogative of mercy was the Infanticide Bill of 1936. Introduced by a number of Labour back-benchers,[17] it would have exempted the killing of infants up to the age of eight years from the death penalty, and would have widened the definition of the mother's state of mind to include 'distress and despair arising from solicitude for her child or extreme poverty or other causes'.

Whether it would have passed through Parliament is very doubtful, but in the event it lapsed – a minor casualty of the skirmishing over the King's Abdication. The Home Secretary and the Lord Chancellor, who saw 'a number of difficulties' in amending the 1922 Act, would promise no Government legislation for this purpose.[18]

Finally Lord Dawson of Penn, who had given medical evidence in at least one case of infanticide, successfully introduced a Bill which became the Infanticide Act of 1938. It made it clear that the child could be of any age under twelve months, and to make the length of this period plausible the woman's mental imbalance was to be attributable either to the birth of the child or to the consequent lactation (not a few psychiatrists in fact spoke of 'lactational insanity', although this is no longer a fashionable diagnosis).

Since the 1938 Act was passed on the eve of the 1939–45 war – a period for which no relevant criminal statistics have been published – it is not possible to assess the effect of this legislation on the numbers of women found guilty of infanticide. The annual post-war figures were undoubtedly higher, but that could be due to many other causes. Indeed, the form of the published statistics renders it difficult to measure the extent to which the system has become readier to classify a crime as infanticide. The statistics do not tell us how many women were originally charged with murder or manslaughter for the homicide of their last-born children in their first year of life, so that we have no 'number at risk' to which to relate the numbers eventually found guilty of infanticide. We know[14] that as a result of the 1922 Act no mother who killed her 'newly born' child was found guilty of murder – at least from 1927 to 1936: but we do not know whether the wider definition of the victim in the 1938 Act was equally effective, although we do know that it is now much rarer for women to be indicted for murder.

Probably the best measure of the courts' decreasingly punitive attitude towards this crime is the declining percentage of women who have been sentenced to imprisonment for it. Table 4 shows the annual numbers of women found guilty of infanticide, and how many of them were sentenced to imprisonment, released on recognisance, put on probation or dealt with in other ways, such as committal to a psychiatric institution.

TABLE 4. Women found guilty of infanticide and how courts dealt with them (the statistics from which this table is calculated will be found in Appendix C)

Years	Recognisances or discharge	Probation	Imprisonment	Otherwise[a]	Total (=100%)
1923–27	42·4%	5·1%	49·1%[b]	3·4%	59
1928–32	34·4%	18·1%	42·6%[c]	4·9%	61
1933–38	44·0%	22·7%	33·3%	Nil	66
1939–45	No statistics published				
1946–50	24·4%	49·0%	22·3%	4·3%	139
1951–55	15·0%	55·0%	16·2%	13·8%	80
1956–60	9·5%	76·2%	3·2%	11·1%	63
1961–65	5·6%	68·1%	1·3%[d]	25·0%	72

[a] Most of these cases were no doubt committed to institutions for mental defectives or, more recently, to mental hospitals. In 1964 and 1965 the published statistics made it clear that all women not dealt with by discharge, probation, or imprisonment were dealt with by hospital orders.
[b] In 1923 one of these women was sentenced to 4 years' penal servitude, another to 3 years' penal servitude.
[c] One of these women was sent to a borstal.
[d] She was sent to prison for 6 months or less.

In the first few years after the new crime was created, almost half the women convicted of it were sent to prison, two of them for three and four years of penal servitude. Table 4 shows a steady transition to an entirely different pattern of disposal, in which nine out of ten are either committed to mental hospitals or put on probation (in many cases on condition that they accept psychiatric treatment). In the last eight years only one woman has been sent to prison for this offence – in 1964, for six months or less.

This remarkable shift in sentencing pattern must be viewed against a perspective in which there has been a general shrinking in the use of imprisonment. In 1923 nearly two-thirds – 64 per cent – of all persons convicted by higher courts were sent to prison, as compared with two-fifths – 40 per cent – in 1965. There are other types of offence which are now dealt with much more humanely than formerly. In 1923 a man convicted at Assizes of indecency with another man or boy went to prison in three out of four cases (72 per cent); but in 1965 higher courts sent rather less than 6 per cent of such men to prison: the rest were fined, discharged, or put on probation. Nevertheless, the virtual abandonment of prison sentences as a means of dealing with a crime involving the taking of human life is one of the most striking developments in the history of our sentencing policy.

Because the Home Secretary invariably respited a death sentence imposed on a mother who killed her young children, a cynic[19] has suggested that the only objective achieved by the Infanticide Acts has been to save Her Majesty's judges from the harrowing experience of pronouncing the death sentence in such cases. Certainly one of the noticeable features of the parliamentary debates on the various bills was the frequency with which judges past and present recalled the distress they had suffered on these occasions. In fact, however, the Acts achieved more than this. By removing the label of 'murder' from this form of homicide and substituting a new and technical term which lacked emotional association it made it psychologically possible for the judges' attitudes towards it to change in the way which is demonstrated by the sentencing statistics. I have already drawn attention elsewhere[20] to this variety of 'legal realism': the tendency to assume that legal names and definitions of crimes correspond to subdivisions in nature. This leads people to assume, for example, that the acts which the law labels as 'murder' are, so to speak, a natural subspecies of 'crime', whose members have more in common with each other than any of them have with acts that are classified under other headings, such as manslaughter. The power of such labels to arouse our feelings is demonstrated by the way in which opponents of the reform of the law on abortion use the argument that abortion is really 'murder'. Even criminologists slip into this way of thinking when they study samples of 'murders' but not of 'attempted murders'.

Had the Act of 1922 allowed the label of 'murder' to remain attached to this type of homicide, and simply provided that it was not to be punishable with death – as the Homicide Act of 1957 later did for some other subdivisions – it is very doubtful whether judicial or popular attitudes towards it would have changed as rapidly. Even if the 1922 Act had provided that this form of homicide was to be 'manslaughter' and not 'murder', this would have substituted a label with a weaker but still powerful impact. The choice of a label that had no traditional associations was one of the most important features of the legislation. 'Infanticide' is now so clearly distinguished from 'murder' that in England even criminologists ignore the former when writing about the latter.[21]

Taken at their face value, however, the Acts are still an odd piece of legislation. In the first place, they provided the infanticidal mother with a very half-hearted exemption, which recognises that she was in a disordered state of mind but does not go to the length of conceding a special verdict. She was neither to be acquitted, nor to be found guilty but insane; but to be convicted of a crime which was expressly equated with manslaughter. It was an intermediate verdict of the same nature as that which was introduced thirty-five years later under the name of 'diminished responsibility'.

On the other hand, unlike the murderer who pleads insanity or diminished responsibility, the infanticidal mother does not, at least on the face of it, have to satisfy the court that her act was the result of her disorder. All that she need produce is evidence that at the time the balance of her mind was disturbed by the birth or subsequent lactation: not that the disturbance was sufficiently severe to deprive her of knowledge of the nature and quality of her act, or knowledge of its wrongness, or the capacity to control herself. If section 1(1) of the Act of 1938 is read literally, her counsel could safely say to the court 'She knew that she was killing the child, and that this was morally and legally wrong. She had not lost her self-control, and could have refrained if she had wanted to. Her temporary disorder was in fact quite unconnected with what she did. But you have had evidence that at the time the balance of her mind was disturbed by reason of her not having fully recovered from the effect of giving birth to the child, and so you must find her guilty not of murder but of infanticide.' This was of course the last thing that the draftsmen had in mind. Implicit in their wording is the presumption that if at the time the balance of her mind was disturbed for the reasons given then there must have been sufficient causal connection between this disturbance and the act to reduce her responsibility for the act. This presumption is of course quite foreign to English law; in the case of both the defence of insanity and the defence of diminished responsibility the causal connection must be established and not presumed. Yet although the presumption is foreign to the law, it is by no means foreign to the jury-room. As the Gowers Commission were told by Lord Cooper, juries simply ask themselves whether the accused was or was not mad; and if the answer is that he was they return a special verdict, without agonising about the severity of the madness or its connection with the deed.

In other words, the Infanticide Act of 1922 was not merely an Act for the sparing of the judge's feelings; it was also an Act for the simplification of his summing-up. So far as this specialised kind of homicide was concerned, it acknowledged the fact that juries paid no attention to the sort of questions which were prescribed by the M'Naghten Rules.

The statutes contain other oddities. If the mother, instead of or as well as killing her own latest-born child, intentionally kills another of her children or someone else's child, such a killing cannot be treated as infanticide. Yet the depressed mother who kills all her young children is by no means uncommon. The distinction between killing the child to which she last gave birth and killing other children made sense only when the aim was to accord special treatment to the mother who kills within a very short time of parturition. As soon as the objective was widened to include mothers who had resumed their place in their families, the distinction became illogical, although the illogicality does not seem to have troubled anyone since the 1938 Act. As so often, it could be, and was, left to the prerogative of mercy to ensure that common sense prevailed. More recently, the Homicide Act of 1957 has made it possible for mothers in this position to plead diminished responsibility. The consequence is that a woman is occasionally convicted at the same trial of the infanticide of her last-born child and the manslaughter of her firstborn.

Yet the most unusual and interesting feature of the Acts is not their amateurish draftsmanship but the way in which they attempt to single out and define a special sort of criminal act for the very purpose of creating a virtual presumption that the author of the act was not fully responsible by reason of mental illness. There are acts, such as arson, in the case of which one can say with a substantial degree of probability that the author is mentally ill or – more probably still – subnormal. Similarly, women who are detected in shoplifting often benefit from a popular disposition to attribute this behaviour to the mental disturbances of menstruation or the menopause (the extent to which this is justifiable is not at the moment the point). It is not the law, however, which creates these assumptions: merely psychiatric experience and the exploitation of it by the defence. Yet if a mother kills her last-born child in its first year of life, the law more or less invites us to treat her as having done so in an abnormal state of mind. It is not easy to point to any other situation with which it deals in quite this way.

Perhaps the closest analogy is the assumption that persons who commit or attempt suicide are mentally ill. No doubt this is true oftener than it is false; but equally certainly some suicides are simply more realistic and courageous than the ordinary person. The assumption is encouraged by the regularity with which coroner's inquests used to return findings of 'suicide while the balance of his mind was disturbed' – a practice which made it possible to allow the suicide a Christian burial. Significantly, the Infanticide Acts use this very phrase; and it is likely that in much the same way the undeniable fact that *most* mothers who kill their babies soon after giving birth to them are in a highly disordered state of mind has led eventually to the assumption that *all* mothers who kill their children are disordered. The assumption is fostered not merely by our stereotyped notions about normal maternal feelings, but also by the processes of the law itself, which have in a sense set the official stamp of approval on this belief.[22] It is an interesting example of myth-making by legislation.

Notes

1 See the article by B. Jacobs in (1943), 89, *Journal of Mental Science,* 242–, which is based on a study of 152 cases.
2 G. Aschaffenburg, tr. 1913, *Crime and its Repression* (1903, tr. Boston, 1913); M. Grünhut, *Penal Reform: a comparative study* (Oxford University Press, 1948), 408.
3 See the evidence of M. Chédieu to the Capital Punishment Commission of 1864–6, op. cit. ch. 6 n3, minute 1397. In practice, the *droit de grâce* was almost invariably invoked to save the woman.
4 Ibid., minute 2120.
5 21. Jac., c. 27, 'An Act to prevent the destroying and murdering of bastard children'.
6 43 Geo. III., c. 58.
7 24 & 25 Vict., c. 100.
8 Hale, *Historia Placitorum Coronae,* I (London, 1736).
9 19 & 20 Geo. 5, c. 34.
10 See A. H. Dymond, *The Law on its Trial* (London, 1865), 97; and the Home Secretary's evidence to the Capital Punishment Commission of 1864–6 (loc. cit.), minute 1453.
11 Ibid., minute 1467–.
12 Ibid., minute 2193.

13 Ibid., minute 187.

14 This can be inferred from the Home Secretary's reply to a parliamentary question in Hansard (Commons), 1937, vol. 332, col. 2093, which disclosed that in the decade 1927–36 he did not have to reprieve any mother who had killed her child while it was much under four weeks of age.

15 The woman may be charged with murder but committed for trial for infanticide; or committed for murder, tried for murder, and found guilty of infanticide; or put on trial for murder, but have her plea of guilty to infanticide accepted; or she may simply be charged with infanticide in the first place (in which case she usually pleads guilty).

16 R. v. O'Donoghue (1927), 20 Cr. App., R. 132–.

17 Why *eight* years? Recent legislation had made this the earliest age at which a child could be found guilty of a criminal offence, and although the logic of adopting it for this bill is not clear I can think of no other explanation.

18 Hansard (Commons) for 15 April 1937, col. 1165.

19 D. Seaborne Davies. See his article in *The Modern Approach to Criminal Law* (ed. L. Radzinowicz and J. W. C. Turner) (London, 1945).

20 In *The Aims of a Penal System* (James Seth Memorial Lecture for 1966) (Edinburgh, 1967).

21 The only modern exception in English criminological literature known to me is J. D. J. Havard's *Detection of Secret Homicide* (London, 1960), where ways of killing babies are described.

22 'It is very seldom, where the Act applies, that we cannot find some evidence to justify reducing a murder charge to infanticide at an early stage.' (From a letter from the Department of the Director of Public Prosecutions, for whose help on this as on many other subjects I am grateful.)

Chapter 8. Diminished Responsibility in Scotland

A third of a century after the first of the Infanticide Acts the law of murder was modified by an importation from Scotland. This chapter is an attempt to explain how the Scots developed a concept which had no parallel in English law – the concept of diminished responsibility. For in the sixteenth century their law seems to have dealt with the insane by much the same test as its English counterpart. There is a record of the trial of one Jasper Lauder for murder in 1554. His defence asked for trial by jury on the grounds that

> at the tyme of committing thairof, and lang of befoire, and as yit, continualie, the said Jasper has bene furious and wantand [wanting] the use of resoune, doand [doing] in all the said tyme . . . furious and daft dedis [deeds], lyke as at lenthe is contentit in ane Inventour [contained in an inventory]. . . . And sua is comparit of the law [and so is comparable at law] to ane infant, pupill or beist . . . quharethrow [wherefore] he could nocht contract, trespass or do any sic deid . . . quherbj he mycht be oblist [whereby he might be liable] to punishment of his persoune. . . .

He was granted trial by jury, but his defence failed to produce the inventory, and he was beheaded. His trial illustrates the brutal speed with which a case that appeared straightforward could be disposed of in those days: the homicide took place on 1st May, the hearing on 7th May, and his assize and execution on 10th May.[1]

It is clear from the wording of his 'allegeance' – which failed only because it was not supported by the necessary evidence – that it was the same defence as would have been recognised by an English court. It rests upon the same comparison with children and wild beasts as was drawn by Bracton and his successors. The insistence that he had been 'continualie' mad suggests that the possibility of lucid intervals was also recognised: certainly it is discussed in the next century by Mackenzie. It would be mistaken, however, to regard the 'wild beast' analogy or the notion of 'lucid intervals' as conclusive evidence of English influence, for both can be found in Continental jurists, and were more probably derived from them.

Sir George Mackenzie of Rosehaugh (1636–91), more commonly known as 'the Bluidy Mackenzie', was a contemporary of Hale's, and his treatise on *The Laws and Customs of Scotland in Matters Criminal* was completed in 1674, within a few years of Hale's *Historia Placitorum Coronae*.

As the king's advocate in Scotland, Mackenzie prosecuted covenanters and witches with equal fervour, and was chiefly responsible for the use of torture to extract confessions from those he accused. By one of the many contradictions in his character, however, he took a more enlightened interest in disorders of the mind, and on the subject of the insane offender his views were unexpectedly liberal. It is clear that the law which he was discussing still resembled in its principles the law of England. Only absolutely furious persons were excused from punishment, and those who had lucid intervals were in danger of losing the benefit of even this exemption. But according to Mackenzie the onus of proving that the act was done in a lucid interval lay on the prosecution, whereas in England the defence had to prove the contrary:

> ... when a man is proved to have been once furious the law presumes that he still continues furious, till the contrair be proved, for madness is too sticking a disease; and is seldom or never cured. And this presumption should rather hold in the committing of crimes than in anything else, for the committing of a crime looks liker the madness than the lucid intervals. . . .[2]

Mackenzie was being independent rather than original. Until the Act of Union Scots lawyers were influenced at least as strongly by Continental jurists, and Mackenzie, who had studied in Holland, borrowed many of his arguments, including this one, from Matthaeus, the Dutch legal writer of the previous generation. There is a paragraph in Matthaeus' *De Criminibus* (1644) which might be translated almost into Mackenzie's words:

> ... yet once a man has been furious, or is furious at intervals, we shall presume that his crime is more likely to have been committed in his fury, ... since fury is a sticking disease [morbus durabilis].[3]

But Mackenzie goes further than this. He says earlier:

> Possibly that judge would not be much mistaken who would remit something of the ordinary punishment in all crimes committed, even where the lucid intervals are clearly proved: for where madness has once disordered the judgement, and more where it recurs often, it cannot but leave some weakness, and make a man an unfit judge of what he ought to do, *est tantum adumbrata quies, intermissio, sed non resipiscentia integra*[4]: and as our proverb well observes 'once wood, ay the worse'. . . .[5]

Finally, he makes a case for an even bolder concession:

> It may be argued that since the law grants a total impunity to such as are absolutely furious therefore it should by the rule of proportions lessen and moderate the punishments of such, as though they are not absolutely mad yet are Hypochondrick and Melancholy to such a degree, that it clouds their reason; *qui sensum aliquem habent sed diminutum*,[6] which the lawyers call *insania*. . . .

Mackenzie is discussing here one form of the 'partial insanity' which Hale dismisses so firmly. We saw in chapter 2 that the latter recognised not only insanity which consists of a 'particular dementia in respect of some particular discourses, subjects or application', but also the kind which is

'partial in respect of degrees'. Both Hale and Mackenzie instance wha
would now be called 'anxiety states' or 'depressive states'. 'This', say
Hale, 'is the condition of very many, especially melancholy persons, wh
for the most part discover their defect in excessive fears or griefs, and ye
are not wholly destitute of the use of reason.' But, says Hale, 'this partia
insanity seems not to excuse them in the committing of any offence for it
matter capital. . . .' Mackenzie draws the opposite inference: 'Since th
law grants a total impunity to such as are absolutely furious, it should b
the rule of proportions lessen and moderate the punishments of such. . . .

The contrast between the two contemporary lawyers, both writing wit
practical experience of the application of their doctrines, is striking, an
since in all probability it marks the point at which the Scottish lawyer
began to diverge on this subject, it is worth examining the reason. Para
doxically, Mackenzie was more generous to the partially insane because hi
notion of the function of punishment was more retributive. It is significan
that he prefaces his argument with a quotation from the Digest:

> Do not exact any punishment from him whom the misfortune of
> his destiny excuses: by the madness itself is he punished
> enough. . . .[7]

This argument was known to lawyers such as Coke, who coupled it rathe
unthinkingly with the doctrine that a crime is not committed by a mad
man who acts without the intention to harm. Here again, however, Mac
kenzie's debt was not to them, but to Matthaeus, from whom he wa
borrowing freely. His originality lay in the inference which he drew from
the maxim. If the 'unhappy fate' of the 'absolutely mad' is a sufficien
substitute for punishment, partial insanity should be regarded as a partia
substitute. Although this argument fell into disuse among later Scots an
English jurists, it crops up in odd places. Prichard used it in 1842 whe
discussing the criminal responsibility of the man whose conscience fight
a losing battle against the impulses of 'instinctive insanity':

> Such persons must be admitted to be morally guilty and to deserve
> to suffer. But the calamity with which we know them to be
> afflicted is already so great, that humanity forbids our entertaining
> the thought of adding to it. Perhaps all that we ought to aim at in
> such a case is to secure the community against the evils to which
> it may be exposed.[8]

The generation after Mackenzie saw the Act of Union with Englan
and the imitation of English culture against which so many latter-da
Scots are in revolt. The ways in which the Scots legal system diverge
from that of England were glossed over and reduced. By the time of Baro
Hume (1757–1838) Mackenzie's doctrine that partial insanity shoul
mitigate the punishment was honoured in a rather shamefaced way. Bot
Hume, writing late in the eighteenth century, and Alison, writing early i
the first half of the nineteenth, make it clear that ostensibly insanit
offered the accused the same protection as it did in England. If manifes
(and sufficiently severe) at the time of his assize it could bar his trial; if i
intervened between sentence and execution it could postpone the pains o

death. If he could be shown to have suffered from 'a complete alienation of reason' at the time of his act it excused him. Mackenzie's generous divergence from Hale over the onus of proof where lucid intervals were involved was glossed over by Alison:

> The proof of insanity lies upon the pannel to establish; and in the case of an insane person having lucid intervals, it lies upon him to show that the criminal act was committed during the continuance of the disease, *unless those intervals were of short duration.* . . . Upon the whole, however, the remark of Mr. Hume appears well founded, that the point should be left for the consideration of the jury, rather than made the subject of any unbending preconceptions. . . .[9]

Hume wrote:

> With regard to the result of a verdict finding the defence of furiosity proved, it cannot well be any other than the entire acquittal of the pannel [the accused], 'cum satis furore ipso punitur'. . . . As to the inferior degrees of derangement, or natural weakness of intellect, which do not amount to madness and for which there can be no rule in law: the relief of these must be sought either in the discretion of the prosecutor, who may restrict his libel [charge] to an ordinary pain [penalty], or in the course of application to the King for mercy. Yet I find that in one case, that of Sommerville (1704), though perhaps not to be approved of as a precedent, a middle course was taken, by absolving the pannel from all corporal pain, but decreeing for a fine to the fiscal, and asythment [compensation] to the widow and children of the deceased.[10]

This is a transparent attempt to disguise the difference between the Scottish and the English approach to the problem of partial insanity. Hume is arguing that the legal principle is the same (without realising that the maxim '*satis furore ipso punitur*' is really un-English); and he is insisting that cases of partial insanity can escape punishment only by one of two extra-legal devices – the discretion of the prosecutor or the royal prerogative of mercy. Sommerville's case, in which the court itself recognised his partial insanity as a legal ground for mitigating punishment, is an awkward one for Hume (although Mackenzie would have approved), and has to be dismissed as a judicial error.

But underneath the pretence of agreement there lay real heterodoxy. Although partial insanity was not usually recognised as a defence it was taken into account after conviction by the practice of allowing – or advising – the jury to recommend a pardon:

> If it appear from the evidence that the pannel, though partially deranged, was not so much so as to relieve him entirely from punishment, the proper course would be to find him guilty; but on account of the period of infirmity of mind which he could not control, recommend him to the royal mercy.[11]

Indeed, if the crime were such that the court had a choice as to the nature or severity of the punishment, evidence as to the convict's state of mind would be heard after he had been found guilty. In 1835, after one William

Braid had pleaded guilty (to what crime is not recorded), a Dr Traill was examined 'to show that the state of the pannel's mind had diminished his responsibility, although it did not take it entirely away'. Since this is recorded in Bell's notes to the 1844 edition of Hume, the phrase 'diminished responsibility' is at least as old as that.

Even in Hume's day, however, juries would sometimes either misunderstand the judge's advice or interpret the law in their own way, and Hume records cases in which they should, by his lights, have convicted the pannel and left him to the royal mercy, but instead acquitted him.[1]

Moreover, even when Hume was dealing with insanity as a defence (as distinct from a mitigating factor), he was more liberal than his English contemporaries in the interpretation of what Hale would have called 'total insanity'. Even if the accused had known that he was committing murder and that murder in general was wrong, Hume would still have regarded him as 'absolutely mad' if, for example, he had lost 'all true observation of facts, all understanding of the good and bad intentions of those who are about him'. This part of his Commentaries was so apposite to M'Naghten's paranoid attitude to the Tories that Cockburn (himself a Scot) read out the entire passage in his speech for M'Naghten's defence, and like Hume glossed over the independence of Scots law on this and other matters.

This was the state of affairs in 1867, when Lord Deas tried Dingwall for the murder of his wife. Like the Bluidy Mackenzie, Deas was not normally a merciful man, although it was said that handsome women and respectable gentlemen could expect lighter sentences from him than ordinary members of the criminal classes.[13] Certainly Dingwall, though by now a forty-five-year-old alcoholic, had been of good family. In his youth he had served in the Indian Army, when he was said to have had sunstroke; but for the last twenty years he had been living on his property as a minor laird in Aberdeenshire and elsewhere, and spending most of his money on drink. After his return to this country he had had convulsions which 'might have been epileptic', but his most obvious symptoms were clearly those of alcoholism. Soon after his return he had entered 'Dr Poole's Retreat' in an attempt to cure himself, but the regime there seems to have been so permissive that he could get drunk whenever he wanted. A few years later, in 1851, he began to have attacks of *delirium tremens*, and was known locally as 'the wud laird' (that is, 'the mad laird'): but doctors who were asked to certify him as a lunatic would not agree that he was more than 'weak-minded, wayward, and eccentric'. One of the marks of his eccentricity was that he would kindle his own fire in the mornings using a knife of which he had – perhaps significantly – blunted the point for safety.

By the end of 1866 he was living in lodgings in Stonehaven with his wife, who was ten to fifteen years older. By New Year's Eve he had had his daily allowance of whisky (a glass before each meal) but went out to drink about half a dozen more glasses at various houses nearby; for it was Hogmanay, when Scots custom obliges householders to give whisky to any friend or total stranger who presents himself at the door. He returned late with a bottle of whisky, but his wife succeeded in hiding it and his money. There was a quarrel over this, but they eventually went to bed. A little later he got out again and while his wife was dozing stabbed her with a carving knife. She did not die for several days, and in her dying declaration tried to defend him by saying that he was always kind to her when not under drink, but that drink 'threw him into a sad state of excitement, so that he did not know what he was saying or doing . . . in these states he had often threatened to put an end to his own life and hers'. He was tried in Aberdeen before Lord Deas.[14]

In his charge to the jury, Lord Deas pointed out that there had been no allegation of idiocy or what the law called 'furiosity', nor of insane delusions:

> . . . If the jury believed that the prisoner, when he committed the
> act, had sufficient mental capacity to know, and did know, that
> the act was contrary to the law, and punishable by the law, it
> would be their duty to convict him.

As for intoxication, the accused had had a good deal to drink, but was accustomed to it.

> There remained the question whether the offence was anything
> short of murder. . . . It was very difficult for the law to recognise
> it as anything else. On the other hand, however, he could not say
> that it was beyond the province of the jury to find a verdict of
> culpable homicide if they thought that was the nature of the
> offence. The chief circumstances for their consideration with this
> in mind were
> 1st, the unpremeditated and sudden nature of the attack;
> 2nd, the prisoner's habitual kindness to his wife; of which there
> could be no doubt, when drink did not interfere;
> 3rd, there was only one stab or blow; this while not perhaps like
> what an insane man would have done, was favourable for the
> prisoner in other respects;
> 4th, the prisoner appeared not only to have been peculiar in his
> mental constitution, but to have had his mind weakened by
> successive attacks of disease. It seemed highly probable that he had
> had a stroke of the sun in India, and that his subsequent fits were
> of an epileptic nature. There could be no doubt that he had had
> repeated attacks of *delirium tremens*, and if weakness of mind could
> be an element in any case in the question between murder and
> culpable homicide, it seemed difficult to exclude that element
> here.
> His Lordship had anxiously considered that question, and had come
> to the conclusion that the element was not inadmissible. Culpable
> homicide, in our law and practice, included what in some countries
> was called 'murder with extenuating circumstances'. Sometimes
> the crime of culpable homicide approached the very verge of
> murder; and sometimes it was a very minor offence. The state of
> mind of a prisoner might, his Lordship thought, be an extenuating
> circumstance, although not such as to warrant an acquittal on

ground of insanity; and he could not therefore exclude it from the consideration of the jury here, along with the whole other circumstances, in making up their minds whether, if responsible to the law at all, the prisoner was to be held guilty of murder or of culpable homicide.[15]

The Scots have an almost superstitious reverence for the effects of alcohol, particularly when these are associated with Hogmanay, and the jury took only half an hour to agree upon the course which Lord Deas had unmistakably pointed out to them. Dingwall was found guilty of culpable homicide, and sentenced to ten years' penal servitude.

The effect of Lord Deas' innovation was to achieve by means of the jury's verdict what had normally been left to the royal prerogative of mercy – the substitution of a lesser penalty than death. We have seen in chapter 7 how a similar result was brought about in England in cases of infanticide, although it took legislation to do so. To innovate in this way by mere judicial guidance to the jury would have been unthinkable in contemporary England, with its statutory definition of murder and its equally precise test of criminal insanity. In Scotland, where the M'Naghten Rules were merely interesting news, and the boundary between murder and culpable homicide was less clearly defined by statute and precedent, it was less remarkable.

Certainly neither Lord Deas nor his colleagues seem to have had misgivings about his expedient. Deas himself continued to steer juries into similar verdicts until he retired in 1887, and his fellow judges followed his example.[16] By 1909, if not earlier, the phrase 'diminished responsibility' – which, as we have seen, had been used in Bell's description of Braid's case – was being used by judges.[17] Occasionally the simple-minded jury failed to appreciate the subtlety of the solution which they were being offered. In the case of Miss Abercrombie, a servant girl who had killed her illegitimate baby after a difficult birth, the medical evidence did not really support a verdict of insanity, and the judge, emphasising this, hinted at a verdict of culpable homicide: the jury, however, acquitted her as insane.[18]

But by the nineteen-thirties the stage had been reached at which the defence of insanity was rarely offered in a Scots court to a charge of murder. Either the accused was found 'insane in bar of trial' or he pleaded diminished responsibility. Moreover, the Lord Advocate seems to have been willing to accept medical evidence of diminished responsibility and reduce the charge itself to culpable homicide. Thus in practice almost all the cases which forced the jury to weigh the accountability of the accused in the light of his mental state were those in which the Lord Advocate's Crown Office was not satisfied that responsibility *had* been diminished.

Until recently it has been a disputed question whether the defence was confined to murder or could be offered to other charges. Lord Keith and Professor T. B. Smith have argued from some Victorian cases[19] that it was not restricted to murder; but in the cases which they cite it was used as the basis of a plea *in mitigation of punishment* – that is, in the way described by Hume, and not as a plea intended to alter the nature of the charge. It is true that Lord Deas himself implied in one of these cases (M'Lean's) that

without being insane in the legal sense, so as not to be amenable
to punishment, a prisoner may yet labour under that degree of
weakness of intellect or mental infirmity which may make it both
right and legal to take that state of mind into account, not only in
awarding punishment, but in some cases even in considering
within what category of offences the crime shall be held to fall.

But it should be noted that the court of which he was the spokesman on
that occasion had been asked to consider only the sentence of an already
convicted man, so that the re-classification of his offence was not really in
issue.

What was probably the last word on this side-issue was uttered by the
Lord Justice General (Lord Clyde) in 1963. A man charged with causing
death by dangerous driving (and other offences connected with the accident) offered a special defence which the court seems to have taken for
one of diminished responsibility (although it seems more likely that it was
a misunderstood attempt to set up the quite different defence of automatism – see chapter 10). Lord Clyde ruled very firmly that

. . . diminished responsibility is a plea applicable to murder. It is
not open in the case of a lesser crime such as culpable homicide.[20]

Notes

1 See H. Arnot, *A Collection and Abridgement of Celebrated Criminal
   Trials in Scotland* 1536–1784, 11 (Edinburgh, 1833 ed.), pt. 2, 363.
2 Mackenzie, *The Laws and Customs of Scotland in Matters Criminal*,
   1678 ed. (London, 1674), pt. 1, tit. 1, section 8.
3 Matthaeus, *De Criminibus ad Lib.* XLVII *et* XLVIII *Dig. Commentarius* (Amsterdam, 1644), Prolegomena, Cap. 11, 6: 'sin quandoque
   furiosus fuerit, aut per intervalla furiat, in furore potius admissum
   crimen aestimabimus . . . quod furor sit morbus durabilis'.
4 'It is only a false calm, an interval, not a complete
   recovery of reason.'
5 'Once mad, ever the worse.' The Lowland Scots 'wood' or 'wud' is
   the descendant of the Anglo-Saxon 'wód', meaning 'mad'.
   Dingwall was known as 'the wud laird'.
6 'Who have a certain amount of awareness, though reduced.'
7 'Non exigas ab eo, quem fati infelicitas excusat, quicquam: furore
   ipso satis punitur', Digest 1, 18, 14.
8 J. C. Prichard, *On the Different Forms of Insanity in relation to
   Jurisprudence* (London, 1842), 178.
9 Sir Archibald Alison, *Principles of the Criminal Law in Scotland*
   (Edinburgh, 1832), 658.
10 Baron Hume, *Commentaries on the Law of Scotland respecting the
   description and Punishment of Crimes*, 1 (Edinburgh, 1797), ch. 1.
11 Alison, op. cit., (n9), 652.
12 Hume, loc. cit. (n10).
13 See Lord Keith's article, 'Some Observations on Diminished
   Responsibility' in (1959), 4, *Medico-Legal Journal* (Cambridge).

M

14 Although the report in Irvine shows that Lord Neaves went on circuit with Lord Deas, it does not make it clear that Lord Neaves assisted at this trial: it was common practice for two judges to go on circuit together at this time. It cannot therefore be inferred – as has been suggested – that Dingwall's case was regarded in advance as likely to make legal history.

15 HM Adv. v. Dingwall (1867), 5 Irvine 466.

16 See Lord Keith, loc. cit. (n13), and HM Adv. v. Granger (1878), 4 Coup. 86; HM Adv. v. Ferguson (1881), 4 Coup. 552; HM Adv. v. Brown (1882), 4 Coup. 596; HM Adv. v. Brown (1886), 1 White 93.

17 Lord Keith, loc. cit. (n13), says that he cannot find an earlier example of its use by a judge.

18 HM Adv. v. Abercrombie (1896), 2 Adam 163.

19 HM Adv. v. M'Lean (1876), 3 Coup. 334 (housebreaking); HM Adv. v. Wilson (1877), 3 Coup. 429 (firing hayricks); HM Adv. v. Small (1880), 4 Coup. 388 (theft); HM Adv. v. Fergusson (1894), 1 Adam 517 (fire-raising).

20 HM Adv. v. Cunningham (1963), J.C. 45: S.L.T. 345.

Chapter 9. **Diminished Responsibility Imported**

The advantage of the Scottish expedient over the defence of insanity lay not so much in the types or degrees of disorder which it could take into account, nor even in the less intellectual definition of what it could take into account, but in its fundamental logic. Whereas the English law allowed only two possibilities in the case of a man who was fit to stand trial – that he was or was not so insane as not to be accountable for his act or omission – the Scots allowed a third: that he was sufficiently disordered to deserve not complete exemption from the usual punishment but a mitigation of it.

The solution of an intermediate verdict had obvious attractions for English lawyers who chafed in the narrow harness of the M'Naghten Rules. We have seen how dissatisfied Lord Deas' English contemporary, Stephen, was with the Rules. Discussing cases in which self-control was weakened by insanity Stephen actually suggested that

> . . . the law ought . . . where madness is proved, to allow the
> jury to return any one of three verdicts: Guilty; Guilty, but his
> power of self-control was diminished by insanity; Not Guilty on
> the ground of insanity.[1]

Had his suggestion been adopted, the defence of diminished responsibility would have been introduced into English law about seventy years earlier than it was. As it turned out, no notice was taken of the suggestion. Not even the Atkin Committee or the two medical associations which gave evidence to it in 1922 seem to have considered it, although the Medico-Psychological Association's evidence was drafted by doctors who were aware of the Scottish system, for they instanced it to show that it was possible to do without a legally defined criterion of responsibility.

By the time of the Gowers Commission, however, the British Medical Association had broadened its criticisms, and urged that the 'oversimplification' of the English law should be remedied by introducing the plea of diminished responsibility as an alternative to the defence of insanity. They received not only support from Scottish psychiatrists (Drs Henderson and Yellowlees) and from the Institute of Psychoanalysis, but also the approval of a leading member of the English bench, Lord Denning, although, since the latter's written evidence did not deal with insanity, he was probably taken by surprise:

> . . . Would you be in favour of introducing that Scottish doctrine

into the law of England? – I should like to know how it works in
Scotland. If the juries apply it well in Scotland, all well and good.
My own doubt is whether it is too vague. Subject to that qualifi-
cation I should be in favour of introducing it. . . .[2]

Other witnesses opposed the idea firmly, among them the Royal Medico-Psychological Association, the redoubtable Sir Norwood East (doyen
of the prison medical service, and author of well-known texts on forensic
psychiatry), Dr Hopwood of Broadmoor, and Sir John Anderson, who
was probably the only man to have been both the chief civil servant at the
Home Office (1922–32) and later Home Secretary (1939–40). Anderson
thought it would be hard to draft a statutory definition of diminished
responsibility, and that in any case the use made of it in Scotland between
the wars had weakened the deterrent effect of capital punishment (an
argument for which he did not offer any evidence). The psychiatrists
thought that it would place too much responsibility on medical witnesses,
and would give rise to conflicting testimony which would confuse the
jury.

The Royal Commission's members included two Scots, Montgomery
(a Professor of Scots Law), and Mann (a Labour Member of Parliament),
and the former at least was a strong supporter of the doctrine. The majority,
however, were against its introduction, and the Commission came to the
rather awkward conclusion that 'although the Scottish doctrine of diminished responsibility works well in that country, we are unable to recommend its adoption in England'. (Would it be unfair to paraphrase this as
'We can hardly recommend its abolition in Scotland in the face of the
evidence, but not enough of us are in favour of introducing it in England'?)
In order to support this conclusion they had to reason rather more subtly
than their witnesses. They rejected most of the objections to diminished
responsibility (which would have led to the conclusion that it should be
abolished north of the Border) and relied on a somewhat formal argument.
If diminished responsibility were introduced into English law, it would
have to become part of the general law applying to offences other than
murder. But their terms of reference were restricted to the law of murder,
and they did not think 'that so radical an amendment of the law of England
would be justified for this limited purpose'. They took refuge in their
much more daring proposal that juries should be able to decide between
life and death sentences, taking into account extenuating circumstances
such as the mental state of the murderer.

The proposal to entrust the jury with such a decision was a most surprising one, coming from so conservative a body. It would have meant a
major innovation in the English sentencing system, which allots no official
part to the jury after they have convicted the accused (if one ignores the
recommendation to mercy). It would probably have discredited the distinction between capital and non-capital murders even sooner than did
the Homicide Act of 1957. Certainly this proposal was one of the most
criticised parts of their report. This apart, however, the argument against
the introduction of diminished responsibility was based on an obviously
faulty assumption: that this could not be done without making it part of

the general law. It is possible that the Commission were misled by Scottish witnesses who insisted that it was part of the general law of Scotland; historically, as we have seen, this was at best doubtful, and in practice certainly no longer true. In any case, there were already the analogies of provocation and infanticide to demonstrate that both common and statute law could modify criminal responsibility for homicide without affecting the general law.

Even had this not been so, that part of the argument which appeals to the Commission's terms of reference is also weak. Had the Commission been unanimously in favour of the proposal it could have defied this technicality as other Commissions and Committees have done in similar circumstances.

The fate of the Gowers Report has already been described in chapter 6. The Government, whose Ministers seem to have been as divided as Parliament on all the important issues, announced early in the next session (1955–6) that they could not accept any of the Commission's major recommendations. This was not because they had proposals of their own for amending the law: on the contrary, they were hoping to maintain the *status quo ante*. Thus, while they rejected the proposal to abrogate or at least amend the M'Naghten Rules, they also rejected the only other courses which the Commission had seriously considered – the giving of discretion to the jury and the introduction of diminished responsibility.

The Cabinet's unwillingness to propose any legislation provoked a group of their own supporters to take the initiative. The Inns of Court Conservative and Unionist Society appointed a committee of barristers and legally qualified Members of Parliament, under the chairmanship of Sir Lionel Heald, who had been the Conservative Government's Attorney-General until the year before. The Heald Committee produced a short, crisp report[3] which recommended changes in the law regarding provocation, constructive malice, accomplices, and the defence of insanity in trials for murder. Over the last of these they seem to have had great difficulty, for they sought advice from Dr Max Grünhut, the Oxford criminologist. Originally a continental lawyer, Grünhut was predisposed in favour of diminished responsibility, and after listening to his advice the Heald Committee consulted the Scottish Lord Advocate, then W.R.Milligan, QC. The outcome was that they recommended, instead of attempts to improve the M'Naghten Rules, the adoption of the Scottish expedient so far as murder was concerned, pointing out that it was no innovation to provide a special defence which was confined to a specific crime.

The Heald Report seems to have dislodged the Cabinet from its precarious seat on the fence, and in the House of Commons' debate which took place in the month after its publication the Home Secretary (Gwilym Lloyd George) indicated that the Government were seriously reconsidering their attitude to diminished responsibility:

> It may be illogical to confine diminished responsibility to murder,
> but that objection does not seem to me to be conclusive. Murder
> is *sui generis* because the penalty is death. I am not clear that,
> were it thought right on other grounds to introduce a special

defence of diminished responsibility in respect of murder, it would
be wrong to do so without also introducing it in relation to quite
different offences for which the penalty is not death. . . .[4]

Later in the debate Mr Butler (then Leader of the House) gave a rather
odd example of the sort of doubts that were still worrying the Government:

. . . it would be very difficult to translate this practice into English
law if only for one reason: in Scotland the jury act by majority.
I am bringing out these facts because I have made it my business
to try to master the subject as best I can in order to show that
there will be difficulty in this respect. . . .[5]

His reasoning is not easy to follow. Why should it be easier for a system
which accepted majority verdicts from juries to avail itself of diminished
responsibility? Were English juries more likely to fail to reach agreement
over the application of this test than over the application of the M'Naghten
Rules?

The credit for resolving such doubts as these should probably go to the
Lord Chancellor of that period, Lord Kilmuir, a Scottish member of the
English Bar. Certainly this is the straightforward interpretation of a phrase
which he let drop in the House of Lords ('. . . when I made up my mind
that the Scottish doctrine of diminished responsibility could be introduced
into English law . . .')[6]

However that may be, when the Government published its Homicide
Bill later in the year it contained a clause providing for a defence of
diminished responsibility. The meat of the clause lay in the first sub-
section:

Where a person kills or is a party to the killing of another, he shall
not be convicted of murder if he was suffering from such
abnormality of mind (whether arising from a condition of arrested
or retarded development of mind or any inherent causes or induced
by disease or injury) as substantially impaired his mental responsibility for his acts or omissions in doing or being a party to the
killing.

The following subsections provided that it was for the defence to raise this
issue, and that if the defence were successful in doing so the accused became liable to be convicted of manslaughter (just as in Scotland he would
be convicted of culpable homicide). The effect of this (which was not
stated in the Bill) would be to free the judge from the necessity of pronouncing sentence of death (or life imprisonment if the murder belonged
to the new category of 'non-capital murder') and to allow him a choice
between life imprisonment, imprisonment for a specified term, a fine, a
probation order, or an absolute or conditional discharge. Indeed, if the
necessary medical evidence were forthcoming at the stage when he was
considering sentence, he could commit him to a mental hospital, but was
not compelled to do so as he would have been by a verdict of 'guilty but
insane'.

The attempts to amend this clause during its passage through Parliament were not very determined, and the Attorney-General and Lord

Chancellor successfully resisted them. It was of course the words in parentheses which gave rise to most discussion. Scots judges had employed phrases such as 'weakness of mind' (Deas in Dingwall's case), 'aberration of mind', 'unsoundness of mind', 'a state of mind bordering on, though not amounting to, insanity' (Alness in Savage's case),[7] 'partial insanity', 'great peculiarity of mind' (Moncrieff in Muir's case),[8] 'infirmity or aberration of mind or impairment of intellect' (Cooper in Braithwaite's case).[9] The English draftsmen deliberately chose the widest possible term, 'abnormality', and then proceeded to qualify it by listing the ways in which it might be caused. In doing so, they followed very closely the words of the definition of 'mental defectiveness' in the Mental Deficiency Act of 1927, which read '. . . a condition of arrested or *incomplete* development of mind existing before the age of eighteen years whether arising from inherent causes or induced by disease or injury'. In the 1957 version 'retarded' has been substituted for 'incomplete', and the requirement that the condition should have existed before the age of eighteen has been omitted, since it would have excluded conditions which were not classified by psychiatrists as 'mental defectiveness'.

On the other hand, the parenthesis was obviously meant to limit the scope of the defence to states of mind which were recognised as pathological by psychiatrists or neurologists – that is, to what might be described as 'casualties' – as distinguished from states which were abnormal in other ways (for example, as a result of extreme religious or political views). At the Committee stage in the House of Commons Mr Silverman proposed that the phrase should be amended so as to read 'abnormality of mind (however arising)'. He himself gave no clear example of the sort of case which might otherwise be excluded, but his supporters instanced people who were partners in suicide pacts, or who were merely 'simple' without suffering from 'arrested or retarded development of mind'. However that might be, it was pointed out that their amendment would include murderers who were merely possessed of exceptionally bad tempers; and the amendment was not accepted. Another unsuccessful proposal of the abolitionists would have shifted the onus of proof from the defence to the prosecution.

In the upper house, Lord Chorley made a mild attempt to widen the meaning of abnormality of mind, and also moved a more interesting amendment which would have made detention during Her Majesty's pleasure the automatic result of a successful defence under this clause. His object was to eliminate the possibility of a fixed sentence of imprisonment, after two thirds of which a man could claim his freedom although he might still be regarded by the authorities as dangerous. This was rejected by Lord Kilmuir on the grounds that there would also be cases in which the accused had virtually recovered by the time of trial, and in which it would be unduly severe to deprive the judge of discretion. He seems to have assumed that Her Majesty's advisors would not act with sufficient speed and flexibility to deal suitably with such cases.

A linguistic feature of the statutory definition which is worth some notice is the way in which it refers to 'mental responsibility' as if responsibility were a quality of the mind. It is something which can be 'impaired', a word which modern usage applies to intelligence, memory, hearing, and sight. Compare this with the use of 'responsible' in the Trial of Lunatics Act of 1883, where the question is whether the accused is 'insane so as not to be responsible according to law for his actions'. There 'responsibility' clearly refers to the legal position of the accused and can be paraphrased as 'accountability'. The same is true of Lord Deas' usage in Dingwall's case, where he glances at the question whether the accused was 'responsible to the law at all. . . .' But in section 2 of the Homicide Act it does not make sense to paraphrase 'mental responsibility' as 'mental accountability' or 'answerability', for in our usage it is the individual as a whole, not his 'mind' which is accountable or answerable. The change was not of course a sudden innovation on the part of the draftsmen of the bill. The transition from one meaning to the other can be observed in the language of Scots judges. In 1923 Lord Alness was still using 'diminished responsibility' in the older sense: 'the prisoner . . . must be only partially accountable . . .' But in 1939 Lord Normand, in Kirkwood's case, twice used the phrase 'impaired responsibility', and once the phrase '. . . mental weakness, or weakness of responsibility . . .'[10] If these two Lords Justice General were representative, the shift of meaning took place in Scotland between the wars.

The transition is interesting because it illustrates the way in which a new concept may be formed. In the period from Deas to Alness the doctrine was simply that certain states of mind could justify a court in holding that an offender did not deserve the full punishment for his offence. There could be more than one such state of mind: let us call them A, B, C, etc.: the doctrine gave them no collective name, and did not assume that they had anything in common. But for Lord Normand and the draftsmen of the bill the doctrine seems to go one step further and imply that such states (diverse as their causes might be) do have something in common – an impairment of some *mental* faculty which is called 'responsibility'. What began as a term for a man's penal status had become a psychological concept, although not one that scientific psychologists recognise. It is probable that the English judges would have had – or professed – fewer difficulties over the interpretation of this section if the draftsmen had avoided this usage.

The Act received the Royal Assent in March 1957, and a month later the new defence was offered for the first time.[11] Shirley Campbell, a 21-year-old coloured mill girl, had been asked by her married friend to sit with her baby one evening while the friend and her husband went to the cinema. The baby's crying annoyed Miss Campbell, who seems also to have had a grudge against its mother over some unpaid debts; she strangled it and went quietly home to her lodgings. The two psychiatrists called by the defence testified that she was of low intelligence, 'very unstable, impulsive, rather aggressive, sensitive about her colour . . . a girl with a gross personality defect . . . a psychopathic personality'. At least one of them also said that she was not within the scope of the M'Naghten Rules, but both thought her within the scope of section 2 of the new Act. No medical evidence was called to rebut this defence, and the judge himself said to the jury 'You may think – and I don't mind telling you I would think so in your place – that this case comes within that section. . . .' The jury took nine minutes to agree, and she was sentenced to life imprisonment.

The relationship between the old and the new defences gave rise to disagreement. There were cases in which the accused pleaded diminished responsibility yet was considered by the Crown to be the sort of person who ought to be committed to a mental hospital during Her Majesty's pleasure. But should the Crown be allowed to attempt to persuade the jury that the proper verdict was 'guilty but insane'? In Bastian's case[12] Mr Justice Donovan ruled that they could, in spite of the arguments of defence counsel, Mr F.H.Lawton, QC. But counsel had his revenge a few years later, when, after his elevation to the bench, he ruled the opposite in Price's case.[13] His reasoning was interesting, for it illustrated the extent to which the law was still hypnotised by the fiction that a verdict of 'guilty but insane' was an acquittal (see chapter 11). Lawton argued first that it would be paradoxical that the prosecution should ask for an acquittal. Second, that if they succeeded the accused would be deprived of the right to appeal, again because the verdict was treated as an acquittal (this had been true since 1914, and was not Lawton's fault). Third, that in any case Parliament had not said in the Act that the prosecution could do this (a curious argument, since most procedural matters of this sort are determined by the courts themselves).

It was obviously undesirable, however, that a combination of defence tactics and such reasoning should prevent the court from arriving at the verdict which seemed to them to fit the medical evidence, and the Criminal Law Revision Committee's report of 1963[14] recommended that it should be made clear by statute that whether the accused offered a defence of insanity or diminished responsibility the prosecution should be allowed to adduce or elicit evidence in favour of the other verdict. The prosecution's right to bring evidence in favour of diminished responsibility when the accused was pleading insanity had been recognised in Nott's case[15] and had not subsequently been challenged; but it was thought best to deal with it too in the statute. Ironically, this was the very report which recommended that 'guilty but insane' should be replaced by the older wording which pretended to be an acquittal (see chapter 11). These and other minor amendments were made in the Criminal Procedure (Insanity) Act of 1964.

There were other false starts. In a substantial number of cases the reports which the defence and the prosecution obtained from psychiatrists were unanimous that the responsibility of the accused had been substantially impaired by abnormality of mind; and the prosecution were inclined to allow the defence to plead not guilty to murder but guilty to manslaughter by virtue of section 2 of the Homicide Act, without themselves challenging the defence. At first the courts insisted that the decision between murder and manslaughter must be left to the jury, and the prosecution were obliged to cross-examine the defence's psychiatric witnesses without having any evidence to offer in rebuttal. By the end of 1963, however, it was apparent that the judges were no longer insisting on what was more or less a formality, and in the following year no less than 30 out of 41 such pleas were openly accepted by the Crown, although it was not unheard of for a judge to insist on hearing the psychiatric evidence, perhaps to assist him in deciding on sentence.

The judges were also unsure how much assistance they should give to the jury in interpreting the section. Ten months after the passing of the Act, when summing up in Spriggs' case[16] Mr Justice Jones simply handed the text of the section to the jury and left them to puzzle it out for themselves. Spriggs appealed on the ground that the jury should have had more help from the judge, but in the Court of Criminal Appeal Lord Goddard said 'I cannot see that a judge . . . can do more than call the attention of the jury to the exact terms of the section. . . .' In the following year, however, Mr Justice Paull in Walden's case[17] not only gave the jury the text of the section but added that it was meant to cover the man who was 'walking on the borderline between being sane and insane'. The jury decided that Walden did not come within this interpretation, and Walden appealed. In view of Lord Goddard's dictum in Spriggs' case the appellant's argument that the judge should not have added what he did could hardly fail; but fail it did. Lord Goddard was no longer presiding over the Court of Criminal Appeal, and Mr Justice Hilbery explained that the decision in Spriggs' case did not mean that the judge was not entitled, if he wished, to illustrate what the section meant! (Walden was therefore hanged.) As we shall see, it had in fact become quite common for the judge to interpret the words of the section to the jury. By 1964 the Court of Criminal Appeal had completed its swing, and dealt very sharply with Mr Justice Paull in Gomez' case[18]. Paull was by then taking the original line that: '. . . it is for the jury to say what it means. They can use their brains just as well as I can use mine on this section' (after which he appears to have read it to them without even giving them a copy). The Court of Criminal Appeal criticised this strongly, and called it 'a non-direction'.

As to what the section did mean, some judges were at first as restrictive as they could be. In this they were certainly encouraged by the Crown, who argued in Spriggs' case that 'mind' meant 'intelligence', a view for which counsel found more support in the Oxford Dictionary than in legal or psychological texts. Since the judge was determined not to offer his own interpretation of the section he did not warn the jury against this one, and since the Court of Criminal Appeal upheld his caution they did not challenge it either.

Slightly less restrictive was Mr Justice Paull's suggestion to the jury in Walden's case that 'abnormality of mind' meant a state on the 'borderline' of insanity within the sense of the M'Naghten Rules. Since this had some support from the *dicta* of Scots judges, and was not contradicted on appeal, it seems to have been followed for a time by some judges, for example by the Chief Justice of the Bahamas in Rose's case.[19] But in 1960 Byrne's case[20] at last elicited a considered interpretation from the Court of Criminal Appeal under the new Lord Chief Justice, Lord Parker.

Patrick Byrne was a 27-year-old Irish labourer. In December 1959 one of the girls in a YMCA hostel at Birmingham discovered him peeping in at her window. He burst into her room, strangled her, and indulged in perverted sexual behaviour with her body, which he also mutilated. He might never have been caught had he not voluntarily given himself up to the police some weeks later. At his trial he pleaded diminished responsibility, and called medical witnesses who testified that he was a sexual psychopath, that is, a person suffering from violent perverted sexual desires which he finds difficult or impossible to control; that this was an abnormality of mind within the terms of the Act; but that when not under the influence of these desires he was normal. Mr Justice Stables told the jury that if Byrne killed his victim under an abnormal sexual impulse which was so strong that he found it difficult or impossible to control, but was otherwise normal, section 2 of the Homicide Act did not apply to him. The jury found Byrne guilty of non-capital murder, and Byrne appealed on the ground that they had been misdirected.

In the Court of Criminal Appeal the Lord Chief Justice – now Lord Parker – agreed that the jury had been misdirected, and gave what is now the accepted interpretation of 'abnormality of mind'. It is, he said:

. . . a state of mind so different from that of ordinary human beings that the reasonable man would term it abnormal. It appears to us to be wide enough to cover the mind's activities in all its aspects, not only the perception of physical acts and matters, and the ability to form a rational judgement as to whether the act was right or wrong, but also the ability to exercise will-power to control physical acts in accordance with that rational judgement.

Complete inability would clearly entitle Byrne to the benefit of this defence; difficulty in controlling his actions might entitle him, depending on the jury's estimate, on the balance of probabilities, as to whether the difficulty amounted to *substantial* impairment. The decision made no difference to Byrne, who was now to serve a 'life' sentence for manslaughter instead of non-capital murder: but for the courts it marked the end of a phase. Until this case judges had been left very much to their own devices so far as guidance to the jury had been concerned, and the Court of Criminal Appeal's policy appeared to be one of non-interference.

The courts now had an authoritative interpretation, which they could safely give to juries with no danger of being corrected on appeal. What is more, the interpretation was a wide one, 'wide enough to cover the mind's activities in all its aspects'. It made it clear, for example, that at last the defence could *openly* be based on so-called 'irresistible impulse', which had been outlawed since the nineteen-twenties. For the heart of Byrne's defence was that his abnormality substantially impaired his 'mental responsibility', not because he did not know what he was doing, nor because he did not know that it was wrong, but because he could not control his impulse.

Byrne's case also marked the stage at which it became plain that the English version of diminished responsibility was more generous to the accused than the original Scottish notion. The adopted child had outgrown its twin. Compare Lord Parker's interpretation in Byrne's case with Lord Cooper's in Braithwaite's case:

> You will see . . . the stress that has been laid in all these formulations upon weakness of intellect, aberration of mind, mental unsoundness, partial insanity, great peculiarity of mind and the like. . . . To carry the matter just a stage further in view of the evidence that we had from Dr Robertson and Dr Harrowes, *I am going to take the responsibility of telling you, in so many words, that it will not suffice in law, for the purpose of this defence of diminished responsibility merely to show that an accused person has a very short temper, or is unusually excitable and lacking in self-control. The world would be a very convenient place for criminals and a very dangerous place for other people, if that were the law.* It must be much more than that. . . .[21]

Although that was said in 1945, the words which I have italicised were still being quoted with approval in 1963 by Lord Wheatley in the case of Burnett, a psychopathically hot-tempered man who had murderously attacked both his mistress and her husband when they showed signs of becoming reconciled.[22] In view of what Cooper said about lack of self-control, Byrne's appeal would probably have been unsuccessful in Scotland.

Moreover, as we shall see in volume II, 'psychopathy' is accepted in an English court as an abnormality of mind which *may* substantially impair responsibility, but in no Scottish case has this yet happened. Both Carraher, who was tried in 1938,[23] and Burnett, tried in 1963, were called psychopathic by their medical witnesses, and both failed to establish defences of diminished responsibility. It can be argued, of course, that the cases in which Scottish psychiatrists used the term 'psychopathic' (with which they are more sparing than their English colleagues) were less convincing than cases such as Byrne, and that no Scottish court has said that 'psychopathic disorder' can never be the basis for this defence. Moreover, it is relevant that the Secretary of State for Scotland did not recommend a reprieve for Burnett, which he would presumably have done had there been strong grounds for questioning his responsibility at the time of his act.

It could be a mistake, however, to infer that it was the ruling of the Court of Criminal Appeal in Byrne's case which made the English interpretation so much wider than the Scots'. Such an inference would assume that before Byrne's case all judges had been as cautious as Jones, J. or as restrictive as Stable, J. The cases which figure in the law reports are far from typical; they are those in which a new point of procedure or interpretation is raised. As for the Court of Criminal Appeal, it never deals with a case in which the defence succeeds. If the cases in the reports make legal history it is a one-sided sort of history. In 1958, for example, while a handful of cases such as Bastian's, Spriggs', and Matheson's were being noted in law reports and discussed in legal journals, there were altogether 27 successful defences of diminished responsibility, the great majority of which were reported only in the daily press.

It is fairly certain that in the more typical cases it was not the judge's summing-up but the psychiatric evidence which was decisive. If the medical evidence was all in favour of the defence a jury which rejected it would have their verdict quashed by the Court of Criminal Appeal, as that court declared as early as March 1958.[24] It is true that even if the medical witnesses were unanimously unfavourable to the accused the jury were still free to find in his favour, and in at least one case they did: but such cases must have been exceptional. As for the case in which medical witnesses differ 'it is to the jury, after a proper direction by the judge, that the decision . . . is entrusted'.[25] In other words, the jury – and therefore the judge – come into their own only where the psychiatrists disagree.

We do not, unfortunately, know how often this happened. But we have a valuable analysis by Lady Wootton of the medical evidence and other information about the first 73 cases in which this defence was offered – a series extending from April 1957 to June 1959.[26]

Her study showed what a wide variety of conditions were accepted by juries as satisfying the definition in the Act. In no fewer than 53 of these cases the defence succeeded at the trial itself; in two others the accused was found 'guilty but insane'; and in two more the Court of Criminal Appeal substituted a conviction for manslaughter on the grounds of diminished responsibility.[27] In other words, about three in every four such defences succeeded in one way or another; an observation which demonstrates how exceptional were the cases which made law.

Indeed, Lady Wootton found it difficult to put her finger on the characteristics which had differentiated the successful from the unsuccessful cases. Eventually she concluded that 'so far as juries are concerned . . . a previous history of mental disorder is the type of evidence most likely to prove convincing'. Even so, there was a case in which a man charged with capital murder succeeded in this defence in the face of two medical opinions to the contrary and in the absence of any history of mental instability.

Even in the majority of cases in which the medical evidence favoured diminished responsibility, the grounds on which it was based were varied in the extreme:

In most of the medical reports in which diagnosis of diminished responsibility is reached, reference will be found to 'emotional immaturity', 'mental instability' or 'psychopathic personality'. . . Yet if we . . . ask by what kind of evidence is the presence of emotional immaturity, mental instability or psychopathic personality established, the answers are wide-ranging. . . . An 'abnormal' state of despair induced by the need to care for an imbecile child or by a diagnosis of cancer in a beloved relative, leading in each case to a 'mercy killing': a 'reactive depressed state' associated with the breaking of an engagement or the discovery of unfaithfulness in a spouse: 'mixed emotions of depression, disappointment and exasperation' causing a 'lack of control' over the defendant's actions in similar circumstances: inability to hold down a job: even an attempt at suicide *after* the commission of the offence . .

all these have been adduced as at least contributory evidence of diminished responsibility.[26]

It was tempting to infer from these observations – as Lady Wootton at first did – that the Homicide Act had flung wide the half-closed door by which the mentally abnormal could escape conviction for murder. But the statisticians soon showed that its effect was neither as spectacular nor as simple as this. Gibson and Klein[28] compared the percentages of murderers committed for trial who benefited from the loopholes of 'insanity on arraignment', 'guilty but insane', or 'diminished responsibility' in the years immediately before and after the Act, and drew attention to the startling fact that in both periods the combined percentages totalled very much the same. A comparison which extends over a longer period confirms their observation, as figure 2 shows. This diagram is based on the Criminal Statistics from 1946 to 1963. It shows sliding three-year averages (i.e. the percentage shown for 1947 is the average percentage for 1946, 1947, and 1948); and is based on persons committed for trial for murder in those calendar years. Gibson and Klein's figures are for a shorter period, are not averaged, and group murderers according to the year of the homicide. But the same picture emerges.

Two separate trends are discernible. First, there has been the recent reduction – to be discussed in chapter 14 – in 'murderers'[29] who escaped trial altogether by reason of insanity. This was compensated by the gradual increase in the percentage of 'murderers' who were found 'guilty but insane'. But as soon as the defence of diminished responsibility became available, this percentage too began to fall. The steady fall in both findings of 'insane on arraignment' and findings of 'guilty but insane' has been compensated by verdicts of 'diminished responsibility', *but no more*. These trends suggest that section 2 of the Homicide Act has done no more than take over the sort of case which previously would have been accepted by courts as within the M'Naghten Rules.

This takeover has been most obvious in trials for capital murder, when a defence of insanity has been almost completely replaced by the new defence, although the former is still not quite unheard of in trials for non-capital murder (and occasionally, of course, in trials for other non-capital

TABLE 5. 'Murderers' committed for trial (with successful defences of insanity in brackets)

	for capital murder	for non-capital murder
1957 (after the Homicide Act)	7 (none)	44 (3)
1958	11 (1)	50 (6)
1959	11 (4)	63 (11)
1960	18 (none)	68 (9)
1961	15 (none)	73 (5)
1962	4 (none)	62 (8)
1963	6 (none)	59 (2)
1964	8 (none)	72 (1)
1965 (before suspension of death penalty)	17 (none)	51 (1)

FIGURE 2. 'Murderers' found 'guilty but insane', 'insane on arraignment', or of diminished responsibility, 1947—63

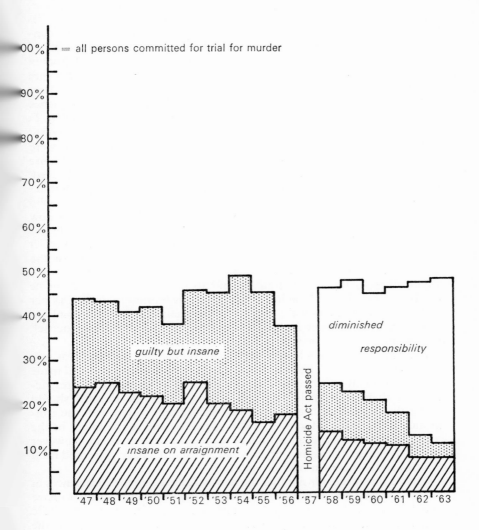

Percentages are shown as sliding three-year averages for 1946—8. They are also shown cumulatively: thus in 1946—8 the percentages found 'insane on arraignment' or 'guilty but insane' *together* averaged 44 per cent.

offences). Although the Criminal Statistics show only successful defences of insanity, we know[30] that unsuccessful defences are uncommon. The figures are therefore a fairly reliable indication of the rarity with which it is offered in capital cases (see Table 5). Clearly counsel is readier to attempt a defence of insanity when the consequence of failure is not the death sentence.

Indeed, at first sight it is surprising that counsel should still think the defence of insanity worth attempting even in trials for non-capital murder. If it is easier to show on the evidence that a client is suffering from diminished responsibility, why embark on the more difficult task of convincing a judge and jury that he did not know the nature and quality of his act, or did not know that it was wrong? The answer is probably that in those cases in which they did attempt this counsel wanted to make sure that their clients were sent to a hospital and not to prison. For, at least until the Mental Health Act 1959 came into operation,[31] the consequence of a successful defence of diminished responsibility was imprisonment in all but a handful of cases. Of the 100 diminished responsibility cases dealt with in that period (March 1957 to November 1960) all but eight were given prison sentences, most of them for 'life' or long fixed terms of more than three years. (Most of the lucky eight were put on probation.) Indeed, it is hardly unfair to say that the only unmistakable change in penal practice which resulted from the new defence was that some murderers who would presumably have been committed to mental hospitals were now sent to prison instead. Consequently, in a case in which his client's life was not at risk counsel had something to gain by attempting to obtain a verdict of insanity, which would allow the judge no choice but to entrust the accused to Her Majesty's pleasure and a mental hospital.

Nevertheless, the swing from the old to the new defence cannot be wholly accounted for by capital cases, which are a minority (about 15 per cent) of those committed for trial. The explanation must lie not only in the tactical attractions of diminished responsibility for defending counsel, but also in the preferences of medical witnesses.

Their preference for a looser label than 'M'Naghten madness' was not, of course, surprising. The evidence to the Gowers Commission had made it clear that many psychiatrists felt the Rules to be so excessively restrictive that they made their own minds up whether the accused should escape the death sentence and testified accordingly, often with the connivance of the judge. Moreover, however precise and subtle might be the examination and cross-examination of the medical witnesses, and however correct the judge's summing-up, the issue must often have presented itself to juries as 'Is this man mad or isn't he?'

What is unexpected is not that the new defence eased the consciences of judges, counsel, and psychiatrists in this way, but that it seems to have done little more than this. Surely 'murderers' like Byrne would not have been found insane before 1957? If so, why have they not added to the total percentage of 'murderers' who are found to be abnormal in one way or another? Have such cases, though prominent in the law reports, been so exceptional that they have not noticeably affected the statistics? The answer may be that they are just beginning to be numerous enough to make their effect noticeable: for as figure 2 shows, the overall percentage seems to have been climbing very gradually since 1960.

Even so, it is remarkable that between them defence counsel and psychiatrists did not make more use of their new freedom. The explanation is not that they did not try to do so, for – in the first fourteen months at least – they were unsuccessful in roughly one out of four cases in which they offered the defence.[32] Another possibility is that the Director of Public Prosecutions acted as a limiting factor by instructing his counsel to challenge this defence more often than they had challenged the defence of insanity. On the whole this is unlikely, for even in 1964, when the number of successful defences of diminished responsibility was higher than ever before, three out of four were cases in which the Director of Public Prosecutions had agreed not to oppose the defence, since he had no evidence that would justify him in doing so.[33]

There are more likely explanations, however. One is that prison medical officers functioned as a restraining influence. Nowadays the prison medical officer invariably furnishes the court, the defence and the Director of Public Prosecutions with a report on the mental state of prisoners accused of murder. If he is clearly of the opinion that the prisoner is within the scope of the M'Naghten Rules or of section 2 of the Homicide Act, the prosecution would not try to rebut such a defence. If his report were to the clear effect that the accused was outside the scope of these defences, he would almost certainly be called on to give rebutting evidence. The prison medical officers of the local prisons are therefore involved more often than any other psychiatrists in making up their minds whether the mental state of the accused was a ground for excusing him from the consequences of his act. Unlike most other psychiatrists, they have also to examine large numbers of accused and convicted persons who are mentally normal. Thus whereas psychiatrists in mental hospitals usually have to decide merely what disorder the patient is suffering from, and how severe it is, the prison medical officer has to decide first *whether any disorder is present*, and is doing so constantly.

A constant succession of decisions may well produce a capacity for consistency; and consistency may reach a point at which it becomes difficult for the decision-maker to adjust to a new criterion. It is not unlikely that this process has been at work among hard-worked medical officers of prisons, and accounts for the phenomenon which I am trying to explain.

But so long as it is possible for the defence to find psychiatrists who are prepared to testify to the impaired responsibility of the accused in the face of a sceptical prison medical officer, and so long as juries are inclined to favour the defence in disputed cases, the prison medical officer cannot be the only restraining factor. We must suppose that there is something in the nature of the cases which has prevented juries from accepting every disputed defence of diminished responsibility. The most likely possibility is suggested by Lady Wootton's observation that in her early sample the type of evidence which was most likely to convince juries was a history of

N

mental disorder before the crime. If so, we have only to suppose that the percentage of persons committed for trial for murder who had previously been recognised as disordered is fairly constant in order to explain the constancy shown by figure 2.

There are of course other features of the accused's crime or previous record which are likely to sway juries. For example, both before and after the Homicide Act a woman who killed her children and her husband never failed, if brought to trial, to escape conviction on grounds of mental abnormality. At the other end of the scale a man who kills in the course of a planned acquisitive crime will find juries sceptical of psychiatric evidence on his behalf (as Terry the bank robber did). A glance at Gibson and Klein's comparisons of murders in the six years 1955–60 [28] shows how constant, on the whole, have been such factors as the relationships between murderer and victim, the methods used, and the motives for the crime. The only marked exception to this was a sharp increase (from 7·6 per cent to 19·6 per cent) in the percentage of murders by men which were committed for gain: a change which might well have reduced the readiness of juries to entertain defences based on mental abnormality.

The suspension of the death penalty for murder in 1965, and its replacement by a mandatory sentence of imprisonment for 'life', has reduced, without eliminating, the incentive to plead diminished responsibility. The plea is no longer an escape from sentence of death; but it still has the function of liberating the court from a fixed penalty. What *would* reduce section 2 of the Homicide Act to desuetude would be legislation which allowed judges the same freedom in sentencing convicted murderers as they have in sentencing persons found guilty of attempted murder, manslaughter, or infanticide – a development which now seems less unlikely than it used to.

Was Lord Kilmuir's decision that Lord Deas' expedient should be forcibly introduced into the English law of murder a sound one, or was it, as Mr R.F.Sparks has argued in a trenchant article,[34] justified neither by theory nor by subsequent practice? So far as the theoretical justification is concerned, Sparks' argument is that mental disorder cannot be a logical reason for mitigating a man's punishment, only for excusing him from it altogether. This argument seems to be based on the rather old-fashioned view that a man either is or is not capable of conforming to the requirements of the criminal law in a particular situation, and that he cannot be in an intermediate state, although experience suggests that some people conform without seriously thinking of doing otherwise, others try to conform and succeed, others again try without succeeding, and some do not try at all. Admittedly the notion of an intermediate state is foreign to the traditional principle of English law that a man is either fully accountable for his act or not accountable at all (although there are exceptions even to this). But that does not make it either inconceivable or nonsensical from the point of view of retributive punishment. (Indeed, as we have seen, it had its origins in an essentially retributive view of penal measures.) If, on the other hand, the aim of the court's sentence is seen as the reformation of the offender and the protection of society, an expedient which allows the court to decide between psychiatric, custodial and supervisory measures for a mentally disordered offender makes more sense than one which compels the court to commit him to a mental hospital (as Mr Sparks himself would agree).

Sparks' objection to the way in which courts have actually used their sentencing powers in practice is a sounder one. Two-thirds of all diminished responsibility cases in the years 1957–62 went to prison, one-third for fixed terms, one-third for 'life'. But since his article was written this picture has changed. In 1964 and 1965, out of 70 men and 18 women who were dealt with under section 2 of the Homicide Act, only 27 men and 2 women were imprisoned: two thirds have sunk to one third. Even that fraction may, of course, have been too high: but this could be argued only on a close examination of each case. What is still hard to defend – except as part of a retributive tariff – is the fixed-term prison sentence which is still imposed in a handful of such cases each year.

The two most relevant features of our present position, however, seem to be these. On the one hand we have a penal system which provides a fixed penalty for murder (formerly death, now 'life'). On the other hand we have mental abnormalities which seem to conduce to murder, not all of them such as will respond to psychiatric care or treatment. In this situation an expedient which sets the court free to choose between psychiatric, custodial, or supervisory measures seems preferable to the traditional one which automatically excludes all but psychiatric measures.

Notes

1 J. F. Stephen, *History of the Criminal Law of England* 11 (London, 1883), 175. This was written before the Trial of Lunatics Act of 1883 altered the wording of the English verdict (see chapter 11).
2 Royal Commission on Capital Punishment, Minutes of Evidence, Day 9 (1950), HMSO.
3 *Murder: some suggestions for the reform of the law relating to murder in England* (Inns of Court Conservative and Unionist Society; Crawley, 1956).
4 Hansard (Commons) for 16 February 1956, cols. 2553–4.
5 Ibid., col. 2642.
6 Hansard (Lords) for 7 March 1957, col. 358.
7 HM Adv. v. Savage (1923), J.C. 49.
8 HM Adv. v. Muir (1933), J.C. 46.
9 HM Adv. v. Braithwaite (1945), S.C.(J.) 55.
10 HM Adv. v. Kirkwood (1939), J.C. 36.
11 See the *Yorkshire Post and Leeds Mercury* for 27 April 1957.
12 R. v. Bastian (1958), 42 Cr. App. R. 75.
13 R. v. Price (1963), 14 Cr. App. R. 21.
14 Criminal Law Revision Committee: Third Report: *Criminal Procedure and Insanity*, Cmnd. 2149 (HMSO, 1963).
15 R. v. Nott (1958), 43 Cr. App. R. 8 (circuit case).
16 R. v. Spriggs (1958), 42 Cr. App. R. 69.
17 R. v. Walden (1959), 43 Cr. App. R. 201.

18 R. v. Gomez (1964), 48 Cr. App. R. 310.

19 Rose v. R. (1961), 45 Cr. App. R. 102, P.C.

20 R. v. Byrne (1960), 44 Cr. App. R. 246.

21 HM Adv. v. Braithwaite (1945), S.C.(J.) 55.

22 The proceedings were, rather surprisingly, reported only in the press.

23 See G. Blake (ed.), *The Trials of Patrick Carraher* (London, 1951).

24 R. v. Matheson (1958), 42 Cr. App. R. 145.

25 The Court of Criminal Appeal in R. v. Jennion (1962), 46 Cr. App. R. 212.

26 See Baroness Wootton's 'Diminished Responsibility: a layman's view' in (1960), 76, *Law Quarterly Review*, 224; and *Crime and the Criminal Law* (London, 1963) for a less detailed analysis of a later series of cases. Since she had access to unpublished information from Home Office files she did not identify her cases by name.

27 These must have been the cases of Matheson (n24) and Dunbar (1958), 41 Cr. App. R., 182. In Dunbar's case the Court of Criminal Appeal did not take the view that the defence should have succeeded; they simply thought that the jury had been misdirected.

28 E. Gibson, and S. Klein, *Murder: a Home Office Research Unit Report* (HMSO, 1961).

29 The term 'murderers' is used, in inverted commas, as a less cumbersome way of referring to persons committed for trial on charges of murder.

30 For example, from the useful summary of trials for murder from 1957 to 1962 in *A Calendar of Murder* by T. Morris and L. Blom-Cooper (London, 1963). It is worth adding that juries were more likely to be generous to a desperate defence if the alternative was the death sentence, so that the unknown percentage of unsuccessful insanity defences was probably smaller in the case of capital murder charges than non-capital murder charges.

31 For its effect on the disposal of cases of diminished responsibility see volume II.

32 See Wootton, loc. cit. (n26).

33 I am indebted for this information to the Director of Public Prosecutions and his staff.

34 R. F. Sparks '"Diminished Responsibility" in theory and practice' in (1964), 27, *Modern Law Review*, 9.

Chapter 10. **Automatism and Drunkenness**

Very occasionally in the chronicles of the criminal law there appear references to a condition which has come to be known by the name of 'automatism'. In this condition, it is said, a person may perform apparently purposeful actions 'automatically', without being in conscious control of his bodily movements.

What this condition must be like is not easy for those who have not experienced it to conceive. We are familiar with states of unconsciousness, in which the central nervous system is doing no more than playing its part in the regulation of breathing and heart-beats, and is neither initiating nor controlling movements of the head, limbs, or torso. But in this condition the body engages in no activity of the kind which is normally regarded as 'purposeful'. Again, we have all experienced reflex actions, such as sneezing, or the blinking of an eye at a puff of wind. Certainly these take place without our volition, although they can sometimes be made to take place voluntarily, and with practice many can be prevented from taking place by conscious effort. Rather similar to reflex movements are spasmodic twitches of leg, arm, or face muscles, which, if very repetitive, are labelled 'tics'. But 'automatism' usually refers to more complex forms of behaviour.

It is sometimes applied by psychiatric textbooks to stereotyped movements which persist when they are no longer appropriate. These are commonest in elderly patients, especially in sufferers from the special form of cerebral degeneration known as Pick's disease. This form of automatism does not involve complex sequences of movements, so that it is only by rare accident that they lead to incidents which could conceivably form the basis of a criminal charge.

There are conditions, however, in which more complex sequences do take place. These are of a kind which are normally carried out with a purpose, and by a person who is paying some attention to what he is doing, but which seem to involve the person concerned in doing things which are quite inconsistent with his normal desires and behaviour, and of which he afterwards has no recollection, or only a faint and inaccurate memory.

The first of these conditions to be recognised was the comparatively frequent phenomenon of sleep-walking. Although this was described as early as classical times, and is mentioned briefly in most modern textbooks of psychiatry, most pronouncements on the subject are impressionistic and based on very little in the way of scientific observation. There is evidence that the brains of *some* sleep-walkers function abnormally.[1] On the other hand, the popular belief that the sleep-walker is deeply asleep is denied by Oswald, the experimental psychologist of sleep, who says that 'there is no reason to suppose that even the genuine sleep-walker's cerebral cortex is functioning at a level of vigilance lower than drowsiness. The essence of this disorder is almost certainly disorientation while preoccupied'.[2] Whatever this state may be, it seems to be one in which a fear, an anxiety or a hostility which the sleep-walker might or might not acknowledge in his normal waking moments may be manifested in words or deeds.

Nowadays this abnormality is dismissed by most textbooks as a transient and unimportant disturbance of childhood:

> Children who cry out or talk in their sleep often sleep-walk too:
> and there is a connection between somnambulism and night terrors.
> For all these symptoms a subsequent amnesia is the rule; but
> unlike the child with *pavor nocturnus* the typical sleep-walker shows
> *little sign of affect*, walks slowly and deliberately, and engages in
> no dramatic action. Although perception is reduced or narrowed
> he seems to find his way and avoid objects. . . .[3]

Although the authors of this textbook say that the typical sleep-walker 'engages in no dramatic action', it has for long been recognised that occasionally he may do someone serious injury. As early as 1313 the Council of Vienne was responsible for a resolution to the effect that if a child, a madman, or a sleeper killed or injured someone he was not to be held culpable. This is recorded by the sixteenth-century Spanish canonist Diego de Covarrubias (1512–77), who explains that the act of a sleeper is not of itself a sin, unless in his waking state he deliberately arranges matters so that he will commit the act in his sleep. Covarrubias instances two possible sins, nocturnal pollution by the emission of semen, and killing or harming of another human being:

> It follows of course . . . that a person who was asleep at the time
> of the homicide is not at fault, for the obvious reason that he was
> asleep when he killed his victim; such a one lacks understanding
> and reason, and is like a madman. . . . For this reason the misdeed
> of a sleeper is not punished, unless it so happens that in his
> waking state he knew very well that in his sleep he would seize
> weapons and attack people. For then if he did not take care to
> prevent himself from doing harm in his sleep to someone, certainly
> he should be punished, although not in the usual way. . . .[4]

Later Continental jurists made other exceptions. Matthaeus[5] thought that the mother who killed her child by overlying it in her sleep should not be completely excused, because she should have known that it was dangerous to sleep so close to it. He also thought that punishment – though not the full punishment – was deserved by the sleep-walker who killed someone if in his waking state he harboured enmity against that person – a doctrine which seems to be based on an almost psychoanalytic insight into the sleep-walker's behaviour, although the jurists' reason for laying it down was probably the ease with which sleepwalking could be offered as an excuse in such circumstances. English lawyers were sufficiently insulated from their Continental contemporaries from the fourteenth century onward to prevent the importation of this 'defence'; but in Scotland Mackenzie was influenced by Matthaeus on this as on other points:

Such as commit any crime whilst they sleep, are compared to Infants . . . and therefore they are not punisht, except they be known to have Enmity against the person killed; or that Fraud be otherways presumable: *quo casu* they may be punisht *extra ordinem* [i.e. more lightly].[6]

That such crimes must have occurred very occasionally can be inferred from modern cases: Simon Fraser could have battered his baby to death as easily in the fifteenth as in the nineteenth century. That they were ignored by lawyers can be explained. As we shall see, the cases of Colonel Culpeper and Esther Griggs were recorded not by law reporters but by newswriters. In neither case did the outcome make legal history, in the first case because the jury's verdict was twisted into a special finding of insanity, in the second because the grand jury threw out the indictment before it came to trial. Even in Scotland Simon Fraser's case was regarded as very irregular, if not bad law; and Ritchie's case has now been disowned by the Lord-Justice General. As recently as 1961 Boshears' case was ignored by law reporters. For the lawyer these cases were either no news or bad news.

Colonel Cheyney Culpeper, whose trial occurred in 1686, ten years after Hale's death, was a brother of the quarrelsome Lord Culpeper. He seems to have been a 'famous dreamer', and in one of his dreams he shot not only a Guardsman on patrol but also his horse. At the Old Bailey his defence was that he had been asleep, and he produced nearly fifty witnesses to testify to the extraordinary things which he had done in this state. A contemporary newsletter[7] says that 'the jury at first brought it in manslaughter, but were sent out again, and considering that he might be distempered to do such a rash action found it special'. In other words, they returned a special verdict of manslaughter while he was insane. A few days later the Palace instructed the Chief Justice to forbear from putting the sentence into execution, and a few weeks later his pardon was signed.[8] The case was ignored in the contemporary law reports.

By the end of the eighteenth century the phenomena of 'mesmerism' and mesmeric trances had aroused popular interest in sleep and sleep-like states. In France words like 'somnambulism' and even 'vigilambulism' were coined. Popular psychiatrists such as Pagan and Winslow included somnambulists in their books; but when they came to crimes by somnambulists they had to borrow from continental authorities such as Marc and Georget. The two most overworked anecdotes in the literature of this period are the stories of the sleep-walking monk who stabbed his abbot's empty bed, and of Bernard Schedmaizig's attack on the man who aroused him from a bad dream (Schedmaizig's name became almost unrecognisably garbled by English printers). In a book called *The Philosophy of Sleep*, published in 1830, Robert Macnish revived the tale of Colonel Culpeper, but in an oversimplified version in which the colonel was acquitted. Daniel Tuke borrowed the story unaltered from Macnish for his book *Sleepwalking and Somnambulism* (1884); but neither book attracted the attention of lawyers. In 1853 at the Old Bailey a young servant girl called Sarah Minchin, who had stabbed one of her master's children in the small hours of the morning, offered a defence based on sleep-walking, but was not believed: and her case attracted no attention. Had she been tried a few years later she might have been more fortunate, for in 1862 an English psychiatric textbook for the first time described an example of violence committed by a sleep-walker that was at once indigenous, authenticated, and dramatic. This was the first revision of Bucknill and Tuke's well-known *Manual of Psychological Medicine*. These two celebrated asylum superintendents had evidently kept their eyes on the newspapers when preparing their second edition, for they noticed that in January 1859 a woman called Esther Griggs had been charged at Marylebone Police Court in unusual circumstances. The constable, Sergeant Simmons, who had been virtually an eye-witness of her actions, gave evidence:

> At half-past one o'clock this morning, while on duty in East Street, Manchester Square, I heard a female voice – 'Oh, my children! save my children!' I went to the house, No. 71, from whence the cries proceeded, and the landlord opened the door. I went upstairs, accompanied by two other constables, and while making our way to the first front room I heard the smashing of glass. I knocked at the door, which I found was fastened, and said, 'Open it; the police are here.' The prisoner, who was in her nightdress, kept on exclaiming, 'Save my children!' and at length, after stumbling over something, let me and my brother officers in. When we entered we found the room in total darkness, and it was only by the aid of our lanterns that we could distinguish anything in the room. On the bed was a child five years old, and another three years of age by her side. Everything in the place was in great confusion. She kept on crying out, 'Where's my baby? Have they caught it? I must have thrown it out of the window!' The baby must have been thrown out as I was going up stairs, for before getting into the room I heard something fall. I left a constable in charge of the prisoner, and I ascertained that the child, which had been thrown from the window, had been taken to the infirmary. *She told me that she had been dreaming that her little boy had said that the house was on fire, and that what she had done was with the view of preserving her children from being burnt to death.* I have no doubt that if I and the other constable had not gone to the room, all three of the children would have been flung out into the street. . . . From the excited state in which the prisoner was I did not at the time take her into custody. I had understood that the surgeon had said it was a species of nightmare which the prisoner was labouring under when the act was committed. The window had not been thrown up. The child was thrust through a pane of glass, the fragments of which fell into the street.[9]

She was saved from going to trial by the grand jury, which refused to find a true bill against her. They were thus in effect acquitting her of responsibility for what she had undoubtedly done, a decision which strictly speaking should have been left to the petty jury at a proper trial: Baron Alderson had already refused to accept a similar decision from a grand jury which had been so impressed by evidence of a woman's insanity that it decided she should not go for trial.[10] As usual, the case did not reach the law reports.

The case which is usually regarded as the earliest example of the defence of sleep-walking in a British court eventually occurred in Scotland.[11] Since Hume and Alison are as silent on the subject of sleep-walking as English institutional writers and Mackenzie's brief remarks seem to have been forgotten, the credit for the decision in Fraser's case must go to the ingenuity of the defence and the open-mindedness of the Lord Justice General rather than to any superiority of Scots legal principles. By this date (1878) the investigations and experiments of French psychiatrists and psychologists had popularised the notion of 'somnambulisme' as something which could occur not merely in children or mesmerised subjects, but as a result of a pathological disturbance in adults (Lady Macbeth being a dramatised example). Maudsley's *Responsibility in Mental Disease*, which had been published in 1874 and had sold so well that a second edition was required within the year, had drawn attention to 'somnambulism' after epileptic fits, and had suggested that many adult somnambulists would be found to be undiagnosed epileptics. Certainly Simon Fraser[11] had a spectacular history of somnambulism.

He was charged with the murder of his baby son during the night of 9th April 1878 by battering his skull in against the wall of his room. He pleaded not guilty, and further pleaded that 'at the time the crime was committed he was asleep'. He had dreamed, he said, that he was attacking a wild beast which had jumped into the bed, and he told the same story not only to the neighbour whom he summoned but also to the physician. His father and sister both testified that he had been prone to sleep-walking from an early age, and that at different times while in this state he had struck his father, tried to strangle his sister, attempted to pull his wife out of what he thought to be a burning house, and entered 'the water' to rescue his sister from supposed drowning. At this point the foreman of the jury intervened to say he thought it unnecessary to continue the case as the jury believed that the prisoner was not responsible for his actions: but the Lord Justice General thought that the medical evidence ought to be heard. Of the three asylum superintendents who gave evidence only one, Dr Yellowlees, thought that Fraser had been insane at the time of his act, and he overstated his case by coining the word 'hypnomania' in order to provide Fraser with an impressive diagnostic label. All three doctors agreed, however, that Fraser had been unconscious of what he was doing, and not responsible.

At the Lord Justice General's suggestion the jury returned a verdict that the pannel (i.e. the accused) killed his child but that he was in a state in which he was unconscious of the act which he was committing by reason of somnambulism, and that he was not responsible. It is by no means clear whether this was a conviction or not, and the Solicitor General, who simply suggested that the case should be adjourned for two days to allow consideration of 'what arrangements should be made with reference to the accused', may not have been quite certain himself. At the resumption of the case Fraser gave an undertaking that in future no one but himself would sleep in his room, an undertaking in which his father 'concurred'. Counsel for the Crown refrained from moving for sentence, and the Court 'deserted the diet *simpliciter*', dismissing him from the Bar. These formalities certainly do not confirm the assumption, which one finds in later writers, that the result of Fraser's case was an acquittal; if it had been, how could the court 'desert the diet', or Crown Counsel refrain from moving for sentence? It sounds very like an improvised analogy to the special verdict which English juries were allowed by statute to return in cases of insanity (and which, according to Hale, the common law allowed them to return in the seventeenth century).

But such cases were no more than nine days' wonders, of which lawyers themselves took no notice. An *obiter dictum* of Stephen's refers to the possibility of the commission of crime in a state of 'somnambulism'. Discussing the case of a lady who had committed bigamy in the belief that her husband had been drowned, he said

> . . . in every case knowledge of fact is to some extent an element of criminality as much as competent age and sanity. To take an extreme illustration, can any one doubt that a man who, though he might be perfectly sane, committed what would otherwise be a crime in a state of somnambulism, would be entitled to be acquitted? And why is this? Simply because he would not know what he was doing.[12]

It is clear that Stephen regarded his illustration as quite imaginary; probably he had never heard of Esther Griggs or Simon Fraser.

In the twentieth century similar cases continue to be recorded by the newspapers but ignored by law reporters. In 1936 a man called Stone was acquitted of an offence against a girl who lived in his house, on the grounds that he was asleep. In 1949 a soldier, Price, attacked his corporal with a bayonet while awaking from a dream (like Schedmaizig), and was acquitted.[13] But a case which occurred in 1951 is of more than ordinary interest because of a remark made by a medical witness. Paltridge, a thirty-four-year-old naval officer who was said to be 'a perfect husband', went to bed with his wife as usual one night, but telephoned the police in the early hours of the morning to ask for an ambulance and a doctor for his wife, saying 'She has a cut in her head. I did it.' What he seems to have done was to try to strangle her and then hit her with an axe which he must have fetched from downstairs, where he had been chopping wood the day before. His defence was that he had been asleep. A psychiatrist supported his story, and said that on two occasions in the last year and a half he had been consulted about husbands who had tried in their sleep to strangle their wives. He thought that Paltridge had probably been wandering about downstairs in his sleep and picked up the axe because he had been using it earlier in the day. It was probably fortunate for the accused that his wife recovered and testified to his virtues as a husband. The jury took only ten minutes to acquit him.[14]

The case which has attracted most attention in recent years, however, was that of Boshears. He was a twenty-nine-year-old staff sergeant at an American Air Force base in England. On New Year's eve in 1960, when his wife was away in Scotland, he went to a public house, where he met a twenty-year-old girl, Jean Constable, whom he knew. Miss Constable had just made the acquaintance of a young man called Salt, whom she introduced to Boshears. The sergeant invited them both back to his flat, where they drank vodka. Salt and Miss Constable had intercourse on two occasions during the evening when Boshears left them together, but all three ended by sleeping side by side in front of the living-room fire. Salt decided, however, to go home about one o'clock; the girl said she was too tired to move, and stayed. A neighbour testified that about this time she heard a girl in Boshears' flat sobbing in a muffled way, and saying 'You don't love me' or 'You do love me'. Boshears said in evidence at his trial that after going to sleep the next thing he remembered was that he felt

. . . something scratching and pulling at my mouth. I was not awake but this woke me and I found that I was over Jean and I had my hands round her throat. Jean was dead and I panicked. . . .

Later he tried to conceal his crime by dumping her body in a ditch. In cross-examination he admitted that he 'knew' he had committed a crime, but said that he thought the crime was manslaughter. His defence, however, was that since he had been asleep it was not a crime at all. The judge, in his summing-up, agreed that if he had been asleep his act was not voluntary and he should be acquitted. He was very sceptical, however, and asked the jury whether they had ever heard of such a thing. Since it was the sort of thing which only forensic psychiatrists were likely to have heard of, it was hardly a fair question. Nevertheless the jury, after an absence of nearly two hours, surprised everyone by acquitting Boshears.[15]

Again the case was reported only in the press, but this time more notice was taken. As in M'Naghten's case, it was the House of Lords (in its political capacity) which gave expression to the feeling of disquiet. Lord Elton put down the question whether, as a result of a recent case in which the defendant was acquitted of a charge of murder on the ground that he was asleep, they (i.e. HM Government) are considering bringing about a change in the law to make possible a verdict of 'guilty but asleep' (which would, he pointed out in debate, at least make it possible to detain the accused). Lord Bathurst, the Home Secretary's spokesman in the upper house, replied that the circumstances were without precedent and demonstrated no need for a change in the law. As we have seen, however, they were not entirely unprecedented. It would have been more accurate to say that they were exceedingly rare and had not so far occurred in a case which had reached the Court of Criminal Appeal.

Moreover, Lord Elton's proposal (whether entirely serious or not) was certainly not unprecedented, for it was based on the very reasoning that had led to the Act of 1800 and the procedure of the High Court in Fraser's case. In his view it was unsafe to let people who might kill in their sleep go completely free, without any legal way of minimising the future risk to others. Detention, which Lord Elton envisaged, would not be morally or economically justified in most such cases; but to require an undertaking of the kind that Fraser gave, to sleep alone, would be neither unjustifiable nor totally unenforceable. Similar conditions are often imposed by courts when they deal with offenders by means of conditional discharge or probation. The problem may be rare, but it is gradually becoming less rare.

Bed is not the only place where it is dangerous to fall asleep: the wheel of a car is another. In 1925 a mining engineer called Ritchie, who had knocked down a pedestrian in a Scottish village after a long day's driving, was acquitted in the High Court after evidence had been given that he had absorbed carbon monoxide into his blood and was consequently in a state of 'mental dissociation'. There were several unsatisfactory features, however, in the case, which is now regarded in Scotland as wrongly decided,[16] and in any case he seems to have been more than asleep. Nevertheless a defence based on sleep is not only plausible in motoring cases but also attractive, since most traffic offences are deliberately defined so that it is no defence to argue that one did not mean to do what one did (whether it is breaking the speed limit, ignoring lights or hitting pedestrians). Virtually the only defence which can be considered is one which seeks to show that one was not in command of one's body at the time, and thus, as Lord Goddard has put it, 'could not be said to be driving'.

Such a defence seems more likely to impress magistrates than judges. Butterworth, who had been working long hours at a factory, was overcome by drowsiness at the wheel of his car one night in 1945 and drove into a column of American soldiers who were marching on the same side of the road, injuring sixteen of them. He contended that as he was asleep he could not be held responsible for his actions, and the justices agreed. The police prosecutor, however, appealed on the point of law, and Mr Justice Humphreys directed the justices to convict, saying that 'if a driver allows himself to be overtaken by sleep while driving he is guilty at least of the offence of driving without due care and attention'.[17] Nor is the defence of automatism now confined to cases where the accused was, or claims to have been, asleep. Baxter, who had ignored traffic lights, convinced the magistrates that he had some kind of 'blackout' and was therefore not responsible. Again there was an appeal, and Goddard, like Humphreys, recognised that there could be situations in which the motorist could not be said to be driving (Humphreys instanced being struck by a stone or attacked by a swarm of bees; Goddard suggested a stroke or epileptic fit). But it seemed to Goddard that the magistrates had been too credulous in accepting the story of the blackout without medical evidence and they were directed to convict.[18]

What is popularly called a 'blackout' is nowadays recognisable as the last resort of a desperate defendant. An example is the case of Harrison-Owen, a man with a long record of housebreaking and larceny. At about 1 a.m. on a spring morning in 1951 the hostess of a house where a party was in progress found him in one of her upstairs rooms (he seems to have found the keys of the house in her car). At first he maintained he was looking for lodgings, but while a guest was summoning the police he bolted. When he gave evidence at his trial he seemed at first to be suggesting that he was insane, later that he had been drunk, but finally that he had had a blackout. The judge unwisely decided that in order to let the jury see how plausible this was the prosecution should cross-examine him on his previous record, and the jury not unnaturally rejected his defence. His conviction was quashed by the Court of Criminal Appeal on the ground that the nature of the defence did not justify the cross-examination as to his previous convictions.[19]

Nevertheless, psychiatrists do recognise mental states which can loosely be called 'blackouts', and in which people are capable of complex and apparently purposive behaviour. As we have seen, nineteenth-century psychiatrists such as Maudsley (who was by no means inclined to give criminals the benefit of the doubt) recognised that somnambulistic states might be a feature of epilepsy. His contemporary, Crichton-Browne, chose 'Dreamy Mental States' as the subject for his Cavendish Lecture in 1895; and although many of his cases were evidently epileptics, many were not. The state sometimes takes the form known as a 'fugue', in which the person wanders away from his usual surroundings, sometimes taking a train or bus, so that he is found miles away in a confused state.

A cerebral tumour – especially in the temporal lobe of the brain – may produce a state in the patient resembling the twilight state or fugue of the epileptic.

> Objectively he seems to be far away, dreamy; subjectively he
> finds the environment endowed with a strange, bizarre quality. . . .
> Visual hallucinations . . . commonly . . . take the form of com-
> plicated visual scenes which pass before the patient with the
> vividness of a dream. . . . There follows a period of involuntary
> behaviour of varying duration in which he may pass a hand across
> his face, adjust his clothes, or move some object in the room.
> More complicated and organized forms of behaviour may occur, in
> which the patient wanders from the place where his attack com-
> menced, and carries out activities of which he has no subsequent
> memory. . . .[20]

An example was Charlson, a 'devoted husband and father', who suddenly and inexplicably attacked his ten-year-old son. He had seen a rat in the river outside his window and asked his son to come and look at it. The rat had gone, and Charlson's foot (according to his later statements) happened to kick against a mallet on the floor. He seems to have picked it up to put it away, but suddenly struck his son on the head with it and then threw him out of the window. Later he found himself some distance away in his car with the feeling that something dreadful had happened to his son, and he drove back to his home, where the police had by then arrived. Medical evidence not only brought out the fact that several of his blood-relations had suffered from cerebral disorders – in one case a tumour – but also found symptoms in his history that suggested a cerebral tumour, although (for some reason) the prison medical officer was not prepared to say definitely that this was present. Mr Justice Barry's summing-up was favourable to Charlson, and he concluded with the words:

> If he did not know what he was doing, if his actions were purely automatic and his mind had no control over the movement of his limbs, if he was in the same position as a person in an epileptic fit and no responsibility rests on him at all, then the proper verdict is 'not guilty'. . . .

Charlson was therefore acquitted.[21]

A state of 'automatism' can also be produced by certain substances. The effect of carbon monoxide on Ritchie has already been described. An overdose of insulin seems to have produced a similar state in the accused in the case of Watmore v. Jenkins. He was a 46-year-old diabetic who took regular doses of insulin. Recently, however, he had suffered from jaundice (which increases the blood-level of a substance that reduces the effectiveness of insulin) and had therefore been prescribed increased doses. In June 1961 he was driving home in his car when he crashed into a parked vehicle, and was consequently charged with driving under the influence of drugs, dangerous driving, and driving without due care and attention. Jenkins (who had driven for twenty years without a conviction) could not remember what had happened after he passed a point about five miles away from the accident; but evidence was given that his car had swerved from side to side, hit a kerb, crashed through traffic lights, and been driven for some distance on the wrong side of the road.[22]

More commonly, however, no organic cause can be discovered, and the 'dissociated state' or 'fugue' is ascribed to 'hysteria', one of the great havens in the long odyssey of psychiatric diagnosis. As a result of Freud's writings, the 'hysteric' is nowadays regarded as suffering from a conflict between different aspects of his personality – often between his instinctive desires and impulses and a rigid virtue which is the result of a strict upbringing. His inability to face this conflict consciously or resolve it rationally may drive him into dramatic symptoms. These may take the form of paralysis of a limb or of his vocal muscles, or occasionally of periods during which he seems to assume a different 'personality', and of which he may later have little or no recollection. When these periods recur he is sometimes described as suffering from 'dual' or 'split' personality, of which examples have been described by William James (the Rev. Ansell Bourne), Morton Prince (Miss Beauchamp), and Thigpen and Cleckley ('Eve'). More often, there is a single episode in which the 'hysteric' escapes from some intolerable situation by resigning from his normal personality, with its strict code of responsibility, and runs or wanders away. Soldiers with high standards of discipline and courage who 'desert' positions of danger are often diagnosed by psychiatrists as suffering from 'hysterical fugues'. Under the influence of French nineteenth-century psychiatrists these states are sometimes called 'hysterical somnambulism'.

The dangers of the defence of automatism were obvious. If successful, it exempted the accused not only from any penal measure which the court might have thought fit to impose but also from any compulsory precaution which might prevent him from repeating his dangerous behaviour. Ritchie remained free to drive his car. Charlson need not have submitted to any special care or treatment if he did not wish to. The reluctance of Humphreys and Goddard to see magistrates accepting motorists' dozes and blackouts is understandable. The logical course would have been to ask for legislation to allow the court to insist on precautions in such cases. Failing this, the higher courts at first simply discouraged such defences by scepticism. In the last decade, however, a new possibility has occurred to them: that if the evidence in favour of 'automatism' could be regarded as evidence of insanity, the jury could be told to return a special verdict.

This was the solution arrived at in Kemp's case. Kemp was an elderly man of blameless reputation, devoted to his wife. He suffered from arteriosclerosis, and was consequently depressed; but his depression may well have been a rational reaction to his state of health, and he showed no other signs of abnormality. One night in 1956, however, he made an apparently motiveless attack on his wife with a hammer, and was charged with causing her grievous bodily harm with intent to murder her. In his defence at Bristol Assizes before Lord Devlin medical evidence was given that his arteriosclerosis had, as it often does, interfered with the blood supply to his brain, causing a temporary lapse of consciousness. His counsel therefore argued that, like Charlson, he was entitled to an acquittal. The prosecution contended that the proper verdict was 'guilty but insane', since on the evidence of the defence's witnesses the explanation of the fact that he did not know what he was doing had been that he was labouring under a 'defect of reason, from disease of the mind', so that he came within the meaning of the M'Naghten Rules. The defence tried to rely on a distinction between 'disease of the mind' and 'purely physical' disease.

Lord Devlin, who gave a most lucid explanation of the psychiatric distinction between functional and organic causes of mental disorder and its relevance to the present issue, decided that the M'Naghten Rules had not been intended to differentiate between diseases of mental and physical origin. He therefore directed the jury that on the whole of the medical evidence they ought to find that Kemp's disorder was a disease of the mind, with the result that his defence led not to an acquittal but to a special verdict of insanity.[23]

The consequence of Kemp's case is that English courts now recognise two sorts of automatism, which have been nicknamed 'insane' and 'noninsane automatism'. The former describes a defence based on what appears to the court to be a disease of the mind, and enables the judge to direct the jury (if they accept the defence) to bring in a special verdict of insanity. The latter refers to a defence which, if successful, can lead only to an acquittal, because it is based on a state which is not regarded as a disease of the mind, such as sleep, concussion, or an attack by a swarm of bees.

The most recent case of importance occurred in Northern Ireland in 1961. Bratty, a twenty-six-year-old Irishman, had strangled a young girl, who was a neighbour of his, while giving her a lift home in his car. He dumped her body by the side of a country road and drove away until his car broke down. They do not appear to have had sexual intercourse, but her underpants had been removed. Bratty's story was that

> . . . coming back again, just about halfways up the road from her
> house, I had some terrible feeling and then a sort of blackness.
> Just with that I took one look at her, caught her, threw her right
> over the back of the seat into the back. I caught her with my
> two hands. When I caught her with my two hands I took one of
> her stockings and put it round her neck. I tightened the stocking.
> Afterwards I went down the road a piece . . . took her out of the
> car and left her on the side of the road. . . . I didn't mean to do
> what really happened. . . . I apologise for what happened. I don't
> think it would have happened only that terrible feeling came over
> me at the time. I don't know really what caused it at all.

On the basis of medical evidence which was not very strong or definite,
his counsel suggested that he had been suffering from psychomotor epilepsy, in other words, a seizure which resulted in 'automatic' behaviour.

Since the Homicide Act of 1957 did not apply to Northern Ireland,
Bratty's murder was a capital offence, and the defence of diminished
responsibility was not open to him. Counsel asked the jury to find 'one of
three separate and completely independent verdicts'. The proper verdict
he submitted, was one of 'Not guilty', since Bratty had been in a state of
automatism. If this were rejected, the verdict should be manslaughter,
not murder, since 'his mental condition was so impaired and confused, and
he was so deficient in reason' that he was not capable of forming the necessary intent. If neither of these points were acceptable, at least he was insane within the meaning of the M'Naghten Rules. But the judge (Mr
Justice McVeigh) refused to leave the issue of non-insane automatism to
the jury, because in his view it rested solely on evidence of what was really
a disease of the mind; what he did leave to them was the issue of insanity.
The jury were simple men, and convicted Bratty of murder. Both the
Court of Criminal Appeal for Northern Ireland and the House of Lords
upheld the course taken by the judge (Bratty was, however, reprieved).[24]

In doing so their Lordships clarified several points on which there had
hitherto been doubt. Lord Denning's definition of 'disease of the mind'
has already been mentioned in chapter 6. Again, we have seen that if the
defence is insanity it is for the accused to produce evidence of it, but this
evidence need not satisfy the jury 'beyond reasonable doubt', only 'on a
balance of probabilities'. Kilmuir now laid it down that if the defence is
non-insane automatism

> . . . once the defence have surmounted the initial hurdle to which
> I have referred and have satisfied the judge that there is evidence fit
> for the jury's consideration, the proper direction is that, if that
> evidence leaves them in a *real state of doubt* the jury should acquit
> (my italics).

It is clear from the context that he was distinguishing from the evidential
burden where the defence was one of insanity. Since automatism automatically negatives *mens rea*, and since it is for the prosecution to prove
mens rea, evidence of non-insane automatism throws onto the prosecution
the task of satisfying the jury beyond reasonable doubt that the accused

nevertheless had *mens rea*. If they are left 'in a real state of doubt' (which must mean the same as 'reasonable doubt') on this point, they should accept the defence and acquit.

At this point, however, Kilmuir was talking about non-insane automatism. It is equally clear that if the defence amounted to 'insane automatism' the burden of proof was that which lies on the accused if the defence is insanity: he must not only introduce evidence worth putting to the jury but must also satisfy them 'on a balance of probabilities' that the insanity was such as to negative *mens rea*. Neither the Lords nor the Court of Criminal Appeal have yet tried to justify this state of affairs, in which a man whose defence is that he was asleep need only raise a reasonable doubt in the jury's mind, whereas a man whose medical witnesses testify that he was suffering from cerebral arteriosclerosis must do better, and satisfy them on a balance of probabilities.[25]

DRUNKENNESS AS A DEFENCE

Although it has been considered somewhat similar to the defence of automatism, the modern defence of drunkenness has met with even more discouragement in the course of its development, largely because of the disapproval which drunkenness itself incurs. In strict law, mere drunkenness has never been an excuse, and it is only recently that it has come to be accepted as a mitigating factor by sentencers: in the eyes of Coke and Blackstone it aggravated the offence. Since Hale's day, however, if not earlier, it has been recognised that long periods of drinking may produce a state of permanent or intermittent insanity, which may or may not be such as to come within the M'Naghten Rules or the definition of diminished responsibility. Hale also conceded that if a man became drunk 'by the unskilfulness of his physician or by the contrivance of his enemies' he would have a defence; but this defence is almost unheard of (I recollect, but cannot trace, a newspaper report of a case in which a motorist charged with driving while drunk successfully defended himself on the ground that he had become drunk through the contrivance not of his enemies but his friends, who had put spirits in his beer).

Coke and Hale, however, belonged to a comparatively sober age. By the middle of the eighteenth century cheap and powerful distilled spirits were being imported from Scotland and the Continent; 'geneva shops' had sprung up in the expanding industrial cities; drunkenness was an everyday sight, and alcoholism a social problem. Blackstone, writing in the second half of the century, merely echoed Coke; but Bentham thought that 'perfect intoxication', like insanity, should exempt an offender from punishment. His argument was the purely utilitarian one that in such cases punishment would be inefficacious, since it would not deter the offender from repeating his offence: an argument which has its fallacies.[26] Many a jury, however, when faced with a man who had broken the law when in drink, must have said to themselves 'There but for the grace of God go I', just as modern juries do when trying some motoring offenders. There are cases in the Old Bailey Sessions Papers in which the accused is clearly using drunkenness as a defence. In 1790 Patrick Hill was acquitted

O

of stealing a sheep on the grounds that, as he put it, he was 'so drunk I could not see through a story ladder'; and it was clear from the questions put from the bench that his drunkenness was the central point of his defence.[27] Since the Sessions Papers seldom record what the judge or recorder said to the jury, we do not know exactly what his reasoning was. A little later, when we find cases that are better reported, some judges were certainly making cautious concessions to the new tolerance. In a trial for murder in 1819 Mr Justice Holroyd held that although voluntary drunkenness cannot excuse, nevertheless if the material question is (as in the case of murder) whether the act was premeditated or done only 'with sudden heat and impulse', the intoxication of the accused could properly be taken into consideration.[28] It is true that in a later case of 1835 his decision was overruled as too wide and dangerous in its application;[29] but there were several trials in the eighteen-thirties in which the jury were told that they could take intoxication into account in deciding, for example, whether the accused really thought he was defending himself against attack, or (in another case) whether he was sufficiently provoked to reduce his crime from murder to manslaughter.

But the usual form of the defence is that the accused was so drunk that he did not intend to do what he did. In 1838, for example, a drunken man called Cruse seized a neighbour's child who was in his room and battered its head against a beam. When he and his wife were tried for attempted murder, the judge (Patteson, J.) said to the jury: 'A person may be so drunk as to be utterly unable to form any intention at all, and yet he may be guilty of great violence. If you are not satisfied that the prisoners, or either of them, had formed a positive intention of murdering this child, you may still find them guilty of an assault': the jury did so.[30]

In later cases men charged with murder have been found guilty of the less serious charge of manslaughter for the same reason. In R. v. Meade (1909) the accused had drunkenly attacked his wife and killed her with a blow of his fist, and was convicted of murder. The Court of Criminal Appeal said that the jury should have been told to return a verdict of manslaughter if the prisoner was so drunk as not to know that what he was doing was dangerous.[31]

In at least one early case the defence resulted in a complete acquittal. In 1852 a woman called Moore was indicted for the offence of attempting suicide. She and her husband had quarrelled violently, and in order to separate them someone living in the same house had pushed her out of the house into the garden. There was a thirty-eight-foot well in the garden, and as she was being pushed out of the house the woman said she would throw herself into it, which she did (she was fortunate in being pulled out without much injury). A witness told the court that at the time the accused had been 'so drunk as not to know what she was about'. The judge (Jervis) asked the jury 'If the prisoner was so drunk as not to know what she was about, how can you say that she intended to destroy herself?'; and she was acquitted.[32] No doubt the fact that no actual harm had resulted from her act, and that there was no lesser offence of which she could have been convicted, contributed to this result. Not all attempted suicides were so fortunate: Doody, who was found hanging in the water-closet of an inn two years later, offered the same defence, but failed, probably because it was hard to believe that he could have strung himself up by his scarf without intending suicide.[32]

That judges could still fail, however, to distinguish adequately between the defences of drunkenness and insanity was demonstrated by Beard's case. Beard was a night-watchman who drunkenly raped a thirteen-year-old girl in his factory, and in placing his hand over her mouth to stifle her screams caused her to die. The judge (Bailhache, J.) told the jury that the defence of drunkenness could be accepted only if they believed that the accused did not know what he was doing, or that it was wrong: the jury brought in a verdict of murder. The Court of Criminal Appeal thought that instead they should have been asked whether Beard knew that what he was doing was dangerous; and a verdict of manslaughter was substituted. The case was complicated, however, by the fact that Beard had caused the girl's death while in process of committing a felony of violence – namely rape – which he *must* have intended, and at that date this was enough to make his crime murder. The House of Lords therefore restored the original verdict (although Beard was in fact reprieved on the ground that it would be inhumane to reimpose a death sentence which had been cancelled).[33]

In delivering the decision, the Lord Chancellor (Birkenhead) made it clear that the M'Naghten test was relevant only if drink had produced insanity; but that evidence that drunkenness had rendered Beard incapable of forming the specific intent essential to the crime should be taken into consideration, along with other proved facts, in deciding whether he had had that intent. Short of these two situations, drunkenness which merely caused him to give way more readily to some passion was no defence. The last of these points was driven home in 1954 by the case of R. v. McCarthy, when it was decided that the fact that intoxication rendered the accused more easy to provoke was not relevant: the provocation must be sufficient to cause a reasonable man to lose his control to the same extent as the accused had.[34]

The case of Di Duca confirmed that drunkenness had no more chance of coming within the meaning of 'abnormality of mind' in the definition of diminished responsibility than it had of coming within the M'Naghten Rules. (Di Duca had battered a secondhand dealer to death with a washbasin while burgling his shop, and had alleged, among other things, that he was drunk, and therefore suffering from abnormality of mind induced by 'injury'.[35])

What is not yet clear is whether a mental disorder which is not by itself sufficient to bring the accused within the scope of the M'Naghten Rules or the defence of diminished responsibility would be accepted as within the scope of one or the other if it were sufficiently intensified by drink. Gallagher, a psychopath who drank whisky to give himself the courage to kill his wife, failed both with a defence of insanity and with a defence of drunkenness; but he had formed the intention to kill before he took the whisky.[36]

Consider an actual case[37] which might well have raised the issue, although the defence in fact took a safer course which avoided doing so. A man in his fifties was twice tried for murder in very similar circumstances. He seems to have been a 'quiet, reserved man' leading a peaceful unmarried life with his parents until the age of about 40, when his aged father committed suicide and his mother died soon afterwards. From this time onward he incurred a series of convictions for minor larceny or malicious damage, interspersed with occasional stays in mental hospitals, once after a suicidal attempt, on other occasions due to periods of depression. He seems to have had occasional sexual relations with prostitutes whom he picked up in public houses. On one occasion he took a middle-aged widow, known for her heavy drinking, back to his room. There seems to have been some sort of drunken quarrel in which he put his hands round her neck and she collapsed and died, although it was not certain that this was due to strangulation. When he came to his senses he put her body under his bed and went to sleep, but next day gave himself up to the police. A specialist psychiatric examination revealed no evidence of sufficient mental disorder to justify a defence of insanity or diminished responsibility; but at his trial the court seem to have accepted the defence that he had no intention of doing her serious harm, and he was found guilty of manslaughter, for which he was sentenced to a year's imprisonment. A few weeks after his discharge from prison he picked up another middle-aged woman and took her home to continue their drinking. Again there seems to have been a struggle, and he came to his senses to find her strangled. Once more he put her under the bed, but eventually gave himself up to the police. Psychiatric examination produced the same results as before: but he succeeded in the defence that he was too drunk to prove the necessary intention. This time, however, his sentence for the manslaughter was life imprisonment. The judge may have regarded him as more to blame for allowing himself to get into the same situation again, or may simply have been more impressed with his dangerousness to the public.

Let us suppose, however, that the defence had been one of diminished responsibility. The doctors had testified:

a. that he suffered from some abnormality of mind which even without drink had made him behave with violence, but not violence against other people;

b. that in all probability, therefore, his violence to women when he had taken drink was to be attributed partly to his abnormality, partly to the drink; without *both* he would not have done what he did.

What should the judge's direction to the jury have been?

There are several other aspects of the relationship between drunkenness and *mens rea* on which the law is at present far from clear or logical. Nor is it by any means certain that courts will treat the effects of other drugs on exactly the same principles as the effects of alcohol. A complete review of the subject, however, would take us outside the scope of this book. What is relevant to its theme is one feature which defences based on non-insane automatism and on drunkenness have in common. The courts seem to regard both as the beginnings of slippery slopes, and therefore resist them in practice while recognising them in theory. The nature of these defences, and the lightness of the evidential burden which they place on the accused, mean that they can be abused by unscrupulous defendants; and not many people have scruples when they are faced with serious charges. It is arguable that the law would be in a simpler and more satisfactory state if, instead of relying on the ingenuity of the Court of Criminal Appeal and the Law Lords, Parliament had legislated (as it did in the case of insanity) so as to provide an intermediate verdict of the kind (although not in the wording) suggested by Lord Elton.

Notes

1 See the article by C.M.Pierce and H.H.Lipcon, 'Somnambulism, Electroencephalographic Studies and related findings' in (1956), 7, *U.S. Armed Forces' Medical Journal*, 1419–. They compared 34 naval ratings whose history included sleep-walking (including sleep-walking before entry into the navy in every case) with 60 non-sleep-walking controls. They found, for example, abnormal electro-encephalograms in seven of the sleep-walkers but only one of the controls. Nearly half the sleep-walkers, but none of the controls, suffered from nocturnal bed-wetting, another feature which suggests neurologically abnormal sleep.

2 I.Oswald, *Sleep* (London, 1966).

3 Mayer-Gross, Slater and Roth, *Clinical Psychiatry* (London, 1954 ed.), 250.

4 Diego de Covarrubias y Leyva (Leyden, 1568), *In variis civilis ac pontifici juris titulos relectiones*, pt. III: 'Subsequitur statim . . . dormientem ipsius homicidii tempore, nempe quia dormiens aliquem occiderit, minime fore irregularem: quia is intellectu ac ratione caret, ac furioso similis est . . . qua ratione dormientis delictum minime punitur: nisi eo casu, quo ipse vigilans satis cognitum habebat, quod dormiens arma capiebat, ac homines persequebatur. tunc enim si non adhibuit diligentiam, quam debuit in praecavendo, ne dormiens alicui noceret, profecto puniendus erit, licet non poena ordinaria.'

5 Matthaeus (1644), *De Criminibus ad Lib.* XLVII *et* XLVIII *Dig. Commentarius*, ch. 2, 13.

6 *The Laws and Customs of Scotland in Matters Criminal* (1678), pt. I, tit. L, VI.

7 In the *Calendar of the Domestic State Papers of James* II.

8 See documents 150 and 174 in Public Records Office file SP44/337.

9 J.C.Bucknill and D.H.Tuke, *A Manual of Psychological Medicine*, 2nd ed. (London, 1862), 213–14.

10 See R. v. Hodges (1838), 8 Carrington & Payne, 195.

11 HM Adv. v. Fraser (1878), 4 Couper, 78.

12 Obiter, in Tolson's case (1889), 23 Q.B.D. 168.

13 See Glanville Williams, *The Criminal Law: General Part* (London, 1961 ed.), 483n.

14 See *The Daily Telegraph* for 20 February 1952.
15 See *The Times* and *The Guardian* for 17 and 18 February 1961.
16 See Lord Clyde's remarks in HM Adv. v. Cunningham (1963), J.C. 45., S.L.T. 345.
17 Kay v. Butterworth (1945), 110 J.P. 75.
18 Hill v. Baxter (1958), I Q.B. 277.
19 R. v. Harrison-Owen (1951), 35 Cr. App. R. 108.
20 Mayer-Gross, Slater and Roth, op. cit. (n3), 434.
21 R. v. Charlson (1955), I All. E.R. 859.
22 Watmore v. Jenkins (1962), 2 Q.B. 572.
23 R. v. Kemp (1957), I Q.B. 399.
24 Bratty v. A.G. for Northern Ireland (1962), 46 Cr. App. R. I, H.L.
25 As Professor Cross has pointed out in his article 'Reflections on Bratty's Case' in (1962), *Law Quarterly Review*, 236.
26 J.Bentham, *The Principles of Morals and of Legislation* (London, 1780).
27 Hill's case (1790), Sessions Papers, case 276.
28 R. v. Grindley (1819), cited by Russell in *Crimes and Misdemeanours* 2nd ed. (London, 1826), 8.
29 R. v. Carroll (1835), 7 Clarke and Payne, 145.
30 R. v. Cruse and his wife (1838), 8 Carrington & Payne, 541.
31 R. v. Meade (1909), I K.B. 895 C.C.A.
32 R. v. Moore (1852), 3 Carrington and Kirwan, 319; and R. v. Doody (1854), 6 Cox 463.
33 R. v. Beard (1920), A.C. 479.
34 R. v. McCarthy (1954), 2 Q.B. 105; (1954), 2 All. E.R. 262.
35 R. v. Di Duca (1959), 43 Cr. App. R. 167.
36 A.G. for Northern Ireland v. Gallagher (1963), A.C. 349; 45 Cr. App. R. 316.
37 The case is not in the law reports, and since I have included certain facts which were not made public at the trial I have refrained from identifying it.

Chapter 11. **Insanity and Treason**

Sovereigns have always found the exemption of the insane from punishment a difficult doctrine to swallow when their personal safety or honour has been involved. The autocratic Henry III made short work of a madman who tried to assassinate him:

In the XIX yere of the Kyng [i.e. 1235] at Wodstok, cam in a clerk, which feyned him a prophete, and sumtyme feyned him a frentick, which had upon him to scharp knyves, with which he had slayn the Kyng had not a holy woman sent him warnyng. So was he taken and sent to Coventre, there drawen and hanged. Men sey that he was sent be on [i.e. by one] William Marys that was outlawed, and dwelled in a ylde [island] betwix Cornwayle and Wales. Thei that dwelle there clepe it Lundy.[1]

Unless we take this more or less official version at its face value, Henry's expedient for disposing of this problem was to dismiss the insanity as 'feyned'.

Henry VIII went further, and simply amended the law when it seemed likely to protect the elderly Lady Rocheford. She had acted as a go-between for Catherine Howard in her adultery with Thomas Culpeper. Culpeper and his abettor Dereham were tried for treason by the King's Council on 1st December 1541 and executed nine days later. Lady Rocheford was also examined by the King's Council and would have been dealt with at the same time, but, according to a deciphered letter from Chapuys, the Spanish ambassador, to his sovereign, she went mad on the third day of her imprisonment:

She recovers her reason now and then, and the King has sent her to be with the Admiral's wife, and gets his own physicians to visit her, desiring her recovery that he may afterwards have her executed as an example.[2]

Henry was determined that Lady Rocheford should not escape the block; but he did not want to override the law too obviously. His solution was to introduce a bill which in effect provided that persons who committed high treason while in their senses, and confessed what they had done to the King's Council, but then happened to 'fall to madness or lunacye' should be the subject of a special Commission of Oyer and determiner of Treasons. This Commission should hear evidence from four of the King's Council to the effect that the accused was sane at the time of his treason and his examination, but had since become insane. Thereupon the Commission should impanel a jury to try the indictment without the necessity for any arraignment or plea of guilty or not guilty. If the jury found the accused guilty, he or she should suffer the penalties for high treason.

This hasty piece of legislation, which Parliament passed in time to allow Lady Rocheford to be beheaded on the same day as her Queen, was dignified by being entitled 'An Act for due Process to be had in High Treason in Cases of Lunacye or Madness'.[3] Its preamble was an attempt to justify its provisions:

> Forasmuch as sometime some persons, being accused of High
> Treasons, have, after they have been examined by the King's
> Majesty's Council, confessed their offences of High Treason, and
> Examinations and Confessions thereof, as is afore said, have fallen
> to Madness or Lunacy, whereby the condign Punishment of their
> Treasons, were they never so notable and detestable, hath been
> deferred spared and delayed; and whether their Madness of Lunacy
> by them outwardly shewed were of Truth, or falsely contrived
> and counter feited, it is a Thing almost impossible to judge and
> try. . . .

Although the plural is used, I can find no evidence of any other case resembling that of Lady Rocheford. Probably this was no more than a feeble attempt to gloss over the fact that the bill was aimed solely at Lady Rocheford.

The Act must have been repugnant even to Henry's immediate successors, for they quickly passed one which provided that henceforth trials for treason would be governed by the common law.[4] Certainly Elizabeth's Council seemed anxious to observe the correct procedure when dealing with John Somervile, the young Catholic gentleman who set out to shoot the Queen in 1583. After succumbing to a 'frantic humour' that midsummer, he became convinced that it was his destiny to free his religion from persecution and that he must die for the common good (notice how many assassins have suicidal intentions: Hadfield was another example). Somervile was heard to say that he would go to the court and shoot the Queen with his dag; and he set out for London, attacking some people with his sword on the way. He made no secret of his plan, and when arrested implicated his unfortunate parents-in-law and a priest: his father-in-law was beheaded as a result. Somervile himself gave the Queen's Council more trouble, for not only was he said to be a lunatic, but he also made no reply when asked whether he pleaded guilty or not guilty. This was a common gambit of men of property, for it avoided the conviction and consequent forfeitures which would ruin their families (it did not save their lives, for they were pressed slowly to death by means of the *peine forte et dure* unless they gave way and made their plea). But was Somervile's silence the result of real or feigned madness? The Council asked the justices to decide, and they impanelled a jury for the purpose. It was agreed that if this inquest declared his madness to be real his trial should be deferred until his recovery; but if not he should be tried. Presumably the inquest went against him, for he is said to have pleaded guilty (although it is possible that he was simply assumed to have done so). He was sentenced to be beheaded, but like Townley and many another insane prisoner he had the last word. He was found strangled – probably by his own hand – in his cell at Newgate.[5]

Nevertheless there seems to have been some confusion about the position of the madman whose offence was high Treason. Coke speaks with two contradictory voices on the subject. In his commentary on Beverley's case he says that

> ... in some cases *non compos mentis* may commit high treason, as if he kills, or offers to kill, the King, for the King *est caput et salus reipublicae, et a capite bona valetudo transit in omnes* (is the head and protector of the state, and from the head all derive their health); and for this reason their persons are so sacred, that none can offer them any violence: but he is *reus criminis laesae Majestatis, et pereat unus ne pereant omnes* (guilty of the crime of lèse majesté, and one must die lest all do so).[6]

The same argument has been used more recently to justify the creation of offences of strict liability in the attempt to control traffic, the sale of bad food and similar dangers: the potential harm is regarded as so great that the offender must be dealt with even at the risk of penalising the man who could not help what he did. The difference is that the penalty is not death, but a fine or, in the last resort, imprisonment.

In the Third Part of his Institutes, however, Coke recognises that this point of view is out of date:

> The ancient law was, that if a mad man had killed or offered to kill the king, it was holden for treason; and so it appeareth by king Alfred's law before the conquest, and in lib. 4 in Beverley's case. But now ... he that is *non compos mentis* and totally deprived of all compassings and imaginations, cannot commit high treason by compassing or imagining the death of the king. ...[7]

Hale agrees that insanity is a defence to a charge of high treason,[8] and though Dalton notes Coke's inconsistency subsequent legal writers follow the same line.

It is certainly assassination rather than cuckoldry which is the occupational risk of monarchs: and most would-be assassins are mentally ill. George III was attacked at least three times by lunatics. The first of these attacks occurred in 1786, when a domestic servant called Margaret Nicholson tried to stab him with a small knife at Windsor, under cover of handing him a petition which turned out to be blank paper. She was arrested and examined by Thomas Monro of Bethlem (who was later called in to attend the King himself), and – since her crime was treason – finally brought before the Privy Council. The occasion must have been an impressive one, for in addition to the Archbishop of Canterbury and the newly created Home Secretary (Lord Sydney) there were present three dukes, two earls and three other peers. Her conduct, and the other oral and written evidence which they received, convinced them that she had long been insane, and the Home Secretary committed her to Bethlem, although it was said at the time that as a State prisoner she ought properly to have been sent to gaol.[9]

Four years later, John Frith threw a stone at the king's carriage while it was on its way to the House of Lords. He too was interrogated by an impromptu Privy Council, including Pitt himself and his Attorney-General; but this time the result was that he was committed for trial on the charge of high treason. The proceedings are described in chapter 14, which deals with insanity on arraignment. The third attack was of course Hadfield's. He too underwent preliminary examination by the Duke of York, who may have acted as a member of the Privy Council; and like Frith he was committed for trial.

The gradual transfer of power from the sovereign to the prime minister diverted a few madmen to this new target. Spencer Perceval was shot by Bellingham, and M'Naghten's intended victim was Peel. But even a constitutional monarch seems to capture the imagination of the mentally disordered more easily than the most charismatic of politicians. After Frith's attack on George III two Bow Street Runners were seconded for the protection of the royal person, and after the formation of the Metropolitan Police constables were stationed outside Buckingham Palace. The Runners, however, seem to have been more effective at arresting than at frustrating offenders. Soon after the young Victoria's coronation an army officer called Goode, who thought he was the son of George IV and entitled to recognition as King John II, forced his way into her presence and shouted at her 'You are an usurper, I will yet have you off the throne!' In court he threatened to impale and disembowel the royal family and the Dutch and Russian embassies, and was found unfit for trial.[10] In the following year the Master of the Household complained to the Home Secretary that a partially insane and partially drunk man had been found seated in the Palace's picture gallery a few minutes after the queen had passed through it on her way to bed. The incident provided an excuse for replacing the Runners with two inspectors of the new police, although leaving the Runners responsible for the Queen's safety at Windsor.[11] They may have been more effective there, for in the next year (1839) a lunatic called Shockledge was arrested when he tried to enter the castle.[12] But there were more serious incidents to come. On six occasions pistols were fired at Victoria, and on the seventh she was struck on the head with a brass-knobbed cane, by another insane officer in her army.

The first of these assailants, all of whom were young men, was Edward Oxford. He had obviously acted with knowledge of what he was doing, for he had bought a pair of pistols more than a month earlier, and had practised with them before he waylaid the royal carriage in the park. After missing with one pistol he said 'I have got another', and fired it too; and he was afterwards able to describe what he had done. On the other hand, medical and other witnesses testified to his insanity; several members of his family had been insane; and the attempted assassination seems to have been connected with an imaginary secret society called 'Young England', notes about which were found in his lodgings. Although his insanity was less marked than Hadfield's, and may have been no more than feeble-mindedness, his youth probably told in his favour, and he received a special acquittal under the Act of 1800.[13] Moreover, the judges seem to have been anxious to avoid the sort of miscarriage of justice which had led to the execution of Bowler (see chapter 4).

By no means all of Victoria's assailants, however, were excused on the grounds of insanity, if indeed this defence occurred to their counsel. John Francis, 'a little swarthy ill-looking rascal', fired a pistol at her in Green Park in May 1842. The pistol misfired, and he slipped away in the crowd; but the royal couple, who disliked suspense more than danger, deliberately drove over the same route next day with their equerries (but no ladies-in-waiting) surrounding them. Francis fell into the trap, and was caught in the act of firing a pistol at the Queen. The pistol was loaded only with powder, but his act was treason, and he was sentenced to death.[14] Though the idea of his being executed was 'painful' to the Queen, she appears to have accepted the necessity for it. It was the Home Secretary who, after consultation with the judges, advised that the sentence be commuted to transportation for life, on the grounds that the pistol had not been loaded with ball. Victoria was relieved, but pessimistic about the effect upon potential imitators; and two days after his reprieve there was indeed another incident of the same kind. William Bean, almost a dwarf but 'certainly not a simpleton', fired a pistol loaded with tobacco, paper and a little powder at her.[15]

The necessity of charging youths such as Oxford, Francis, and Bean with the capital crime of high treason placed the judiciary and the executive in an awkward dilemma. On the one hand it seemed inhumane to condemn to death weak-minded bunglers, especially when it was by no means certain what harm they meant to do. On the other hand, to acquit them on the ground of insanity was to stretch that defence much further than had hitherto been done. Nor can Peel have relished the solution of a reprieve which could be misunderstood as condonation of the practice of sniping at Her Majesty. By the time William Bean came to trial, an Act had been passed 'for the further Security and Protection of Her Majesty's Person'.[16] In effect, it distinguished between genuine attempts to kill or harm the sovereign and merely pointing firearms, firing blank charges, throwing things at her, or striking her. These were no longer to be high treason, but a lesser offence, dignified by the title of 'high misdemeanour'. The punishment was to be seven years' transportation, or not more than three years' imprisonment, with or without hard labour, and with or without whippings. Bean himself was sentenced to only eighteen months' imprisonment.

Less fortunate was William Hamilton, an unemployed Irishman, who fired his landlady's pistol, charged only with powder, at Her Majesty as she was driving down Constitution Hill. 'This time', wrote Victoria to Leopold, 'it is clear it was a wanton and wicked wish to frighten, and will be tried and punished as a misdemeanour.'[17] Hamilton was sentenced to seven years' transportation. In the next year, Lieutenant Pate, a former cavalry officer whom even Prince Albert recognised as deranged, was also sentenced to transportation for striking Victoria on the head with his cane in Piccadilly. But by the middle of the nineteenth century transportation to Australia was resented by the respectable descendants of eighteenth-century convicts, and Queensland had the impertinence to suggest that her malefactors be transported to England. From 1854 to 1867 a few Englishmen were transported to Gibraltar and Bermuda; but that was the end. Edward Oxford, who had spent twenty-eight years in Broadmoor and was now middle-aged, was released on condition that he emigrated; but whither we do not know. It is said that in Broadmoor, as he read the news of later attacks on Victoria, he remarked, 'If only they had hanged me, the dear Queen would not have had all this bother.'[18]

It was a sentiment which his Queen herself would have endorsed. By the time of M'Naghten's acquittal in 1843 she had become understandably restive, and complained to Peel that

> The law may be perfect but how is it that whenever a case for its application arises it proves to be of no avail? We have seen the trials of Oxford and MacNaughten conducted by the ablest lawyers of the day – and they *allow* and *advise* the Jury to pronounce the verdict of not guilty on account of insanity, whilst *everybody* is morally convinced that both malefactors were perfectly conscious and aware of what they did.[19]

The emphasis, as usual, is Her Majesty's. There is no trace here of the failure to understand the criminal law for which, as we shall see, she was later ridiculed. She was correct in assuming that, by the legal tests of her day, Oxford and M'Naghten should have been convicted. At most she can be accused of ignoring the signs of change; but these were faint indeed.

When, in 1872, the seventeen-year-old Arthur O'Connor fired a pistol loaded with blank at her outside Buckingham Palace, transportation was obsolete, and he was sentenced to a year's imprisonment and the birch. Victoria was incensed, and caused her private secretary, Sir Henry Ponsonby, to write to the Prime Minister, now Gladstone, about 'the singular leniency of the sentence and the ill-judged charge of Baron Cleasby'.[20] She 'did not desire that more painful punishment should be awarded, but that such criminals should be compelled to excile [sic] themselves'.[20] Finally, in a postscript that was obviously dictated from the heart:

> The Queen must say she is shocked at only one year's imprison-ment considering how much she was alarmed at the time and she fully expects we shall have more of these things.[20]

As usual, the Queen was right: ten years later Roderick Maclean fired a pistol at her as she was about to descend from her carriage at Windsor Station. He was at once attacked by two loyal boys from Eton wielding umbrellas. The Queen was becoming used to such experiences. 'It is worth being shot at – to see how much one is loved', she wrote to her eldest daughter, a consolation which she had crossly rejected when Lord Hardwicke offered it to her after Lieutenant Pate's attack.[21] This time, however, the pistol was found to have been fully loaded, and Maclean was tried for the capital offence of treason. Like Oxford, he was acquitted on

the grounds of insanity, and the Queen was so disturbed that she insisted
on a change in the law:

Windsor, April 23, 1882

. . . if this was the necessary effect of the law, Her Majesty thinks
it worth consideration whether the law should not be amended. . . .

. . . Punishment deters not only sane men but also eccentric men,
whose supposed involuntary acts are really produced by a diseased
brain capable of being acted upon by external influence.

A knowledge that they would be protected by an acquittal on
the grounds of insanity will encourage these men to commit
desperate acts, while on the other hand certainty that they will not
escape punishment will terrify them into a peaceful attitude -
towards others.[20]

She was not alone in believing that even the mentally ill could be deterred:
the eminent psychiatrist Dr Harrington Tuke had said so to the Royal
Commission of 1866.

Her solution – which was at least subtler than Henry VIII's – was to
alter the form of the special verdict so that it sounded like a finding of
guilt. Although neither she nor her advisers seem to have realised it, this
had something very like a precedent in the special verdicts which were
occasionally returned by juries before 1800. Gladstone was at first cautious: 'ignorant of the law, he does not venture an opinion. . . .' After
consulting the Lord Chief Justice and the Attorney-General, however, he
told her that he had 'urged' a change in the form of verdict.[22] A few
months later, when the Trial of Lunatics Bill was ready, he was almost
claiming the credit for it:

. . . By this most proper change, as Mr Gladstone hopes, there
will be a complete extinction of the risk subsisting in the prior
condition of the law. Then – an inducement might offer itself to
morbid minds for the commission of crime by an apparent declaration of innocence in the teeth of the facts.[20]

It is said that the origins of the Bill were privately explained to the Opposition; and certainly it was allowed to pass through both Houses without
serious debate.

The effect of the change was nominal, since the result of a special verdict continued to be detention in an asylum during Her Majesty's Pleasure.
The Judicial Statistics continued – until they were overhauled in the
eighteen-nineties – to record such cases as 'acquitted as being insane'. For
a short time after the creation of the Court of Criminal Appeal in 1907 it
seemed as if the special verdict would be treated as a conviction, at least
so far as appeals were concerned, but the traditional view soon prevailed.
An epileptic called Ireland, who had stabbed a woman, was regarded by
the prison medical officer as insane, although Ireland later claimed to have
feigned insanity. At his trial he did not set up the defence of insanity, but
the judge questioned the prison medical officer, and Ireland was found
'guilty but insane'. His counsel succeeded in convincing the Court of
Criminal Appeal that this amounted to a conviction, and could therefore
be the subject of an appeal (he failed, however, to convince them that in

this particular case it was unjustified).[23] A year and a half later the Lord Chief Justice, who had not presided at the hearing of Ireland's case, did his best to escape from that decision without openly calling it a mistake. He reasoned that what could be the subject of an appeal was the finding that the accused had done the act charged, but not the finding that he was insane, and did his best to ignore the fact that in Ireland's case it was the latter which had been under consideration by the court.[24] Finally, Felstead's case in 1914 provided an opportunity to have the matter considered by the House of Lords, who firmly laid it down that the special verdict was an acquittal, and could not be the subject of an appeal.[25] For the same reason, as we saw in chapter 9, some judges have taken the view that the prosecution cannot ask for a special verdict, since that would amount to asking for an acquittal.

Lawyers, however, have done less than justice to Victoria's reasoning. The oversimplified assumption that she did not understand the doctrine of *mens rea* was encouraged by the fact that she belonged to a sex which was supposed to be weaker in jurisprudence as well as in other matters. Matthaeus mentions a Queen of Castile who flouted the law by executing a madman for wounding her husband, and comments, 'I am not surprised that it should have been a woman who punished a frenzied man.'[26] The attitude of Victorian lawyers was much the same. Sir Herbert Stephen (who may have heard the story from his father, Fitzjames Stephen) wrote in 1920 to *The Times*:

The form of the verdict displeased the Queen. She overlooked the fact that crime, generally speaking, compromises both an un-lawful act and an unlawful intention, and that a man who is 'guilty' of one and not of the other is not 'guilty of the crime. . . . The Queen maintained that, whether or not the man was guilty of high treason, he was 'guilty' of firing a pistol at her. She said that the verdict in such cases ought to begin not with the words 'not guilty' but with the word 'guilty'. Her constitutional advisers did not agree with her view, but could not persuade her to accept theirs. They therefore explained to the leaders of the opposition party the real reason for their proposal to alter the form of the verdict, and the Act of 1883 was passed without controversy. . . .[27]

Sir Herbert Stephen's unchivalrous and unwarranted explanation was adopted and perpetuated not only by Lytton Strachey's biography of Victoria but also by the Atkin Committee on Insanity and Crime, of which Sir Herbert was a member.

The Committee recommended that the verdict should be 'that the accused did the act (or made the omission) charged, but is not guilty on the ground that he was insane so as not to be responsible, according to law, at the time.' No action, however, was taken on any of its recommendations. Thirty years later, the Royal Commission on Capital Punishment came to a similar conclusion; but as we have seen none of its recommendations on insanity were adopted. In 1963 the Criminal Law Revision Committee, which had been asked to tidy up a number of loose ends in the procedures for dealing with insanity in the criminal courts, agreed with

10. Downing Street,
Whitehall.

Mr Gladstone with his humble duty transmits to Your Majesty a short Memorandum written by the Attorney General, which explains succinctly, and as he believes accurately, the change now to be effected in the law as to the _form_ of verdicts in cases of criminal lunacy.

By this most proper change, as Mr Gladstone hopes, there will be a complete extinction of the risk subsisting in the prior condition of the law, that an inducement might offer itself to morbid minds for the commission of crime by an apparent declaration of innocence in the truth of the facts.

Aug. 20. 1883.

its predecessors and recommended (*inter alia*) a simple verdict of 'not guilty by reason of insanity'. None of its other recommendations were controversial, and the bill which was introduced soon afterwards to give effect to them had an easy passage through both Houses, in the course of which Sir Herbert Stephen's slander on Victoria was again recited, this time by Lord Gardiner.

The Bill also created a right of appeal against the verdict, and made it clear that the prosecution *could* ask for such a verdict. Thus one Gilbertian situation was replaced by another. Instead of a verdict which sounded like a conviction but was treated as an acquittal, we now have a verdict which sounds like an acquittal but is treated as a conviction. On the whole, the Queen seems to emerge from the affair with more credit than the lawyers. For her, the Act of 1883 was a harmless means to a reasonable end – the discouragement of insane and unpredictable attacks by means of a nominal deterrent which made no difference to the actual fate of the attacker. It is a remarkable fact that up to the passing of the Act she suffered seven such attacks, but after it none, although she lived another eighteen years.

Even if her logic had been as simple as Sir Herbert Stephen made out, it would not necessarily have been ridiculous. In a legal system in which the practical effect of an acquittal is normally the liberation of the accused, while a conviction renders him subject to a penal measure, how should we classify a verdict which is intended to subject him to indefinite detention in a mental hospital? It is a poor sort of acquittal. If it has anything in common with either of the ordinary verdicts, it is with the one which says 'guilty', since at least both render the accused liable to restraint. But the most remarkable feature of the whole story is the universal assumption that the verdict must contain the word 'guilty', and that there could not possibly be a third sort of verdict which merely labelled the accused 'not responsible for his act by reason of insanity'. In practice the special verdict *was* no less different from the other two, but the inclusion of the word 'guilty' had so hypnotic an effect that this was overlooked.

Notes

1 John Capgrave, *The Chronicle of England* (1420 ca.), pub. 1858 by Treasury authority under the direction of the Master of the Rolls, London.
2 From entry 1401 in the *Calendar of State Papers of Henry* VIII, vol. XVI. The entry is a translation of a deciphered original in the *Spanish Calendar* VI. I. 209 at Vienna.
3 33. Henry VIII, c. 20.
4 1 & 2 Phil. & Mary, c. 10 (1554–5).
5 See the State Papers (Domestic) of Queen Elizabeth and (for the procedural aspects) Savil's Reports (CV and CXXI in the English Reports).
6 Coke, *Reports*, pt IV, 123B.
7 Coke, *Institutes*, III, ch. I.
8 *Historia Placitorum Coronae*, I (London, 1736), ch. IV.
9 See the Privy Council minutes for 1786, pp. 357–.

10 See *The Times* for 20 November 1837, and 7 Adolphus & Ellis 536.
11 See Henry Goddard's *Memoirs of a Bow Street Runner* (London, 1956), editor's notes, p. 166.
12 See file H.O.45/O.S.964 in the Public Record Office. After Shock-ledge had spent nearly six uneventful years in Bethlem someone, perhaps the Home Secretary himself, wrote 'liberate' on his papers.
13 R. v. Oxford (1840), 9 Car. & Payne, 526.
14 See *The Times* for 31 May, 4, 18 and 22 June, 1842.
15 See the Queen's Journal for 17 June and 1 and 4 July 1842, and E. Longford's *Victoria, R.I.* (London, 1964).
16 5 & 6 Vict., c. 51.
17 In a letter of 22 May 1849: see A.C.Benson (ed.), *The Letters of Queen Victoria* (London, 1907).
18 See G.W.Keeton, *Guilty but Insane* (London, 1961).
19 See A.C.Benson, op. cit. (n17), 581.
20 From unpublished correspondence in the Royal Archives at Windsor, which is published by gracious permission of HM the Queen.
21 E.Longford, op. cit. (n15), 192, 446.
22 See P.Guedalla (ed.), *The Queen and Mr Gladstone* II (London, 1933), Ir. 855 et seq.
23 R. v. Ireland (1910), 4 Cr. App. R. 74, 87.
24 R. v. Machardy (1911), 6 Cr. App. R. 256, 272.
25 R. v. Felstead (1914), 10 Cr. App. R. 129.
26 Op. cit. (ch. 8 n3), Cap. 5, 'A femina autem punitum esse hominem furiosum non miror'.
27 See *The Times* for 16 December 1920.

Chapter 12. **The King's Mercy**

This chapter is concerned with the form in which the oldest expedient for exempting the insane from punishment has survived. We saw in chapter 1 that in Norman times homicides who were excused by self-defence, infancy, or madness were dealt with by invoking the power of the king to remedy defects in the law: 'the king must be consulted'. The king not only excused them from the penalty but also gave directions for their safe-keeping. Even when in the nineteenth century the procedure for committing insane criminals to custody was embodied in the statutes the fiction that it was the sovereign who decided where and how long they should be detained was preserved, and was not finally abandoned until the Criminal Procedure Insanity Act of 1964 was passed.[1]

More important, even when insanity, infancy, and self-defence came to be recognised as grounds for acquittal, as they seem to have been at various times in the Middle Ages, the king's power to pardon in such cases could not be regarded as superseded, although lawyers' explanations of the position seemed slightly forced. 'At common law', wrote Joseph Chitty as late as 1820, 'where a person indicted for manslaughter or murder is found by the jury to have killed . . . in his own defence or by misfortune, he is obliged to crave the King's pardon, to which, however, he is entitled as a matter of right. It is now usual to avoid expense by directing a general verdict of acquittal.'[2] So useful a tree could not be allowed to wither away. For in the Middle Ages the royal pardon was so profitable an institution that it would have been unthinkable to allow it to fall into disuse. The king could use it to oblige a powerful lord, to protect his entourage, to improve his public image, and of course to supplement his other sources of income: pardons were sold for money. Like the institutions of sanctuary and benefit of clergy, the king's pardon became a wide back-door through which felons escaped the penalty for their crimes, and from the fourteenth century there recur records of protests from Parliament, burghers and others against the wholesale freedom with which the power was used. By Richard II's reign the granting of pardons had become one of the tasks of his officers, and most of them were issued under warrant of the privy seal without reference to the king himself. These seem to have been less objectionable than those in which the king took a personal hand, for in 1390 a petition of Parliament asked that all pardons should bear the privy seal – in other words, should have gone through the proper channels in his small bureaucracy. The proper channels, however, seem to have been equally irresponsible, for in 1406 Henry IV directed his Chancellor, Treasurer, Keeper of the Privy Seal, and other officers not to grant pardons except on the advice of the King's Council.[3]

Equally objectionable was the blank pardon, in which the name of the accused could be filled in later, and the blanket pardon, which covered any crime that the holder might have committed. Although Richard bound himself to abandon these practices, they persisted or were revived long after his reign. In the middle of the fifteenth century scores of pardons were issued to cover 'all trespasses, contempts, violation of the statute of liveries, murders, rapes, rebellions, riots, felonies, conspiracies, maintenances, embraceries and treasons'.

Nor was it only the king and his chancery who used this convenient power. In Tudor times it was being exercised by the lords of the Welsh Marches, that remote and lawless tract, in much the same way as colonial governors exercise it in this century. As part of the consolidation of his authority over this area Henry VIII took this power away from them and confined it to the king himself. In the Act of 1535–6[4] which did so, he attributed the existing state of affairs to 'sondrye giftes of the King's most noble Progenitours', but this was probably no more than official mythology. A predecessor *may* have delegated this power for reasons of tact or administrative convenience: but it is equally likely that the insubordinate Lords of the Marches simply assumed this power during the anarchic fifteenth century, and that Henry was the first monarch who felt strong enough to bring them to heel.

A few years later, in 1542–3, Henry decided that it was time to establish the English judicial system in Wales, and the Act by which he did so contains an interesting clause providing

Item, That from hensforthe no maner of person or persones for
Murther or Felony shall be put to his Fyne, but suffre according
to the Lawes of the Realme of Englande, excepte it pleas the Kinges
Majestie to pardone him or them. And if the said Justices see
cause of pitie or other consideracion they may reprie the prysoner
till they hav advertised the Kinges' Majestie of the matur.[5]

Almost certainly this tells us how the royal prerogative was meant to operate in England at this period. Communication with the king could be a lengthy business. Consequently, if the judge (or local justices, who had to deal with many cases of felony during the periods when the judges of assize were afraid to travel) thought that a felon deserved mercy, they would not simply pronounce sentence of death on him but would 'reprie' him – that is take him back to prison – until the King could be consulted. This practice was the origin not only of the term 'reprieve' but of an even greater delegation of responsibility to the judges in the post-Tudor era which will be described later in this chapter.

We saw in chapter 1 that by the end of the fifteenth century – and perhaps earlier – it was established that a person who had clearly been sufficiently insane at the time of his felony could be acquitted by the justices themselves, without going through the old formality of consulting the king. This must have almost eliminated the need to use the expedient of pardon to save the insane from capital punishment. Certainly none of the many medieval pardons which have been extracted by historians from contemporary records deals with a case of insanity. It is true that, by Henry VIII's reign, it seems to have been accepted as a principle that a criminal who had been sane enough at the time of arraignment to stand his trial, and who had been, in the view of the jury, sane enough at the time of his crime to be found guilty of it, should nevertheless have his execution deferred if after sentence he manifested a sufficient degree of insanity. This seems to be implied, for example, by the preamble of the bill which Henry VIII introduced to enable him to execute Lady Rocheford (see chapter 11):

> Forasmuch as sometime some persons, being accused of High Treasons, have, after they have been examined before the King's Majesty's Council, confessed their Offences of High Treason, and yet nevertheless after the doing of their Treasons, and Examinations and Confessions thereof, as is aforesaid, have fallen to Madness or Lunacy, whereby the condign punishment of their Treasons, were they never so notable and detestable, hath been deferred, spared and delayed. . . .[6]

This does not allow us to assume, however, that either traitors or felons who 'fell to madness or lunacy' after conviction were at this date regarded as entitled to a *pardon*. It is more likely that what they were granted was a delay of execution. Henry's statute used the words '*deferred*, spared, and *delayed*'. Moreover, when we come to the first detailed exposition of the law regarding reprieves and stays of execution – in Hale's *History of the Pleas of the Crown* – this seems a reasonable interpretation of it.

Hale, writing in the second half of the seventeenth century, held that there were three sorts of reprieves, or stays of judgment or execution. First he lists those which were at the king's command (*ex mandato regis*). A second sort consists of those which were at the judge's discretion (*ex arbitrio judicis*), and were granted sometimes because the judge doubted the guilt of the accused, sometimes because the crime seemed to merit leniency. The third sort are enjoined by law (*ex necessitate legis*). The only example of this sort given by Hale is the pregnant woman, who must not be put to death while pregnant, but must be after she had been delivered of her child.[7] To which category did the reprieve of the lunatic belong? Certainly the fact that Henry VIII found it necessary to legislate before he could put Lady Rocheford to death is almost conclusive evidence that it was *ex necessitate legis*; there is no suggestion in Hale's passage that reprieves of the other two kinds were other than discretionary.

Moreover, it is highly probable that, like the pregnant woman, the convicted or sentenced felon who later fell to madness or lunacy was entitled only to a deferment of execution. As we shall see in the next chapter, even Lord Normanby's bill of 1840 was consistent with this principle. It was well known that some madmen quickly recovered their senses; indeed, the term 'lunatic' was reserved by purists for those whose madness was periodic. It is worth noting that nearly all the justifications which lawyers offered for the principle that a sentenced felon who later fell to madness should not suffer the penalty were arguments that necessitated its deferment and not its cancellation.

Continental ecclesiastics seem to have taken different sides over the question whether a man who did wrong before going mad could justly be the subject of corporal punishment after he had done so. Diego de Covarrubias (see chapter 10) followed earlier authorities in arguing that this was unjust. 'For', he pointed out, 'the strongest reason for a penalty is that it inflicts suffering upon the punishable person: a reason which is clearly lacking in the case of the insane person.'[8] Although the sentence is not completely unambiguous, he seems to imply that the madman is incapable of suffering, perhaps because he is incapable of experiencing apprehension. If so, it would be consistent to punish him when he had recovered his senses.

The same is true of the argument which Coke used in commenting on Henry's Act. 'The principal end of punishment is, that others by his example may feare to offend, *ut poena ad paucos metus ad omnes perveniat* (in order that the penalty may touch a few, but the feare thereof touch many): but such punishment can be no example to madmen.'[9] His logic, of course, was far from strong, for as was pointed out by Sir John Hawles, Solicitor-General to William III, 'the terror to the living is equal, whether the person be mad or in his senses.'[10] Hale and Hawles agree that the main justification is that if the madman were sane he might be able to give a reason why he should not be executed; but Hawles adds a third argument. 'It is inconsistent with religion, as being against Christian charity to send an offender quick, as it is stiled, into another world, when he is not of a capacity to fit himself for it.'[10] Hume offers what seems to be the same argument: that the offender is not spiritually ready for death.[11]

Blackstone gives two reasons. One is Hale's – that if sane he might have offered a reason why he should not be executed. The other is more interesting, for it echoes the words of the Digest: the madman is punished by his very madness.[12] It is the only one of the five arguments against executing a madman which is not entirely consistent with the principle that he should be hanged when he has recovered his senses.

If I am correct in supposing that until Queen Victoria's reign strict legal theory allowed only a respite and not a commutation of a sentence for the criminal who 'fell to madness' after conviction, it does not necessarily follow that there were no cases in which the king took into account the criminal's state of mind when considering whether to substitute a lesser punishment. This is most unlikely, for several reasons. It is clear from Hume[13] that by the eighteenth century permanent commutation of the death sentence could be expected in Scots cases in which it was clear that the accused had almost, if not quite, satisfied the test of insanity at the time of his crime. Did English judges never recommend a similar course? After all, by George III's reign a large number of death sentences was commuted every year to transportation or even imprisonment, for reasons such as the youth of the accused, his previous good conduct, or simply what the judge described vaguely as 'favourable circumstances'. Indeed, so far as the provinces were concerned the judges' power of reprieve had developed into something very like a delegated power of pardon; and they could virtually commit the King to substituting a lesser penalty. Even when, in an attempt to increase the deterrent effect of capital punishment in cases of murder, an Act of 1752 decreed that convicted murderers should be executed on the next day but one after sentence (thus allowing practically no time for private attempts to secure the royal mercy), the judge was empowered to grant a stay of execution if there appeared to be 'reasonable cause'.[14]

Very large numbers of judges' reports on capital cases, and private recommendations or petitions for mercy, covering most of the reign of George III, are preserved in the Public Record Office.[15] It is unfortunate that Arnold's case occurred too early to fall within this period, for we know that on the intercession of Lord Onslow his death sentence was commuted to imprisonment, and that he spent the rest of his life in Southwark Gaol.[16] But the State papers of George II contain only one letter about Arnold: Lord Onslow's note about arrangements for the trial which is referred to in chapter 3; so that we cannot be sure whether it was Arnold's state of mind or some other consideration – such as the survival and magnanimity of his victim – which prevailed.

The Home Office papers for 1787, however, include a document which is worth reproducing in full because it illustrates several features of the way in which the insane criminal could be dealt with:

To the King's Most Excellent Majesty

I most humbly Certify unto Your Majesty That at the last Assizes holden at Nottingham in and for the County of Nottingham MATTHEW CLAY was Tried before me for Burglary and in the course of the Trial Evidence was given of the said Prisoner's Insanity and such Evidence was submitted by me to the consideration of the Jury who tried him. But they notwithstanding found him Guilty of the said Offence. Whereupon I respited Judgment. And it being represented unto me that his Father is willing to receive and take care of him in case Your Majesty shall be graciously pleased to extend your Royal Mercy to him I do most humbly recommend him to Your Majesty for a Pardon on Condition that his Father do enter into a Recognizance in the sum of Twenty pounds before one of Your Majesty's Justices of the peace in and for the said County of Nottingham that due Care shall be taken of the said Matthew Clay to prevent him from committing any Offence for the future. Dated this twenty sixth-day of January 1787.
H. Gould[17]

Here is a case, thirteen years before Hadfield's trial, in which the judge had been so impressed with the evidence of the insanity of the accused that he had not only put it to the jury but, when they were too stupid to take the hint, had put off the execution and asked the king to grant him a

To the King's most Excellent Majesty

I most humbly Certify unto Your Majesty That at the last Assises holden at Nottingham in and for the County of Nottingham Matthew Clay was Tried before me for Burglary and in the course of the Trial Evidence was given of the said Prisoner's Insanity and such Evidence was submitted by me to the consideration of the Jury who tried him But they notwithstanding found him Guilty of the said Offence Whereupon I respited Judgment thereon. And it being represented unto me that his Father is willing to receive and take care of him in case Your Majesty shall be graciously pleased to extend your Royal Mercy to him. I do most humbly recommend him to Your Majesty for a Pardon on Condition that his Father do enter into a Recognizance in the Sum of Twenty pounds before one of Your Majesty's Justices of the Peace in and for the said County of Nottingham that due Care shall be taken of the said Matthew Clay to prevent him from committing any Offence for the future Dated this twenty sixth — day of January 1787 H Gould conditional pardon. The arrangements for looking after Clay have already been mentioned in chapter 2.

But that was a case in which the judge considered that there had been a miscarriage of justice, and that the accused ought to have been acquitted. Scotland apart, were there cases in which a lesser degree of mental disorder was accepted as a sufficient reason for clemency? In a search through the judges' reports for nineteen years I have found several cases in which the prisoner's 'weakness of understanding' or 'imbecility of mind occasioned by a violent fever' or similar states of mind were mentioned as extenuating circumstances in petitions on his or her behalf, although in most of these cases the judge refused to recognise any mental disorder. When Amelia Gill, for example, was sentenced to seven years' transportation for stealing five yards of printed calico from a shop, the gaoler of York Castle wrote that during her confinement 'she appeared at times of a flighty disposition . . . owing to a Decline in Life'; but the judge wrote 'I have stated the evidence, from which it appears that she was in her perfect senses at the time of the commission of the Fact.' If the sentence was mitigated there were usually a number of favourable circumstances, so that it is impossible to be sure whether the prisoner's state of mind was an important consideration. I found one clear-cut case, however: in 1787 Robert Chamberlayne, aged 20, was sentenced to seven years' transportation for attempted robbery on the highway. His defence (which did not succeed) was insanity, and the keeper of a house for lunatics at Hoxton testified that Chamberlayne had been a patient of his for twelve weeks, while a relative said that both before and after this the accused 'had at times a sort of Madness or Frenzey'. His petition proposed – and the judge agreed with it – that if pardoned Chamberlayne should go to a colony at his own expense.[18]

But clemency could not be counted on even in circumstances which would seem to us overwhelmingly in favour of it. When Decima Chapple was convicted in 1786 of receiving a few stolen articles of clothing, the churchwardens of Bath wrote that 'The object of the petition, in her sixty-sixth year, is sentenced to Fourteen Years' transportation, for doing what she was not conscious to be a crime – Providence not having blessed her with an Understanding capable of clearly distinguishing right from wrong; and her slender capacity now most probably impaired by the infirmities of age'. But the judge's report contained nothing in her favour, and a curt marginal note says 'No alteration of the present sentence'.[19] It is unlikely that Decima Chapple survived the voyage, let alone fourteen years in whatever colony she may have reached.

Although George III was advised by Ministers, and indeed from 1782 onwards had a 'Secretary of State for Home Affairs', the responsibility for these decisions had not yet devolved on the latter. It was the King who took the final decision. Usually he did so in the presence of his Cabinet Council, of which the Home Secretary was a member; and it was the Home Secretary's clerks who had assembled the judge's reports and other documents in provincial cases. But that did not give the Home Secretary any special say in the matter. The real responsibility was divided between the judge and the King. When metropolitan cases, tried at the Old Bailey, came up for discussion, the Recorder of London attended and answered questions about them. In provincial cases it was the judge whose report usually settled the matter, although if the judge happened to be available he sometimes attended in person. Moreover, although such occasions came to be known as 'hanging cabinets', the decisions were regarded as the king's own responsibility (as indeed they often were). Meetings of the hanging cabinets were not officially regarded as Privy Council meetings, and their decisions were not recorded in Privy Council minutes. It was only when the madman's conduct seemed to amount to treason that the Privy Council took an official hand (see chapter 11). At other times the decision was the King's own.

The judge's share of the responsibility was emphasised as late as 1823. When the Parliamentary campaign to restrict the scope of the death penalty was achieving its first successes, an Act of Peel's[20] allowed judges to do more than grant a respite where felonies other than murder were concerned. If the court was of opinion that the circumstances made the offender 'a fit and proper subject . . . to be recommended for the Royal Mercy' it could refrain from pronouncing sentence of death, and merely record it instead. This seems to have been regarded as making it impossible to carry out the sentence, so that the judge was in effect committing the king to a pardon. (No doubt the pardon was usually a conditional one, requiring the felon to be transported or confined in an asylum or prison.) At a time when the death penalty was becoming so controversial Peel was probably trying to reduce to the minimum the cases in which the hanging cabinet could be held responsible for the decision between life and death.

At this stage, the machinery which brought the prerogative of mercy into play seems to have worked thus. At a provincial assize a judge would *pronounce* sentence of death on all murderers (of necessity) but only on other felons if they seemed to be undeserving of mercy. (In deserving cases he would simply allow the death sentence to be *recorded*, thus ensuring that a lesser penalty would be substituted.) If a murderer seemed an 'object of mercy' he would reprieve him for consideration by the king, whose decision would almost certainly confirm his view. At the Old Bailey, on the other hand, while death sentences were occasionally respited by the judge, they would usually be *pronounced* not only on murderers but on other convicted felons whose crimes were capital; and they would be left to the 'hanging cabinet' to deal with. The reason for the difference between provincial and metropolitan practice was of course the much greater speed with which metropolitan cases could be brought before the king.

In all probability the hanging cabinets seldom spent time in discussing capital cases from the provinces. If the judge had recommended mercy, that was that. If he had not, any plea on the condemned person's behalf, was probably put forward by the Home Secretary. It was usually only in metropolitan cases, therefore, that the cabinet had to arrive at a decision. Edward Gibbon Wakefield says 'that on average about twenty such cases were decided at a sitting, which might last a few hours or occasionally less than an hour. The Recorder of London would attend and present state-ments on all the cases (some but not all of which he himself would have tried). Wakefield referred to the cabinet as a 'Court of Appeal', but em-phasised that it heard no evidence and was bound by no known rules.[21]

If the king in council decided against mercy, the condemned man had one more chance. Like his provincial counterpart, he could be pardoned by the king himself. By Wakefield's time this usually meant that if the Home Secretary advised the king in the prisoner's favour the king would take this advice. Earlier secretaries of state for home affairs had not been strong men, and it was not until Peel's first term in this office, from 1822 to 1827, that the Home Secretary's advice in the matter of the death sen-tence began to be recognised as the last word. Peel himself had to take George IV to task more than once for commuting capital sentences at the instance of courtiers after appeals for mercy had been officially refused.[22]

Notes

1 See the following chapter.
2 J. Chitty (junior), *A Treatise on the Law of the Prerogatives of the Crown* (London, 1820), 94.
3 See Sir Harris Nicholas (ed.), *Acts of the Privy Council* (1834–).
4 27 Henry VIII, c. 24.
5 34–5 Henry VIII, c. 26, s. XXXII.
6 33 Henry VIII, c. 20.
7 M. Hale (1736), *History of the Pleas of the Crown*, II ch. 57. In the eighteenth century the woman was said to 'plead her belly'. Strictly speaking she had to be 'quick with child': in other words, the child must be palpably moving. But, as Hale says, the jury of women tended to be 'gentle to them in their verdicts'.
8 Diego de Covarrubias, loc. cit., Part 3. 'Nam ratio potissima poenae in hoc extat, quod afficiat afflictione ipsum puniendum: quae quidem ratio in furioso defiicit manifeste.'
9 *Third Institute* (1641), cap. 1.
10 See his *Remarks on the trial of Mr Charles Bateman* (Howell's *State Trials*), XI, 476.
11. Baron Hume, *Commentaries on the Law of Scotland respecting Trial for Crimes* (Edinburgh, 1797) ch. XVII.
12 Blackstone, *Commentaries on the Laws of England*, IV (Oxford, 1765–9), ch. 31: 'furiosus solo furore punitur'.
13 Hume, loc. cit.
14 25 Geo. II. c. 37, 'An Act for better preventing the horrid crime of murder'.
15 For the period 1760–75, convenient summaries have been printed in the Calendar of Home Office Papers (1878). But for the rest of George III's reign the originals themselves have to be searched.
16 See chapter 3.
17 In volume H.O. 47/6 of Home Office Papers in the Public Record Office, by whose permission it is reproduced here.
18 Ibid.

19 In Volume H.O. 47 4 of Home Office Papers in the Public
Record Office.
20 4 George IV, c. 48.
21 Edward Gibbon Wakefield, *Facts relating to the Sentence of Death
in the Metropolis* (London, 1831).
22 See N. Gash, *Mr Secretary Peel* (London, 1961), ch. 9.

Chapter 13. The Home Secretary's Mercy

Although it was Peel who asserted the right of the Cabinet to decide whether a reprieve was justified or not, it was not until 1837 that the decision passed effectively into the hands of the Home Secretary.

The accession of Queen Victoria meant that the meetings of the King's Council were presided over by an eighteen-year-old girl, with whom, as Fitzjames Stephen said, 'it would have been indecent and practically impossible to discuss . . . the details of many crimes then capital'.[1] Within a few weeks the Central Criminal Court Act of 1837 had been passed, and capital cases from the Old Bailey need no longer be reported to the sovereign. The judge could henceforward refrain from pronouncing the death sentence in deserving cases and merely order it to be recorded, as the 1823 Act allowed him to do in cases other than murder.

That judges sometimes intervened in this way to save the lives of insane felons is demonstrated in the case of Charles Westron, tried for murder in 1856. Doctors had testified that his capacity to distinguish right from wrong had been impaired, but could not swear that he was quite unaware of the wrongness of killing a man. The jury found him guilty, but recommended mercy on the ground that he was 'predisposed to insanity'. Mr Justice Wightman, after consulting Mr Justice Willes, who had assisted at the trial, ordered the death sentence to be recorded instead of pronouncing it, and thus ensured its commutation.[2]

This expedient was very soon supplemented by another piece of legislation which was eventually to have embarrassing consequences. At the time of Victoria's accession the law allowed persons under sentence of imprisonment or transportation to be transferred to a lunatic asylum by warrant of the Home Secretary if two physicians or surgeons certified that the offender was insane.[3] In 1840 the Home Secretary (Lord Normanby) introduced a little bill which did not, he said, 'contain anything either of novelty or difficulty'. Henceforward, if a prisoner appeared to be insane there was to be an inquiry by two justices of the peace and if they as well as the doctors certified that the prisoner was insane it would be 'lawful' for the Home Secretary to order his transfer to an asylum. More important, this procedure was to apply not merely to persons sentenced to imprisonment or transportation, but to every sort of criminal prisoner, including those under sentence of death.[4]

It is doubtful whether the implications of including this group of prisoners were really appreciated. For the Act – which both Houses accepted with virtually no debate – provided for the return of prisoners to prison if they recovered their sanity but said nothing about hanging those who had been under sentence of death. It was not long, however, before this very eventuality arose. Dalmas, who committed a murder on Battersea Bridge in the early eighteen-forties, was under sentence of death when he was certified as insane and transferred to Bethlem. Shortly afterwards he was certified sane and sent back to prison. The death sentence was commuted to transportation for life, and there has been no subsequent case in which a prisoner in similar circumstances has been hanged.[5]

This case reminds us of the similarity between the reprieve of the pregnant woman and the reprieve of the lunatic. The death penalty was not cancelled, merely postponed until the prisoner recovered sanity or was delivered of the child, as the case might be. As far as pregnancy was concerned this was still assumed to be the rule as late as 1849, when Charlotte Harris was found to be pregnant after her conviction for poisoning her husband. Dymond, the campaigner against the death penalty, says that after the birth 'a disposition was manifested by the Executive to carry out the sentence', but that a memorial to the Queen by forty thousand women secured the commutation of her sentence. Dymond assumed that this case set a precedent; if so, a way of circumventing it was soon devised. For in 1863 Alice Holt's trial for murder was postponed until she was no longer pregnant, and she was hanged![6]

It should not be assumed, of course, that during this period only prisoners who were certified insane were reprieved. In 1855 Thomas Corrigan stabbed his wife in a temporary frenzy which was believed to be the result of habitual drinking; and although he cannot have been certifiably insane at the time when Sir George Grey was persuaded to consider his case, the death sentence was commuted at the last moment to transportation for life.[6]

Sir George Grey must have played a considerable part in the formation of Home Office policy during this period. After a short career as a barrister and a longer one as a Member of Parliament, he was Home Secretary from 1845 to 1852, from 1855 to 1858, and from 1861 to 1866. His oral evidence to the Capital Punishment Commission in 1865 revealed a highly legalistic attitude to the use of the prerogative. 'The duty of the Secretary of State is not to make the law but to administer it. . . .'[7] Dymond, as Secretary of the Society for the Abolition of Capital Punishment, found Grey especially resistant to the idea of reprieving murderers on the grounds of insanity[6]; and as Townley's case was to demonstrate, he certainly interpreted his powers very narrowly.

The judges' discretion was virtually abolished in 1861, when the law dealing with offences against the person was codified. The draftsmen of the Offences against the Person Act[8] simply provided that the court *must pronounce* the death sentence for murder. Since the Act did not deal with treason, arson of the royal dockyards, or armed piracy, the judges' power to record the death sentence for these offences was untouched, and for some reason has remained so ever since. The reasoning which led to its abolition in cases of murder was not, so far as I can discover, publicly stated. It may simply have been that improvements in communications and the creation of an organised bureaucracy in the shape of the Home Office made it unnecessary to preserve the older expedient for ensuring clemency. The change was regretted by some – for example, by Sir George Grey – and there were occasional attempts to restore the judges' discretion in the course of the next half-century: the last of these was in 1909.[9] But this was a clock that could not be turned back.

Thus from 1861 the Home Secretary became virtually the only dispenser of mercy. This did not, at this early date, mean that he automatically considered the use of the royal prerogative in *every* capital case. That this was far from being so was disclosed by Sir George Grey when he gave his oral evidence to the Capital Punishment Commission in 1865 and frankly admitted that the recent case of the murderer Köhl was known to him only from the newspaper. 'Not a single letter or communication', he said, 'was addressed to the Home Office upon the subject; and the case seemed so clear that there was nothing to induce one to communicate with the judge, and the sentence was carried into effect, I believe, with universal consent. . . .' Conscious that perhaps this did not sound too well, Sir George added: 'But this is rather an exceptional case.' Even the Home Office's own records do not make it possible to establish the exact date when it became the practice to review every case. What is certain is that in 1882 prison governors were instructed that every case in which a prisoner was sentenced to death must be reported at once to the Home Office.[10] This can be interpreted either as the beginning of the modern practice of automatic review, or as an attempt to remedy a defect which had come to light in the existing arrangements for automatic review. The most that can be said with certainty is that the practice was adopted at some date between 1865 and 1882.

If a reprieve was being considered, the Home Secretary invariably consulted the judge who had tried the case. This is illustrated by the reprieve of Celestine Sommers,[11] who in 1856 took her ten-year-old stepdaughter to the cellar and cut her throat. Her defence was that her responsibility for her action had been impaired by distress at her husband's conduct, and although this was unacceptable in law the Home Secretary, Sir George Grey, reprieved her on the grounds of insanity. (She was later transferred to an asylum, and there died insane.) In those days a reprieve could occasionally be as unpopular as the refusal of one, and Grey had to face both criticism in the newspapers and a question in the House of Commons.[12] The questioner asked whether the judge had been consulted, and what his opinion had been. Sir George replied that, without any good grounds for doing so, it would be contrary to all precedent to disclose the judge's confidential communications.

If, on the other hand, the evidence of the accused's insanity was disputed at the trial, he had little hope of a reprieve at this period. Luigi Buranelli, who ran amok with a pistol in his lodgings in 1855, was not reprieved in spite of his history of eccentric behaviour, his depressed ramblings about suicide, and strong testimony on his behalf by several psychiatrists. The Crown had brought medical and lay witnesses to rebut the defence of insanity, and their evidence secured a conviction. Even a memorial by five doctors, including the well-known John Connolly of Hanwell, did not persuade Sir George Grey to interfere with the law.[13]

How did Home Secretaries reason when they had to consider such cases? It is unfortunate that since the beginning of Victoria's reign, if not earlier, they have felt a need for reticence about the use of the prerogative. Sir John Graham told John Bright in 1844 that 'it was not consistent with his duty' to discuss the case of Mary Furley, who had thrown herself and her child into a pond, but had herself been rescued.[14] But Home Secretaries are politicians first, and their ability to keep their mouths shut has varied, especially under strong attack. Grey's lips were unsealed in 1864 by his anxiety to defend himself in the House of Commons over Townley's case.[15]

Townley was a man from a respectable Manchester family whose fiancée in Derbyshire had broken off the engagement because she preferred someone else. He wrote asking her to see him, and when he arrived from Manchester they went for a long walk, at the end of which he cut her throat. Making no attempt to escape, he said to the people who found them: 'I told her I would kill her. She knew my temper', and behaved with 'apparent indifference'. His defence was insanity, and Forbes Winslow was the chief medical witness. (It is interesting to note that both his interviews with the prisoner had been conducted in the presence of the prison governor and without any disclosure of his name or purpose to the prisoner.) Townley had showed several clear symptoms of insanity, saying that six conspirators were plotting his destruction, and that he had as much right to deal with his unfaithful fiancée as with any other property of his; he had no remorse, and recognised no man's right to judge him. On the other hand, Winslow seemed to admit under cross-examination that Townley knew he was breaking the law. Baron Martin, who referred to several earlier cases but made no mention of the M'Naghten Rules, told the jury in effect that the question for them was whether Townley knew that his act was contrary to the law of God and punishable by the law of the land. Townley was convicted and sentenced to death.[16]

Immediately after the trial Baron Martin wrote to the Home Secretary that the conviction was in his opinion just, but that two doctors had declared Townley 'absolutely insane'. Grey asked Martin what his view was, but Martin hedged. The Lunacy Commissioners were then asked to examine the prisoner, but reported that, though not of sound mind, he had been responsible for his act within the meaning of the M'Naghten Rules. Townley's family, however, were well-to-do and his lawyers were resourceful. A scrutiny of Lord Normanby's Act of 1840 showed them what could be done. At the same time as the Lunacy Commissioners' report there arrived at the Home Office a certificate by three local justices and two doctors that they had examined Townley and that he was insane. It was now only forty-eight hours before the time fixed for the execution, and although there were legal flaws in the certificate Grey decided to respite the prisoner, and shortly afterwards transferred him to Bethlem.

There, at Grey's request, he was examined yet again by Meyer of Broadmoor, Hood of Bethlem, and two other doctors, who said unequivocally that he was of sound mind. Townley was transferred again, this time to the penitentiary at Pentonville, where he put an end to the tragi-comedy by committing suicide.

Grey was well aware of the theoretical arguments of Coke, Hawles, and Hale against hanging madmen. But did he ask himself whether the public hanging of Townley would deter others? Or whether Townley was too mad to meet his Maker, or to offer last-minute evidence in his favour? He did not. If he asked any definite question it was whether Townley might not after all have been so insane at the time of his act as to have come within the M'Naghten Rules. Bramwell's evidence to the Capital Punishment Commission shows that he too believed that this was the real issue for the Home Secretary.

In fairness to Grey and Bramwell it must be remembered that until 1907 there was no properly constituted court of appeal, and that the Home Office consequently had to review thousands of cases each year in which miscarriages of justice were alleged. It was both natural and desirable that the Home Secretary should not regard the defence of insanity as completely disposed of by the trial, since a hostile judge, jury, or prison doctor, or an incompetent counsel or medical witness for the defence, could occasionally ruin this defence. What is not so easy to understand is how the Lunacy Commissioners and Grey could assume that the *only* relevant question for them was whether the accused had been 'M'Naghten-mad' when he committed the murder. The mere fact that the 1840 Act allowed a certificate that the prisoner was insane *when examined* should have suggested otherwise, for in the case of an offender sentenced not to death but to imprisonment the examination might take place years after the crime. The explanation seems to be that neither the Commissioners nor the Home Office at this time drew a clear distinction between insanity at the time of the act and supervening insanity. They may simply have assumed that a certificate of insanity at the time of examination was merely the best available evidence of insanity at the time of the act.

The case aroused almost as much public concern as M'Naghten's. *The Times*[17] saw nothing wrong with Townley's conviction, and wrote scathingly of 'the scientific theories of Dr Forbes Winslow' which had raised doubts as to the prisoner's insanity. Winslow had to defend himself publicly against attackers who included his own psychiatric colleagues: Maudsley and Lockhart-Robertson produced a hastily written pamphlet which disowned Winslow's criteria of insanity.[18] But there was even more indignation over the way in which, as *The Times* put it, 'the authority not only of the judge and jury, but of the Queen herself, is set aside by two magistrates and two medical practitioners'. The Derbyshire magistrates demanded an investigation into 'the origin and conduct' of the inquiry which had forced the Home Secretary's hand.[19] Since, however, the inquiry had apparently been conducted in accordance with the statute, it was the Act of 1840 which was really under fire, and Grey quickly introduced a bill to amend it.[20]

For all its length and imposing verbiage, however, the bill made only a few changes in the law. Henceforth, the certificate could not be given by any justices, but only by those officially appointed to visit the place where the prisoner was confined. Since local gaols – where most executions took place – were still the responsibility of the justices, Grey refused to take away from them the choice of medical examiners, but merely stipulated that these should be on the newly created Medical Register. Finally, the bill made it plain that if a prisoner under sentence of death was later certified as sane he must return to prison to be hanged. Although this grim provision reflected traditional theory, if not practice, it was probably intended merely to pacify those members of parliament who would have liked to see Townley hang; for, as I have said, there have been no cases since Dalmas' in which this was actually allowed to happen.

An unobtrusive little amendment made it not merely lawful but *obligatory* for the Home Secretary to act upon the justices' certificate that a prisoner was insane. Grey had been criticised for not having the strength of mind to exercise the discretion which the 1840 Act gave him and let Townley hang; and this may have been his way of protecting himself and his successors against future attacks from the same quarter. He could have defended it on the ground that the obligation already existed in common law – an argument used by one of his successors in 1922. However this may be, the *statutory* obligation was tacitly dropped twenty years later. By 1884 local gaols as well as convict prisons were the responsibility of central government, and the Home Secretary had taken over the justices' duty of appointing doctors to examine prisoners whose sanity was in doubt. The manœuvre of 1864 had lost its point, for the Home Secretary could hardly shelter behind the authority of doctors whom he himself had seen fit to appoint. In any case, the impropriety of binding the Home Secretary to exercise what was in essence a royal prerogative must have become more obvious. The Criminal Lunatics Act of 1884 (which dealt mainly with other matters)[21] merely provided for the holding of the medical examinations, and was silent as to the appropriate action by the Home Secretary.

What the 1884 Act did oblige the Home Secretary to do was to order an examination in certain circumstances. Although the justices were no longer responsible for local gaols, each gaol had, then as now, a visiting committee of justices; and if any two of these certified that there was reason to believe a prisoner under sentence of death to be insane the Home Secretary had to appoint two legally qualified medical practitioners to examine the prisoner. He also had to do so if 'by any other means' there appeared reason to doubt the prisoner's sanity. The doctors were to report on this in writing, and they, or a majority of them, could certify that he was insane. As in the Acts of 1840 and 1864, the issue was not the murderer's state of mind at the time of his crime, but his sanity at the time of examination. It is by no means certain, however, what question the Home Secretary was meant to put to himself after reading their report. Grey, for example, would have argued that his task was still to decide whether the prisoner had been sane when he killed, and that the doctors were asked to consider his sanity at the time of examination because that was the best that could be expected of them. The Atkin Committee, however, were told in 1922 that the official instructions to the medical examiners directed them to investigate the prisoner's mental condition both now and at the time of the murder, and long before then the Home Office must have been asking itself at least two questions:

a. Was this a case in which a defence of insanity (whether offered or not) should have succeeded: that is, in lawyer's slang, was the act committed in a state of 'M'Naghten-madness'?

b. If the answer to a was 'No', was the responsibility of the accused nevertheless impaired by his mental condition at the time?

For by 1884, as we have seen, the narrowness of the M'Naghten Rules was beginning to be appreciated, and the Home Secretary's right to look beyond them was becoming not only recognised but welcomed.

Not long before 1884 there had been another change in procedure. Originally, as we have seen, the execution of the insane prisoner was merely respited until he recovered his sanity, as happened, for example, in Dalmas' case. But when insanity at the time of the crime came to be recognised as a mitigating circumstance the logical course was to commute the sentence to a lesser penalty by means of a conditional pardon; and that was what happened in some of the cases which I have cited from George III's reign. By the eighteen-seventies it seems to have become the normal practice to commute the death penalty, not merely respite it, whatever the reason for deciding that the law should not take its course, so that the practice of respiting the execution of the insane had fallen into disuse.[22] This must have happened after Dalmas' case, which very probably established the principle that once respited the sentence should not be carried out. Certainly the distinction between a commutation and a permanent respite is a fine one. However that may be, it seems to have been decided in 1879 that the traditional procedure should be revived: thenceforth the insane murderer's death sentence was 'respited until further signification of Her Majesty's Pleasure'. Her Pleasure never was signified, but meanwhile the insane prisoner was transferred by a statutory warrant to Broadmoor (or, later, to other mental hospitals).

From 1884 onward, although the hardening tradition of Ministerial reticence makes published information about individual cases even scarcer, some light of a more diffuse kind is provided by the statistical and general statements which the Home Office supplied to the Atkin Committee of 1922 and the Royal Commission on Capital Punishment of 1949–53.[23] The Atkin Committee were told that 58 statutory inquiries had been held since 1900, and that this represented 10 per cent of all convictions for murder. Since they were also told that the corresponding percentage for the period 1884–1922 was 11 per cent, it can be inferred that a murderer had at least as good a chance of a statutory inquiry during the period 1884–99 as during the period 1900–22. (Indeed, it is noticeable that during the 1914–18 war only 3 out of 78 condemned men were the subject of statutory inquiries, and that none were reprieved.) Both before and after the time of the Atkin Committee, however, it was extremely rare for a woman to be the subject of a statutory inquiry: between 1900 and 1948 only four such inquiries are recorded (in 1911, 1934, 1940, and 1948). Since 11 per cent of the 1,178 persons sentenced to death in this period were women, it is at first sight remarkable that only 2 per cent of the inquiries related to women. The explanation is almost certainly that women were much more likely to be reprieved automatically (especially if their crime was infanticide) or on non-psychiatric grounds, so that there were correspondingly fewer cases in which the decision between life and death turned on a psychiatric report (see table 6).

TABLE 6. Death Sentences, medical inquiries and resulting reprieves from 1884 to 1960 in England and Wales

Period	A Death sentences	B Medical inquiries (as % of A)	C Resulting certificates of insanity (as % of B)	D Other[b] reprieves on grounds of mental condition (as % of B)	E C+D as % of A
1884–99		About 13%[a]	About 30%[a]	(?)	(?)
1900–22	599	10·0%	25·0%	16·7%	4·2%
1923–39	349	13·2%	32·6%	13·1%	6·0%
1940–48	230	30·9%	24·0%	22·6%	14·4%
1949–60[c]	269	38·2%	13·6%	21·4%	13·4%

[a] Inferred from percentages given by the Atkin Committee.
[b] Unfortunately this column does not include reprieves on grounds of mental condition which were decided upon without a medical inquiry.
[c] For this period, *informal* as well as statutory medical inquiries are included. The figures were supplied by the Home Office.

The Atkin Committee were also told that of the 58 inquiries held between 1900 and 1922, 36 – two-thirds – were held at the suggestion of the trial judge or the newly created Court of Criminal Appeal, no doubt as a result of the medical testimony at the trial.

From the late nineteen-twenties onward there was a more or less steady rise in the percentage of death sentences which were followed by a medical inquiry (column B). Until the period 1940–48 this was accompanied by a corresponding rise in the percentage of death sentences which were commuted on psychiatric grounds (column E). But the further extension of medical inquiries (no doubt stimulated by the discussions of the Royal Commission) did not produce a corresponding increase in the percentage of cases which were reprieved as a result. The most probable explanation is that by 1949 the stage had already been reached at which any male murderer who had a chance of being reprieved on the grounds of his mental condition was more or less sure to be the subject of a medical inquiry; and that the psychiatrists' distinction between normality and abnormality was such that the wider use of inquiries merely resulted in an increased number of cases which they diagnosed as normal.

By 1903 – if not earlier[24] – it was clearly the Home Office's practice to distinguish at least two types of case. One was the case in which the medical inquiry resulted in a certificate that the condemned person was insane. In such cases he or she was invariably reprieved and transferred to an asylum; and the Home Office took the view that a certificate of insanity made a reprieve obligatory. That this was their view was made plain in 1922, when the reprieve of True, after his defence of insanity had been rejected both by the jury and by the Court of Criminal Appeal, led to a storm of disapproval (the case is described in chapter 6). Like his predecessor Grey, the Home Secretary of the day, Mr Shortt, found that his lips were less firmly sealed than everyone had supposed. He defended himself in the House of Commons by explaining that both the trial judge and the Lord Chief Justice had pointedly drawn his attention to the medical evidence given in True's favour; that three psychiatric experts had subsequently certified that True was insane; and that he was therefore 'bound by the law of the land' to reprieve him.[25] Since the statute no longer bound him to do so, it was the common law to which he was referring (he cited Coke, Hale, Hawkins, Blackstone, Hawles, and Stephen); and he implied that someone who had been 'certified insane' was clearly 'mad', 'non compos mentis', or 'of non-sane memory', to use the words of those authorities.

The other type of case was one in which the medical inquiry did not result in a certificate of insanity but in which either the inquiry or some other source of information suggested that *at the time of the crime* the prisoner had been insane or so mentally abnormal as to justify a reprieve.[26] Unfortunately the published statistics relating to this type of case are not as exhaustive as those relating to certificates of insanity. Both are confined to the cases in which statutory medical inquiries were held; but whereas prisoners under sentence of death were certified as insane only after a medical inquiry, it had always been possible for a lesser degree of mental disorder to be brought to the Home Office's notice without an inquiry. This seems to have been *more* likely in the early part of this century, since at some later stage it became the practice to order a medical inquiry whenever a plea of insanity had been unsuccessfully raised at the trial, and by the time of the Royal Commission of 1949–53 it was also the practice to order one whenever the question of the condemned man's mental condition was raised 'by any other means, such as a report from the [prison] medical officer, or because of the obscurity of the motive or for any good and sufficient reason'.[27] By the time the Commission reported, however, the practice had been slightly modified so that if some mental abnormality was suspected, but was not thought to amount to certifiable insanity, an informal non-statutory inquiry was held: statutory inquiries were confined to cases in which the abnormality seemed likely to be certifiable.[28]

Consequently so far as non-certifiable murderers are concerned the table cannot be used to compare the different decades from 1900 to 1948. What can be inferred is that reprieves based wholly or partly on insanity or mental abnormality at the time of the crime were at least as frequent as those based on certificates of insanity at the time of the inquiry.

Like Sir George Grey, twentieth-century Home Secretaries treated these cases as discretionary, and did not feel 'bound by the law' as they did when presented with a certificate of insanity at the time of the inquiry. Understandably, they have not attempted to define the degree of abnormality which is sufficient to tip the balance. Clearly it included 'very low intelligence', even if this did not amount to certifiable mental defect.[29] It also included cases in which a murder had been committed 'without premeditation as the result of some sudden excess of frenzy and the prisoner . . . previously had no evil animus towards the victim', especially if he was 'weak-minded or emotionally unstable to an abnormal degree'. Other examples given by the Home Office to the Royal Commission were genuine survivors of suicide pacts, and 'cases where the crime is premeditated but is due to great mental stress and is prompted by motives which excite sympathy' (as in mercy-killings).[23]

Home Secretaries have been even more cautious in offering justifications for the practice of reprieving the certifiably insane or the mentally abnormal. Shortt, though he cited Coke, Hale, Hawkins, Blackstone, Hawles, and Stephen to prove that he was bound by the common law, refrained from dwelling on their explanations of it, which are, as we have seen, far from impressive. The Atkin Committee, being lawyers, were more respectful to the institutional writers, and argued that 'many [*sic*] of the reasons given for the merciful view of the common law continue to have force even under modern conditions. Everyone would revolt from dragging a gibbering maniac to the gallows'. If they had reflected they would surely have conceded that 'modern conditions' greatly weakened two out of the three traditional reasons. The abolition of public executions made Coke's argument irrelevant as well as illogical; and Hale's argument – that if sane the condemned man might be able to produce a sound reason why he should not be hanged – was greatly weakened now that the condemned man's interests were so well looked after by his lawyers. As for Hawles' argument that an insane man was spiritually unready for the next world (which not even Hawles regarded as the main objection) – were the Committee such devout Christians that they set store by it? Equally odd was their remark that 'everyone would revolt from dragging a gibbering maniac to the gallows', which sounded as if it was meant as an endorsement of one or more of the traditional justifications, but if so could hardly have been more unfortunately phrased. Why should it be more revolting to hang a 'maniac' than a woman, a seventeen-year-old boy or a decrepit old man? Must the maniac be 'gibbering' before it becomes revolting?

A more logical justification was suggested by Lord Hewart, who opposed Lord Darling's attempt to legislate on the lines recommended by the Atkin Committee (see chapter 6). Lord Hewart suggested that the medical inquiry should be concerned only with a single, simple question: 'If this condemned person is now hanged, is there any reason to suppose from the state of his mind that he will not understand why he is being hanged?' Although this suggestion would have appealed to Covarrubias, it had little attraction either for the Home Office or for humanitarians in general, for it was clearly intended to reduce the number of cases in which the inquiry led to a reprieve. Nevertheless, given certain assumptions about the purpose of the death penalty, it was at least more logical than the traditional justifications which the Atkin Committee had so piously repeated. If, as Covarrubias and Hewart no doubt believed, the primary aim of a penalty was retributive punishment, it could well be argued that the penalty would achieve its aim only if the offender understood why it was being imposed. This argument is not open, however, to someone who believes that the primary aim of a penalty such as hanging is the protection of society by deterrence or elimination. The Atkin Committee would have been more realistic if they had contented themselves with the observation that for at least four hundred years it had been accepted that common law forbade the execution of a madman, although the institutional writers' explanations were obviously speculative and odd: and that since 1884 certifiable insanity had been accepted as the modern equivalent of 'madness'. Any further attempt to justify the practice would have involved them in one sort of difficulty or another, as Lord Goddard was to argue to the Gowers Commission.

The Atkin Committee had no fault to find with the 1884 Act or the way in which it was being used by Home Secretaries, although one member – Sir Herbert Stephen – argued that the Home Secretary should not necessarily reprieve all murderers who were certified as insane. By the early nineteen-fifties, however, the Home Office had come under the displeasure of Lord Goddard, a King's Bench judge since 1932 and Lord Chief Justice since 1946. He told the Royal Commission:

> It happens over and over again . . . that where the issue of insanity has been tried and decided by a jury, who have found a prisoner sane, an inquiry has been held . . . an inquiry be it observed held in private with no representation of the prosecution or the convict, by persons who are not guided by a judge and who need give no reasons for their findings, with the result that the verdict of the jury is reversed. . . .[30]

He argued that the 1884 Act was not meant to work in this way, but to provide for cases in which the prisoner had either been in a position to offer a defence of insanity but had failed to do so, or else had become insane after conviction. He conceded that there must be 'borderline cases' in which 'a condition of mental instability', not necessarily amounting to insanity, seemed to the Home Secretary to justify mercy; but they were outside the scope of the 1884 Act. What he objected to was what seemed to him the use of the 1884 Act to reverse the jury's verdict.

The Royal Commission might well have wondered how Lord Goddard was able to tell the difference between a case belonging to the borderline category which he was prepared to accept and a case in which the jury's verdict was being reversed. Was it not in any case probable that a prisoner who could produce enough evidence of insanity to put before a jury, though not enough to satisfy them that he came within the Rules, would fall into the borderline category?

The Royal Commission's report did in fact defend the Home Office, although in a slightly different way. As it pointed out, the 1884 Act said nothing which excluded the prisoner who had unsuccessfully attempted a defence of insanity. Another incontrovertible point – by this date – was that the Home Secretary was not merely permitted but *obliged* to respite the death sentence if the prisoner were certified insane. The Commission's most important argument, however, was that the inquiries were concerned with insanity 'in the medical sense', which was wider than insanity of the kind that satisfied the M'Naghten Rules.

What the Commission were saying in a roundabout way – for they could hardly do so directly – was that for some considerable time the Home Office had been using the prerogative of mercy in such a way as to remedy the shortcomings of the M'Naghten Rules. They had done so by reprieving murderers who had failed to satisfy the Rules, but nevertheless seemed to have been not fully responsible for their crime. Although the Prison Medical Officers were careful to tell the Commission that they did not know the Home Secretary's reasons for reprieving any prisoner, they explained the reprieve of mentally retarded murderers by saying 'there was diminished responsibility'.[29] In other words, the Home Office's use of the prerogative was anticipating the Homicide Act of 1957 in this as in other types of cases. But to admit this openly would have been to meet Lord Goddard head-on; for it would have implied that the hours spent by counsel, judges, and juries in reading, hearing, and discussing evidence as to whether the accused knew the nature, the quality, or the illegality of his act were virtually a waste of time. More precisely, and even more objectionably, it would have implied that the only cases which the *courts* really saved from the gallows on the grounds of mental disorder were those which the Home Secretary would *not* have regarded as calling for a reprieve! It was a situation in which the Home Office's heart was in the right place but could not be worn on the sleeve.

The passing of the Homicide Act in 1957 reduced the scope for reprieves in two ways. The distinction between capital and non-capital murder meant that four out of five convicted murderers were no longer sentenced to death, while the new defence of diminished responsibility allowed courts to take into account states of mind which had hitherto been grounds only for mercy and not for special verdicts. The number of medical inquiries, statutory and informal, fell to a mere trickle, and two years later the statutory inquiry was quietly abolished in a schedule of the Mental Health Act, 1959. Occasionally, however, the Home Office still had to consider whether a murderer who had omitted to plead either insanity or diminished responsibility, or who had unsuccessfully done so, should nevertheless be reprieved because of his mental condition. One such case was that of Peter Hirst, a twenty-three-year-old painter and decorator who shot one of his neighbours. Although no realistic motive was revealed, and Hirst had suffered from acute depression and delusions of persecution, no defence of insanity or diminished responsibility was offered, and he was sentenced to death. Although not certifiably insane, he was reprieved, no doubt because of his mental condition. Spriggs, whose unsuccessful defence of diminished responsibility is mentioned in chapter 9, was also reprieved, almost certainly for similar reasons. Vivian Teed, on the other hand, who had battered a postmaster to death in the course of robbing his post office, was not reprieved after his defence of diminished responsibility had failed, although he was said to be psychopathic and had many previous convictions for violence.

What began as the king's mercy in the days before the Conquest has in effect been the Home Secretary's mercy since the accession of Queen Victoria, whose youth and innocence made it necessary to exclude her from detailed discussion of the crimes involved. Since 1837 it has been the Home Secretary's function to come to a decision, and all that is expected of the sovereign is a signature on a pardon. In her later years Queen Victoria showed a disposition to question some of the recommendations for mercy which were submitted to her – especially those which involved female murderers – but she was dealt with by Sir William Harcourt almost as firmly as George IV had been by Peel.[31] (Nor have modern Home Secretaries attempted to share this responsibility with the Prime Minister or Cabinet. They have consulted Ministerial colleagues, and in particular Law Officers; but the decision has been theirs, and not a collective one.) As for the fiction that the sovereign has a say in the *disposal* of the insane offender, this was almost entirely abolished when the Criminal Procedure (Insanity) Act of 1964 realistically substituted detention in 'a hospital specified by the Secretary of State' for detention at Her Majesty's Pleasure.

The suspension of the death penalty in 1965 automatically put an end to the most spectacular use of this prerogative, although the Home Secretary still has to review the occasional death sentence imposed in the Channel Islands or the Isle of Man, to which the 1965 legislation did not apply. On the mainland this function of the Home Office is now confined to the remission of lesser penalties or the issue of free pardons, either to remedy miscarriages of justice or to take account of mitigating circumstances. Very occasionally the reason for an intervention of this kind is the offender's mental condition. Now and again it is established that for one reason or another a court failed to take account of the mental state of the accused at the time of his offence; and the remainder of his prison sentence has been remitted. Slightly different is the case in which a person receives psychiatric treatment in prison for a mental disorder which is regarded as the cause of his offence and is then released before the end of his sentence in order to assist the process of rehabilitation: but such cases are not common. A comparatively frequent use of the prerogative, however, is the remission of fines imposed on offenders who subsequently enter mental hospitals for what are likely to be lengthy periods: they are thus saved from becoming liable to imprisonment as 'fine defaulters' if they do not pay.[32]

These unspectacular and unpublicised transactions serve almost as well as the reprieve of insane murderers to demonstrate the important function which is still performed by this ancient institution. As my introductory chapter pointed out, a certain amount of rigidity is probably one of the essential features of a penal system: offenders must not have too great an expectation of being able to bend the system to suit themselves. Yet this very rigidity creates a need for an extra-legal device which can occasionally be brought into play, as the *deus ex machina* was by the Greek dramatists, to solve the otherwise insoluble problem. This particular *deus ex machina* has also operated as a harbinger of future changes in the law. The history of infanticide, or of diminished responsibility (to say nothing of reprieves for young felons or for survivors of suicide pacts) show that alterations in the law of murder have time and again been preceded by several decades in which the Home Office quietly applied principles in accordance with contemporary sentiment but not yet recognised by the law. In this respect at least the Home Office could claim that what it does today the legislature will do tomorrow, or perhaps a little later.

Notes

1 In his *History of the Criminal Law of England*, (London, 1883).
2 See A.H.Dymond, *The Law on its Trial* (London, 1865), 210.
3 The development of the law on this subject will be dealt with in volume II.
4 3 & 4 Vict. c. 54 (The Insane Prisoners Act, 1840).
5 See the references to his case in the debate on Townley's case (Hansard, 1864, 8 February, col. 247) and para. 369 of the Gowers Commission's report (Cmnd. 8932).
6 See Dymond, op. cit. (n2).
7 Report and Minutes of Evidence before the Capital Punishment Commission 1864–6 (British Sessional Papers, 1866, vol. XXI).
8 24 & 25 Vict. c. 100.
9 In one of the debates on infanticide: see chapter 7.
10 I am indebted to the Home Office for this information.
11 Or Celestina Somner(?). Her name is differently spelt by Dymond, op. cit. (n2), p. 13, and minute 1468 in the evidence to the Capital Punishment Commission of 1864–6.
12 See Hansard (Commons) for 1856, vol. CXLII, col. 428.
13 See Dymond, op. cit. (n2).
14 See Hansard (Commons) for 1844, vol. LXXIV, cols. 106–7. The justification for this traditional reticence is the subject of an interesting article by G.Marshall in the journal *Public Law* (spring 1961).
15 See Hansard (Commons) for 8 February 1864.
16 R. v. Townley (1863), 3 Foster and Finlason's Nisi Prius Reports, 839.
17 In a leading article of 12 January 1865.
18 C.Lockhart-Robertson and H.Maudsley, *Insanity and Crime: a medico-legal commentary on the case of George Victor Townley* (London, 1864). Originally an article intended for publication in the *Journal of Mental Science*, this was published in advance because of the interest aroused by the case.
19 See *The Times*, 15 January 1865.
20 27 & 28 Vict. c. 29, The Insane Prisoners Act, 1864.
21 47 & 48 Vict. c. 64.

22 See para. 460 of the Gowers Commission's report (n5).
23 See both the report and the Home Office's memorandum of evidence (Day 1).
24 This is inferred from table 3 of the Home Office's memorandum of evidence to the Gowers Commission (n5).
25 Hansard for 13 June 1922, cols. 210–.
26 See Sir Edward Troup, *The Home Office* (London, 1925).
27 See Sir Frank Newsam's oral evidence to the Gowers Commission (1949, Day 1).
28 See para. 362 of the Gowers Commission's report (n5).
29 See the evidence of the prison medical officers to the Gowers Commission (1949, Day 8).
30 Ibid., Day 11.
31 See A. G. Gardiner's *Life of Sir William Harcourt* (London, 1923).
32 This paragraph is based on information supplied by the Home Office.

Chapter 14. **Insanity on Arraignment**

This final chapter is concerned with the legal rule which sometimes post-pones or prevents the trial of the accused on the ground that he is so disordered mentally that it would not be just to proceed with the trial. Although nowadays this rule saves more offenders from punishment than does the defence of insanity, its origins and development have received very little attention from legal historians.

The decision whether an insane offender could be tried has for centuries been complicated by the way in which he has been linked in the minds of courts with two other awkward sorts of malefactor – the deaf-mute and the man who refuses to plead. Indeed, the practice of exempting the deaf-mute from trial may well have preceded – in England at least – the practice of excusing the insane, whether from trial or punishment. The 'Dooms of Alfred', which were probably announced in the last quarter of the ninth century, provide that 'if a man be born dumb or deaf, so that he cannot acknowledge or confess his offences, his father must make *bōt* for his misdeeds'.[1] The so-called laws of Henry I, which were probably a description of pre-Norman customs, say much the same: 'If a person be deaf and dumb from birth, so that he cannot put or answer questions, his father must pay his forfeitures'; and the next provision deals with 'the insane and evildoers of a like sort', as we saw in chapter 1. Clearly, at least so far as misdeeds punishable with forfeitures were concerned, the deaf-mute was like a child: his father must pay.

Since most outbursts of insane violence are eventually followed by a phase in which the madman is at least calm enough to converse, communication with him is seldom quite as difficult as with the deaf-mute, although some extremely withdrawn schizophrenics may be even more *incommunicado*. It is therefore understandable that a society which recognised the hopelessness of interrogating the deaf and dumb might take longer to accord the same exemption to the insane. In any case, if my suggestion in chapter 1 is correct, it was not until the days of petty juries, in the thirteenth century, that the obviously insane offender would even be brought to trial. However that may be, the difficulty of trying him was certainly recognised by 1353, for there is a record of a discussion in that year between Edward 111's itinerant justices, in which one mentions the indictment for homicide of a man who could neither speak nor hear, and the problem of what to do. Another justice, Hill, said that he had a case in which a man had killed four people when he was 'enrage'; Hill had decided not to try him until he recovered his senses, but remanded him to prison. What had happened next was not clear; but eventually the accused had been pardoned by the king. The implication seems to be that Hill had at first intended that the man should eventually be tried. Perhaps his recovery was despaired of; perhaps it was realised that the outcome was bound to be a royal pardon, so that there was little point in trying him first.[2]

But for medieval and Tudor judges the offender who seemed too insane to try was a minor part of a more complex problem. The commonest difficulty with which they had to contend at the outset of a trial for felony or treason was presented by the man who simply refused to plead 'Guilty' or 'not guilty'. Unless he uttered the necessary words, reverence for the ritual of the law made it unthinkable to proceed with the trial, with the result that he could not be convicted and executed. More important still to the Exchequer, his property would not be forfeit. But to take this course for the sake of one's dependants called for great fortitude, since the courts' remedy was to order the man who refused to plead to be subjected to the *peine forte et dure*, which consisted of slowly pressing him to death under an increasing weight, unless his endurance gave out in the process and he consented to plead. (The *peine forte et dure* was not officially abolished until 1772, and was actually used as late as 1736 to compel a man to plead to a charge of murder.) Consequently, if a prisoner made no reply when asked for his plea – as was quite likely if he was a madman or deaf-mute – the first question for the court was 'Is he mute of malice, or by the visitation of God?'

The court was unlikely to decide in favour of 'the visitation of God' unless presented with very striking evidence of this. It would, for example, accept evidence that the accused had been deaf and dumb from birth. But in such cases the trial was not halted; since it could be assumed that if able to speak the accused would have pleaded, a plea of 'not guilty' was entered for him, and a relative who was accustomed to communicate with him by signs would do his best to help.

But there was another confusing factor. Deaf-mutes have such great difficulty in communicating with other people – a difficulty which is not wholly overcome even by the special training techniques of the twentieth century – that unless they are exceptionally intelligent they often appear mentally retarded, as indeed for practical purposes they are. (In many cases their dumbness is itself merely the consequence of their complete inability to hear and thus to imitate the sound of other people's voices.) In a way, the law recognised this. As Hale put it, the man who was deaf and dumb from birth was

in presumption of law an ideot, and the rather, because he hath
no possibility to understand, what is forbidden by law to be done,
or under what penalties; but if it can appear, that he hath the
use of understanding, which many of that condition discover by
signs to a very great measure, then he may be tried, and suffer
judgment and execution, tho great caution is to be used therein.[3]

In practice, courts did not always use the great caution which Hale rightly advised. As late as 1787 Elizabeth Steel – who could speak but not hear – was put on trial for grand larceny. She would not plead, and the jury found her mute by the visitation of God. She was remanded for some months while the judges discussed, in the light of what Hale had said, whether she could be tried. They decided that if no plea could be got from her by signs a plea of 'not guilty' should be entered for her. She was arraigned again, and when asked to plead said 'You know I cannot hear.' After the jury had again found her mute by the visitation of God she was tried, convicted, and sentenced to seven years' transportation.[4]

Somervile's case, already described in chapter 11, is important because it shows us the Elizabethan judges struggling with the problem. Somervile, when arraigned, would plead neither 'guilty' nor 'not guilty', 'and appeared in open shew to be lunatick or madd'; and one of the points which the Chief Justice and his colleagues had to decide was the correct procedure to be followed. They must have wondered whether he was simply trying to avoid a traitor's death, and they agreed that in the first place there should be an 'inquest of office' to decide whether his lunacy was real or feigned. If it was dismissed as feigned, he should not be condemned to the *peine forte et dure*, as he would have been if the indictment had been for felony, but should be sentenced for high treason. But if the inquest decided that his lunacy was real, the trial should be deferred until he recovered.[5]

The inquest which they proposed, although it was to be held by twelve jurors, was modelled not on the petty jury which tried indictments for felony, but on the civil inquests which were held as a result of writs from the Chancellor 'de lunatico inquirendo', and which decided whether the subject of the writ was mentally competent to manage his own affairs. But since in most cases a jury was about to be impanelled to try the guilt of the accused, it must have been a natural and early development to use this jury to decide whether he was fit to be tried.

Coke and Hale agree that an insane person ought not to be tried. As usual, it is Hale who is the more informative and precise:

If a man in his sound memory commits a capital offense, and
before his arraignment he becomes absolutely mad, he ought not
by law to be arraigned during such his phrenzy, but be remitted
to prison until that incapacity be removed; The reason is, because
he cannot advisedly plead to the indictment; and this holds as well
in cases of treason, as felony, even tho the delinquent in his sound
mind were examined, and confessed the offense before his
arraignment. . . . And if such person after his plea, and before his
trial, become of *non sane memory*, he shall not be tried. . . .

But because there may be great fraud in this matter, yet if the
crime be notorious, as treason or murder, the judge before such
respite of trial . . . may do well to impanel a jury to enquire *ex
officio* touching such insanity, and whether it be real or counterfeit.[3]

Hale even deals with the case of the person who was clearly insane at the time of his crime as well as the time of his trial, a not unlikely state of affairs:

> . . . If a person of *non sane memory* commit *homicide* during such
> his insanity, and continue so till the time of his arraignment, such
> person shall neither be arraigned nor tried, but remitted to gaol,
> there to remain in expectation of the King's grace to pardon him.[3]

He distinguishes clearly between the two stages at which the trial might have to be halted because it was recognised that the accused was not fit to be tried:

> . . . But in case a man in a phrenzy happens by some oversight,
> or by means of the gaoler to plead to his indictment, and is put
> upon his trial, and it appears to the court upon his trial, that he
> is mad, the judge in discretion may discharge the jury of him,
> and remit him to gaol to be tried after the recovery of his under-
> standing. . . .[3]

Several points are worth noting in Hale's exposition. First, that, like his account of insanity as a defence, it is expressly limited to capital offences. Second, that to qualify for the deferment of his trial the accused must be 'absolutely mad'. Third, that the impanelling of a jury appears to be at the judges' discretion, and not obligatory.

So much for legal theory in Hale's day. The trial of Bateman in 1685, a few years after Hale's death, shows that in practice the accused had to be very disordered indeed before he could hope for a postponement of his trial. Charles Bateman was an elderly surgeon who had been injudicious enough to attend to Titus Oates after his first flogging in 1685. Later in the same year he himself was accused, on rather doubtful evidence, of playing a minor but treasonable part in Lord Russell's plans for an insurrection in support of the Duke of Monmouth. When brought to trial at the Old Bailey he asked for a postponement, saying that he was 'very much indisposed' (he was described later as 'to all appearance moped mad'). The Recorder of London, though evidently determined that he should be convicted, was sufficiently impressed with his state to grant him a few hours respite and – an unprecedented concession – the help of his son to present his case. Although the evidence sounded suspiciously like that of professional informers, he was convicted and sentenced to death. The whole proceeding was strongly criticised by Sir John Hawles (1645– 1716), one of William III's solicitors-general. Hawles thought that Bateman was not fit to be tried, and pointed out that the court had put itself in the wrong by allowing his son to defend him: either he was fit to defend himself, or he was not fit to be tried at all.[6]

However that may be, the evidence of the Old Bailey Sessions Papers suggests that it was not until the middle of the eighteenth century that the insane prisoner had any real chance of being found unfit for trial. It is probably no coincidence that the first example which I could find occurred in 1756, about the time when the chances of an acquittal seem to have increased (see chapter 3). In that year Robert Dyle was indicted for murder, but 'his appearance at the bar seeming to discover he was not right in his senses, the following evidences were sworn, for the Middlesex jury to determine whether he was, or was not, of sound mind and memory, fit to take his trial. . . .' Among the witnesses was his lawyer, who had tried to take instructions from him for his defence but had found the task impossible. 'I don't think' he told the court 'he is capable of attending to or minding the evidence, or remembering it when he has heard it' – a remark which to some extent anticipates the criteria that were to be laid down by nineteenth-century judges. The jury found Dyle 'not of sound mind and memory' and there is no record of any subsequent attempt to try him'.[7]

From this date onward, the Sessions Papers provide occasional examples of similar findings, although it is sometimes not certain whether the accused was acquitted or excused from trial. Juries themselves may not have been clear in their minds about the distinction. By 1786 the climate of opinion was such that Margaret Nicholson, whose puny attack on George III has been described in chapter 11, was not even arraigned, but simply consigned to Bethlem. It was, of course, the Privy Council and not a mere magistrate who took this somewhat irregular course; and a few years later, in Frith's case, the Privy Council themselves followed a more orthodox procedure.

As George III was driving in state to the House of Lords on 21st January 1790, a stone was thrown at his coach by a tall man dressed in a scarlet coat, black breeches, a striped waistcoat and a cocked hat with an orange cockade. This colourful figure was seized and taken to the Treasury in nearby Whitehall, where he was interrogated for four hours by the Attorney-General, Pitt, Grenville, and other members of the Privy Council, after which he was committed to prison for further examination. At least one of these examinations was conducted by one of the king's physicians, all of whom were, of course, only too well versed in the symptoms of insanity. The assailant was found to be John Frith, whose name had appeared on a libel against the king which had been found pinned on the whalebone in the courtyard of St James' Palace about two weeks earlier. The result of these interrogations was that he was committed to Newgate for trial on a charge of high treason. His trial took place on 17th April before the same Lord Chief Justice, Kenyon, who later tried Hadfield for treason. Like Hadfield, Frith was assigned well-known counsel, in this case Mr Shepherd and Mr Garrow, both of whom later became law officers of the Crown. They asked for a postponement in order that they could procure more evidence, probably relating to Frith's sanity; but Frith himself objected strenuously. After some argument the judges decided that a jury should be sworn to inquire whether the prisoner 'be of sound mind and understanding or not. . . .' Frith's counsel then asked him to tell the court why he thought he was fit to plead. Frith began with a rather muddled and irrelevant but not obviously insane protest about the way in which he had been examined by the king's physician. After a few minutes, however, counsel asked him to tell the jury what had happened at Liverpool, whereupon Frith's deluded state rapidly became plain:

Prisoner. When I first arrived at Liverpool I perceived I had some powers like those which St Paul had; and the sun that St Paul gives a description of in the Testament: an extraordinary power

that came down upon me – the power of Christ; in consequence
of my being persecuted and ill-used the public wanted to receive
me as a most extraordinary kind of man. . . . When I went to St
Thomas's church I was there surprised to hear the clergyman
preach a most extraordinary sermon upon me as if I was a god. . . .

He made several more deluded statements of this kind, attributing a pain
in his ear to witchcraft ('it is in the power of women to annoy men publicly, even throughout the whole continent'). After several lay witnesses
had related other strange ideas of his, Lord Kenyon addressed the jury.
He pointed out that the question was not whether Frith was insane at the
time of his act, but whether he was now sane or insane. 'The humanity of
the law of England, falling into that which common humanity, without
any written law, would suggest, has prescribed that no man shall be
called upon to make his defence at a time when his mind is in that situation as not to appear capable of so doing. For however guilty he may be,
the enquiring into his guilt must be postponed to that season when, by
collecting together his intellects, and having them entire, he shall be able
so to model his defence as to ward off the punishment of the law. . . .'
Taken literally, his test was a generous one: unless the accused had all his
wits, his trial must be postponed. As we shall see, however, his successors
were less generous. The protesting Frith was found insane by the jury and
'remanded for the present': but, as in Dyle's case, there is no record of a
subsequent trial.[8]

In at least one case of this period, however, the accused was brought
back for trial later. In 1794 Susannah Milesent, charged with stealing a
petticoat, was found insane and unfit to be tried at one Old Bailey session,
and was remanded to Newgate to be arraigned again at the next session
but one. This time no objection to her trial was raised, and she pleaded
guilty. Her replies to questions, however, were very inconsequential, and
other witnesses from Newgate, including 'a nurse in the sick ward', confirmed that she had acted insanely. The jury found her 'deranged and not
in a sound mind', and although the record is not entirely unambiguous
this probably amounted to a special verdict. (The report of the proceedings
is so vivid and circumstantial that I have reproduced the whole of it in
Appendix E.)

The Act which was passed a few years later, after Hadfield's trial, dealt
not only with cases such as his, in which a defence of insanity had been
accepted, but also with cases like Frith's. It provided that if a person was
either found insane on arraignment by a jury impanelled for the purpose,
or – at a later stage of the trial – appeared insane to the jury which was
trying him, the court should direct this finding to be recorded, and order
him to be kept in 'strict custody' until His Majesty's Pleasure was known.
Although Hale would have confined this provision, like the defence of
insanity, to treasons and felonies, the section was drafted in such a way
that it applied to any offence for which the accused might be indicted –
that is, to misdemeanours as well.

This section was used to deal with offenders whom we would not today
label 'insane'. Esther Dyson, who was arraigned in 1831 for cutting off

the head of her bastard child, was a deaf-mute. Communicating by signs through an interpreter she pleaded 'not guilty', but the interpreter could not make her understand the next step in the proceedings, which was the exercise of her right to challenge jurors. The judge (Parke) told the jury that the question was whether she had 'sufficient reason to understand the nature of this proceeding, so as to be able to conduct her defence with discretion'. The jury decided that she was 'insane', and she was accordingly dealt with under the Act of 1800.[9] The term 'insane' as used in those days of course included idiots as well as madmen, and Esther Dyson may well have appeared dull-witted to the jury. But the practice of dealing with the deaf and dumb as 'insane', and ordering their detention during Her Majesty's Pleasure, continued through Victoria's reign, and was upheld in this century in the case of R. v. the Governor of Stafford Prison,[10] when Lord Alverstone said that it was 'in accordance with common sense and with the proper administration of the criminal law'. His argument was, in effect, that for the purposes of section 2 of the Act of 1800 'insanity' simply meant such a 'failure of intellect' as prevented the accused from following the proceedings.

From Esther Dyson's case onward judges became more precise in explaining to juries exactly how insane the prisoner must be in order to be found unfit for trial. Hale had said at one point that he must be 'absolutely mad', but Mr Justice Parke told the jury that the question was whether Esther Dyson could understand the nature of the proceedings so as to be able to conduct her defence with 'discretion'. A few years later, in the case of the deaf and dumb Pritchard, indicted for bestiality, Baron Alderson told the jury to consider whether the accused was 'of sufficient intellect to comprehend the course of proceedings in the trial so as to make a proper defence – to know that he might challenge any of you to whom he may object, and to comprehend the details of the evidence' (the jury thought he ought not to be tried). It was these words which became the most authoritative definition of the test of fitness to plead.[11]

Although the judicial definition of unfitness was now somewhat stricter than it had been – for example in Frith's case – in practice a prisoner's chances of benefiting from it were increasing slightly, and were shortly to rise very markedly, as we shall see when we come to the statistics. In Scotland a situation was eventually reached in which 'insanity in bar of trial' was so widely interpreted that the defence of insanity became very rare indeed. Although English practice never approached that, it reached a stage at which the Director of Public Prosecutions was able to tell a meeting of prison medical officers at the Home Office in 1948 that the modern tendency of the courts was in favour of a finding of unfitness for trial if this was at all possible. He told them that judges did not like trying persons who were stated to be certifiably insane but fit to plead. In other words, there would be a presumption that a prisoner who was certifiably of unsound mind or mentally defective was also unfit to plead.[12] In the following year the prison medical officers who gave evidence to the Gowers Commission made it clear that they simply equated unfitness to plead with certifiability, and that their evidence was hardly ever

R

challenged.[13] (The criteria of certifiability have never been defined unanimously, but a contemporary textbook explained that 'the patient must be demonstrably suffering from a mental disorder, which in practice means a psychosis, and he must be a danger to himself or others, incapable of managing his affairs, or in need of treatment which he refuses. . . .') As we shall see, Alderson's test was appealed to now and again, but in most cases the prison medical officer simply asked himself 'Would I certify this patient?'

This should draw our attention to a point which must be made repeatedly in this chapter: that the key to this escape route for the insane offender has been in the hands of the prison doctor ever since such an official came into existence. This will become plain when we consider the statistics, which are available from 1834 onward.

In the early years, findings of unfitness for trial were even less frequent than successful defences of insanity. In the eighteen-thirties an average of only eleven offenders a year were dealt with in this way. Even in the nineteen-fifties the annual average was only forty-eight, although this was now greater than the numbers found guilty but insane. The trend so far as murder trials are concerned can be seen in table 3 in chapter 5. But for several reasons it is more illuminating to study the figures for offences other than murder. Since these offences were not subject to the death penalty during the period we are considering, medical witnesses had less incentive to give the accused the benefit of the doubt, and the defence had less incentive to use 'the preliminary issue' as a tactic. The figures, too, are larger. Table 7 shows persons found unfit for trial for offences other than murder for various periods from 1834 to 1965. They are shown as rates per 100,000 persons brought to trial in order to allow for wide fluctuations in the total numbers of persons arraigned, which ranged from more than 30,000 in 1848 to just under 5,000 in 1916 (a decline which was largely due to the increasing numbers who were tried summarily).

As in table 3, I have grouped the years not into decades or quinquennia but into periods of uneven length separated by what seem to be 'landmarks' – that is, events which may have influenced the rates. Where there was no obvious landmark or this sort I have simply adopted the landmark which was used in table 3.

What is clear is that the sharpest rise in the rate of findings of unfitness for trial occurred in the late eighteen-sixties: to be more precise, about 1868. This was an eventful decade for the penal system. Broadmoor was opened in 1863. Penal servitude was made more severe in 1865. The Capital Punishment Commission reported in 1866. It is difficult, however, to find in any of these a plausible explanation of the doubling of the rate that we are considering.

The most likely cause is to be found in the Prison Act of 1865,[14] which at last imposed a certain amount of efficiency upon the gaols which had been run so haphazardly by local justices. Nationalisation did not come until 1877, but the Act of 1865 closed the least satisfactory local gaols and laid down strict rules for the conduct of the rest. Most important of all, it provided for regular medical inspection of all prisoners by the prison

TABLE 7. Persons found unfit to plead or unfit to be tried from 1834 to 1965 shown as mean rates per 100,000 persons brought to trial (trials for murder are excluded: see facing page)

Period	Mean rate	Landmarks (see text)
1834–36	31·3	
		Pritchard's case (1836). Counsel allowed to address court (late 1836)
1837–40	47·0	
		Act allowing certification of untried prisoners
1841–43	39·0	
		M'Naghten's case
1844–53	42·9	
1854–65	48·9	
		Prison Act, 1865
1866–77	106·0	
		Prison Commission takes over local gaols, 1877
1878–84	117·4	
		Prison Standing Order 138 (1885)
1885–94	163·1	
		Gladstone Committee on Prisons reports, 1895
1895–1900	162·8	
		Prison Standing Order 302 (1900)
1901–07	213·3	
		Court of Criminal Appeal created, 1907
1908–13	179·1	
		Mental Deficiency Act, 1913
1914–18	252·6	
		First World War ends, 1918
1919–24	236·3	
		Atkin Committee reports, 1922
1925–29	230·6	
		Commons Committee on Capital Punishment, 1930
1930–38	164·7	
1939–45		No figures published for the period of the Second World War
1946–53	162·4	
		Royal Commission on Capital Punishment reports, 1953
1954–56	187·3	
		Homicide Act, 1957
1957–60	141·3	
		Mental Health Act comes into operation (late 1960)
1961–65	94·0	

Source: The Judicial and Criminal Statistics of England and Wales from 1834 to 1965.

surgeon. It is true that each gaol already had its part-time surgeon, but his attention to the inmates was often intermittent and perfunctory. Now he had to see every prisoner at least once each week. It was the local gaols and not the centrally controlled penitentiaries to which prisoners awaiting trial were remanded, and it was therefore the gaol surgeon who was most likely – or perhaps I should say 'least unlikely' – to detect the signs of insanity. The Act came into operation early in 1866, and the rise in the numbers of prisoners found unfit to plead seems to begin in the year 1868. Certainly the connection would be more certain if it had begun a year earlier; but it is not improbable that it took a little time for surgeons to become accustomed to the new regime.

By this time, however, a new complication had been introduced by the Act of 1840 which regularised the transfer of insane prisoners to asylums. This was the Act which Lord Normanby had introduced with the assurance that it did not contain 'anything either of novelty or difficulty' (see chapter 13). Not only did it lead to the embarrassing case of Townley (*ibid.*), but it irritated the courts. For as well as sentenced offenders, prisoners *awaiting trial* could be transferred by the Home Secretary's warrant, given on a certificate of insanity signed by two justices of the peace and two doctors. Although the Act did not say what should be done about the trial in such cases, it seems to have been assumed that while in the asylum the accused could not be tried. When this was done with Dwerryhouse (who had scalped a woman), his trial was first of all deferred until the next Assizes. At the next Assizes counsel produced an affidavit from the asylum governor to the effect that the accused was hopelessly insane and was unlikely to recover, and explained to Mr Justice Patteson that the new statute allowed the Home Secretary to keep the accused in any asylum until he was fit to be brought before the court. 'Where is that statute?' exclaimed the judge. 'If justices of the peace were to pronounce upon a prisoner's insanity, a door might be open to the most grievous abuses. The proper tribunal to determine if he is in a state to take his trial is a jury. . . . A man might be put into a lunatic asylum and kept there until the witnesses were dead. We are too gingerly in acting about insane people.'[15] But the courts must have come round to the acceptance of this dangerous provision, for in a later case of the same kind the clerk simply told the judge that the correct thing to do was to postpone the trial *sine die*.[16] On at least one occasion (in 1870) the prosecution forced the hospital to produce the accused for trial by means of a writ of *habeas corpus*, but after a confused discussion the jury decided that he was insane and unfit to be tried.[17]

Some judges continued to mistrust this power of the executive, and in 1885 Marshall's case led to a public outburst from Baron Huddleston. Marshall had been committed for trial on the charge of murdering a young girl, but was transferred to Broadmoor before trial on the order of the Home Secretary. Although Sir William Harcourt had himself signed the order, the document produced to the court was signed only by one of his officials, and this gave the judge a point of attack. A question was put down in the Lords by the Earl of Milltown, but Harcourt seems to have satisfied him privately that his department had not acted improperly. Nevertheless, the Home Secretary gave instructions that the power of transfer before trial should be used with great caution. A Standing Order informed medical officers of local prisons that

. . . in the case of untried prisoners, especially if charged with offences of a grave nature, the Secretary of State [sc. the Home Secretary] desires that the prisoner's insanity should, if possible, be publicly decided by the verdict of a jury, and that the prisoner should, for this purpose, be left to stand his trial, unless there be strong reasons to the contrary. He proposes, therefore, to order the removal of untried prisoners, only in cases where it may appear, for special reasons, to be advisable or necessary. . . .[18]

The result, as we can see in table 7, was a rise in the frequency with which prisoners were found unfit to plead. The instruction remained in force until the Mental Health Act of 1959 introduced new procedures and criteria for the transfer of disordered prisoners.

In theory, of course, it remains true that whether the accused has been transferred to a mental hospital by the Home Secretary before arraignment or as a result of a finding by the jury that he was unfit to plead or be tried, the trial is merely deferred until he is in a proper state to be tried. In practice the trial eventually takes place only if he is suspected of having feigned the disorder or if he makes a very quick recovery. Sometimes the accused himself feels that his detention without a trial is unjust and demands a chance to prove his innocence. His demand is not always granted, since it may be based on obvious delusion, but occasionally it is; and at least one accused, Pickering, was eventually acquitted.

Pickering's story, however, was unusual in many respects.[19] In 1958 Boucher, a lodger at a Salvation Army hostel, was drowned in a dock; with him were three men (including Pickering, lodging at the same hostel), who said that he had fallen in accidentally. The coroner's inquest found the death accidental, but Pickering later confessed to the police that he had pushed Boucher because the latter had refused to lend him half a crown, and one of his companions confirmed this. Pickering had a long history of schizophrenia with delusions, and at his trial was found unfit to plead and sent to Broadmoor. A month or two later, at his own request, he was re-examined by two Broadmoor doctors and allowed to stand his trial. He now pleaded not guilty, maintaining (as he had done at first) that Boucher had slipped by accident, and claiming that his mental state at the time of his confession prevented him from recalling it. His companion now retracted his testimony that he had seen Pickering push Boucher, and as the Director of Public Prosecutions offered no evidence Pickering was acquitted. (Later, as a result of a newspaper investigation, he swore to a Commissioner for Oaths that he lived constantly under the impulse to commit murder, had in fact pushed Boucher, and had feigned insanity at his first arraignment. A few months after his acquittal he was arrested as a 'prowler' in Lincolnshire and committed for observation to a mental hospital, where he was put in the same ward as Boucher's brother, who had had a nervous breakdown after the drowning. Pickering was allowed to leave hospital a few weeks later, and shortly after that was imprisoned for stealing an axe. He was alleged to have said 'I stole it because I wanted to chop the head off a child.'

Six months later he was released from prison but taken back to the same mental hospital under the compulsory powers of the Lunacy Acts. The hospital discharged him a few months later, and on the following day he was arrested in a nearby town for stealing a tin of polish from his lodging. This earned him two month's imprisonment. A few months later he was again in court, on charges of housebreaking and larceny. This time he was remanded for medical examination and was committed to another of the special mental hospitals, where he was still a patient late in 1966.)

Another awkward question was 'Up to what stage in the trial should it be possible to raise the issue of fitness to plead?' The later the better from the point of view of the defence, if there was any chance that the prosecution's evidence might prove unconvincing. It may have been for this reason that in 1876 the legally qualified chairman of Worcester Quarter Sessions followed a somewhat unusual course in the trial of Berry for pocket-picking. Berry was a deaf-mute, and after the jury had found him mute by the visitation of God a plea of 'Not Guilty' was entered for him. The trial was conducted with the help of an interpreter, and eventually the Chairman summed up the evidence and asked the jury whether Berry was guilty or not. He also asked them, however, whether in their opinion Berry was capable of understanding, and had understood, the nature of the proceedings. It is hardly surprising that the conscientious jury found him both guilty and incapable of understanding the proceedings. The Court for Crown Cases Reserved held that the trial should have been halted and Berry dealt with as unfit to be tried. (In an *obiter dictum* Kelly, C.B. seemed to be saying that there were precedents for ordering a verdict of not guilty in such a case, but he did not cite them.) Thereafter it seems to have been assumed that the proper time to raise the question was before the impanelling of the jury: indeed, it came to be known by the cryptic title of 'the preliminary issue'.[20]

Forty-eight years later, however, Devlin took a more flexible point of view in Roberts' case. Roberts, another deaf-mute, was arraigned for murder and found mute by the visitation of God. The prosecution submitted that the preliminary issue should be tried next, but the defence counsel, who knew that the strength of the prosecution's case lay in statements by Roberts which might well be ruled to be inadmissible as evidence, asked that the general issue of guilt should be tried first. Mr Justice Devlin agreed, pointing out that otherwise an innocent man might be committed to Broadmoor and investigations which might uncover the true culprit might not take place. A plea of 'Not Guilty' was entered, and defence counsel (who saw no need to have the proceedings interpreted to his client) simply objected that the statements attributed to Roberts had not been made voluntarily. The court adjourned to enable the judge to make inquiries as to whether Judges' Rules for the interrogation of suspected persons had been followed. The upshot was that the Crown decided to offer no further evidence, and Roberts was automatically acquitted.[21]

Not all of Devlin's colleagues, however, approved of the course which he had followed. In R. v. Beynon, for example, Mr Justice Byrne refused to allow a similar request by the defence, and agreed with the prosecution that Devlin's attention should have been drawn to the Act of 1800. He seems to have assumed that the Act of 1800, which referred only to persons found insane *on arraignment*, excluded the possibility of such a finding at a later stage and did not attempt to meet Devlin's commonsense argument that the accused might conceivably be innocent; perhaps it was not conceivable in Beynon's case. Beynon was found unfit to plead, and detained.[22]

As for the burden of proof, this has swung to and fro over the last century. In the early cases which I have cited it seems to lie on the defence. In 1853 it was ruled in Davies' case[23] that it lay on the Crown to prove fitness to plead, but in the following year Mr Justice Cresswell said in Rebecca Turton's case[24] that the presumption was that the accused was sane, and it was for the defence to bring evidence to the contrary. That was all very well in theory; but in practice it was hardly reasonable to expect the accused to raise the preliminary issue unless he were represented by counsel. How could he do so if he did not understand what was going on? Cresswell's ruling was not completely unrealistic, since the Act of 1836 had given the accused the right not merely to be advised by counsel but also to have a speech on his behalf made by counsel after the close of the prosecution's case. It had not automatically *provided* him with counsel; but in cases of murder it was the practice by 1853 – if not earlier – for the court to assign counsel to a prisoner who could not afford one.[25] As we shall see, however, it was by no means unheard of even at the end of the century that prisoners should be arraigned for other serious crimes without being represented. It was probably for this reason that towards the end of the century it became the practice of most, if not all, prison medical officers to send a report to the clerk of assize or quarter sessions if it seemed that the court should be aware of the prisoner's mental condition. The judge and prosecution were thus in a position to question the prisoner's fitness for trial even if the defence did not do so.

That judges were willing to do so is illustrated by the case of William Hillard,[26] who was arraigned at Durham Assizes in 1899 for the attempted murder of his wife. He did not have counsel and pleaded guilty. When evidence was being given Mr Justice Grantham, who questioned some of the witnesses himself, became suspicious of Hillard's state of mind and sent for the prison medical officer. His evidence was to the effect that Hillard had been insane at the time of his attack on his wife, and though improved was still not quite sane. (It is interesting to note how rigid was the sentencing philosophy of that time: since Hillard had pleaded guilty the judge, though sympathetic, felt obliged to sentence him to five years' penal servitude, and thought that all he could do was to bring Hillard's case to the Home Secretary's attention!) Although the prison medical officer had in fact reported his view of Hillard's mental condition to the clerk of assize, the latter had evidently not told the judge, who complained to the Home Office. The result was the issue to prisons of a standing order which made it clear that prison medical officers were expected to send such reports to courts. It may well have been this standing order which was responsible for the markedly higher rate of findings of unfitness to plead in the first years of this century that can be observed in table 7.

The practice was described succinctly by the Court of Criminal Appeal in Dashwood's case in 1943, when Mr Justice Humphreys said

> . . . the court acts in such a case on information conveyed to it
> from any quarter. It does not matter whether the information
> comes to the court from the defendant himself or his advisers or
> the prosecution or an independent person, such as, for instance,
> the medical officer of the prison where the defendant has been
> confined.[27]

Shortly after Dashwood's case, however, at least one judge, Mr Justice Stable, began to take a stricter line. The system of dock briefs and the successive extensions of legal aid (which had begun in 1903) had made it less and less likely that a person would ever be tried on a serious charge at a higher court without the help of counsel, although of course many a petty offender continued to be dealt with summarily without the attention to his mental state which a lawyer might have secured for him. If the accused had a legal adviser it was not unreasonable to expect the latter to study any report which the prison medical officer might have supplied, and even, if it was likely to be in his client's interests, to obtain a second opinion. It was probably for this reason that in 1946, when Crown counsel was about to call the prison medical officer to testify that one Evelyn Aglington was unfit to plead, Mr Justice Stable cut him short with the remark 'My absolute invariable practice is that I will not allow the Crown to call evidence of insanity: it is purely a matter for the defence'.[28] His attitude did not of course take into account the possibility that the defence might be embarrassed by a client who insisted on being tried, or even on pleading guilty, when obviously unfit to make such decisions; and he does not seem to have distinguished clearly enough between the defence of insanity and the issue of fitness to plead.

It was probably Stable – although one or two other judges may have followed his lead for a time – to whom the prison medical officers were referring when they told the Gowers Commission in 1949 that they had recently met with a change of attitude on the part of judges:

> Up to quite recently we reported to the Director of Public
> Prosecutions and when the case came to court it was usually
> raised by the prosecution; counsel announced in court that there
> was a preliminary issue. But within the last nine months I have
> had two cases where it has been ruled by the judge that that issue
> should be raised by the defence. . . .[13]

It may have been for this reason that from 1949 there was a temporary decline in the frequency with which the accused was found unfit for trial. This can be seen in figure 3, which shows the post-war rates of these findings. (In order to reduce chance fluctuations from year to year, which would distract the eye from the long-term trend, the rates are shown as three-year moving averages: that is, the rate shown for 1947 is the average

FIGURE 3. Persons found unfit for trial from 1947 to 1964 shown as three-year
moving average rates per 100,000 persons for trial

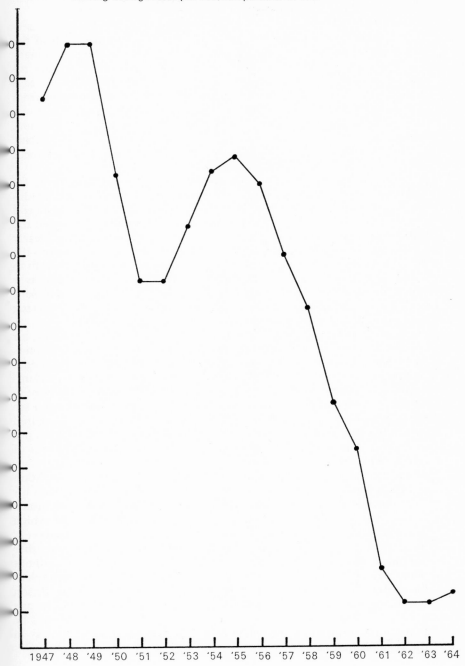

rate for 1946, 1947, and 1948; the rate shown for 1948 is the average for 1947, 1948, and 1949; and so on. Persons tried for murder are included, but if they are excluded a similar trend appears.)

Not all judges, however, were as strict as Stable. In Roberts' case (described above) Mr Justice Devlin, as he then was, could have solved the dispute by ruling that the prosecution could not raise the preliminary issue, but he did not; and that was in 1953. Whether the temporary resurgence of findings of unfitness in 1953, 1954, and 1955 was due to a swing away from Stable's point of view is impossible to say. Certainly from 1959 the Lord Chief Justice felt able to say in Podola's case[29] that it was 'now well established' that the issue could be raised by the prosecution, the defence, or the court itself; and since he did not refer to any specific case it must be inferred that the judges had simply come to an agreement among themselves.

This state of affairs had not been envisaged by Cresswell in 1853; for his ruling that the accused must be presumed fit to plead unless the defence brought evidence to the contrary was clearly too simple to meet a situation in which not only the defence but the prosecution or even the judge could raise the issue. The more sophisticated rule which was clearly needed was provided by Mr Justice Salmon in R. v. Sharp. It was to the effect that the normal presumption must still be that the accused was fit to plead, but that if in any case the court had reason to doubt his fitness it must inquire into it, *and the onus is then on the Crown to prove that he is fit to plead*.[30] There the matter rested until Podola's trial in the following year, which will be described shortly.

The Court of Criminal Appeal had not sorted out these difficulties, for in 1908, in Jefferson's case[31] it had decided that since a finding of fitness to be tried was not a conviction, it was not within the court's jurisdiction. Although the British Medical Association suggested to the Atkin Committee on Insanity and Crime in 1923 that there should be some way in which a retrial could be ordered in such cases, the Committee could see nothing wrong with the present state of affairs. They had been assured that in practice whenever a person found unfit to plead had later been put on trial he had *in all cases* been found guilty but insane. That was of course before Pickering's case.

The Royal Medico-Psychological Association argued to the Atkin Committee that it was always best if possible to let the accused stand his trial, for two reasons. One was that the risk that an innocent but insane person might be dealt with as a criminal lunatic, an argument which assumes that he is more likely to establish his innocence if tried as soon as possible than if the trial is postponed until he has improved. The other argument was that people detained at His Majesty's Pleasure without being convicted have a sense of grievance; but at most this is an argument for trying them *eventually*. The Atkin Committee accepted the Prison Commissioners' Standing Order as satisfactory, and made only one positive recommendation on the entire subject – that nobody should be found unfit to plead on the evidence of less than two doctors 'unless in the very plainest cases'.

As we have seen, the Government took no action on the major recommendations of the Atkin Committee, and even this harmless minor one
seems to have been ignored; for the Gowers Commission were told that
in the early nineteen-fifties it was usual for such findings to be made on
the evidence of a single medical witness, usually the prison medical officer.
The Royal Commission endorsed the Atkin Committee's view, and this
time it was put into practice, although it was not made statutory. They
refused, however, to accept the suggestion of some witnesses that anyone
who had been certified insane or mentally defective should automatically
be regarded as unfit for trial. The Commission argued that it was desirable
that persons charged with criminal offences should if possible be tried,
and that even certifiably insane or defective persons were often able to
plead and follow the proceedings. They did not deal with the problem of
appeals.

Some of the doubts and difficulties which have been described were
cleared up or at least reduced by Podola's case in 1959, which may well
come to be regarded as the last case of major importance in the series
which began with Hadfield and included M'Naghten, True, and Byrne.

Guenther Podola was a German criminal who had been deported from
Canada a few months before his encounter with the British police. He had
been trying to blackmail a Mrs Schiffman, and was arrested in a telephone
kiosk in South Kensington Underground Station. He shot and killed one
of the detectives who arrested him, and made his escape. Four days later
he was traced to a small hotel. When the police charged the door of his
room the door fell on top of him, with a policeman's weight behind it;
and after a short struggle he was taken to Chelsea police station. A police
surgeon who saw him there about half an hour later found that he would
obey instructions but would not answer questions, and thought that he was
suffering from 'withdrawal' from a frightening situation, and possibly
from concussion. He was taken to hospital, where a consultant also thought
he was suffering from 'withdrawal' and concussion. When he was arraigned
his counsel submitted that he had lost his memory for 'all events before
July 17' (the day after his recapture in the hotel), and was therefore unfit
to plead. The prosecution argued that Podola's amnesia was feigned, and
even if it were genuine it could not justify a finding of unfitness to plead,
in support of which they produced evidence that while in hospital he
obviously remembered, for example, how chess was played.

After hearing argument on the subject of the burden of proof, Mr
Justice Edmund Davies (as he then was) ruled that it lay on the defence,
but could be discharged by showing *on a balance of probabilities* that the
accused was unfit for trial. His ruling, which contradicted Mr Justice
Salmon's recent pronouncement, was clearly intended to place such cases
on all fours with the defence of insanity. (It is difficult to see how it would
meet the situation in which the judge or prosecution raised the issue
against the wishes of the defence; but it was upheld by the Court of
Criminal Appeal). A jury was then impanelled, and the issue was subdivided for them. In the first place they were asked to decide whether
Podola's amnesia was genuine. After nine days of medical evidence they

decided that it was not, and so escaped the second question, which would
have been whether it unfitted him for trial. Podola then pleaded 'not
guilty', but was found guilty and sentenced to death. In view of the Court
of Criminal Appeal's decision in Jefferson's case, Podola did not attempt
to appeal; but the Home Secretary invoked his little-used power to ask
the appellate court to hear and determine the case as they would have
done had it been an appeal against conviction. In doing so they expressly
disowned Mr Justice Darling's ruling in Jefferson's case and took the view
that Podola could have appealed against his conviction on the ground that
it was the result of a misdirection on the subject of fitness to plead.

Their decision, delivered by Lord Parker, upheld Mr Justice Davies'
ruling as to the burden of proof. Strictly speaking, that was that: Podola's
conviction stood. But in everyone's mind was the uneasy question 'What
if the jury were wrong, and his amnesia was genuine?' For the medical
evidence in his favour had been impressive, even if it had not quite convinced the jury. Lord Goddard and his four colleagues therefore made it
plain that, even if Podola had really lost his memory for the relevant
period, that did not of itself render him 'insane so that he could not be
tried'. In coming to this rather startling conclusion they relied largely on
precedent. They rightly rejected defence counsel's contention that in the
passage quoted from Hale 'sound memory' referred to powers of recollection; undoubtedly it meant no more than 'sound mind'. They also rejected
the suggestion that in Scotland hysterical amnesia was accepted as con-
stituting unfitness for trial.

Having disposed of these two red herrings with impeccable logic, they
argued that Alderson's test in Pritchard's case was still 'firmly embodied
in our law'.[29] Nobody had suggested that Podola could not plead, did not
know of his right to challenge jurors, or was unable to follow the evidence;
and his counsel's argument that his loss of memory meant that he could
not comprehend the details of the evidence did not convince the court. Accordingly, Podola would have been fit for trial even if his amnesia had
been genuine. The Court did not ask itself whether Alderson had intended
to describe *all* the disabilities that might render a man unfit to make a
proper defence; or merely those from which Pritchard might conceivably
have been suffering. Nor did it consider that in 1836 Alderson might never
have heard of loss of memory. The court's reasoning was at once correct
and contrary to commonsense. The law has often been criticised unfairly
for failure to adapt itself to new scientific ideas, especially in psychiatry;
but in this case the criticism was unquestionably justified.

At that date Podola's crime was capital for several reasons: he had committed murder while resisting arrest, his weapon was a firearm, and his
victim was a policeman on duty. The shooting of unarmed policemen
arouses particular alarm and horror in Britain (much more than the
shooting of unarmed bank clerks or the strangling of children), and unlike
most murderers whose states of mind have brought their cases before the
Court of Criminal Appeal, he was allowed to go to the scaffold. Had his
conviction depended on the question whether his amnesia was genuine,
there would probably have been just enough doubt in the minds of the

Home Office to tip the scale in favour of a reprieve. But by saying so clearly and firmly that his conviction was proper even if he really had lost his memory Lord Goddard and his fellow judges had turned that doubt into an irrelevancy.

The last word – for the moment at least – was uttered by the Criminal Law Revision Committee in 1963 when they produced their report on criminal procedure and insanity.[32] The Home Secretary had asked them to consider the revision of the law in terms which gave them a broad hint that there should be a right of appeal against a finding of unfitness to plead; and this they duly recommended. They also discussed, in considerable detail, the stages at which it should be possible to raise the issue, and – not without disagreement – decided in favour of a procedure under which the latest stage at which it could be raised was the opening of the case for the defence, thereby upholding Lord Devlin. Unlike the reports of the Atkin Committee or the Gowers Commission, this one was not linked to any controversy of political interest, such as capital punishment: like all the reports of the Criminal Law Revision Committee, it was presented as a series of technical recommendations for overdue procedural reform, with a draft bill annexed. It was accepted and implemented in the Criminal Procedure (Insanity) Act of 1964 with virtually no dissent.

The Act also made it clear that the question of the fitness of the accused for trial could be raised by anyone ('at the instance of the defence or otherwise'); and dealt with the question as to when a new jury must be empanelled. These too were uncontroversial provisions. It made one alteration in the law, however, which could be criticised. The Criminal Law Revision Committee had recommended that the result of a special verdict or of a finding that the accused was under disability should be either an order committing the accused to a hospital specified by the Home Secretary or an order for his immediate release. Their reasons for this proposal were not made entirely clear, and when the Bill was introduced in Parliament this was one of the few points on which it differed from the Committee's draft. It provided simply that in such cases the court must make an order committing the accused to 'such hospital as may be specified by the Secretary of State'. What may not have been realised is that the result was to tie the hands of the executive in a way in which they had not hitherto been tied. For under the Act of 1800 the 'place' and 'manner' of the custody was to be decided by the sovereign, not the court; but under the Act of 1964 it must be a hospital. Since in twentieth-century practice virtually every special verdict or finding of unfitness for trial had resulted in committal to a hospital, one might dismiss the change in the law as nominal were it not for the case of the deaf-mute. In fact nearly all deaf-mutes who are unfit to be tried seem to have been considered suitable patients for a special or ordinary mental hospital. Occasionally, however, one had been dealt with by a short period of custody in prison or committal to a home for the deaf. Henceforth the court will be obliged to commit him to a hospital named by the Home Secretary. It is true that the hospital need not be a *mental* hospital[33]; but if the deaf-mute does not require a stay in a mental hospital it does not necessarily follow that another kind of hospital is appropriate. It is ironical that the deaf-mute, who was the first to be recognised as unfit for trial, should now be overlooked among the mentally disordered.

By 1964, however, the downward trend in the relative frequency of findings of unfitness had reached a very low level, as can be seen from table 7 and figure 3. The rate per 100,000 persons arraigned was less than it had been 100 years before. The decline was apparent both in trials for murder – as can be seen from table 3 in chapter 5 – and in other trials on indictment. The explanation is not obvious. Trends of this sort, which take place over a relatively short span of time, are usually the effect of some procedural change. It would be tempting to attribute this one to the courts' post-war insistence that the preliminary issue could be raised only by the defence, if it were not for the fact that this seems to have been a short-lived innovation on the part of no more than a few. It is conceivable, too, that an increasing number of judges were insisting that the preliminary issue should be settled before the general issue, as Mr Justice Byrne did in 1957 in Beynon's case; this might have discouraged a few counsel from raising it in circumstances like those of Roberts' case. Situations, however, in which the defence is so confident of succeeding on the general issue that it will sacrifice its chances on the preliminary issue must be rare indeed. Nor can the decline be attributed to the Mental Health Act of 1959, which did not come into operation until late in 1960. Although the rates seem to have settled down at a stable level soon after that, the trend began years earlier.

I have been able to obtain the views of seven prison medical officers[34] whose experience covers this period, and from which two factors appear to be of major importance. In the first place there seems to have been an increasing tendency to take the view that the guilt or innocence of the accused should be determined before he is committed to indefinite detention. The evidence given to both the Atkin Committee and the Gowers Commission had emphasised not only the grievance felt by inmates, of Broadmoor and other hospitals, at their detention without trial, but also the possibility that an innocent person might occasionally be dealt with in this way. These were not entirely new points, but the publication, from 1949 onwards, of the evidence given to the Commission, and the eventual appearance of its report in 1953, gave them wide currency, and they are now stock arguments in any discussion of the subject.

The other factor was the introduction of the phenothiazine group of tranquillising drugs in the nineteen-fifties, and especially chlorpromazine. This began to be used for the treatment of schizophrenia in 1952, and by 1955 its effect on the country's mental hospitals was beginning to be felt. It was in that year that a decline began in the numbers of male and female in-patients in their twenties and thirties, the age-group in which one's first admission for schizophrenia is most likely. The effect of chlorpromazine is a rapid reduction in the emotional symptoms of the schizophrenic, the excitement of the manic patient, and the agitation of some depressed patients; and it is these patients who are responsible for a large share of the serious crimes committed by mentally disordered people.

Whether the drug should be regarded as a 'cure' for any mental disorder is now very doubtful. What it undoubtedly does is to relieve sufferers from these disorders of much of the emotional disturbance which prevents their communicating with others and behaving as rationally as their delusions or confusion will permit. Many a schizophrenic, maniac, or depressive prisoner who would previously have been too disturbed could now be rendered fit for trial.

Unlike the defence of insanity, however, the preliminary issue of fitness for trial can hardly be regarded as obsolescent. There will always be the occasional case in which both justice and common sense will require that the trial be postponed or dispensed with because of the mental condition of the accused. What is open to question is whether the present procedure for identifying such cases is the best possible. Certainly the Act of 1964 has made it about as flexible as could be expected of any transaction in our higher courts. One might ask, perhaps, why magistrates should not be allowed to consider the issue at the stage of committal for trial, especially if the defence is willing that they should do so. To argue that only a jury, assisted by a judge, can be entrusted with this task is not only implausible but also unrealistic; for ever since 1840 it has been possible for doctors, and especially those attached to prisons, to prevent altogether the appearance of the accused in court, at least until his condition improves.

Notes

1 See Miss A.J.Robertson's *The Laws of the Kings of England from Edmund to Henry* I (Cambridge University Press, 1925).
2 From the Liber Assisarum for 26 Edward III, plea 27: 'Skipwith dit a les Justices que . . . un fuit endict de mort de un home qui ne puit ne parler ne oier, &c. que serra fait &c. Hill: un est endict devant moy que il occist iiii homes quant il fuit enrage [sc. furiosus?] et ieo ne luy voile arrain tanque il ad son seine, mes luy commaunde al prison tanque &c. et puis quant &c le Roy luy dona sa peas. . . .' I am indebted to Mr J.M.Kaye for helping me to trace this reference.
3 *Historia Placitorum Coronae*, I, ch. IV.
4 R. v. Steel (1787), 2 Leach 507.
5 See the contemporary law reports (1583), 1 Anderson, 104, and Savile, 57. *The Dictionary of National Biography* gives a short account of the episode, without legal details (S. v. Somervile).
6 See F.T.Hargraves' *State Trials* (1776), vol. IV, cols. 161–; and for Sir John Hawles' comments cols. 203–.
7 Dyle's case (1756) O.B.S.P., 271.
8 See Howell's *State Trials*, XXII, cols. 307–, and Old Bailey Sessions Papers, 1790, pp. 360–.
9 R. v. Dyson (1831), 7 Carrington & Payne, 305: 1 Lewin 64.
10 R. v. the Governor of Stafford Prison (1909), 2 K.B. 81. The
11 prisoner's name was Emery.
   R. v. Pritchard (1836), 7 Carrington & Payne, 303.

12 I am indebted for this information to the Director of Public Prosecutions and his staff.

13 Minutes of Evidence taken before the Royal Commission on Capital Punishment, 1949–53, Day 8 (1949, HMSO).

14 28 & 29 Vict., c. 126.

15 R. v. Dwerryhouse (1847), 3 Cox (Criminal Law Cases), 291 & 446.

16 R. v. Blackwell (1857), 7 Cox 353.

17 R. v. Peacock (1870), 12 Cox 21.

18 See *The Times* for 10 February 1885 (the case seems to be unreported otherwise). I am indebted to the Home Office for helping me to trace the connection between this case and Standing Order 138 (as it originally was); and to the Prison Department for permission to examine and quote from their series of Standing Orders. The rest of the Standing Order deals with procedural matters. For the full text in a later form see the appendices to the Atkin Committee's report (1924, Cmd. 2005).

19 I have pieced Pickering's story together from sources which include T. Morris and L. Blom-Cooper, *A Calendar of Murder* (London, 1963), and the *Empire News*, 11 January 1965.

20 R. v. Berry (1876), 1 Q.B.D. 447.

21 R. v. Roberts (1954), 2 Q.B. 329; 37 Cr. App. R. 86.

22 R. v. Beynon (1957), 2 Q.B. 111; 41 Cr. App. R. 123.

23 R. v. Davies (1853), 6 Cox 326.

24 R. v. Turton (1854), 6 Cox 395.

25 See the 12th edition of Archbold's *Criminal Pleading*, published in 1853 (London): the 11th edition does not mention the practice, which suggests, although it does not prove conclusively that it was instituted between the two dates. The edition of 1900 differs from the previous one of 1886 in saying that the practice applied to 'serious crimes' as well as murder. Since Hillard, accused of attempted murder in 1899, did not have counsel it is a fair inference that the extension of the practice to serious crimes other than murder took place about that time.

26 This is unreported; and I am indebted to the Home Office for drawing my attention to the Public Record Office file concerning it.

27 R. v. Dashwood (1943), 28 Cr. App. R. 167; K.B. 1.

28 I am indebted to the Director of Public Prosecutions and his staff for my information about this case, which was not reported. The comments are of course my own.

29 R. v. Podola (1960), 43 Cr. App. R. 220, C.C.A. For a full account of the crime, the trial and the proceedings in the Court of Criminal Appeal, see R. Furneaux, *Guenther Podola* (London, 1960).

30 R. v. Sharp (1958), 41 Cr. App. R. 197.

31 R. v. Jefferson (1908), 1 Cr. App. R. 95.

32 Criminal Law Revision Committee: third report: 'Criminal Procedure and Insanity' (1963: Cmnd. 2149: HMSO): see paras. 13–37, but especially 32 and 34.

33 See the definition in s. 147 of the Mental Health Act, 1959, which is

applied to the Criminal Procedure (Insanity) Act, 1964, by s. 8 of that Act.

34 Drs Angus, Brown, Fenton, Knox, Oldham, Terry, and Wray, all of whom took a great deal of trouble and provided me with valuable information. I am also grateful to Dr Pickering, Chief Medical Officer of the Prison Department, for distributing my questions to the prison medical officers concerned.

Epilogue. The End of an Old Song

In my preface I referred to the way in which the development of the criminal law on the subject of the insane has been oversimplified. At the risk of oversimplifying my own attempt at history let me outline the main stages through which the law seems to have passed. In the era of compensation the problem presented by insane violence was easily solved by the rule that it was for the madman's kin to pay for the injuries which he had caused and keep him out of trouble. I have suggested that this custom survived into the era of official punishment, so that someone who committed a felony but was locally known to be mad was not presented for trial. When the Plantagenets succeeded in bringing criminal trials under central control, and petty juries took the place of trial by ordeal, the question whether the man accused of felony was sane or not was still decided by these local men, but they were no longer allowed to exempt him from trial: it was for the king to pardon him. This was a cumbersome procedure, and was eventually replaced by one which allowed the jury not only to decide that the accused was insane but also to acquit him.

From the judges' point of view, however, if not the juries', it was not every sort of insanity that justified an acquittal. If the criminal act had been committed in a lucid interval, insanity was no excuse. The insanity must have deprived the offender of reason at the time of his act, so that he did not know what he was doing. Later, the analogy of the child offender suggested to lawyers that the madman might not be able to distinguish right from wrong; and this became part of the test. Hadfield's case opened their eyes to the possibility that he might have known what he was doing, and that it was wrong, but have been impelled to do what he did by a delusion. M'Naghten's acquittal, however, was not based on his delusion so much as on the irresistible force of his impulse. The M'Naghten Rules were, in effect, an admission that he should not have been acquitted, and and the defence could still be justified only by ignorance of the nature of the act, ignorance of its wrongness, or a delusion which, if true, would have justified the act. A defence based on irresistible impulse, though acceptable to some judges, was not officially countenanced until the Lord Chief Justice defined diminished responsibility in 1960.

But are juries really swayed by these distinctions? To Hale the English jury, properly instructed by a judge, seemed the best possible arbiters of such issues. Lord Cooper was more cynical about Scots juries, and believed that all they asked themselves was "Is this man mad or is he not?" Recent research suggests that American juries at least are less naive than this, if not quite so sophisticated as Hale assumed; and that the nature of the test which they are instructed by the judge to apply does make a difference to the likelihood of their returning a special verdict.[1] However that may be, the fact remains that one of the most striking observations which emerge from my statistical approach to the last two hundred years has been the almost complete absence of any connection between the changes in courts' behaviour, as reflected in the statistics, and the cases which have made legal history. So far as general trends are concerned, Hadfield, M'Naghten, True, Windle, Byrne, and Podola might never have existed.

In any case, the king's ancient power to pardon insane felons has been preserved, and from the eighteenth century onward has been used with increasing frequency to extend mercy to madmen whom the strictness of the judge or the perversity of the jury had convicted. By the twentieth century the royal prerogative was used in such a way that the contest in court over the criminal responsibility of the insane murderer became academic: if he was really insane he would be saved from hanging, whatever the court decided. The prerogative also anticipated the Infanticide Acts by nearly a century, so that this paper victory did not save a single life.

The difficulty of trying a person with whom one cannot communicate rationally had been recognised in the case of deaf-mutes before the Conquest, and by the middle of the fourteenth century, if not before, it was accepted that a madman too might sometimes be, for the moment at least, unfit for trial. Since this was an even rarer event than the defence of insanity, courts tended to improvise principles for dealing with it when it confronted them. It was not until the creation of a prison medical service that it became a numerically important avenue of escape for the insane; and with the introduction of the tranquillising drugs in the nineteen-fifties the frequency of such findings declined again.

As for the special verdict itself, from the lawyer's point of view Queen Victoria's intervention in 1883 was little more than the beginning of a bad joke which lasted until 1964. If seen more objectively, however, it was the most striking incident in the long-drawn conflict between justice or expediency – or, since these words are apt to have emotional overtones, between the approaches of the moralist and the utilitarian.

To the moralist, justice requires that a man who is not to blame for the harm he has done should not be penalised for it. Young children, madmen, sleep-walkers, and people who do harm by accident should be exempt from the penal system. To the administrator with a utilitarian outlook it is obvious that this idealistic principle will result in avoidable harm. Children and madmen will repeat their offences; sleep-walkers cannot help going to sleep again; some people are accident-prone or even careless. Moralists and utilitarians compromise on this issue by various devices. Delinquent children are dealt with by a social service which is carefully distinguished from the penal system, even if the child finds the distinction a difficult one to grasp. Very frequent types of negligence – for example, in the driving of motor cars – are defined as crimes. Madmen are put under restraint by their nearest and dearest, and not as a punishment.

This at least was the theory from Saxon times until the eighteenth century, when legislation to deal with vagrants also provided statutory powers to confine troublesome lunatics. The importance of the Act of 1800 was that it expressly made it the function of a *criminal court* to order the confinement of an insane offender at the same time as it pronounced him 'not guilty'. Although Queen Victoria's special verdict was meant as a deterrent which would have no effect on the actual fate of the insane offender, and was, if anything, less paradoxical than an acquittal which meant detention, it troubled the moralists because of the injustice of the word 'guilty'. Presumably they are now satisfied by the re-insertion of the word 'not'. What is most interesting, however, is the hypnotic effect of the ancient question 'How say you, are you guilty or not guilty?' The words 'not guilty' must be one of the most ambiguous phrases in English law. They may mean that what was done was not criminal, or that it was not done by the accused, or that it was done by him in circumstances which excuse him morally. Yet the law tries to preserve the fiction that there are only two verdicts, guilty or not guilty. Even a finding that is obviously of a third kind, such as the special verdict of insanity, must be disguised as one or other. From 1800 to 1883 it was disguised as an acquittal; from 1883 to 1964 it was disguised as a conviction; now it is again disguised as an acquittal. But one does not solve a dilemma by shifting from horn to horn.

What is often forgotten is that the two horns of this dilemma date from an era in which the penalty was automatically dictated by the conviction. When 'guilty' meant death, the only question of practical importance was 'Is this man guilty or not?' As soon as courts were allowed discretion to choose between penalties, the two-verdict system began to become out of date, although the law has not yet fully accepted this.

It is not only the two-verdict system that is historically linked to a mandatory death penalty: so is the defence of insanity. Until the eighteenth century it was acceptable only 'in capitals' (to use Hale's phrase). When capital punishment was virtually restricted to murderers, it became comparatively rare for insanity to be offered as a defence to any other indictment. After the Homicide Act of 1957 provided the easier plea of diminished responsibility, the defence became rarer still. Its only peculiar advantage is now that it forces the court, instead of merely permitting it, to commit the accused to hospital instead of prison (or whatever other course would be permissible). In a system which makes a point of conferring on courts as much freedom of choice as possible at the stage of sentencing, this is an anachronism. The point at which the obsolescent becomes obsolete is always hard to identify, but the defence of insanity must be close to it.

It is the same principle, that there should be only two alternatives, which is at the heart of the conflict between the criminal law and modern psychiatry. The psychiatrist, and to an even greater extent the clinical psychologist, sees most mental disorders as extreme forms of differences of degree. Just as it is a question of degree how fat one must become before one is in need of a physician, so it is often difficult to say whether this person or that is of subnormal intelligence or is merely stupid. The test is often an operational one. Is he too stupid, or too confused in his thinking, or too impulsive in giving way to his desires, to keep out of trouble without care or treatment?

In contrast, the criminal law has little use for delicate shades of colour, and prefers to deal in black and white. When counsel insists that a witness answer 'Yes' or 'No' he is not merely employing a useful tactic: he is speaking with the voice of the law. And in criminal liability as in many other matters the law sees only differences in kind, not differences of degree. The accused must be either liable to punishment or not liable. Not until the stage of sentencing has been reached can differences of degree be taken into consideration and allowed to operate in mitigation. It was as a mitigating circumstance that partial insanity was recognised by the Bluidy Mackenzie and found its way into the Scots law of sentencing. It is worth noting, however, that the effect of Dingwall's case was not merely to elevate partial insanity to the status of a defence but also to change it from a question of degree to a question of kind: how else could it be used to distinguish between two legally distinct crimes, murder and culpable homicide?

Lawyers are often accused of being unsympathetic to the psychiatric point of view because they have not troubled to acquaint themselves with it. Certainly judges sometimes give the impression of a rather hasty use of textbooks. Lord Chief Justice Goddard, in his carefully prepared judgment on Rivett's appeal,[2] explained that schizophrenia was 'a modern and perhaps more imposing name for what used to be called *dementia praecox*'. So far so good: but he went on to translate *dementia praecox* as 'defect of mind existing from an early age'. His translation was neatly reminiscent of the Mental Deficiency Acts; but in fact *dementia praecox* does not mean this, even in a literal translation. A reasonable English equivalent would be 'premature deterioration of the mind', which is what schizophrenia was first thought to be. Other judges, however, have shown not only a sounder grasp of psychiatric diagnoses but also an ability to explain them with a clarity that psychiatrists must – or should – envy: Devlin is an example. The great Fitzjames Stephen had read his Maudsley and – even more surprisingly – the German Griesinger to good effect.

Even the most sophisticated of judges or counsel, however, tends to regard a psychiatrist's diagnosis as the exact equivalent of a physician's. A physician can say with certainty whether a man's leg is broken or not, and if it is broken whether he could have walked on it after it was broken. Why should not a psychiatrist be able to say whether the accused is mentally defective, and if so whether he could have understood the nature of his act? This view is encouraged not merely by the simpler or less up-to-date form of psychiatric textbook but also by the way in which the psychiatrist is compelled by the legal process to express himself. The criminal trial is a game in which the objective is to transform what the psychiatrist wants to say into a firm basis for an irrevocable decision between two clean cut alternatives, expressed in language intelligible to twelve men from whom any practising lawyers or doctors are virtually excluded by the process of selection. The rules say that this must be managed by subjecting him to questioning by two or even three lawyers, at least one of whom is supposed to do his best to expose any weaknesses in what the psychiatrist has to say.

In a contest of this sort the psychiatrist is like a wrestler who is compelled to box. He must achieve an objective which does not appeal to him by gymnastics for which he is not trained. Psychiatrists are accused by lawyers of obscurantism and jargon; and this is quite as justifiable as psychiatrists' complaints of lawyers' superficiality. To a considerable extent, however, the psychiatrist's jargon is forced on him by his situation. He may, for example, believe that mental subnormality is not a disability which, like a broken leg, can be diagnosed *before* asking whether it prevents a man from doing something, but a diagnosis which can be made only *by* asking what he can do. Since the typical judge and counsel are at least as intelligent as the typical psychiatrist, this point is by no means beyond them. But if the jury is to come to a decision, what is wanted is a confident assertion that the accused is or is not suffering from some form of mental disorder, and that as a result he could or could not have performed whatever feat of comprehension or self-control is considered relevant. The more esoteric the name of the disorder the more incapacitating it sounds.

The psychiatrist is therefore tempted – one might almost say invited – to slap an impressive label on the accused in order to ensure that he arrives at what seems to the psychiatrist to be the right destination. He may not like the wording on the label; if allowed to write it himself he might well produce a more accurate and less categorical description. But ready-made labels are recognised and acknowledged where home-made ones are not.

Some of these labels, like the slogans of over-enthusiastic advertisements, have been so widely used that they have ceased to impress and begun to amuse or even irritate lawyers, although they may – for all we know – still carry weight with jurors. A nineteenth-century example is the collection of 'manias' which alienists used to fire, like grape-shot, at judges and juries – monomania, kleptomania, pyromania, erotomania, and Yellowlees' unforgettable 'hypnomania'. A more modern example, 'psychopathy', will be discussed in the next volume. Nevertheless the court expects the psychiatrist to produce a diagnostic label when he appears in the witness-box. If he were to say 'I cannot put a name to this man's disorder; all I can say is that it is a disease of the mind and that it prevented him from knowing what he was doing' he would carry less authority than the colleague who began 'This man is suffering from schizophrenia of an unusual kind . . .' The witness-box may be the place for truthfulness but not for intellectual honesty.

None of these observations, however, dispose of the incompatibility between the legal and psychiatric approaches to the problem of criminal responsibility. The literature on this subject is enormous, but what is common to all psychiatric attacks on legal tests of responsibility is the assertion that the tests are too narrowly selective; that is, that they reject as 'responsible' too many of the offenders who are submitted to them. In assessing the strength of attacks of this sort, however, one must distinguish between those which accept the law's fundamental justification for its concern with 'responsibility' and those which do not.

This justification is primarily moralistic and retributive. Originally, in the minds of the Roman jurists, it took the form of excusing the madman *because he was punished enough* by his madness. Although, as I have pointed out on page 27, we are still capable of such reasoning, it had at least one inherent weakness; for punishment is surely something that is imposed on someone if, because, and after he has done something wrong, whereas the madman is mad whether he does something wrong or not. (A believer in predestination might find a way round this point, but that is a digression.) In any case, as soon as the penalties of the criminal law are seen as having utilitarian aims, such as general deterrence or the correction of the individual, the Roman argument ceases to apply. The justification on which the codes of Western Europe and America have based their reasoning is that *the madman is not to blame* for the harm he does. This argument is of course at its strongest when the penalty is thought of as retributive punishment, but it does not cease to have force if penalties are regarded as entirely utilitarian measures, designed to deter potential imitators, correct the individual offender, or protect society at large. For, as Professor Hart has pointed out,[3] it is still a fundamental principle of our criminal law that one should not be liable to its penal measures unless one has, without sufficient excuse, infringed one of its prohibitions.

Whether this can be upheld as a moral principle or only as a rough rule of expediency is not for the moment a relevant question.[4] It is the most defensible form of the lawyer's retributive justification for exempting the insane from the ordinary penalties of the criminal law. If a psychiatrist does not want to meet the lawyers on this ground, he must put forward – as some have done – an alternative justification for this exemption: that to treat the mentally disordered as patients instead of criminals will more effectively achieve the utilitarian aims of correction and protection. That royal Benthamite Queen Victoria would have asked at this point why the psychiatrist ignores general deterrence, and in the next volume we shall see how far it can be safely assumed that correction and protection are achieved by psychiatrists. At the moment, however, we are concerned with the psychiatrist who accepts at least Hart's version of the retributive justification for excusing the insane.

This being so, the disagreement is over the answer to the question 'What should be regarded as a sufficient excuse in the case of the mentally disordered offender?' The lawyers have been willing to accept as excuses certain types of causal connection between the disorder and the act. What the psychiatrists want may be clearer after we have considered the possible types of causal connection, of which I can distinguish at least fourteen:

1. The disorder may have rendered a man an automaton, so that

his bodily movements were not those that he would have decided
to make had he been in a normal state. An example is the driver
of a car who has an epileptic fit.

2. It may deceive him as to the nature of his physical act. He may
   think he is saying something harmless, but in fact be uttering
   obscene words.

3. It may deceive him as to the identity of his victim. Fraser thought
   he was defending himself against a wild beast when he was
   really battering his baby to death.

4. It may deceive him as to the situation in which he is placed. If
   it is conceded that sleep-walking is a mental disorder, an
   example is Esther Griggs, who threw her baby out of the window because she thought the house was on fire.

5. It may deceive him not as to the nature of his act, nor as to the
   physical situation in which it is performed, but in such a way
   as to give him grounds for believing that his act was not criminal. When Male thought he was a reincarnation of one of the
   Prophets and had the right to the food which he took from the
   supermarket, he was in this situation.

6. There are other ways in which the disorder might make a man
   ignorant of his act's criminality. Low intelligence might prevent
   him from realising that his behaviour with a child was an indecent assault.

These were the situations which English law officially recognised in the
second half of the nineteenth century. With good reason, psychiatrists
pointed out that the list ignored causal connections that were not cognitive
in nature. It assumed, too, that a man could be mad north-north-west but
sane and completely rational in all other directions. The situations which
seemed to cry out for inclusion were those in which

7. the disorder distorts his ethical views. Windle, who does not
   seem to have been deluded in any other way, thought it right to
   give his depressed wife a fatal dose of aspirin.

This situation is now officially recognised in the criminal codes of several
common-law countries, although not, as we saw in chapter 6, in England
itself.

8. The disorder may either
   (a) intensify normal impulses or desires or other reactions to a
       degree which makes it difficult or impossible for a person
       with normal self-control to resist them;
       or
   (b) weaken the offender's control over desires, impulses, etc.,
       of normal strength.

In practice it is seldom possible to distinguish between these two situations. But if one is able to compare a man who yields only to one sort of
temptation, and then only after resisting it, with one who yields without
much hesitation to a variety of temptations, it is plausible to regard the
former as an example of (a), the latter as an example of (b).

9. The disorder may provide him with an abnormal motive, as in

the case of coprophilia. Sometimes it is a desire which can be satisfied only by breaking the law: examples are what used to be called 'kleptomania' or sadism such as Byrne's.

10. The disorder may provide him with a motive in another way. He may be greatly disturbed by its symptoms and be trying to ignore or control them. Circumstances which remind him of these symptoms or threaten to weaken his control over them may provoke him to violence. A case of this sort (Gorshen's) is described by Professor Diamond, who was one of the defendant's psychiatric witnesses. Gorshen, a Russian immigrant to California, had brief recurrent intervals in which he was tormented by perverted sexual and sadistic images, and he was beginning to lose his sexual potency. In a brawl with him his foreman used a Russian obscenity which in some way fitted in with the fantasies he feared, and in spite of a policeman at each of his elbows Gorshen shot him. 'The essence of my testimony', writes Diamond, 'was that Gorshen killed not because he was insane but rather as a defense against insanity', and 'Only by killing could he retain his sanity and avoid incarceration in the hell of his visions.' As a result of this case the Californian courts now seem to recognise something rather like 'diminished responsibility'.[5]

These situations have now come to be officially accepted in most, if not all, versions of the English law, either as a result of revisions of the M'Naghten Rules or through the introduction of the defence of diminished responsibility.

Nevertheless, so strong has been Isaac Ray's influence that many psychiatrists would like the law to make further concessions. The Medico-Psychological Association, for example, proposed to the Atkin Committee that the defence of insanity should be accepted unless it had been proved to the jury's satisfaction that the offender's crime was 'unrelated to his mental disorder'.[6] Although 'unrelated' is a rather vague term, they seem to have meant that the offender should be excused if his disorder was to any extent the cause of his crime: if, *but for* his disorder, he would not have committed it. Taken at its face value, this proposal would include at least four more situations:

11. The disorder may cause a person to underestimate the seriousness with which his crime is regarded by the law. I have been present at an interview with a man of low intelligence who shot and killed his neighbour because he believed that she was spreading rumours that he was a homosexual. He knew that this was a crime but did not think it a serious one, and repeatedly said that he thought he would get two years for it.

12. It may lead him into situations in which even the mentally normal person would be strongly tempted to commit the offence. The unemployable and penniless schizophrenic who, for one reason or another, will not go near lodging-houses or other places where he could legitimately get food and a bed is eventually

driven to steal something to eat or to sleep where he should not.

13. It may simply mislead him into underestimating his chances of being caught. This may happen because he fails to take into account his own incompetence, as the chronic housebreaker of low intelligence does when he overlooks the fact that his finger-prints are well known to the police. Or he may fail to realise that anyone's chances of detection would be high in the circumstances. A striking example of this was Ley, the Australian politician who suspected a youth of sexual relations with his former mistress, and carried out an elaborate plot to murder him with the aid of two hired accomplices (one of whom betrayed him as soon as it became clear that murder was involved).[7]

14. It may give him a more rational assurance of impunity. One of Forbes Winslow's many anecdotes concerned a conversation which he had had with a lunatic. Asked what would happen if he cut Winslow's throat, the lunatic replied that Winslow would die, and it would be murder. When Winslow enquired what the consequences for the lunatic would be, he answered that since he was a lunatic nothing would be done to him.[8] If the lunatic had followed up the conversation by cutting Winslow's throat, he would have provided a neat example of this situation.

Not all psychiatrists who support the 'but-for' proposal in its general form would in fact be happy about all of the situations which a literal interpretation of it must include. Some would say that they did not really have in mind any of these situations; others would argue that situations 11 and 12 but not situations 13 and 14 would provide an excuse for the offender; and so on. It is not easy either to find in the literature or to draft for oneself a formula which accurately represents this point of view. Perhaps what it amounts to is that the offender's act must have been such that in the circumstances only a mentally disordered person would have committed it. This would include situations 11 and 13 but not 14, since in that situation the offender might be relying on an undeserved reputation for insanity. Whether the formula would include situation 12 depends on the interpretation placed on 'in the circumstances'.

Whatever formula they adopt, psychiatrists who would like any of these situations[9] to be added to the official list – and there are psychiatrists who would – have a difficult case to argue unless they are prepared to reject the entire principle upon which the law bases the exemption of the insane from penal measures. If they are prepared to go to this length, they have more than one alternative. They can simply argue, as I have suggested, that a more effective way to correct such offenders is to treat them as patients (in which case they must of course produce evidence that this is so). Or they may resort to more sophisticated moral arguments, as Covarrubias did when he said that the insane were incapable of the suffering which was essential to punishment, or as Lord Hewart did when he suggested that murderers who were too insane to understand why they were being punished should be reprieved. But men whose disorder merely led to situations 11–14 would be unlikely to meet Covarrubias' or Hewart's requirements. Some psychiatrists would excuse such offenders by the simple resort to determinism. But this is a very blunt weapon, since it excuses all offenders. If they wish it to excuse only *some* offenders, they must explain themselves further.

The usual tactic of the psychiatrist who wants to extend the official list to include any of situations 11–14 without retreating off the lawyers' ground and into complete utilitarianism or determinism is to argue that *pure* examples of these situations do not in fact occur. He will say, for example, that a man who believes the penalty for killing his neighbour to be only two years' imprisonment cannot fully appreciate the nature of his act, and is thus really in situation 2, 4, or 5. Or that the vagrant schizophrenic who steals from hunger cannot have the same self-control as the mentally normal tramp simply because he is schizophrenic: in other words, he is also in situation 7 or 8(*b*). Or that the man who, like Ley, grossly underestimates his chances of detection must also be an example of situation 7 or 8.

This seems to be the underlying logic of the psychiatrists' criticism that the law too readily assumes that mental disorder can affect limited and definable aspects of behaviour. If so, it illustrates in an extreme form the way in which the psychiatric notions of one age recoil upon the psychiatrists of the next, whether in court or outside it. For it was the nineteenth-century alienists, with their talk of monomanias, who encouraged lawyers to think in this way: a monomania was a mental disorder which manifested itself in one particular activity or delusion.

The important question, however, to which lawyers might well demand an answer from psychiatrists is whether the latter's criticism is based on empirical evidence or on a presumption. For a suspicious feature of the literature of forensic psychiatry is that – to my recollection at least – it hardly ever describes a case in which the psychiatrist believes that the offender's mental disorder is quite unconnected causally with his offence. Yet it is as certain as *a priori* reasoning can make it that such cases must occur. For there must have been mentally healthy criminals who in the middle of a career of repeated dishonesties have succumbed to a disorder which cannot have been in any way responsible for their earlier behaviour – for example, because it was the result of injury to or infection of the brain. If after the onset of the disorder they continued to commit similar offences, it would be unscientific to suppose that these were in any way attributable to the disorder. No doubt the fact that such case-histories are so hard to find in the literature is partly due to two facts of nature. The disorders associated with most offences – the schizophrenias, the affective conditions, and subnormality of intelligence – are such that it is impossible to point with certainty to a stage in the offender's career when the disorder could not have been latent in him. Disorders in which one can do this with confidence are much rarer, and when they do occur tend to incapacitate the offender, either at once or soon. Nevertheless the absence of such cases from the literature may tell us something about psychiatrists as well as their patients.

The psychiatrist could claim, however, that – such cases apart – clinical experience suggests, without being able to prove conclusively, that a mental disorder affects the whole personality in the overwhelming majority of cases. He could argue that what he is asserting is not that it does so in all cases, but simply that it does so often enough to create what the lawyers might call a presumption. In other words, if it is shown (a) that a man has committed an offence, and (b) that he was suffering from a mental disorder at the time, the probability that the two facts were connected in one of the ways which provides the offender with an excuse is so substantial *that it should be for the sceptic to show that they were not.* In lawyer's language, what the psychiatrist is asking for is a rule that where reliable evidence of mental disorder is produced by the defence it should be for the prosecution to show that this was unconnected with the offence or connected only in one of the ways which are not accepted as an excuse. The psychiatrist could point out that this is roughly how the burden of proof is distributed in, for example, the courts of the USA, although this argument would not appeal to all English lawyers.

Whether the burden of proof ought to be divided in this way is probably an academic question. Nor is this so merely because of the infrequency with which pleas of insanity or diminished responsibility are now offered. For if this is the way in which a psychiatrist reasons it is bound to have a decisive effect upon his evidence. His statement that the offender did not know the nature of his act (or that his state of mind at the time fell into one of the other excusable categories) must in the nature of things be based not on observation but on inference, usually inference from the psychiatrist's interviews with him. If the psychiatrist believes that a man who thinks he will get only two years for shooting his neighbour dead probably did not know the nature of his act, he is apt to state this without explaining his process of inference in detail; indeed, he himself may not be fully aware of it. Since he must be allowed *some* sort of inference if he is to give any evidence at all on the offender's state of mind at the time of his act, it is very difficult to insist that he should not employ *this* sort of inference.

There remains, however, one question which can be asked about any of the situations in my list, although it is not often faced by psychiatrists or lawyers. (Fitzjames Stephen discussed it[10]; but, as so often happened, he was ignored.) If the state of mind in question is accepted as an excuse, is there a sound reason for confining this concession to cases in which the state of mind is the result of mental disorder? The force of this question is most obvious if situation 7 is taken as an example. If Windle is to be excused because his disorder made him think that it was not wrong to put his wife out of her misery with an overdose of aspirin, why should we not excuse someone who holds the same belief merely because he has been brought up in a free-thinking family?

When this question, *mutatis mutandis*, is asked about the other situations the law's answer varies. Sometimes it is hardly conceivable that the situation could arise except as a result of mental disorder: Male's offence is an example. On the other hand, 'automatism' is an acceptable defence whether it is the result of epilepsy or bees (see chapter 13). Ignorance of an act's illegality, however, is hardly ever acceptable if it does not arise from mental disorder. Although this is a feature of most criminal codes, the only sound justification that can be offered for it is expediency: the defence of ignorance would be too easy if it were not also necessary to prove the existence of a special reason for the ignorance, such as mental disorder. Similarly, if lawyers were asked why Windle should be excused but not a sane man who genuinely believes there is nothing wrong in mercy-killing, it is difficult to see how they could avoid falling back on the argument that this would be an excuse which would be too easily offered.

The psychiatrist is thus faced with a choice of positions. He may say 'I am asking lawyers to accept only excuses which they ought also to accept from sane offenders, if it were not for objections of expediency.' If he goes further, and says 'I am asking lawyers to accept from the mentally disordered some excuses which I would *not* expect them to accept from sane offenders', he must show why. I suspect that some psychiatrists do in fact take up this position, and that at the back of their minds is a justification that cannot be expressed in the language either of utilitarianism or of the common law. It is based on compassion rather than logic and comes very close to the old Roman maxim, 'the madman is punished enough by his madness'. If so, it is a sentiment which is at least humane, and none the worse for its antiquity.

This chapter, indeed this volume, has been concerned with the long-drawn-out dialogue between lawyers on the one hand and on the other the priest or, later, the physician: a dialogue which has so far been concerned with the approach of retributive morality to the insane offender. The growing populations, however, of nineteenth-century prisons and asylums eventually forced psychiatrists, administrators, and finally legislators to think in a more utilitarian way about this problem, and the consequences will be the subject of the next volume.

Notes
1 See Dr Rita Simon's experiments with 98 mock juries, reported in her book *The Jury and the Defence of Insanity* (Boston, 1967).
2 R. v. Rivett (1950), 34 Cr. App. R. 87.
3 See Professor H. L. A. Hart's *Prolegomenon to the Principles of Punishment* (the 1959 Presidential Address to the Aristotelian Society) and his *Punishment and the Elimination of Responsibility* (the 1961 Hobhouse Memorial Lecture: Athlone Press, University of London).
4 See my *The Aims of a Penal System* (James Seth Memorial Lecture for 1966) (Edinburgh 1967).
5 See B. L. Diamond, 'The Criminal Responsibility of the Mentally Ill', in (1961–2) 14 *Stanford Law Review*, 59.
6 Report of the Atkin Committee on Insanity and Crime (1924, Cmnd. 2005), 31–2.
7 See C. E. B. Roberts (ed.), *The Trial of Ley and Smith* (London, 1947).

8 See the evidence of Dr Tuke to the Capital Punishment Commission of 1864–6 (Minute 2429).

9 I have not attempted to include in my list

    (i) situations in which criminal omissions are causally connected with mental disorder;

or (ii) cases in which the mental disorder combines with the effect of alcohol or some other drug to produce one of the situations described.

These would complicate the argument by introducing the moral problems raised by negligence, or by indulgence in drugs; and I do not think that they would affect my main point.

10 See his paper to the Juridical Society in 1855 (op. cit. ch. 6, n2).

Table of Statutes

Table of Cases

T

Abbreviations

A.C.	Law Reports, Appeal Cases, House of Lords and Privy Council, 1890–
Ad. & El.	Adolphus and Ellis's Reports, King's Bench and Queen's Bench, 1834–42
Adam	Adam's Justiciary Reports (Scotland) 1893–
All E. R.	All England Law Reports, 1936–
And.	Anderson's Reports, Common Pleas, 1535–1605
bib.	the bibliography of this book
C. & P.	Carrington and Payne's Reports, Nisi Prius 1823–41
C. C. Ct. Cas	Central Criminal Court Cases (Sessions Papers) 1834–1913 (see bibliography)
Crim. L. R.	*Criminal Law Review*
Car. & Kir.	Carrington and Kirwan's Reports, Nisi Prius, 1843–53
Cl. & Fin.	Clark and Finelly's Reports, House of Lords, 1831–46
Co. Inst.	Coke's Institutes (see bibliography)
Co. Rep.	Coke's Reports, 1572–1616
Coup.	Couper's Justiciary Reports (Scotland) 1868–85
Cox C. C.	Cox's Criminal Law cases 1843–1945
Cr. App. R.	Criminal Appeal Reports, 1908–
E.R.	English Reports
F. & F.	Foster and Finlason's Reports, Nisi Prius, 1856–67
Hale, P. C.	Hale's *History of Pleas of the Crown* (see bibliography)
Hume Com.	Baron Hume's *Commentaries on the Law of Scotland*, 1844 edition (see bibliography)
Irv.	Irvine's Justiciary Reports (Scotland) 1852–67
J.P.	Justice of the Peace, 1837–
K.B.	Law Reports, King's Bench Division 1900–52
Leach	Leach's Crown Cases, 1730–1814
Lew. C.C.	Lewin's Crown Cases on the Northern Circuit, 1822–38
L.T.	Law Times Reports, 1859–1947
O.B.S.P.	Old Bailey Sessions Papers (see bibliography)
P.C.	Privy Council
Q.B.	Queen's Bench Reports (Adolphus and Ellis, New Series) 1841–52
Q.B.D.	Law Reports, Queen's Bench Division 1875–90
Russ. & Ry.	Russell and Ryan's Crown Cases Reserved, 1800–23
Sav.	Savile's Reports, Common Pleas, 1580–91
S.C.(J.)	Court of Justiciary Cases (Scotland), 1906–
S.L.T.	*Scots Law Times*, 1893–
S.S.P.	Selden Society Publications
St. Tr.	State Trials, 1163–1820 (see bibliography)
St. Tr. N. S.	State Trials, New Series, 1820–58 (see bibliography)
White	White's Justiciary Reports (Scotland) 1886–93

Appendixes

A   'Murderers' committed for trial, found unfit to plead or insane or of diminished responsibility, 1834–1965.

B   Persons committed for trial and found unfit for trial from 1834 to 1965 (excluding trials for murder).

C   Women found guilty of infanticide etc. from 1923 to 1965, and the measures to dispose of those convicted of infanticide.

D   Lord Mansfield's charge to the jury in Bellingham's case (1812).

E   Susannah Milesent's case.

F   *The Times'* Report of Broadric's trial. Chelmsford Assizes. Trial of Miss Broadric, for the murder of Mr Errington. Before the Lord Chief Baron.

Appendix A. 'Murderers' committed for trial, found unfit to plead or insane or of diminished responsibility, 1834–1965

Source: The Criminal Statistics for England and Wales

Year	committed for trial	found unfit	special verdict	Year	committed for trial	found unfit	special verdict
1834	86	1	5	1873	59	5	5
1835	78	2	8	1874	62	6	4
1836	73	1	7	1875	84	7	10
1837	43	3	5	1876	67	4	7
1838	75	2	7	1877	70	5	6
1839	46	1	1	1878	59	5	7
1840	54	1	3	1879	60	4	3
1841	66	—	5	1880	61	5	5
1842	67	1	3	1881	61	3	10
1843	85	1	6	1882	59	9	7
1844	75	2	1	1883	53	8	7
1845	65	4	5	1884	79	16	—*
1846	68	2	6	1885	65	16	—*
1847	72	5	5	1886	72	2	8
1848	76	—	5	1887	72	10	6
1849	84	4	12	1888	90	19	2
1850	52	7	5	1889	51	6	2
1851	74	1	5	1890	69	5	18
1852	81	6	5	1891	54	1	14
1853	79	3	5	1892	50	—	13
1854	62	3	11	1893	82	3	12
1855	57	3	4	1894	62	9	6
1856	82	3	4	1895	58	9	12
1857	70	5	9	1896	58	1	8
1858	66	4	11	1897	63	3	16
1859	70	3	5	1898	59	5	11
1860	49	3	2	1899	62	6	9
1861	64	2	6	1900	51	4	18
1862	77	7	10	1901	74	9	19
1863	83	6	7	1902	71	5	17
1864	70	1	8	1903	78	4	16
1865	60	1	10	1904	70	6	21
1866	55	5	3	1905	63	4	14
1867	94	2	5	1906	63	2	20
1868	71	8	4	1907	45	5	11
1869	63	1	7	1908	67	9	13
1870	41	4	2	1909	77	5	20
1871	54	5	10	1910	73	2	30
1872	70	5	7	1911	77	5	17

* In 1884 no special verdicts are recorded for *any* offence, and in 1885 only one (for larceny) is recorded, while the 'found unfit' figures for those years are suspiciously high. Queen Victoria's new wording may have caused confusion.

Year	committed for trial	found unfit	special verdict	Year	committed for trial	found unfit	special verdict
1912	63	7	15	1946	68	15	17
1913	67	5	17	1947	74	16	13
1914	55	6	12	1948	87	25	15
1915	47	2	12	1949	68	16	15
1916	54	12	16	1950	77	11	13
1917	48	5	9	1951	55	16	12
1918	57	10	11	1952	83	18	13
1919	83	13	20	1953	66	17	17
1920	90	8	14	1954	60	8	22
1921	63	7	14	1955	79	13	24
1922	60	3	13	1956	79	14	18
1923	58	14	12				
1924	42	3	14				
1925	81	8	24				
1926	57	5	18				
1927	50	6	13				
1928	60	12	12				
1929	50	7	19				
1930	40	7	11				
1931	57	8	17				
1932	64	9	29				

Year	committed for trial	found unfit	special verdict	Year	committed for trial	found unfit	special verdict	diminished responsibility
1933	53	5	18					
1934	61	7	19					
1935	52	6	15					
1936	67	12	20	1957	85	17	5	11
1937	44	14	11	1958	86	10	7	25
1938	54	12	12	1959	95	11	15	21
1939				1960	109	15	9	23
1940				1961	124	12	5	36
1941				1962	100	11	8	34
1942	No statistics published			1963	111	5	2	46
1943				1964	121	11	1	41
1944				1965	128	6	1	47
1945								

Appendix B. Persons committed for trial and found unfit for trial from 1834 to 1965 (excluding trials for murder)

Source: The Criminal Statistics for England and Wales

Year	For trial	Found unfit	Year	For trial	Found unfit
1834	22,365	7	1879	16,328	15
1835	20,635	2	1880	14,708	19
1836	20,911	11	1881	14,725	6
1837	23,569	11	1882	15,201	12
1838	23,019	11	1883	14,606	20
1839	24,397	12	1884	14,328	37
1840	27,133	12	1885	13,521	40
1841	27,654	14	1886	13,902	2
1842	31,242	9	1887	13,220	32
1843	29,506	11	1888	13,660	37
1844	26,467	14	1889	12,048	21
1845	24,238	8	1890	11,905	22
1846	25,039	9	1891	11,641	8
1847	28,761	10	1892	12,166	6
1848	30,272	10	1893	12,214	19
1849	27,732	7	1894	11,971	21
1850	26,761	19	1895	11,458	14
1851	27,886	8	1896	11,045	15
1852	27,429	13	1897	11,152	18
1853	26,980	18	1898	11,395	20
1854	29,297	13	1899	10,840	21
1855	25,915	20	1900	10,098	19
1856	19,355	7	1901	10,709	15
1857	20,199	11	1902	11,317	26
1858	17,789	4	1903	11,800	23
1859	16,604	11	1904	12,086	32
1860	15,942	9	1905	12,259	24
1861	18,262	6	1906	12,693	28
1862	19,924	12	1907	12,552	31
1863	20,735	9	1908	14,055	28
1864	19,436	10	1909	13,672	19
1865	19,554	8	1910	13,606	23
1866	18,790	9	1911	12,866	21
1867	18,877	9	1912	13,221	28
1868	20,021	19	1913	12,442	24
1869	19,255	13	1914	10,743	22
1870	17,537	30	1915	5,962	15
1871	16,215	16	1916	4,955	14
1872	14,731	17	1917	5,538	10
1873	14,834	18	1918	5,847	20
1874	15,133	21	1919	7,800	16
1875	14,630	15	1920	9,040	18
1876	16,011	19	1921	8,871	23
1877	15,820	27	1922	8,371	17
1878	16,268	14	1923	8,068	26

Year	For trial	Found unfit	Year	For trial	Found unfit
1924	7,803	18	1946	17,682	25
1925	8,058	10	1947	20,142	34
1926	7,867	19	1948	22,931	48
1927	7,086	18	1949	19,476	38
1928	7,222	23	1950	18,858	36
1929	7,022	15	1951	19,934	25
1930	8,344	22	1952	22,070	25
1931	8,610	10	1953	20,197	31
1932	10,346	12	1954	18,676	39
1933	9,148	17	1955	18,012	31
1934	8,614	15	1956	19,493	35
1935	8,218	17	1957	22,861	35
1936	8,425	11	1958	27,740	40
1937	9,039	12	1959	29,527	51
1938	9,949	15	1960	30,505	30
1939			1961	34,236	36
1940			1962	32,943	25
1941			1963	25,529	25
1942	No statistics published for		1964	24,209	23
1943	this period		1965	26,783	26
1944					
1945					

Appendix C. Women found guilty of infanticide etc. from 1923 to 1965, and the measures used to dispose of those convicted of infanticide

Source: The Criminal Statistics for England and Wales

Year	of murder[a]	Women found guilty of manslaughter[a]	of child destruction	of infanticide
1923	?	?		16
1924	?	?	Not	9
1925	?	?	applicable	18
1926	?	?		9
1927	?	?		7
1928	?	?		16
1929	?	?	—	11
1930	?	?	—	10
1931	?	?	—[d]	12
1932	?	?	—	12
1933	?	?	—	10
1934	?	?	—	7
1935	?	?	—	11
1936	?	?	—	15
1937	?	?	—	12
1938	?	?	—	11
1939–1945	no figures published			
1946	—	11	—	38
1947	4	13	1	39
1948	2	11	—	19
1949	4	13	—	19[e]
1950	4	12	—	24
1951	—	9	1	14
1952	2	7	—	18
1953	3	6	—	18
1954	2	9	—	17
1955	4	6	—	13
1956	1	10	—	1
1957	1	11	—	16
1958	3	7	—[d]	10
1959	—	16	—[d]	10
1960	—	17	—	16
1961	2	17	—	13
1962	1	20	—	17
1963	2	19	—	13
1964	—	24	—	12
1965	1	24	—	17

(a) Until 1946 only women *for trial* for murder or manslaughter were shown separately.

(d) A woman is recorded as acquitted of child destruction in 1931. In 1958 two *men* and in 1959 three *men* are recorded as found guilty of it.

(e) In this year a man is recorded as found guilty of infanticide, probably as an accomplice. He was sentenced to imprisonment.

Year	Disposal of infanticidal mothers				
	Discharge[b]	Probation	Fine	Prison	Otherwise[c]
1923	2	1	—	13	—
1924	7	—	—	2	—
1925	7	1	—	9	1
1926	5	1	—	3	—
1927	4	—	—	2	1
1928	9	3	—	4	—
1929	—	4	—	5	2
1930	4	1	—	4	1
1931	3	2	—	7	—
1932	5	1	—	6	—
1933	2	1	—	7	—
1934	4	2	—	1	—
1935	6	1	—	4	—
1936	6	3	—	6	—
1937	7	3	—	2	—
1938	4	5	—	2	—
1939–1945	no figures published				
1946	7	22	—	7	2
1947	10	21	—	8	—
1948	6	5	—	7	1
1949	6	7	—	6	—
1950	5	13	—	3	3
1951	2	7	—	3	2
1952	3	10	—	4	1
1953	3	8	—	2	5
1954	1	11	—	2	3
1955	3	8	—	2	—
1956	2	8	—	—	1
1957	—	13	—	2	1
1958	—	7	—	—	3
1959	—	9	—	—	1
1960	4	11	—	—	1
1961	—	12	—	—	1
1962	2	10	—	—	5
1963	—	9	—	—	4
1964	1	8	—	1	2
1965	1	10	—	—	6

(b) Including recognisances without probation orders and conditional discharges.

(c) The great majority of the women in this column were almost certainly committed to institutions for mental defectives or (after 1948) to mental hospitals. The pre-war (but not the post-war) figures *may* include one or two sent to reformatories or approved schools, since separate columns for these are not included in the pre-war tables.

Appendix D. Lord Mansfield's charge to the jury in Bellingham's case

Source: Old Bailey Sessions Papers (1812) *at p. 272. Apart from the asterisks and italics on p. 271 and the note on p. 272, the passage is reproduced as given in the original.*

Lord Chief Justice Mansfield. Gentlemen of the jury, you are now to try an indictment which charges the prisoner at the bar with the wilful murder (here the learned judge was so hurt by his feelings, that he could not proceed for several seconds) of Mr Spencer Perceval, (in a faint voice) who was murdered with a pistol loaded with a bullet; when he mentioned the name of (here again his lordship was sincerely affected, and burst into tears, in which he was joined by the greatest portion of the persons in court) a man so dear, and so revered as that of Mr Spencer Perceval, I find it difficult to suppress my feelings. As, however, to say any thing of the distinguished talents and virtues of that excellent man, might tend to excite improper emotions in the minds of the jury, but would with-hold these feelings which pressed for utterance from my heart, and leave you, gentlemen, to form your judgment upon the evidence which has been adduced in support of the case, undressed by any unfair indignation which you might feel against his murderer, by any description, however faint, of the excellent qualities of the deceased. Gentlemen, you are to try the unfortunate man at the bar, in the same manner, as if he was arraigned for the murder of any other man. The law protected all his Majesty's subjects alike, and the crime was the same whether committed upon the person of the highest and most distinguished character in the country, as upon that of the lowest. The only question you have to try is, whether the prisoner did wilfully and maliciously murder Mr Spencer Perceval or not. It is not necessary to go very minutely into the evidence which has been produced to the fact, as there is little doubt as to the main object of your enquiry. The first thing you have to say is, whether the person charged with having murdered him [*sic*]; and whether that murder had been committed with a pistol bullet. The learned judge then proceeded to read the testimony given by the several witnesses examined. That of Mr Smith, surgeon Lynn, and Mr Burgess, clearly substantiated the fact, that the deceased had died in consequence of a pistol shot which had been discharged into his breast, and that the hand of the prisoner was the hand which had discharged that weapon. With respect to the deliberation that had been proved by other witnesses, and from what I could collect from the prisoner's defence, it seems to amount to a conclusion, that he conceived himself justified in what he had done, by his Majesty's government having refused to redress some supposed grievances. Such dreadful reasoning could not be too strongly reprobated. If a man fancied he was right, and in consequence conceived that if that fancy was not gratified, he had a right to obtain justice by any means which his physical strength gave him, there is no knowing where so pernicious a doctrine might end. If a man fancies he has a right, and endeavours to assert that right, is he to put to death the persons who refuses to give him any reparation to that which he supposes himself entitled. By the same reason every person who presided in a court of judicature refusing to give to a suitor in an action, what he requires, would be liable to revenge equally atrocious. In another part of the prisoner's defence, which was not, however, urged by himself, it was attempted to be proved, that at the time of the commission of the crime he was insane. With respect to this the law was extremely clear, if a man was deprived of all power of reasoning, so as not to be able to distinguish whether it was right or wrong to commit the most wicked, or the most innocent transaction, he could not certainly commit an act against the law; such a man, so destitute of all power of judgment, could have no intention at all. *In order to support this defence, it ought to be proved by the most distinct and unquestionable evidence, that the criminal was incapable of judging between right or wrong. *There was no other proof of insanity which would excuse murder, or any other crime. There are various species of insanity. Some human creatures are void of all power of reasoning from their birth, such could not be guilty of any crime.* There is another species of madness in which persons were subject to temporary paroxysms, in which they were guilty of acts of extravagance, this was called lunacy, if these persons committed a crime when they were not affected with the malady, they were to all intents and purposes ameniable to justice: so long as they can distinguish good from evil, so long are they answerable for their conduct. There is a third species of insanity, in which the patient fancied the existence of injury, and sought an opportunity of gratifying revenge, by some hostile act; if such a person was capable, in other respects, of distinguishing right from wrong, there is no excuse for any act of atrocity which he might commit under this description of derangement.* The witnesses who had been called to support this extraordinary defence had given a very singular account, to shew that at the commission of the crime the prisoner was insane. What might have been the state of his mind some time ago, was perfectly immaterial. The single question is, whether at the time this fact was committed, he possessed a sufficient degree of understanding to distinguish good from evil, right from wrong, and whether murder was a crime not only against the law of God, but against the law of his country. Here it appears that the prisoner had gone out like another man; that he came up to London by himself, at Christmas last, that he was under no restraint, that no medical man had attended him to cure his malady, that he was perfectly regular in all his habits, in short there was no proof adduced to shew that his understanding was so deranged, as not to enable him to know that murder was a crime. On the contrary, the testimony adduced in his defence, has most distinctly proved, from a description of his general demeanour, that he was in every respect a full and competent judge of all his actions. Having then commented on the evidence of Mrs Clarke, Mrs Billett, and Mary Figgins, his Lordship concluded by advising the jury to take all the facts into their most serious consideration. If you have any doubt, you will give the prisoner the benefit of that doubt; but if you conceive him guilty of the crime alledged against him, in that case you will find him guilty.

- The version of this part of Mansfield's charge to the jury which
will be found in the law reports (see R. v. Offord (1831) 5 Car. &
P. 168n.) is taken from Russell's *Treatise on Crimes and Misdemeanours* (see, for example, the 1826 edition, p. 10):

'. . . In order to support this defence it ought to be proved
by the most distinct and unquestionable evidence that the
prisoner was incapable of judging between right and wrong;
*that in fact it must be proved beyond all doubt, that at the time
he committed the atrocious act with which he stood charged, he
did not consider that murder was a crime against the laws of God
and nature; and that there was no other proof of insanity which
would excuse murder or any other crime. That in the* species of
madness *called lunacy,* where persons are subject to temporary
paroxysms, in which they are guilty of acts of extravagance,
such persons committing crimes when they are not affected
by the malady would be, to all intents and purposes, amenable
to justice; and that so long as they could distinguish good from
evil they would be answerable for their conduct. And that in
the species of insanity in which the patient fancies the existence of injury, and seeks an opportunity of gratifying revenge
by some hostile act, if such a person *be* capable in other
respects of distinguishing right from wrong, there would be
no excuse for any act of atrocity which he might commit
under this description of derangement.'

The source of this version was Collinson on Lunacy, Addendum
636. The passages which appear in one but not both versions, and
which I have italicised, make it likely that these were two independent reports of the same speech.

Appendix E. Susannah Milesent's Case

Source: Old Bailey Sessions Papers (1794) *Case* 627

SUSANNAH MILESENT, whose trial had been put off two sessions ago, on account of appearing insane, was brought to the bar, when Mr Recorder asked her the following questions:

Q. You are brought here to be tried for stealing a petticoat, have you any objection to be now tried? – I a'nt no objection to be now tried.

Q. Are you guilty of stealing this petticoat or no? – Yes.

Q. Who advised you to say that you was guilty? – I do not know, I took it to be married to John.

Q. Who is John? – A young man, a pretty gentleman, he is a gentleman's ostler, a servant, cleans knives.

Q. How long have you known him? – About three weeks, it is only three weeks since I first knew him, since he gave me a glass of peppermint.

Court to Mr Kirby. How long has she been in confinement? – The sessions before last.

Prisoner. As I was coming over the common, I sat down, and he came to me as I sat there; he said he thought it was a pity such a pretty girl as I should be lost, and he took and gave me a glass of peppermint, and he said he would marry me, if I had no objection; and I told him I had no objection; he told me where his master lived, and I went to his master's, but they said if I did not go away from them, they told me they did not know what to do with me. They told me I should see him sit here in a great white wig, but I cannot see none like him; I took the petticoat to be wedded to him, because mine is a nasty old one.

JANE YOUNG *sworn.*

I am a nurse in the sick ward, I have attended her ever since she has been in gaol, from about the 18th of July last, she has acted this part ever since.

Q. How has she conducted herself since that time? – Every time I went to her, as she has done now before Mr Kirby.

Prisoner. I think I have reason so to do, I know you are the greatest enemy I have got.

Witness. She broke the windows in the state side, and on seeing the gentlemen over on the state side was continually calling for John May, and made use of very bad expressions; which on this Mr Stone and all the gentlemen there, cried out for shame.

Prisoner. That is all your spite, because I would not let you do what you wanted with the doctor.

Witness. She is always calling for John May.

Prisoner. Ay, God bless his name.

Witness. And stripping herself.

Court. Can you think she is in a sound mind? – I cannot think that she is in her mind, by her behaviour, from all that I could find.

Q. What sort of answers has she given you? – Very impudent answers.

Q. Has she given direct answers to the questions that hath been put to her? – No otherway than what happened to come in her head.

U

JOHN OWEN *sworn.*

I can only confirm the woman.

Q. How has she behaved since she has been in the gaol? – In a very frenzy bad manner, stripping herself naked and shewing her nakedness.

Q. Did she do any mischief to your knowledge? – Not to my knowledge.

Q. At the time she made this noise, what was that the effect of? – Her general cry was about this Jack May, he was her jewel, she said, and her dear love.

Prisoner. Jack May is a blackguard.

Court to Owen. Did she abuse you at any time? – Very often; sometimes she would lay hold of me and say I was Jack May, and another servant she has laid hold of and said he was Jack May.

Q. Did she give direct answers to the questions that was put to her? – Very ready.

Q. From the knowledge you have had of her, and her conduct, do you believe her to be sound in her mind? – I do not think her to be right in her mind.

JOHN PRIESTLY *sworn.*

I am servant to Mr Priestly.

Q. Have you known this woman ever since she has been in gaol? – [no reply is recorded.]

Q. What has been her conduct? – The same as the woman represented before, in a kind of a mad way.

Q. What have you known her to do? – I saw her break the windows of the ward she was in, and she has took hold of me and called me Johnny May, when I have gone to lock her up in the evening.

Q. Was there any reason for her breaking the windows? Did anybody abuse her that you know of? – None that I saw.

Q. Did she give direct answers to the questions that was put to her ?– No, quite contrary.

Q. Upon your oath, what is your opinion? Do you think she is a mad woman, or a woman in her senses? – I do not think her to be a woman in her senses.

Q. Do you take her to be a mad woman? – I do.

The jury brought in their verdict, we believe her to be deranged and not in a sound mind.

The jury impannelled for the trial of the above cause were as follows:

William Plumendge	Joseph Bevly
Samuel Lee	George Pitcher
Jacob Spinoza	Thomas Harris
Thomas Duckens	James Hurlock
Philip Jortlig	William Ball
William Hyde	George Anderson.

Appendix F. *The Times'* Report of Miss Broadric's Trial.

Source: The Times, 18 *July* 1795

Yesterday morning at seven o'clock came on at the above Assizes, the trial of Miss BROADRIC, for the murder of JOHN ERRINGTON Esq. of Greys in Essex. The indictment charged her with shooting the said John Errington with a pistol value 5s. loaded with gun-powder, and a leaden bullet; to which she pleaded – *Not Guilty.*

Miss Broadric came into Court in deep mourning, attended by a female. At first she appeared greatly agitated, and almost fainting; but on the whole shewed great presence of mind, and behaved with great propriety.

Mr GARROW, as Counsel for the prosecution, made a very humane and excellent address to the Jury, in which he stated, that his was a very painful situation on the present occasion, having formerly been in habits of acquaintance with the gentleman deceased. He thought it, however, but just to the unfortunate Lady at the bar to state a rumour which prevailed, and which he understood was to be the ground of defence – that she was insane. He mentioned this circumstance, as the Counsel on the opposite side could make no reply. Mr Garrow then alluded to Mr Errington's first marriage, and said, that after his divorce he fled for refuge to the charms and accomplishments of Miss Broadric. He then detailed the circumstances of the murder, as related in the evidence.

Mr CONST examined the witness, and called *John Bailey,* footman to Mr Errington, who said that Miss B. came to his master's house on the 13th of May last, and that she asked to speak with him. During this conversation, Mrs Errington was coming down stairs, who returned with Miss B. and conducted her to the room where his master was sitting; that about half a minute after, he heard his mistress scream out, and his master groan, on which he ran up into the room, when his master cried out to him – 'Oh John, I am shot, I am murdered.' His mistress said – 'Take this woman into custody, she has murdered my husband.' Miss B. then laughed, and threw the pistol down, saying – 'Hang me, or do with me as you please.' He (Bailey) then went for a Surgeon and a Constable; and on his return to the house, Miss Broadric was sitting in the parlour below, with some water before her, as if fainting. He saw her put her hand in her right pocket, which led him to suppose she had another pistol about her, on which he approached and held her arms, and on examining he found a pistol loaded, which she declared in a low voice she meant for herself.

The latter part of this evidence was confirmed by the Gardener and a Constable.

Mr *Childers,* a Surgeon, near *Greys,* and Mr *Miller,* also a Surgeon, being examined said, that they went to Mr ERRINGTON's to examine his wounds; that wishing to ascertain what direction the ball had taken they went down stairs, at the desire of Mr Errington, to ask Miss B. what position she was in when she fired the pistol. She minutely described the circumstances, saying she was standing and Mr E. sitting. They both affirmed that the wound was the cause of the death.

The evidence on the part of the prosecution here closed. Mr *Shepherd*, as Counsel for Miss B. then called Miss B.'s Brother-in-law, who proved, that her Mother and Sister had been both afflicted with a constitutional insanity; and that her Sister had died of it.

———, an hostler at an Inn in Whitechapel, deposed, that on the 13th of May last, the prisoner at the bar called at the inn from which the *South End* stage sets out; that it had set off a few minutes before she reached it, on which she seemed much disappointed, and asked if she could not get a conveyance to follow the coach and overtake it, as she was in great haste; that he put a horse to a whisky that was in the yard, and rode after the coach with Miss B. in it. He drove on at a good round trot, but though he did so, she frequently said 'You go too slow', and that she herself drove one horse 803 miles in a week. On mending the horse's pace, she said he went too fast. Near the turnpike he told her to get out her money, that she might not be detained: she took some out, and then said she had no change. He drove her as far as the nine mile-stone, when he overtook the stage. She seemed to be hurrying on, and much fluttered, and her behaviour on the road was such as to convince him she was not in her perfect senses. On his return to town, he told his master that he was sure the passenger he had driven was mad.

A *Chairwoman*, who had been in the service of Miss B. at her house at Kennington, said, Miss B. had frequently asked her, which she thought was the easiest death; that she herself thought drowning was the easiest; that her conversation was extremely odd; and that she left Miss B.'s service, for freat she should find, some morning, she had made away with herself. On Christmas Day her mistress had thrown some scalding water on her because she had not cleaned the stairs to her liking.

Another Young Girl, who had been in Miss B.'s service, spoke also of her whimsical conduct, and said, she was very *maddish like*.

A *Baker* who served Miss B. with bread, said she gave him frequently one shilling or half-a-crown for a three-penny loaf, without desiring any change, and would shut the door in his face, on his offering her change.

Several of her neighbours also gave evidence of Miss B.'s incoherent character. She was described as frequently walking about Kennington, in the attitude of a soldier; doing her exercise, so as to excite the attention of passengers, until one of her neighbours told her of it, when she desisted. She was also described as having a great partiality for a china tea-pot, which was given her by her first attachment, in which, however, she had been heard to declare she was not happy.

This was the evidence brought forward to prove her frequent insanity. The Lord Chief Baron then summed up in a very human and affecting manner, describing the evidence both for and against her with great impartiality. The Jury did not leave the box, but after five minutes consideration, returned a verdict of NOT GUILTY.

Upon the Verdict being given, there was a kind of tumultuous emotion in the Court, as if applauding the Verdict. Certainly, according to the general appearance, it was satisfactory to the majority attending the trial, who seemed to pity the misfortunes of the prisoner.

Mr CONST then applied to the CHIEF BARON, to detain the prisoner in safe custody with a view of having her taken care of, on the Statute of the 8th of Anne, and 17th of George II. the Jury having found her a lunatic. The Chief Baron said this was extremely proper, and accordingly he ordered the prisoner to be DETAINED.

Bibliography

Dates are those of first editions unless otherwise indicated. Reports of committees and commissions will be found under the names of their chairmen; but readers who do not know the chairman's name can look up the committee in the index, where the chairman's name is given.

ALISON, A. *Principles of the Criminal Law in Scotland*, Edinburgh, 1832

ANCEL, M. *Les Codes Pénaux Européens*, 3 vols, Paris, 1957

The Annual Register or a view of the History, Politics and Literature for the year . . ., from 1758 annually, London

ANONYMOUS *A pamphlet on the case of Henry Roberts*, 1747, (quoted by R. Hunter and I. Macalpine, q.v., p. 373 ff.)

idem, Sketches in Bedlam, London, 1823

ARCHBOLD, JOHN FREDERICK *Summary of the Law relating to pleading and evidence in criminal cases . . .*, 1st edition 1812 (references are to editions of 1848, 1853 etc.)

ARNOT, H. *A Collection and Abridgement of Celebrated Criminal Trials in Scotland, 1536–1784*, 1785, republished Edinburgh, 1833

ASCHAFFENBURG, G. *Crime and its Repression*, English translation Boston, 1913 (cited by Grünhut, q.v.)

ATKIN, Lord (Chairman) *Report of the Committee on Insanity and Crime*, Cmd. 2005, HMSO, London, 1924

BARR, the Rev. JAMES (Chairman) *Report from the Select Committee on Capital Punishment*, 1931, HMSO, London (their Special Report dated 1930 merely asks that they be re-appointed in the following session in order to complete their task)

BARROUGH, PHILIP *The Methode of Phisicke, conteyning the Causes, Signes, and Cures of inward Diseases in Mans Body from the Head to the Foote*, London, 1583

BARTHOLOMAEUS ANGLICUS *De Proprietatibus Rerum:* mid-13th century; ms. copies in several libraries (e.g., Bodleian); English translation by John of Trevisa 1398, pub. London, 1495

BATTIE, Dr WILLIAM *A Treatise on Madness*, London, 1758

BENSON, A. C. (ed.) *The Letters of Queen Victoria: 1837–61*, London, 1907

BENTHAM, JEREMY *Introduction to the Principles of Morals and of Legislation*, New York, 1780 (with passages added 1789) Oxford, 1948

BLACKSTONE, Sir WILLIAM *Commentaries on the Laws of England*, 4 vols, 1st edition London 1775–9, (references are to 15th edition)

BLAKE, G. (ed.) *The Trials of Patrick Carraher*, London, 1951

BLOM-COOPER, L.: *see* MORRIS

BOORDE, ANDREW *The Breviary of Healthe*, 2 vols, London, 1547 (vol. I), 1552 (vol. II)

BRACTON, HENRY DE *De Legibus et Consuetudinibus Angliae*, edited by Woodbine 1915, Yale University Press, Oxford University Press.

BRYDALL, JOHN (of Lincoln's Inn) *Non Compos Mentis or, the Law relating to Natural Fools, Mad-Folks and Lunatick persons*, London, 1700 (a series of questions and answers, mostly relating to capacity in civil law)

BUCKNILL, JOHN CHARLES and TUKE, DANIEL HACK *A Manual of Psychological Medicine* (references are to 1st edition 1858 and 2nd edition 1862), London

BURTON, THOMAS *His diary from 1650 to 1659*, 4 vols. (ed. J.F. Rutt), London, 1828

CAPGRAVE, JOHN *The Chronicle of England*, 1464 ca ed. by F.C. Hingeston, in the Series 'The Chronicles and Memorials of Great Britain and Ireland', London, 1858

The Capital Punishment Commission, 1864–6: see Richmond, Duke of

CARSWELL, D. (ed.) *The Trial of Ronald True*, Edinburgh, 1925, (republished 1950)

CATTELL, RAYMOND B. 'The Fate of National Intelligence: test of a thirteen-year prediction' in [1950] 42, *The Eugenics Review*, 136ff, London

CAWTE, E.C.: *see* Watts

Central Criminal Court Sessions Papers: see Old Bailey Sessions Papers

CICERO, MARCUS TULLIUS *Tusculanae Disputationes*, 45 B.C. (in 5 books)

CHITTY, JOSEPH (junior) *A Treatise in the Law of the Prerogatives of the Crown*, London, 1820

COCKAYNE, THOMAS OSWALD (ed.) *Leechdoms, wort cunning and starcraft of early England*, London, 1864

COKE, Sir EDWARD *Institutes of the Laws of England*, First Part (i.e. 'Coke on Littleton'), 1st edition 1628, Third Part (concerning high treason, and other pleas of the crown, and criminal causes), 1st edition London, 1644

idem, Les Reports de Edward Coke . . . &c, 1st edition 1600–15 (1st English translation 1658), London

COSIN, RICHARD *Conspiracie for Pretended Reformation*, London, 1592

COVARRUBIAS or COVARRUVIAS Y LEYVA, DIEGO DE, *In varios civilis ac pontifici iuris titulos relectiones*, Leyden, 1568

COWIE, V. and SLATER, E. 'Psychiatric Genetics', in *Recent Progress in Psychiatry*, vol. III, (ed. E.W.H.T.Fleming), London, 1959

CRICHTON, Sir ALEXANDER *An Inquiry into the Nature and Origin of Mental Derangement*, 2 vols, London, 1798

CRICHTON-BROWNE, Sir JAMES *On Dreamy Mental States*, (The Cavendish Lecture 1895), Cambridge, 1895

Criminal Law Revision Committee: see Sellers

Criminal Statistics: see Judicial Statistics

CROSS, A.R.N. 'Reflections on Bratty's Case', in [1962] 78, *Law Quarterly Review*, London

DALTON, MICHAEL *The Countrey Justice*, London, 1618 (reference is to 1742 edition)

DAVIES, DAVID RICHARD SEABORNE 'Child-Killing in English Law' in *The Modern Approach to Criminal Law*, (edd. L. Radzinowicz and J. W. C. Turner), London, 1945

DIAMOND, B.L. 'Criminal Responsibility of the Mentally Ill', in [1961-2] 14, *Stanford Law Review*, Stanford

idem, 'On the spelling of Daniel M'Naghten's name', in [1964] 25, *Ohio State Law Journal* Columbus

Digest: see Justinian

DYMOND, ALFRED H. *The Law on its trial: a personal recollection of the death penalty and its opponents*, London, 1865

EAST, NORWOOD *An Introduction to Forensic Psychiatry in the Criminal Courts*, London, 1927

ELYOT, Sir THOMAS *The Castel of Helth*, London, 1541

EYSENCK, H.J. (ed.) *Handbook of Abnormal Psychology*, London, 1960

FAIRFIELD, L. and FULLBROOK, E. P. *The Trial of John Thomas Straffen*, London, 1954

FITZHERBERT, Sir ANTHONY *La Nouvelle Natura Brevium*, 1st edition London, 1534, translated and published 1538 as 'The Newe Booke of Justices of Peas made by A. F. Judge, lately translated out of French into English'

FLETA *circa* 1290, in Selden Society Publications (q.v.) vol. 72, London, 1953

FLEMING: *see* Cowie

FULLBROOK: *see* Fairfield

FURNEAUX, R. *Guenther Podola*, London, 1960

GARDINER, A.G. *The Life of Sir William Harcourt*, 2 vols, London, 1923

GASH, NORMAN *Mr. Secretary Peel*, Longmans, London, 1961

GIBSON, E. and KLEIN, S. *Murder: a Home Office Research Unit Report*, HMSO, London, 1961

GILBERTUS ANGLICUS *Compendium medicinae tam morborum universalium quam particularium nondum medicis sed et cyrurgicis utilissimum:* early 13th century. Ms of 1270 *circa* extant: pub. Leyden, 1510, (ed. M. Capella)

GLANVILLE, RANULF DE, putative author of *De Legibus et Consue-
  tudinibus Regni Angliae*, 1180 *circa*, (references are to G.D.Hall's
  1965 edition, Oxford University Press)
GODDARD, HENRY *Memoirs of a Bow Street Runner*, London, 1956
GOLDHAMER, HERBERT and MARSHALL A. W. *The Frequency of
  Mental Disease*, Illinois, 1949, republished as *Psychosis and
  Civilisation*, 1953
GOWERS, Sir ERNEST (Chairman) *Report of the Royal Commission on
  Capital Punishment 1949–53* (Minutes of evidence separately
  published at various dates from 1945 to 1953), Cmd. 8932, HMSO,
  London, 1953
GRÜNHUT, M. *Penal Reform: a comparative study*, Oxford, 1948
GUEDALLA, P. (ed.) *The Queen and Mr. Gladstone*, London, 1933

HADDAN, A.W. and STUBBS,W. (edited, after Spelman and Wilkins,
  by) *Councils and Ecclesiastical Documents relating to Great Britain
  and Northern Ireland*, Oxford, 1869
HALE, Sir MATTHEW *Historia Placitorum Coronae . . . Now first
  published from his Lordship's original Manuscript . . .* London, 1736
HARE, E.H. 'The Origin and Spread of Dementia Paralytica', in [1959]
  105, *Journal of Mental Science*, 594–
HARGRAVE, F.T.: *see State Trials*
HART, H.L.A. *Prolegomenon to the Principles of Punishment*,
  (Presidential Address to the Aristotelian Society), 1959, republished
  in his *Punishment and Responsibility*, Oxford, 1968
idem, Punishment and the Elimination of Responsibility, (Hobhouse
  Memorial Lecture), London, 1962, republished in his *Punishment and
  Responsibility*, Oxford, 1968
HASLAM, JOHN *Medical Jurisprudence, as it relates to insanity, according
  to the Law of England*, London, 1817
HAVARD, J.D.J. *The Detection of Secret Homicide*, London, 1960
HAWKINS, WILLIAM *A Treatise of Pleas of the Crown*, 2 vols, London,
  1716
HEALD, Sir LIONEL (Chairman) *Murder: Some suggestions for the
  reform of the Law relating to murder in England*, Sussex, 1956
HOBSON, Dr J.A. 'Psychiatric Evidence in Murder Trials', in [1955]
  9, *Howard Journal*, London
HOLDSWORTH, Sir WILLIAM *A History of English Law* (references
  are to 7th edition of 1956) London, 1903
HOLINSHED, RAPHAEL *The Chronicles of Englande, Scotlande and
  Irelande . . .* pub. London, 1577–86
Home Office Papers, Calendar of, 1760–1775 published at various dates
  from 1878 to 1899, London. The Calendar consists of transcripts,
  usually abbreviated, of documents preserved in the Public
  Record Office
HOWELL, T.B.: *see State Trials.*
HUME, Baron *Commentaries on the Law of Scotland respecting the
  description and punishment of crimes*, Edinburgh, 1797

HUNTER, RICHARD M.D., M.R.C.P., D.P.R. and MACALPINE, IDA M.D., M.R.C.P. *Three Hundred Years of Psychiatry: 1535–1860: a history presented in selected English texts*, Oxford, 1963

JACOBS, Dr BETTY 'Aetiological Factors and Reaction–types in Psychoses following Childbirth', in [1943] 89, *Journal of Mental Science*, 242

JONES, K. *Lunacy, Law and Conscience 1744–1845: the social history of the care of the insane*, London, 1955

idem, *Mental Health and Social Policy 1845–1959*, London, 1960

Judicial Statistics (England and Wales) 1834– , *Criminal Statistics (England and Wales)* 1857– , HMSO, London. (The annual series of statistics begins with tables of criminal offences committed for trial etc. at assizes or quarter session in 1834 (published 1835). From 1857 the returns include tables of indictable crimes reported to the police, and the results of summary proceedings. From 1893 the tables were enlarged and improved, and new tables added, as a result of the re-organization of the statistics recommended by a Committee in 1892). No volumes were published for the years of the 1939–1945 war.

JUSTINIAN, Emperor, *Digest*, 6th century, (references are to Mommsen's edition of 1870, Berlin)

KEETON, G.W. *Guilty But Insane*, London, 1961

KEITH, Baron 'Some Observations on Diminished Responsibility', in [1959] 4, *Medico-Legal Journal*, Cambridge

KLEIN: *see* Gibson

KUENSSBERG: *see* Watts

LANGTON, CHRISTOPHER *A very brefe Treatise, ordrely declaring the principal partes of phisick etc.*, London, 1547

idem, *An Introduction into Physycke, wyth an universal Dyet*, London, 1550?

LEIGH, D. *The Historical Development of Psychiatry*, vol. I, 18th and 19th century, Oxford, 1961

LIEBERMANN, F. *Die Gesetze der Angelsachsen*, Halle, 1898

LIPCON: *see* Pierce

LOCKE, JOHN *An Essay Concerning Human Understanding*, London, 1690

LOCKHART-ROBERTSON, C. and MAUDSLEY, H. *Insanity and Crime: a medico-legal commentary on the case of George Victor Townley*, London, 1864

LONGFORD, ELIZABETH *Victoria R. I.*, London, 1964

MACALPINE, I.: *see* Hunter

MACKENZIE, Sir GEORGE, of Rosehaugh *A Discourse upon the Laws and Customs of Scotland in Matters Criminal*, Edinburgh, 1674

MACNISH, ROBERT *The Philosophy of Sleep*, Glasgow, 1830

MAITLAND, F.W. (ed.) *Bracton's Notebook*, Cambridge 1887

Malleus Maleficarum: see Sprenger

MARC, CHARLES CHRÉTIEN *De la folie considérée dans ses rapports avec les questions medico-judiciaires*, 2 vols, Paris, 1840

MARSHALL, G. 'Parliament and the Prerogative of Mercy', in 1961, *Public Law* (spring), p. 8 ff., London

MATTHAEUS, ANTONIUS (second of the name) *De Criminibus ad lib. XLVII et XLVIII Dig. Commentarius*, Amsterdam, 1644

MAUDSLEY, Professor HENRY *Responsibility in Mental Disease*, (2nd edition in the same year) London, 1874

MAUDSLEY, H.: *see* Lockhart-Robertson

MAYER-GROSS, W., SLATER, E. and ROTH, M. *Clinical Psychiatry*, London, 1954

MORE, Sir THOMAS *The apologye of syr T. More, Knyght*, London, 1533

MORISON, Sir ALEXANDER *Cases of Mental Disease*, London, 1828

MORRIS, T. and BLOM-COOPER, L. *A Calendar of Murder*, London, 1963

NICHOLAS, Sir HARRIS (ed.) *Acts of the Privy Council*, London, 1834–

NOKES, GERALD DACRE *A History of the Crime of Blasphemy*, London, 1928

Old Bailey Sessions Papers 1684–1834, Central Criminal Court Sessions Papers 1835–1913. The series begins with unbound sheets of reports of occasional sessions, of which some are in a box at the Guildhall Library, some in the Bodleian Library, bound and catalogued with other 17th- and 18th-century news sheets. The complete bound series begins in 1729, from which date it purports to mention every trial in the court. (This was probably not so until about 1740, for in that year the publisher acknowledges a reproof from the bench for the incompleteness of some of his reports, and promises that they will henceforth be complete.) Sometimes only the name and offence of the accused, and the verdict, are given; but usually the main evidence on both sides is reported, more or less verbatim, from short-hand notes; very occasionally the judge's summing up is given in full or part (e.g. in Bellingham's case, q.v. in Appendix D). The most complete series is probably that in the Guildhall Library (although even this has occasional gaps). Other libraries which have the series or parts of it are: the British Museum, the Bodleian Law Library, the Lincoln's Inn Library and the Harvard Law School Library.

The title of the series was changed in 1835 to *The Central Criminal Court Sessions Papers*. The series ends in the spring of 1913 with the trial of Mrs Pankhurst for trying to cause an explosion in someone's house.

OSWALD, I. *Sleep*, London, 1966
Oxford Dictionary, The Concise, 1st edition, Oxford, 1911

PAGAN, Dr J.M. *The Medical Jurisprudence of Insanity*, London, 1840
PIERCE, C.M. and LIPCON, H.H. 'Somnambulism, Electroencephalographic Studies and Related Findings', in [1956, October] 7, *U.S. Armed Forces Medical Journal*, 1419
PLATO *The Laws* (e.g. in E.B. England's edition, 1921, Manchester University Press)
PLATT, ANTHONY MICHAEL *The Criminal Responsibility of the Mentally Ill in England, 1100–1843*, 1965. Unpublished thesis in the Library of the University of California, Berkeley
PLUCKNETT, THEODORE FRANK *Edward the First and Criminal Law*, Cambridge, 1960
PRICHARD, JAMES COWLE *A Treatise on Insanity and other Disorders affecting the Mind*, London, 1835
idem, On the Different Forms of Insanity in relation to jurisprudence, London, 1842

RADZINOWICZ: *see* Davies
RAY, Dr ISAAC *A Treatise on the Medical Jurisprudence of Insanity*, 1st edition 1838 (in U.S.A.), published in England 1839, in London
Registrar-General 'Statistical Review of England and Wales for the year 1960: Supplement on Mental Health', 1964, HMSO, London. (This was the last in a discontinued series.)
REID, D.D. 'Epidemiological Methods in the Study of Mental Disorders', in 1960, *World Health Organization Public Health Papers No. 2*, Geneva
Reports: see Atkin, Gowers, Heald, Richmond, Sellers and Townshend
RICHARDSON, H.G. and SAYLES, G.O. *Law and Legislation from Æthelberht to Magna Carta*, Edinburgh, 1966
RICHMOND, Duke of (chairman) *The Report of the Capital Punishment Commission, 1864–6* (together with the minutes of evidence), HMSO, London, 1860
ROBERTS, C.E.B. (ed.) *The Trial of Ley and Smith*, London, 1947
ROBERTSON, Miss A.J. *The Laws of the Kings of England from Edmund to Henry I*, Cambridge, 1925
Royal Commission on Capital Punishment, 1949–53: see Gowers, Sir Ernest
RUSSELL, WILLIAM OLDNALL *A Treatise on Crimes and Indictable Misdemeanors*, references to 1st edition 1819, 2nd edition 1826, etc., London

SAYLES: *see* Richardson
Scottish Council for Research in Education, 'The Trend of Scottish Intelligence', London, 1949
Selden Society Publications, vols. I–LXXIX, London, 1888–1965

SELLERS, Sir FREDERICK (Chairman) *Criminal Procedure (Insanity)*, (Third Report of the Criminal Law Revision Committee), 1963, Cmd. 2149, HMSO, London

SHAKESPEARE, WILLIAM *The Taming of the Shrew*, London, c. 1591

SHIELDS, J. and SLATER, E. 'Heredity and Psychological Abnormality' in *Handbook of Abnormal Psychology* (ed. H.J.Eysenck), London, 1960

SIMON, RITA JAMES *The Jury and the Defense of Insanity*, Boston, 1967

SLATER: *see* Cowie, and Shields

SPARGO, J.W. *Juridical Folk-lore in England as illustrated by the Cucking-stool*, Duke University Press, 1944

SPARKS, RICHARD F. 'Diminished Responsibility in theory and practice', in [1964] 27, *Modern Law Review*, London

SPRENGER, JACOBUS and INSTITORIS, HENRICUS *Malleus Maleficarum*, 1st edition Cologne, 1474?

State Papers, Domestic, Calendar of, from 1509 to 1704, revised edition published at various dates from 1920, London. The Calendar consists of transcripts, often abbreviated, of documents preserved in the Public Record Office. *See also Home Office Papers.*

State Trials. There are three series:
    edited by F.Hargrave (6 vols, published 1776–81, London), covering the period 1387–1775;
    edited by T.B.Howell (33 vols, published 1816–28, London), covering the period 1163–1820;
    edited by J.Macdonell, and later J.E.P.Wallis, (8 vols, published London, 1823–98, covering the period 1820–1858, and known as 'State Trials (New Series)'.)
    The accuracy of the reports is discussed in G. Kitson Clark's *The Critical Historian*, London, 1967
    References in the Table of Cases are to Howell's or Macdonell's series.

STEPHEN, Sir JAMES FITZJAMES 'On the policy of maintaining the limits at present imposed by law on the criminal responsibility of madmen', in *Papers read to the Juridical Society 1855–58*, London, 1855

idem, A General View of the Criminal Law, London, 1863 (the so-called 2nd edition of 1890 is a rewritten book)

idem, A Digest of the Criminal Law (Crimes and Punishments), London, 1877

idem, History of the Criminal Law of England, London, 1883

STRACHEY, GILES LYTTON *Queen Victoria*, London, 1921

STUBBS: *see* Haddan

THORPE, B. (ed.) *Ancient Laws and Institutes of England*, 2 vols, London, 1840

TOWNSHEND, CHARLES (Chairman) 'Report from the Committee who were appointed to inquire into the State of the private Mad-houses in this Kingdom', in *House of Commons Journal for 1763*, p. 486 ff., London, 1763

TROUP, Sir EDWARD *The Home Office*, London, 1825

TUKE, DANIEL HACK *Chapters in the History of the Insane in the British Isles*, London, 1882

idem, Sleepwalking and Somnambulism, London, 1884

idem, see also Bucknill

VIVES, JUAN LUIS *De Anima et Vita*, Basel, 1538

WAKEFIELD, EDWARD GIBBON *Facts relating to the Punishment of Death in the Metropolis*, London, 1831

WALKER, NIGEL DAVID *The Aims of a Penal System* (James Seth Memorial Lecture for 1966) Edinburgh, 1967

WATTS, C.A.H., CAWTE, E.C. and KUENSSBERG, E.V. 'Survey of Mental Illness in General Practice', in [1964] 2, *British Medical Journal*, p. 1351–

WESLEY, JOHN *The Journal of the Rev. John Wesley* (ed. N. Curnock), London, 1909–1916

WILLIAMS, G. *Criminal Law: the general part*, London, 1953

WINSLOW, L.FORBES *The Anatomy of Suicide*, London, 1840

idem, The Plea of Insanity in Criminal Cases, London, 1843

idem, Lettsomian Lectures on Insanity, London, 1854

WOOTTON, Baroness 'Diminished Responsibility–A Layman's View', in [1960] 76, *Law Quarterly Review*

idem, Crime and the Criminal Law, London, 1963

Index

Cases (for example, M'Naghten's) will be found in the Table of Cases, and statutes in the Table of Statutes. Place-names are included in this index only if they are of importance; for instance, Broadmoor is included but not the Church of St Nicholas at Yarmouth. Commissions and committees are indexed by their titles and dates (for example, the Capital Punishment Commission 1864–6), with a reference to the chairman's name so that they can be found in the bibliography. References are normally to pages and chapters; capital letters indicate one of the Appendixes; bib. refers to the bibliography.

W

as ground for reprieve, 213
distinguished from mental illness,
25, 28, 36, 115, 116, 117
'success-rates' for insane defendants,
68-70, 85, 122-3
suicide
attempts at, 178, 179, 180
automatically attributed to mental
disorder, 136
by mentally disordered (offenders),
33, 94
crime as means of, 75, 107, 184
pacts, 151
surdus et mutus, 31
'surprise bath', 46
swinging chair, 46
Sydney, first Viscount, 185
syphilis, 7, 38, 70

Talbot, Sir George, 131
Templewood, first Viscount, 110
Terry, Dr H., 241
tests of criminal responsibility of
insane, 247-53
in Arnold's case, 56
M'Naghten test, 100, ch. 6 *passim*,
Ray's test, 90, 109, 249-50
'wild beast test', 12, 28, 56, 57
theft, 26, 70
Thigpen, 174
Thorpe, B., 15, 31, 34, bib.
tics, 165
Times, The, 12, 190, 193, 208
Tindal, Sir Nicholas, 92, 98-102,
111-12, 118, 120
Tories as subject of delusions, 91
total deprivation of memory, etc., 28,
38, 56, 62, 77
Townshend, Charles, *see* Committee
on Private Madhouses
Tracy, Mr Justice, 53, 55ff., 64, 101
Traill, Dr, 142
transportation, 84
for Victoria's assailants, 187-8
obsolescence of, 188
treason, 29, 49, 75
ancient law on, 185
and the insanity defence, ch. 11
passim
minor forms of, reduced to 'high
misdemeanours', 187
procedural concessions to persons
accused of, 75

Treasury Counsel, 108
treatment of the insane, 29-31, 45-8
see also asylums, prisons, private
madhouses, bleeding, cupping,
water, whipping, etc.
trebuchet, 48
trespass, 44
trial
by ordeal, 18, 19, 27
confinement without, 19, 80
separate trials of facts and sanity,
106
Troup, Sir Edward, 218, bib.
Tuke, Dr Daniel Hack, 32, 51, 168,
181, 254, bib.
Tuke, Dr Thomas Harrington, 105-6,
121, 189, 254
tumour, cerebral, 117, 173-4
Turner, J. W. C., 137, bib. (s.v.
Davies)
Tyler, Watt, 50

unfitness for trial, 80, 85, 86, 118, 184,
ch. 14 *passim*
amnesia and, 235-6
and Act of 1840, 228-9
becomes a live issue, 222
criteria of, 223, 224
Director of Public Prosecutions and,
225
evidence of at least two doctors on,
234-5
in Scotland, 225
of deaf-mutes, 219-21, 225
prison medical officers and, 225-8
reasons for decrease in frequency
of, 238-9
right of appeal on, 234, 236
statistics relating to, 67, 226-8, A, B
subject of inquest by jurors, 221
when to raise issue of, 230
see also burden of proof, etc.
utilitarian approach, 243-4, 247, 253

vagrants, legislation to deal with, 42,
43, 70
verdict
by majority, 150
changing consequences of, 84
in Hadfield's case, 78-9
public disapproval of, 95
two-verdict system, 192, 244
see also special verdict, acquittals